Two Complete Illustrated Books!
Revised Editions Published by
INNER LIGHT PUBLICATIONS

DRAGONS and UNICORNS

Fact? Or Fiction?

ERNEST INGERSOLL
ODELL SHEPARD

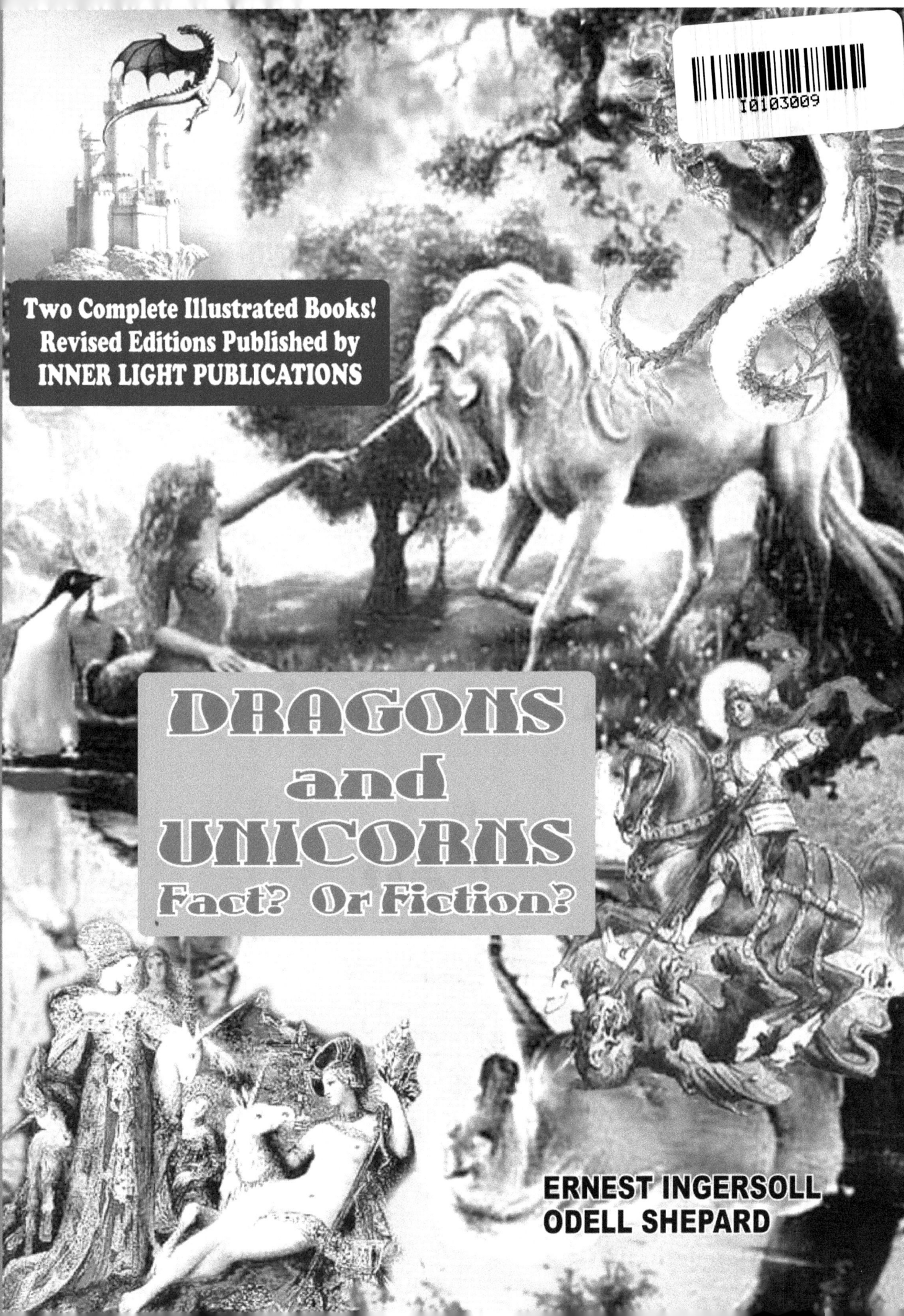

DRAGONS and UNICORNS
Fact? Or Fiction?

Published by Inner Light Publications

MAGICAL COMMUNITY
by Carol Ann Rodriguez

DRAGONS
and
UNICORNS
Fact? Or Fiction?

Revised Edition

ISBN 1-60611-008-x
978-1-60611-008-9

Published by
Inner Light/Conspiracy Journal
Box 753 · New Brunswick, NJ 08903

Staff Members

Timothy G. Beckley, Publisher
Carol Ann Rodriguez, Assistant to the Publisher
Sean Casteel, General Associate Editor
Tim R. Swartz, Graphics and Editorial Consultant
William Kern, Editorial and Art Consultant

Sign Up On The Web For Our Free Weekly Newsletter
and Mail Order Version of Conspiracy Journal
and Bizarre Bazaar
www.ConspiracyJournal.com

Order Hot Line: 1-732-602-3407

REALITY OF THE MYSTICAL BEASTS
Introduction To Expanded Edition
by Timothy Green Beckley

I will never forget my trip to the British Isles to speak before members of the House of Lords.

It's been two decades and my friend who invited me, Brinsley Le Poer Trench, is now deceased. Brinsley was the author of such books as The Sky People, about the visitation of extraterrestrials to our planet in ancient times.

His well written thesis was widely distributed before Eric Von Daniken's popular Chariots of the Gods? Brinsley—aka the Earl of Clancarty—was an actual member of the House of Lords who had championed the reality of the UFO phenomenon for years and had attempted to get the Crown and the Ministry of Defense to release its massive files on the subject.

From time to time, members of the House of Lords would actually hold heated debates on the legitimacy of the topic, taking the sides of both the believer and the skeptic. Brinsley had invited various researchers from all over the world to help him get his point across that UFOs were a subject of "high concern." He requested that I travel "across the pond" to reveal what I knew about the importance of a subject that has fascinated many for decades.

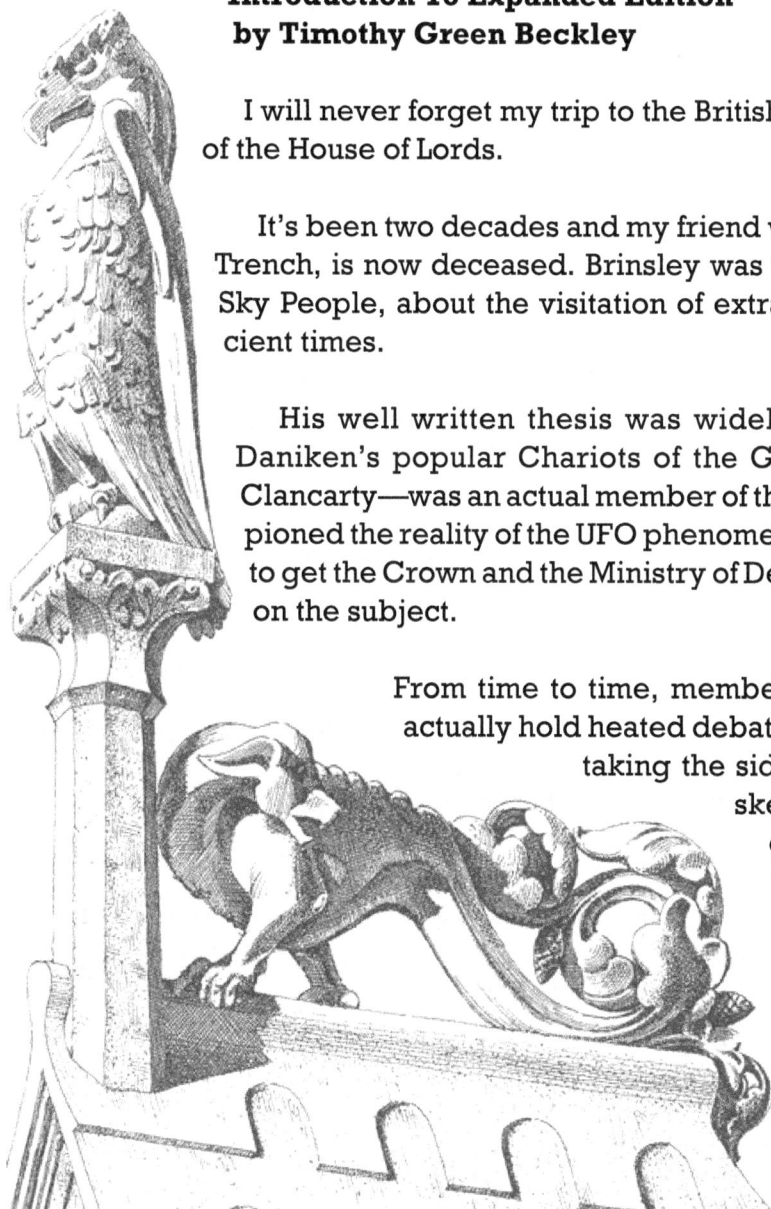

Though our "appeal" was not made in front of the full Lord's body, I did get a chance to pitch my findings before about 50 members of both the House of Lords and Parliament. I must say I was prepared to take my lumps from those who thought Brinsley and I were promoting the "silly season" too early in the year.

Among those with whom I had the opportunity to speak was the famous Lord Hill Norton, head admiral of the British Fleet, who turned out to have had a UFO experience or two of his own, as well as having a definite interest in electrical genius and inventor Nikola Tesla. He also believed that other energy sources were available to us but not being utilized.

Before delivering my presentation, Brinsley had me join with members of the House of Lords. As we all marched together into the main hall, the Lords began taking their seats on the floor below while I was ushered to a seat in the main gallery.

It was, to say the least, an exciting day in my career as an author and journalist. Looking around, I couldn't help but be impressed. The ornamentation was tremendous on the banisters, the stairwells and the chambers. I realized that there was untold centuries of history before me.

One of the things I immediately noticed was the number of wooden carvings of unicorns and dragons to be found above the entranceway and along the many railings. It seems odd, I thought at the time, that such "mythical" creatures would have found a home among such stately gentlemen, many of whom did not even have a taste for UFOs, much less creatures who supposedly only live in our fantasies and our dreams.

Boy, did I find out I was entirely wrong!

In fact, as I traveled throughout England, I discovered figures of unicorns and dragons carved on the sides of churches and old architectural structures....as if they had actually existed at one time or another.

Actually, fourteen hundred years ago, Saint Columba supposedly saw a fearsome dragon in Loch Ness. Plus, there were similar stories throughout the sixteenth and seventeenth centuries that seem to be more than "fairy tales."

While in the U.K. I was introduced to the work of the late F.W. Holiday, a researcher who made a lifelong career out of attempting to prove that dragon-like creatures existed in the various Scottish and Irish lakes, and that carvings of "flying discs" were often directly associated with such "dragons" and serpents.

And as it turns out, other researchers have put their reputation on the line that dragons and unicorns not only may have once walked the earth, but there is still a chance that they could be wandering around very much unabated even to this very day.

In order to tell our story as fully as possible, we have combined two fantastic books that offer evidence that these two creatures are worthy of a credible study and not just a figure of our overworked imagination.

I will now give you the opportunity to make a decision for yourself. But be careful, as it may be a world you will not want to return from.

Timothy G. Beckley, Publisher
MRUFO8@hotmail.com

DRAGONS
AND DRAGON LORE
BY ERNEST INGERSOLL
With an Introduction by
HENRY FAIRFIELD OSBORN
President of the American Museum of Natural History

"There's no such thing in nature, and you'll draw
A faultless monster which the world ne'er saw."

1928
Payson & Clarke Ltd.
New York

INTRODUCTION

I became intensely interested in Dragon Worship and the Dragon Myth during my recent journey in China and Mongolia in support of the Central Asiatic Expeditions of Roy Chapman Andrews. Especially, in the royal city of Peking appears the apotheosis of the Dragon in every conceivable form of symbolism and architecture. The Dragons leading up to the steps of the temples and palaces of the Manchu emperors, and the superb dragon-screen guarding the approach to one of the royal palaces, are but two of the innumerable examples of the universal former belief in these mythical animals, and of the still prevailing beliefs among the common people of China.

For example, one night in a far distant telegraph station in the heart of the desert of Gobi, I overheard two men pointing out Leader Andrews and myself as 'men of the Dragon bones.' On inquiry, I learned that our great Central Asiatic Expedition was universally regarded by the natives as engaged in the quest of remains of extinct Dragons, and that this superstition is connected with the still universal belief among the natives that fossil bones, and especially fossil teeth have a high medicinal value.

Not long after my return from Central Asia, I suggested to my friend, Ernest Ingersoll, that he write the present volume, preparing a fresh study of the history of the Dragon Myth which, now largely confined to China, once spread all over Asia and Europe, as dominant not only in mythology but entering even into the early teachings of Christianity, as so many other pagan myths have done. I knew that the author was well-qualified for a work of this character, because of his remarkable success in previous volumes for old and young, and in his original observations on various forms of animal life, from the American oyster to many birds and mammals. He is especially versed, perhaps, in regard to one very interesting question which is often asked, namely, how far the animals of myth and of legend, like the Dragon, the Hydra, the Phoenix, the Unicorn and the Mermaid, are products of pure imagination, and how far due to some fancied resemblance of a living form or to the tales of travelers. For example, it occurred to me, while examining the giant fossil eggs of the extinct ostrich of China (now known under the scientific name Struthiolithus, assigned by the late Doctor Eastman), that it may have given rise to the myth of the Phoenix or of the Roc. On this point, the author sends me the following very interesting notes:

I have not studied the Unicorn. . . . The Mermaid is usually attributed to somebody's story of seeing a dugong nursing its baby, but I guess the idea goes back to the time when old Poseidon was half man, half fish, and had plenty of watermaidens, half woman, half fish, disporting around him. The first time anyone saw Mistress Venus she was in that 'semi' shape if I remember rightly. . . . I do not find the Roc indigenous in the Far East, and I greatly doubt whether anywhere it had a 'physical' progenitor, or was suggested by any big, extinct, ratite egg. I have discussed this in my "Birds in Legend, Fable and Folklore," and conclude it to be a figment of an ancient boasting storyteller's fancy. . . . The only other imaginary form of importance in China is the Feng—a pheasant-like 'bird' analogous to the Phoenix—and probably hatched in the same sun-nest. . . . As to your query about 'mythical' and 'legendary' animals: My whole thesis in regard to the Dragon is that it is entirely imaginary; and I regard the Hydra (absent from the Chinese mind) as merely an extravagance that arose in the West, perhaps by confusion of snake and octopus.

I feel confident that the present work will arouse a widespread interest among students of animal form and history on the one hand, and of folk-lore, primitive religion and mythology on the other.

HENRY FAIRFIELD OSBORN.
American Museum of Natural History,
December 20, 1927.

CONTENTS

DRAGONS AND UNICORNS—FACT? OR FICTION?

DRAGONS AND DRAGON LORE

CHAPTER ONE

BIRTH OF THE DRAGON

TODAY a solar eclipse is slowly darkening my study window, and when I step out of doors to watch it I hear a man say: The Dragon is eating the Sun.

No dragon exists—none ever did exist. Nevertheless a belief in its actuality has prevailed since remote antiquity, and has become a fact of historic, social, and artistic interest. Millions of persons to-day have as firm a faith in its reality as in any fact, or supposed fact, of their intuition or experience. As an element in the ancient Oriental creation-myths it is perhaps the most antique product of human imagination; and it stalks, picturesque and portentous, through mediaeval legend.

The dragon was born in the youth of the East, a creature engendered between inward fear and outward peril, was nurtured among prehistoric wanderers, and has survived in the hinterlands of ignorance and superstition because it embodied the underlying principle of all morality—the eternal contrast and contest between Good and Evil, typified by the incessant struggle of man with the forces of nature and with his twofold self. In the East the dragon, like the primitive gods, was by turns deity and demon; carried westward, it fell almost wholly into the latter estate, or was transformed into a purely allegorical figure; and it has its counterpart, if not its descendants, in the religious faith and rites of every known land and all sorts of peoples.

The dragon is as old as the sensitiveness and imagination of mankind, and doubtless had assumed a definite shape in some crude, material expression as long ago as when men first began to paint, or to carve in wood and on stone, marks and images that were at least symbols of the supposed realities visible to their mental eyes.

DRAGONS AND UNICORNS—FACT? OR FICTION?

It is needless to repeat that the phenomena of nature must have appeared to primitive man as an immense, contradictory, insolvable mystery, a mixture of light and darkness, sunshine and storm, things helpful to him contending, as if animated, with things harmful, life alternating with death and decay. This is an old story, but it is plain that, in common with the more intelligent animals, man's predominant sensation was fear—fear of his brutish fellows, dread of the jungle and its beasts and ogres, of the desert and its burning drouth, of the wind and the thunderous lightning; most of all terror of the dark, peopled with spirits good and bad. Against the unknown and therefore frightful shapes and noises of the night, the shrieks of the gale, awe of the ocean, the flickering lights and sickening miasma of the bog—all to his half-awakened mind evidence of animate beings above his reach or understanding—man knew of but one defense, which was humble propitiation and neverceasing payment of ransom. Ghosts blackmailed him throughout his terror-stricken life. The only friendly things in nature were sunshine and water—most of all gentle, nourishing rain: what wonder then that the most beneficent spirits and primary deities in all the primitive cults of Europe and Asia, at least, have been those connected with fresh waters. When one attempts to trace to its birth the creature or concept of which we are in search, one is led backward and backward to the very beginning of human philosophy. That origin seems to rest in the earliest discoverable traces of human thought on this earth, when paleolithic man cowered over woodland campfires or watched by night beside Asiatic rivers, now dry, now mysteriously overflowing, or made magic in some consecrated cave; and when wonder was rising slowly—oh, so slowly—in his brain into the dignity of reasoning. These are really very interesting facts, and they appear to have been true during thousands of bygone years. The strange, half-human figures painted on the wall of a cave in southern France by a Magdalenien artist in the Old Stone Age, and labelled 'Sorcerer' by archaeologists, may easily be construed as an attempt to portray an ancestral dragon. Let us try to find the origin of this thing, and to discover not only its meaning, but how or why the Dragon came to be of its present form. It is doubtless a long and complicated story, but there is no call to apologize for either its length or its absurdities.

We have seen that the notion embodied in the word 'dragon' goes back to the beginning of recorded human thoughts about the mysteries of the thinker and his world. It is connected with the powers and doings of the earliest gods, and like them is vague, changeable and contradictory in its attributes, maintaining from first to last only one definable characteristic—association with and control of water. This points unmistakably to its birth in a land where water is the most important thing in nature to human existence—the essential requisite, indeed, for life and happiness. Such are the conditions in the valleys of the Nile and the Euphrates, precisely the regions in which, first of all, mankind began to establish a settled existence and to lay the foundations of civilization in agriculture. The success of agriculture was made possible by the invention of irrigation, through which man obtained command of the water-supply for his fields, and outwitted, so to say, the eccentricities of the rainfall. In timely showers to the right amount, in living streams and their vernal overflows that leave new soil, the rainfall is a blessing; but in the lightning-darting storm, in excessive floods, it may, and sometimes does, be-

DRAGONS AND UNICORNS—FACT? OR FICTION?

come a curse. Primitive men, unlearned in the natural laws by which we now account for the weather, imagined its varying moods to be the result of supernatural powers struggling somewhere in space, on one side for good conditions, on the other towards destruction and chaos; and they invented wondrous and complex stories to explain it. Every change in the weather was attributed to the gods. When rains were favourable, good gods got the credit; when prolonged drouth or devastating storms assailed the locality, men told one another that malignant spirits were at work.

Supreme among the earliest known divinities of Egypt was Re (or Ra). Associated with him was a feminine deity, Hathor, the 'great Mother,' or source of all earthly life. At enmity with Re was a formless being, Set. As Re grew aged mankind (created by Hathor) showed signs of rebellion, instigated by Set, and a council of the gods advised that Hathor be sent down to earth to subdue her insurgent progeny. She complied, received the additional epithet 'Sekhet,' acquired the ferocious lioness as her symbol, and went about cutting throats until the land was flooded with blood. Alarmed at the destruction of his subjects, which threatened to be total, Re begged Hathor-Sekhet to desist. She refused, whereupon Re caused to be brewed a red liquor, a draft of which subdued Hathor's maniacal rage, and so a remnant of mankind was saved. From that bloody time Hathor's reputation fell to that of a malignant spirit, for she, who theretofore had been a beneficent 'giver of life' had shown herself, in the avatar of Sekhet, a demon of destruction. In this skeleton of a legend we have the kernel of Egyptian mythology and religion. Re fades out and Osiris appears, an earthly king deified as a sort of water-god, who becomes more definitely a personification of the Nile in its beneficent aspect. Hathor becomes his consort Isis, and they produce a son Horus whose symbol is a falcon, sometimes accompanied by serpents, and who carries on Re's feud with Set (subsequently murderer of Osiris) under various warrior-methods, such as driving to battle in a chariot drawn by griffins (perpetuated in the Greek gryphon)—perhaps the most primitive incarnations of the dragon. Set is a water-devil whose followers take the form of crocodiles and other dangerous creatures of the great river; and later we read of a gigantic snake-like reptile Apop, which apparently was that long-lived old monster Set, and which later was known among the gods of Greek Olympus as Typhon, a snake-headed giant. Apop had a corps of typhonic monsters at his call. A host of fabulous monsters seem to have been derived, with more or less claim to true ancestry, from these prehistoric creatures of the Egyptian imagination.

While this epic or drama of the development of the human intelligence was in progress in Egypt, exhibiting the Celestial triad at the basis of all cosmic mythology, a similar development of legendary history was proceeding in Mesopotamia. "The Egyptian legends cannot be fully appreciated," we are told, "unless they are studied in conjunction with those of Babylonia and Assyria, the mythology of Greece, Persia, India, China Indonesia and America." We do not find in the opening chapters of the history of either Egypt or Mesopotamia the characteristic dragons we shall encounter later; but we do discover there the germ and its raison d'etre of what later became the conventional forms and properties of the Chinese 'lung,' the hydras and giants of Greek myth, and the hero-stories of mediaeval St. George. "Egyptian literature," Professor G. Elliot Smith assures

DRAGONS AND UNICORNS—FACT? OR FICTION?

us, "affords a clearer insight into the development of the Great Mother, the Water God and the Warrior Sun God, than we can obtain from any other writings of the origin of this fundamental stratum of deities. And in the three legends: The Destruction of Mankind, The Story of the Winged Disk [symbol of Horus], and The Conflict between Horus and Set, it has preserved the germs of the great Dragon Saga. Babylonian literature has shown us how this raw material was worked up into the definite and familiar story, as well as how the features of a variety of animals were blended to form the composite monster. India and Greece, as well as more distant parts of Africa, Europe and Asia, and even America, have preserved many details that have been lost in the real home of the monster."

Physical conditions were much the same in Mesopotamia as in Egypt. Like the Nile, the Euphrates was a permanent river, flowing from the Armenian mountains through a vast expanse of arid, yet fertile, land to the great marshes (now much reduced) at the head of the Persian Gulf. It rose to full banks, or over them, in early summer, fed by melting snow, and the annual inundations along its course were of the highest benefit and importance to the agriculturists settled at least six or seven thousand years ago in its lower basin. As population and tillage increased, irrigation—popularly believed to have been introduced by the gods—became more and more a necessity, and this need of abundant and well-regulated water influenced the local religion, the features of which we have learned from the engraved seals, inscribed tablets, and other evidences exhumed from the ruins of temples and royal houses.

The primitive theory of world-creation and the theogony of these pre-Babylonians are similar to those of Egypt; and the Sumerians, the earliest known permanent residents in the Euphrates Valley, were perhaps allied racially with the men of the Nile country—certainly there was communication between them long before the date of any records yet obtained. There is evidence, moreover, that the peoples whom we know by the earliest 'civilized' remains thus far discovered were preceded in the valleys of both the Euphrates and the Nile by a population far more primitive, which was displaced—in the case of Sumer, presumably by immigrants from southern Persia; for probably the culture represented by Susa is older than that of the cities of Sumer. Both peoples conceived the earth to be an island floating on an infinite expanse and depth of water which welled up around it as an ocean, often imaged forth as an encircling serpent, on whose horizon rested the dome of the sky. At first "darkness was upon the face of the deep," yet the great primeval gods were even then alive,—indistinct, fickle, anthropomorphic originators and representatives of natural phenomena.

The Babylonian god with which we are most concerned is Ea, who seems to stand in about the same relation to the Sumerian myth of creation as did Osiris to the Egyptian. Among the oldest pictures that have come down to us is one of a creature called Oannos-a human figure whose body, from the middle down, is that of a fish. Perhaps it is meant for Ea, who otherwise is represented as a man wearing a fish-skin, as a fish, or as a composite creature with a fish's body and tall. Ea was a water-god, personifying and governing all the waters on the earth, above or under it, including rivers and irrigation canals;

4

DRAGONS AND UNICORNS—FACT? OR FICTION?

nevertheless, although regarded as primarily a personification of the beneficent, life-giving powers of water (as in producing and sustaining crops), he was also identified with the devastating forces of wind and water, as in storms. As Osiris was confusingly reincarnated in Horus, so the earlier Enlil was absorbed in Ea, and gradually Ea in his son Marduk, when he became a sun-god, the slayer of Tiamat the water-demon. Tiamat, chaos personified (with just such a troop of malignant subordinates as attended Set), came out of the murky primeval ocean on purpose to baulk in their creative plans the well-intentioned gods of the air who gave the land the blessed rains on which the people depended for life and happiness. Tiamat was feminine; and this she-dragon, a counterpart of Harbor, heads a long line of 'demons,' good and bad.

The word 'dragon' as we see it written to-day calls to mind the grotesque, writhing figure of Chinese or Japanese ornament; but in this treatise we must accept the term in a far wider scope, as representing supernatural powers in any sense, yet not invariably hateful. As to the matter of sex, demon-women arose very early to vex the sun-gods of Egypt, but they soon became changed in sex, and dragons have been masculine ever since.

What happened to Tiamat is variously explained. Dr. Hopkins' summarizes her history, gathered from the tablets and seals recovered from the ruins of Nippur and elsewhere, thus:

Chaos bred monsters, and then the divine Heaven and Earth, as Anshar and Kishar, ancestors of Anu, Enlil, and Ea, prepared for conflict, to maintain order. . . . The eleven opposing monsters of Chaos are created by Tiamat and headed by Kingu, to whom Tiamat gives the tablets of destiny and whom she makes her consort. The peace-loving gods seem to fear; they send a messenger to Tiamat, "May her liver be pacified, her heart softened" [apparently without effect]. . . . At any rate, we next see Bel-Marduk, at the command of his father, going joyfully into battle after preparing for the conflict by making weapons, bow, lance, club, lightning-bolt, storm-winds and a net wherewith to catch Tiamat. The gods get drunk with joy, anticipating victory and hailing Marduk as already lord of the universe. On Storm (his chariot) he rushes forth, haloed with light, from which Kingu shrinks. Him follow the seven winds. Tiamat, however, fears him not, but when Marduk challenges her, she fights, "raging and shaking with fury," yet all in vain. For Marduk stifles her with a poisonous gas ('evil wind'), and then transfixes her, also taking the tablets from Kingu and netting the other monsters. But Tiamat he cuts in two, making one half of her the sky.

What was Tiamat like in the opinion of the people to whom these fanciful accounts of the work and adventures of the gods in bringing order out of chaos were as 'gospel truth'? The most ancient representation of her is an engraving on a cylinder-seal in the British Museum, which shows a thick-bodied snake, the forward third of its body upreared and bearing two little arm-like appendages, its tongue extended and its head crowned with one goat-like horn. If this portrait is really intended for Tiamat, it shows a queer relationship between this sinister sea-demon and the fish-god Ea, who also appears to

DRAGONS AND UNICORNS—FACT? OR FICTION?

have been part antelope (gazelle or goat), as is shown by antique pictures of him as a combination of antelope and fish, whence a 'sea-goat' came to be the vehicle of Marduk.

The tradition of Marduk's titanic battle with Tiamat seems to have been preserved in the famous story in the Apocrypha of Bel and the Dragon. In the time of the reign of Nebuchadnezzar at Babylon, after the destruction of Jerusalem and the carrying of Judah into captivity, an unconverted Jew named Daniel had risen, with the cleverness of his race, to be the king's favourite and prime minister; and he was naturally hated by the ecclesiastics of the Court, who were justly incensed that a foreigner who persisted in the worship of Yahweh should be so greatly honoured. Scholars disagree as to whether he is the same Daniel who had similar distinction and troubles according to the Book of Daniel, or another man, or whether either of them ever had an existence—but this does not concern us. Among several circumstances not included in the canonical Bible, but narrated in both the Vulgate and Septuagint versions, the one most pertinent to our theme is that in Babylon a huge dragon was worshipped and fed by the people. Daniel refused to pay it homage, and told the king that if permitted he would kill the monster without using any weapons, and so free the populace from its exactions. His majesty consented, whereupon Daniel made a bolus of indigestible materials, mainly pitch (but some say it was a ball of straw filled with sharpened nails), and threw it into the reptile's maw. It was promptly swallowed, wherefore the monster presently 'burst' and died. (One commentator notes that in Hebrew writing the word for 'pitch' looks much like that for 'tornado,' recalling the 'great wind' by which Marduk put an end to Tiamat.) The ungrateful populace, enraged at this Herculean feat demanded Daniel's death, and the king reluctantly cast him into a den of lions kept as royal executioners, where he stayed a full week unharmed, but likely to starve to death—as also were the lions, inhibited by magic from their prey. On the seventh day another Jew, Habbakuk, was cooking dinner for his harvest-hands on his farm somewhere in the country, when he was lifted up by an angel (as once happened to Ezekiel) and carried to the capital with a quantity of provisions to feed the unfortunate reformer. Daniel was thereupon restored to liberty and power as chief magician, and the famishing lions were fed with humbler priests.

Very ancient Babylonian drawings show Tiamat harnessed to a four-wheeled chariot in which is seated a god who, in the opinion of Dr. William Hayes Ward, we may call Marduk. She is drawn as a composite and terrifying quadruped with the head, shoulders and fore-limbs of a lion, a body covered with scaly feathers, two wings, the hind legs like those of an eagle, and a protruding, deeply forked tongue like that of a snake. In another glyph a goddess sits on a similar beast, holding the 'lightning trident.' A third cylinder-design exhibits such a beast standing on its hind legs and with open mouth over a kneeling man. A curious feature of all these representations is that a second, smaller dragon always appears, running along on all fours like a dog, the meaning of which remains unexplained. Another figure, reproduced by Maspero, and said to represent Nergal, an underworld agent of war and pestilence, shows him accompanied by many 'devils' combining horrid animal and human features, and also Nergal's consort Ereskigal, a serpent-wielding queen, the ugliest picture of a woman imaginable. Nergal has here the body, fore-limbs and tail of a big, square-headed dog, four wings, the under and fore-

DRAGONS AND UNICORNS—FACT? OR FICTION?

most two being small and roundish, while the posterior pair reach back beyond the creature's rump like the shards of a beetle; the body is scaly, and the hind legs have the shape of an eagle's. Perhaps what follows will help us to interpret this ugly composition.

All these art-efforts and their like belong to the earliest period, when southern Babylonia was in possession of the Sumerians. Later a different (Semitic) people from the north and west of them became occupants and rulers of Mesopotamia, and we find among their relics at Nineveh and elsewhere seal-cylinders bearing pictures of the conflict between the warrior-god, Bel-Marduk, and the evil genius of the universe, in which the latter is always being struck at, put to flight or killed.

Afterwards in Assyria such figures were grandly drawn, always with a serpentiform head surmounted by two sharp horns, as in that alabaster slab found in the palace of Ashurbanipal at Nimrud, where a storm-god, wielding tridents, fights the traditional monster. "The horned dragon," says Jastrow, "from being the symbol of Enlil . . . becomes the animal of Marduk and subsequently of Ashur as the head of the Assyrian pantheon." These horns long persisted as a royal mark in memory of the fact that Enlil, as Ea, and afterward Marduk, subjugated Tiamat, showing that the conquering dynasty of Ashur assumed their glory and attributes as part of the spoil.

In subsequent and more cultured times an artistically conventionalized image, retaining all the essential elements required by religious tradition, was devised to represent the Evil Spirit, as is shown by the really elegant coloured and glazed tiles that ornament the exterior walls of the magnificent Gate of Ishtar, the approach to the sacred area of Marduk's temple in the ruins of ancient Babylon, an approach built by Nebuchadnezzar four hundred and seventy-five years before the Christian era. Here the dragon reaches its glorification in Assyria, as, in another way, it attained artistic eminence in China and Japan; yet here too it holds tenaciously to the original conception, even then thousands of years old, so impressive and persistent was the underlying reason therefor.

The very earliest representation known, the model so closely adhered to, is the simplest of all, and in its simplicity best reveals its mythical origin. It is an outline cut on an archaic seal found at Susa, in Persia, which unites the head, wings and feet of a bird (the falcon of Horus) with the lioness of Hathor-Sekhet.

Now it is not necessary to assume that ordinary folk in the towns and gardens and pastures beside either of the two great rivers had a full knowledge, or a lively comprehension, of such ideals and co-relations of gods and men as we have traced. The plain farmer, if given by some priest or sheik such an image as a worshipful object, would probably take it to represent a union of his two worst pests—the lion and eagle that ravaged his herds and preyed on his lambs, while his wife would think of it as a combined jackal and hawk, and treasure it as a charm against their raids upon her chicken-yard. The mystical allegory worked out by the philosophers of the time probably escaped them, and still more likely escaped the busy citizens of Memphis, Nippur, or Susa; yet apparently this philosophy is the principle that has vitalized the persistent, although highly variable, idea which is the soul in the dragon.

"The fundamental element in the dragon's powers," declares Professor Smith, "is the control of water. Both the benevolent and the destructive aspects of water were regarded as animated by the Dragon, who thus assumed the role of Osiris or his enemy Set. But when the attributes of the Water-God became confused with those of the Great Mother and her evil Avatar, the lioness (Sekhet) form of Hathor in Egypt, or in Babylon the destructive Tiamat, became the symbol of disorder and Chaos, the Dragon became identified with her also." This means that all these primeval 'gods' were in nature both good and bad, could be either saints or devils; and certainly they played contradictory roles in an amazing way—were dragon, dragon-slayer and the weapon employed, all in the same personage. This wonder-beast ranges from Western Europe to the Far East of Asia, and, in the view of a few extremists, even across the Pacific to America. "Although in the different localities a great number of most varied ingredients enter into its composition, in most places where the dragon occurs the substratum of its anatomy consists of a serpent or a crocodile, usually with the scales of a fish for covering, and the feet and wings, and sometimes also the head, of an eagle, falcon, or hawk, and the fore-limbs and sometimes the head of a lion. An association of anatomical features of so unnatural and arbitrary a nature can only mean that all dragons are the progeny of the same ultimate ancestors."

DRAGONS AND UNICORNS—FACT? OR FICTION?

CHAPTER TWO

WANDERINGS OF THE YOUNG DRAGON

ON THE assumption, which seems fair, that the historic traces of the dragon have led us back to Egypt and Babylonia—and very likely would lead us much farther could we penetrate the obscurities of a remoter past—it is fitting to inquire next how we may account for its presence and varied development elsewhere. Two theories oppose one another in respect to the fact that this and other myths, prejudices, and customs that appear alike, not to say identical, are encountered in widely separated regions, often half the globe apart. One theory explains it on the principle of the general uniformity of human nature and methods of thought, that is, namely: that peoples not at all in contact but under like mental and physical conditions will arrive independently at much the same conclusions as to the origin and causes of natural phenomena, will interpret mysteries of experience and imagination, and will meet daily problems of life, much as unknown others do. This is the older view among ethnologists, and in certain broad features it finds much support, as, for example, in the almost universal respect paid to rainfall and the influences supposed to affect this prime necessity.

Contrary to this view, most students, possessing broader information than formerly, now believe that such resemblances—strikingly numerous—are not mere coincidences arising from a postulated unity of human nature, but are the result of a spread of travellers and instruction from centres where new and impressive ideas or useful inventions have arisen. One of the foremost advocates of this theory of the geographical dispersion of myths and culture, as opposed to local independence of origin, is Professor Smith, quoted in the first chapter, whose books have been of much use to me in this connection. The theory does not deny the occasional independent rise of similar notions and practices here and there, but asserts that it alone accounts for all the important cases, particularly the central nature-myths, of which this of the dragon is esteemed the most important. The doctrine derives its main strength from its ability to show that in the very early, virtually prehistoric, times much closer contact and more frequent intercommuni-

DRAGONS AND UNICORNS—FACT? OR FICTION?

cation than was formerly known or considered probable existed among primitive peoples all over the inhabited world. Assuming that at the dawn of history the most advanced communities were those of Egypt and Mesopotamia (with Elam), which were certainly in communication with one another both by land and by sea forty or fifty centuries before Christ, let us see how widespread, if at all, was their influence.

That the Egyptians were building large, sea-going ships as early as 2000 B.C. is well known. In them they traded with Crete and Phoenicia (whence the Phoenicians probably first learned the art of navigation) and with western Mediterranean ports. They sailed up and down the Red Sea, exploring Sinai and Yemen; visited Socotta, where grew the dragon-blood tree; went far south along the African shore; searched the Arabian coast, gathering frankincense (said to be guarded in its growth by small winged serpents); and made voyages back and forth between the Red Sea and the ports of Babylonia and Elam on the Persian Gulf. What surprise could there be were records available that these Egyptian mariners or those in the ships of the people about the Gulf of Persia sometimes continued on to India. Indeed Colonel St. Johnston elaborates a theory that not only the Malay Archipelago but the islands of the South Pacific, especially Polynesia, were colonized prehistorically by a stream of immigrants from Africa and India, who crept along the shore of the Indian Ocean, and from island to island in the East Indies, gradually reaching Australia and going on thence to the sea-islands beyond; and he and others believe that they carried with them ancestral ideas of supernatural beings, whence they made for themselves fish-gods and sea-monsters which some ethnologists regard as not only analogues, but descendants, of dragons. It is stoutly held, furthermore, that the religion of the half-civilized tribes of Mexico owes its characteristic features of serpent-worship and dragon-like symbols to the teaching of Asiatic visitors reaching middle America via Polynesia; but this is disputed, and I shall be content to avoid this controversy—also as far as possible serpent-worship per se—and confine myself to continental Asia and Europe.

The southwestern part of Persia, or Elam, was inhabited contemporaneously with early Babylonia, if not before, by a people of equal or superior culture, and holding a like religion. Their capital, Susa, was the most important city east of the lofty mountains between them and the valleys of Mesopotamia, and attracted traders and visitors from a great surrounding space. Most numerous, probably, were those from the north, from Iran, the country about the Caspian Sea and the Caucasus Mountains—inhabited by a race that used to be called Aryans; but many came also from Turanic nomads wandering with their cattle in the valley of the Oxus and eastward to the foot of the Hindoo Koosh, and still others from the eastern plains and coast-lands stretching to the Indus valley.

We may suppose these herdsmen and hunters to have been very simple-minded and crude, and their only semblance of religion to have been the rudest fetishism, animated by fear of ghosts and magic. Only the most enterprising among them, or prisoners of war brought back as slaves, would be likely to visit the more educated South, but there they would hear of definite 'gods' with stories behind them of the creation of the world, the gift of precious rain, and of unseen beings of immeasurable power; and they would learn

10

DRAGONS AND UNICORNS—FACT? OR FICTION?

the reason for representing these divine heroes in the forms they saw inscribed on monuments and temples, or in little images given them, thus getting some notion of the philosophy of worship. They would talk of these things by the camp-fire, when they had returned to Iran or Bactria or the Afghan hills, along with their tales of the civilization in Susa, and gradually plainsmen and mountaineers would grow wiser and more imitative. Sailors and merchants also carried enlightening information and ideas, crude as they may seem to us, into the minds of the natives of the shores of India and along the banks of the navigable Indus, whence this news from the West percolated into the more or less savage interior of the peninsula. Later we shall meet with some results of this slow and accidental propaganda.

Meanwhile, a stronger influence was affecting the North Persians. Soon after we first become acquainted with the Sumerians settled in Ur and other places on the lower Euphrates, we learn that they were conquered by Semitic tribes from the West, who created the Babylonian empire. After a while this was overthrown by still more powerful forces higher up the river, until finally the Assyrians became rulers of the whole valley, and ultimately of all Asia Minor north of the Arabian desert. The ancient gods received new names, but the old ideas remained. The antique dragon still stood at the gates of the Assyrian king's palace, and Ea, the fish-god, reappeared on the shores of the Mediterranean as Dagon of the Philistines. But this is running ahead of my story.

North of Assyria, among the mountains of Armenia, dwelt the Medes, a nation of uncertain affinities, but apparently well advanced towards civilization even in the earlier period of Babylon's history. They were not, at least primitively, influenced much by the sea-born myths of their southern neighbours, but held a religious creed combined of sun-worship and reverence for serpents—a conjunction which has had many examples elsewhere.

There was born among them, according to good authorities, about a thousand years before Jesus, a man of good family, now called Zoroaster; but others believe he arose in Bactria, and probably at a much older time. He became the founder of a sect holding far higher ideas than those of any of the religious leaders about them. His sect was called Fire-Worshippers, because it kept fires burning perpetually on its altars as a symbol of the pure life believed to be received constantly from the supreme source of life and prosperity, Ormuzd, the All-Wise. It was thus a reform movement rather than a new religion, and inherited a stock of Medic practices and Vedic legends. Its founders and early communicants were evidently in close contact with the people of northern India many centuries before the era of Buddha or Christ, and were trying to elevate religious ideas which were based on faith in the endless conflict between powers classed as helpful to man or injurious to his interests, so that the same gods might be good at one time and bad at another. "Zoroaster established a criterion other than usefulness to determine whether a power was good or bad, by making an ethical distinction between the spirits." Thus the old nature-gods were still recognized but re-classified on a new spiritual and ethical basis; yet they shrank into subordinate rank beside the Wise Spirit Ormuzd, who was in no sense a nature-god but "spirit only and withal the spirit of truth, purity, and

DRAGONS AND UNICORNS—FACT? OR FICTION?

justice." These refined ideas gradually sank, however, into the meaner old religion that underlay them; and in opposition to Ormuzd, the personification of All Good, arose a host combined of all the old malicious spirits and influences (demons), led by a supreme personification of Evil called by Zoroaster Lie-Demon, who afterward "becomes the Hostile or Harmful Spirit, Angra Mainyu, Ahriman" of Persian writings. "Among the beings opposed to Ormuzd a conspicuous place is taken by the dragon, Azhi Dahaka, whose home is in Bapel (Babylon) a 'druj,' half-human, half-beast, with three heads. . . . This dragon creates drouth and disease." Here we have recovered the trail of the figure we have been studying, and find him travelling eastward with the mark of Babylon still upon him.

The most ancient writings that have come down to us are the Vedas-poems, fables, and allegories recorded in ancient Sanscrit perhaps a dozen centuries before the beginning of the Christian era. They picture weather phenomena as a series of battles fought by a god, Indra, armed with lightnings and thunder, against Azhi, the evil genius of the universe, who has carried off certain benevolent goddesses described allegorically as 'milch-cows,' and who keeps them captive in the folds of the clouds. This fiend was described as a serpent, not because that reptile in life was subtle and crafty, but because he seeks to envelop the goddess of light, the source of the blessed rain, with coils of clouds as with a snake's folds. In the Gathas and Yasnas, or earliest sacred writings of Persia, preceding the Avesta, the 'Bible' of the Zoroastrians, it is asserted that Trita smote Azhi before Indra killed the "monster that kept back the waters." It is a theory of many primitive peoples that an eclipse of the sun or moon means that a celestial monster is swallowing the luminary: the Sumatrans say it is a big snake. Even at this day in China "ignorant folk at the beginning of an eclipse throw themselves on their knees and beat gongs and drums to frighten away the hungry devil." The moon and rainfall are very closely connected in many mythologies.

The forms and characters in which the sky-war appears are almost innumerable as one reads the mythologic narratives of India and Persia; even the summary sketched in his Zoological Mythology (Chapter V), by Angelo de Gubernatis, is bewildering in its changes of persons and scenes and methods, involving an exuberance of imagery in which may be discerned the roots of many an attribute characterizing the dragon-stories of long-subsequent times, such as their guarding of treasure, or kidnapping of women, or the grotesque horror of their appearance. And it was all a matter of weather and of the preciousness of rain in a thirsty land!

Superstition went so far as to imagine that human beings of malignant temper might adopt the character and functions of these celestial mischief-makers. It is related in the book Si-Yu-Ki, written by Hiuen Tsang, the famous Chinese traveller of the 7th century A.D. (Beal's translation), that in the old days, a certain shepherd provided the king with milk and cream. "Having on one occasion failed to do so, and having received a reprimand, he proceeded . . . with the prayer that he might become a destructive dragon." His prayer was answered affirmatively, and he betook himself to a cavern whence he intended to ravish the country. Then Tathagata, moved by pity, came from a long dis-

12

tance, persuaded the dragon to behave well, and himself took up his abode in the cavern. Having interpolated this incident, it may be pardonable to give another, extracted from the Buddhist Records, illustrating how Buddhist influences tended to modify the fierceness in Brahmanic teachings when they had penetrated the minds of Hindoos dwelling in the valley of the Indus, where, probably, the doctrines of the gentle saint began first to get a foothold in India. The lower valley of that river was visited in 400 A.D., by the Chinese traveller Fa-Huan, who reported that he found at one place a vast colony of male and female disciples:

A white-eared dragon is the patron of this body of priests. He causes fertilizing and seasonable showers of rain to fall within this country, and preserves it from plagues and calamities, and so causes the priesthood to dwell in security. The priests in gratitude for these favours have erected a dragon-chapel, and within it placed a resting-place for his accommodation [and] provide the dragon with food. . . . At the end of each season of rain the dragon suddenly assumes the form of a little serpent both of whose ears are edged with white. The body of priests, recognizing him, place in the midst of his lair a copper vessel full of cream; and then . . . walk past him in procession as if to pay him greeting. He then suddenly disappears. He makes his appearance once every year.

Let us now return to our proper path from this Indian excursion. The Persian Azhi, or Ashi Dahaka, is described in Yasti IX as a "fiendish snake, three-jawed and triple-headed, six-eyed, of thousand powers and of mighty strength, a lie-demon of the Daevas, evil for our settlements, and wicked, whom the evil spirit Angra Mainyu made." Darmesteter asserts that the original seat of the Azhi myth was on the southern shore of the Caspian Sea. He says that Azhi was the 'snake' of the storm-cloud, and is the counterpart of the Vedic Ahi or Vritra. "He appears still in that character in Yasti XIX seq., where he is described struggling against Atar (Fire) in the sea Vourukasha. His contest with Yima Khshaeta bore at first the same mythological character, the 'shining Yima' being originally, like the Vedic Yima, a solar hero: when Yima was turned into an earthly king Azhi underwent the same fate." He became then the symbol of the enemies of Iran, first the hated Chaldeans and later the Arabs who persecuted the Zoroastrians. A well-known poem of Firdausi relates the legend of how Ahriman in disguise kisses the shoulders of Zohak, a knight who is Azhi in human form, from which kiss sprang venomous serpents. These are replaced as fast as destroyed, and must be fed on the brains of men. In the end Zohak is seized and chained to a rock, where he perishes beneath the rays of the sun. "Fire is everywhere the deadly foe of these 'fiendish' serpents, which are water-spirits; they are ever powerless against the sun, as was Azhi, lacking wit, against Ormuzd."

Such were the notions and faiths regarding dragons as expressed in the earliest written records we possess of philosophy and imagery among Aryan folk; and they floated down the stream of time, remembered and trusted as generation after generation of these simple-minded, poetic people succeeded one another and gradually wandered away from their northern homes to become conquerors and colonists in Iran and India. Let us note certain stories in modern Persian history and literature exhibiting this survival of the ancient ideas.

DRAGONS AND UNICORNS—FACT? OR FICTION?

In his narrative of his travels in Persia, published in London in 1821, Sir William Ouseley relates that in his time there stood near Shiraz the remains of a once mighty castle called Fahender after its builder, a son of the legendary king Ormuz (or Hormuz). This prince rebelled against his brother on the throne and took possession of Fars, with help from the Sassanian family, long before the founding of Shiraz in the 7th century A.D. The castle was repeatedly ruined and repaired as the centuries progressed, and local wiseacres maintain that in it are buried royal arms, treasures, and jewels hidden by the ancient kings, and these are guarded by a talisman. "Tradition adds another guardian to the precious deposit—a dragon or winged serpent; this sits forever brooding over the treasures which it cannot enjoy; greedy of gold, like those famous griffins that contended with the ancient Arimaspians."

This term 'Arimaspian' seems to have been a name among the more settled people of Persia for the more or less nomadic tribes of the plains and mountains west of them, who in subsequent times, nearer the beginning of our era, are seen following one another in great waves of conquering migration from the steadily drying pastures of what we now call Kurdistan westward to the steppes of southern Russia. The earliest of these known as a definite nation were the Cimmerians, who perhaps reached their special country north of the sea of Azov by migration across the mountains of Armenia and the Caucasus. These were followed and replaced by the Scythians, and they in turn were driven out or absorbed by the Sarmatians. The area they occupied successively north of the Black Sea has been explored by Russian archaeologists, who find that during several centuries previous to the Christian era a substantial though crude civilization existed there, and the worship, or at least a respect for, the snake-dragon prevailed among these peoples. The writings of Prof. M. Rostovtzeff make these investigations accessible to English readers. The dragon-relics discovered make it evident that the notions relating to this matter preserved among the barbarians and peasantry of north-central Europe, which we shall encounter later, were largely derived from these proto-Russians, especially the Sarmatians; and also that they influenced the ideas of the dragon that we shall find in China, with which these early people of the western plains were in constant communication by way of Turkestan, Thibet and Mongolia.

Thus Osvald Siren, author of Chinese Art, in speaking of very early Chinese sculptures, and especially of dragon-figures, remarks:

It seems evident that these dragons are of Sarmatian origin. Their enormous heads and claws are sometimes translated into pure ornaments; their tails into rhythmic curves like the ornamental dragons on the runic stones in Gotland. These two great classes of ornamental dragons, the Chinese and the Scandinavian, are no doubt descendants from the same original stock, which may have had its first period of artistic procreation in western Asia. The artistic ideals of the northern Wei dynasty remained preponderant in Chinese sculpture up to the sixth century (A.D.).

In his famous epic the Shah Nameh, translated by Atkinson, Firdausi describes the

DRAGONS AND UNICORNS—FACT? OR FICTION?

wondrous adventures of the Persian hero Rustem, who like Hercules had to perform seven labours. At the third stage of this task he was alone in a wilderness with his magical horse Rakush, and lay down to sleep at night, after turning the horse loose to graze. Presently a great dragon came out of the forest. "It was eighty yards in length, and so fierce that neither elephant nor demon nor lion ever ventured to pass by its lair." As it came forth it saw and attacked the horse, whose resistance awakened Rustem; but when Rustem looked around nothing was visible—the dragon had vanished and the horse got a scolding. Rustem went to sleep again. A second time the vision frightened Rakush, then vanished. The third time it appeared the faithful horse "almost tore up the earth with its heels to rouse his sleeping master." Rustem again sprang angrily to his feet, but at that moment sufficient light was providentially given to enable him to see the prodigious cause of the horse's alarm.

Then swift he drew his sword and closed in strife

With that huge monster.—Dreadful was the shock

And perilous to Rustem, but when Rakush

Perceived the contest doubtful, furiously

With his keen teeth he bit and tore among

The dragon's scaly hide; whilst, quick as thought,

The champion severed off the grisly head,

And deluged all the plain with horrid blood.

Another hero of popular legend woven into his history by Firdausi was Isfendiar (son of King Gushtask, himself a dragon-killer), who also had to perform seven labours, the second of which was to fight an enormous and venomous dragon such as this:

Fire sparkles round him; his stupendous bulk Looks like a mountain. When incensed his roar Makes the surrounding country shake with fear, White poison foam drips from his hideous jaws, Which, yawning wide, display a dismal gulf, The grave of many a hapless being, lost Wandering amidst that trackless wilderness. Isfendiar's companion, Kurugsar, so magnified the power and ferocity of the beast, which he knew of old, that Isfendiar thought it well to be cautious, and therefore had constructed a closed car on wheels, on the outside of which he fastened a large number of pointed instruments. To the amazement of his admirers he then shut himself within this armoured chariot, and proceeded towards the dragon's haunt. Listen to Firdausi:

. . . Darkness now is spread around, No pathway can be traced; The fiery horses plunge and bound Amid the dismal waste. And now the dragon stretches far His cavern-

15

DRAGONS AND UNICORNS—FACT? OR FICTION?

throat, and soon Licks the horses and the car, And tries to gulp them down. But sword and javelin sharp and keen, Wound deep each sinewy jaw; Midway remains the huge machine And chokes the monster's maw. And from his place of ambush leaps, And brandishing his blade, The weapon in the brain he steeps, And splits the monster's head. But the foul venom issuing thence, Is so o'erpowering found, Isfendiar, deprived of sense, Falls staggering to the ground. As for the dragon-In agony he breathes, a dire Convulsion fires his blood, And, struggling ready to expire, Ejects a poison flood. And thus disgorges wain and steeds. And swords and javelins bright; Then, as the dreadful dragon bleeds, Up starts the warrior knight.

DRAGONS AND UNICORNS—FACT? OR FICTION?

CHAPTER THREE

INDIAN NAGAS AND DRACONIC PROTOTYPES

AT A very early period northern India acquired a mixed population composed of Conquerors and more peaceful immigrants from the west and north, which became amalgamated with whatever remained in the previous inhabitants; and an antique form of Sanscrit spoken by the invaders became the general language. They appear, as far back as they can be traced, to have been an agricultural and cattle-breeding people, using horses, settled mainly in towns and villages, and considerably advanced towards civilization. Their religious ideas, at least within the millennium next preceding the beginning of the Christian era, as we learn from the Vedas, were expressed in a mythology of nature-gods related to the sun and sky and, especially to the weather as affecting grass and crops, with which was mixed a very ancient and fetishistic serpent-worship. In short these ancestral Hindoos much resembled in ideas the people of Elam and Chaldea with whom they were already in communication, but far exceeded them in their reverence of serpents—naturally, perhaps, as these are more numerous and dangerous in India than in Mesopotamia.

Their particular object in serpent-veneration was the deadly cobra, called naga; and every one of these hooded reptiles was regarded as the living incarnation or representative of a great and fearful company of mythological nagas. These were demi-gods in various serpentine forms, uncertain of temper and fearful in possibilities of harm, whose 'kings' lived in luxury in magnificent palaces in the depths of the sea or at the bottom of inland lakes. They were also said to inhabit an underworld (Patala Land), and were believed to control the clouds, produce thunderstorms, guard treasures, and do weird and marvellous things in general. Many feats were attributed to them which could be performed only by beings having human powers and faculties, whence they were said to assume human form from time to time; and stories are told in the writings of 'naga-people'

17

DRAGONS AND UNICORNS—FACT? OR FICTION?

appearing mysteriously and then escaping to the depths of the ocean—probably developed from incidents in which wild strangers had raided the coast and when discovered had fled over the horizon in their boats. The ruder tribes, which were most addicted to cobra-worship, and were despised by the Brahmanic class, were known as Naga men or simply Nagas. This cult persists in remote districts to this day, and is especially vigorous in the rough country of northern Burma and Siam, where temples of snake-worship are yet maintained. Doubtless it formerly prevailed beyond India all over the Malay Peninsula and among the unknown aborigines of China.

It must be remembered in connection with these facts that the semi-civilized inhabitants of the Northwest were largely a maritime people. Living along the great Indus River they early took to the sea and became daring navigators, voyaging far eastward on both plundering and trading expeditions. The civilization of both Burma and Indochina, according to Oldham's investigations, is shown by history as well as legend to be owing to invaders from India, who introduced there not only ideas of a settled life and trade, but taught the notions of naga-worship, and later Buddhistic doctrines and practices throughout southern China, Java, Sumatra and Celebes. Buddha himself refers to such voyages, in which no doubt religious missionaries sometimes participated.

Mingled with this was direct reaching from Babylon and Egypt, as has already been mentioned. "Within twenty years of the introduction of the Phoenician navy into the Persian Gulf by Sennacherib traders from the Red Sea arrived in the gulf of Kiao-Chau, and soon established colonies there." This was in the middle of the sixth century B.C. "They came on ships bearing bird or animal heads and two big eyes on the bow, and two large steering-oars at the stern—distinctly Egyptian methods of ship-building."

Into the Vedic civilization of northern India, was introduced, about the seventh century B.C., the more spiritual and unselfish cult of Buddhism. Its most difficult problem was the overcoming of cobra-worship, and as this proved impossible, the Buddhists were compelled to be content with trying to improve the worst features of ophiolatry among the Naga tribes; but this conciliatory attitude seems to have led to a weakening and corruption of the gospel preached by Buddha and his first apostles. Legends, though conflicting, indicate this. It is related, for example, that a naga king foretold the attainment of Gautama to Buddhahood; and the cobra-king who lived in Lake Mucilinda sheltered Lord Buddha for seven days from wind and rain by his coils and spreading hoods, as is represented in many antique pictures and sculptures. At any rate a schism developed over this matter, resulting in the southern Buddhists teaching less strict doctrine with reference to the old beliefs, which became known as the Manhayana school.

The nagas' ability to raise clouds and thunder when out of temper was cleverly absorbed by this school into the highly beneficent power of giving rain to thirsty earth, and so these dreadful beings became by the influence of Buddha's 'Law' blessers of men. "In this garb," as Dr. Visser' points out, they were readily identified with the Chinese dragons, which were also beneficent rain-gods of water"; and it was this modified, semi-Hindoo, Manhayana conception of Buddhism, with its tolerance of serpent-divinity, which

DRAGONS AND UNICORNS—FACT? OR FICTION?

was carried by wandering missionaries and traders during the later Han period into China and eastward.

Visser ascertained, in his profound examination of this serpent-cult, that in later Indian, that is Greco-Buddhist, art, the nagas appear as real dragons, although with the upper part of the body human. "So we see them on a relief from Gandahara, worshipping the Buddha's alms-bowl in the shape of big water-dragons, scaled and winged, with two horse-legs, the upper part of the body human." They may be found represented even as men or women with snakes coming out of their necks and rising over their heads, which recalls the prime fiends of Persian legend, and also the prehistoric pictures of the more or less mythical Chinese sage Fu Hsi.

The four classes into which the Indian Manhayanists divided their nagas were (quoting Visser):

Heavenly Nagas—who uphold and guard the heavenly palace.

Divine Nagas—who cause clouds to rise and rain to fall.

Earthly Nagas—who clear out and drain off rivers, opening outlets.

Hidden Nagas—guardians of treasures.

This corresponds closely with Professor Cyrus Adler's list (Report U. S. National Museum, 1888), of the four kinds of Chinese dragons: "The early cosmogonists enlarged on the imaginary data of previous writers and averred that there were distinct kinds of dragons proper—the t'ien-lung or celestial dragon, which guards the mansions of the gods and supports them so that they do not fall; the shen-lung or spiritual dragon, which causes the winds to blow and produces rain for the benefit of mankind; the ti-lung or dragon of the earth, which marks out the courses of rivers and streams; and the fu-ts'ang-lung or dragon of hidden treasures, which watches over the wealth concealed from mortals. Modern superstition has further originated the idea of four dragon kings, each bearing rule over one of the four seas which form the borders of the habitable earth."

In a Tibetan picture referred to by Visser nagas are depicted in three forms: Common snakes guarding jewels; human beings with four snakes in their necks; and winged sea-dragons, the upper part of the body human, but with a horned, ox-like head, the lower part of the body that of a coiling dragon. This shows how a queer mixture of Chaldean, Persian and Hindoostanee elements reached Tibet by very ancient caravan roads north of the Himalayan ranges; and it throws light on one possible origin of the four-legged figure adopted by the Chinese, especially in the northern marches of the empire where the inhabitants were open to Bactrian, Scythian, and other western influences.

That composite animal-form of the rain-god of the Euphrates people, the horned sea-

DRAGONS AND UNICORNS—FACT? OR FICTION?

goat of Marduk (immortalized as the Capricornus of our Zodiac), was also the vehicle of Varuna in India, whose relationship to Indra was in some respects analogous to that of Ea to Marduk in Babylonia. In his account of Sanchi and its ruins General Maisey, as quoted by Smith, states that: "As to the fish-incarnation of Vishnu and Sakya Buddha, and as to the makara, dragon or fish-lion, another form of which was the naga of the waters, the use of the symbol by both Brahmans and Buddhists, and their common use of the sacred barge, are proofs of the connection between both forms of religion and the far older myths of Egypt and Assyria." Havell is of the opinion that the crocodile-dragon which appears in the figure of Siva dancing in the great temple of Tanjore, may have been older than the eleventh century when the temple was built. "In the earlier Indian rendering of this sun-symbolism, as seen in the Buddhist 'horse-shoe' arches," says Havell, "the crocodile-dragon, the demon of darkness, who swallows the sun at night and releases it in the morning, is not combined with these sun-windows until after the development of the Manhayana school."

Sun-worship, serpent-worship, phallicism, and dragons are inextricably interwoven in Oriental mythology.

It is in the Indian makara, I think, that we have the 'link' between the Western conception and that of the Chinese as to the shape of this fabulous water-spirit. Yet, all the makaras of Vedic myth are simply a crocodile in simple form, or else are variants of Marduk's sea-goat with two front feet only, varied according to the head and body into antelopes (blackbuck), cats, elephants, etc., all carrying fish-tails. The Chinese dragon, on the other hand, has nothing of the fish about it, but is wholly serpent, except its horned and fantastic head and the fact that it invariably possessed (crocodile-like) four legs and feet which are quite as like those of a bird as like those of a lion. There is evidently some significance in the bird-like feet. Can they be a relic of the introduction ages ago of the Babylonian or Elamite figure of the rain-god, composed by joining the symbols of Hathor-Sekhet and Horus? That is to say, do they possibly represent the long-forgotten falcon of the bright son of Osiris?

"In Chinese Buddhism," Dr. Anderson informs us in his celebrated Catalogue, "the dragon plays an important part either as a fierce auxiliary to the Law or as a malevolent creature to be converted or quelled. Its usual character, however, is that of a guardian of the faith under the direction of Buddha, Bodhisattvas, or Arhats. As a dragon king it officiates at the baptism of the Sakyamuni, or bewails his entrance into Nirvana; as an attribute of saintly or divine personages it appears at the feet of the Arhat Panthaka, emerging from the sea to salute the goddess Kuanyin, or as an attendant upon or alternative form of Sarasvati, the Japanese Benten; as an enemy of mankind it meets its Perseus and Saint George in the Chinese monarch Kao Tsu (of the Han dynasty) and the Shinto god Susano'no Mikoto. When this religion made its way into China, where the hooded snake was unknown, the emblems shown in the Indian pictures and graven images lost their force of suggestion, and hence became replaced by a mythical but more familiar emblem of power."

20

DRAGONS AND UNICORNS—FACT? OR FICTION?

It was mainly—but not altogether, as we shall see—from Indian sources that the now familiar four-footed dragon of China became conventialized through its applications in the several arts of decoration and devotion; and it seems a fair inference that the aggressive Buddhist influence of the early centuries of that sect led Chinese artists to change the smooth, well-proportioned ch'ih-lung of their forefathers, chin-bearded like the ancient sages, into a sort of jungle python with the horrifying head and face characteristic of the countenances of antique Buddhistic images of their demons. To understand how inhumanly terrible these caricatures of malignant beings in the guise of humanity may be, one need only glance at drawings of the temple images exhumed by Sir Aurel Stern from the sand-buried Indo-Chinese cities of Turkestan, which flourished about the time of which I am speaking.

Buddhist artists, at first probably aliens, would be likely to depict the dragon head and face in their attempts to portray the chief 'demon', as they mistakenly regarded the friendly Chinese divinity, after the same horrifying fashion. Then, to impress the people of the North, who saw few dangerous snakes, but who did know and fear tigers and leopards, the artists equipped their frightful-headed serpent with catlike legs, bird's feet, such tufts of hair as decorate and would suggest a lion, and a novel ridge of iguana-like spines along its backbone.

The fully realized dragon, then, as we see it in bronzes or sprawled across a silken screen, is an invention of decorative artists striving, during the last 2000 years, to embody a traditional but essentially foreign idea.

DRAGONS AND UNICORNS—FACT? OR FICTION?

CHAPTER FOUR

THE DIVINE SPIRIT OF THE WATERS

TODAY, WHEN one hears the word 'dragon' one's mind almost inevitably pictures the fantastic figure embroidered in red and gold thread on some gorgeous Chinese garment, or winding its clouded way about the lustrous curves of a Japanese vase. To Western eyes it is hardly more than a quaint conventionalized ornament, but to Orientals, let me repeat, it is an embodiment of all the significance of national history and ancient philosophy—the natural and supreme symbol of their race and culture. Again, the Western man looks on the dragon as something as mythical as the Man in the Moon, but the great mass of the people in China, Tibet, and Korea, at least, believe in the lung (its ancient name) as now alive, active and numerous—believe in it with as firm and simple a faith as our infants put in the existence of Santa Claus, or the Ojibway in his Thunder Bird, or you and I in the law of gravitation. "The legends of Buddhism abound with it; Taoist tales contain circumstantial accounts of its doings; the whole countryside is filled with stories of its hidden abodes, its terrific appearances; . . . its portrait appears in houses and temples, and serves even more than the grotesque lion as an ornament in architecture, art-designs and fabrics." So testifies one who knew!

It is generally agreed that the original Chinese came in from the plateaus west and north of the Yellow River by following its sources down to the plains. This river takes its name (Hoang-Ho) from the hue of its soil-laden current, and that may account, in connection with the golden tint of the venerated sun's light, for the supremacy of yellow in Chinese mythology and political history: it is the national as it was the imperial color until the yellow dragon-flag of the senile empire fell beneath the stripes of the young Republic.

Everywhere the dragon, when first heard of, is associated with the genesis of the arts of civilization in China. Myths relating to it go back to the thirty-third century before

DRAGONS AND UNICORNS—FACT? OR FICTION?

Christ, and to the sage Fu Hsi who then (or, as some say, between 2853 and 2738 B.C.) dwelt in the Province of Honan, and from whom dates the legendary as distinguished from a mythical period before him.

One day Fu Hsi saw a yellow 'dragon-horse'—a horseheaded water-beast of some sort—rise from the Lo River, a tributary of the Hoang Ho, marked on its back with an arrangement of curling hairs expressing somehow those mysterious Trigrams that have survived for the puzzlement of scholars, but are generally considered as the formula or apparatus of a system of prehistoric divination based on mathematics—the theory of the symbolic quality of numbers so widespread and influential in the ancient East. The Trigrams are expounded in that book of unknown antiquity, the Yi King, which is the Bible of the Taoists, and seem to form an attempt at graphic demonstration of the mystical principle at the heart of Chinese philosophy expressed in the terms 'yang' and its antithesis 'yin'. We shall meet these contrasted terms wherever our search may lead us, and shall learn that the sages have found in them, as DeGroot, the foremost expositor of Chinese theology, expresses it, a "clue to the mysteries of nature and an unfathomable lake of metaphysical wisdom."

Be this as it may, the dragon-horse is a strange feature of the history of our subject, and one still among the possibilities of vision to the eyes of the faithful. A native commentary on one of the Classics, written in the second century B.C., and consulted by Dr. Visser, informs its readers that a dragon-horse is the vital spirit of heaven and earth fused together. "Its shape consists of a horse's body, yet it has dragon-scales. Its height is eight ch'ih, five ts'un. A true dragon-horse has wings at its sides and walks upon the water without sinking. If a holy man is on the throne it comes out of the midst of the Ming River carrying a map [i.e., the Trigrams] on its back." Wang Fu, another author of early Han times, says: "The people paint the dragon's shape with a horse's head and a snake's tail. Further, there are such expressions as 'three joints' and 'nine resemblances,' to wit, from head to shoulder, from shoulder to breast, from breast to tail." The nine resemblances referred to seem to indicate nine kinds of animals, parts of which are combined in this imaginary beast. Another description mentions particularly a tail like that of a huge serpent; and Wang Kia asserts in his book, written A.D. 557, that Emperor Muh, of the Chow dynasty, once "drove around the world in a carriage drawn by eight winged dragon-horses." Some kings saddled and rode these prototypes of the classic Pegasus. Certainly horse-like figures with queer little feathery wings and upturned feathery tails appear in art produced under the Han dynasty, and later one finds drawings or sculptures of them showing well-developed wings. Visser quotes a reference, as late as 741 A.D., to the appearance, somewhere in China, of a living blue-and-red example that was heard "neighing like a flute." The dragon-horse is known in Japanese folklore also.

It seems to me very natural and interesting that these earliest recoverable notions of the aspect of the dragon should have conceived of it as having an equine form, reminiscent of the primitive home and habits of the ancestors of these adventurers in the Hoang-Ho Valley in whose nomadic life horses had borne so essential a part; and it is further interesting to observe that in Tibet representations of the dragon, with little resemblance

DRAGONS AND UNICORNS—FACT? OR FICTION?

otherwise to the conventional Chinese model, have the legs and hoofs of the horse instead of those of the lion or the eagle.

Recalling the significance attached by some native commentators to the strange markings on the back of the equine creature which legend says appeared before the sage Fu Hsi, that, namely, they taught him the making and use of the ideographic characters by which Chinese is written, it is worth while to mention a tradition of the legendary emperor Tsang Kie, to whose reign is popularly attributed the introduction of writing as well as other inventions of importance. "One day, the emperor, surrounded by his principal ministers, was thinking of . . . how much had been accomplished, when an immense dragon descended from the clouds, and placed itself at his feet. The emperor, and those who had assisted him in his wonderful discoveries, got upon the reptile's back, which forthwith took its flight to celestial regions." Several early Buddhist heroes and worthies were similarly translated.

The interesting point of resemblance in these legends is that they agree in making the knowledge of writing a divine gift—a fact most appropriate to the pride of the Chinese in literary accomplishments.

The earliest example known to me of a dragon in recognizable Chinese form is shown on some ancient pillars In the city of Yung-Ch'eng near Tientsin.

During an archaeological survey of the coastal district of southern Shansi province, China, wherein much of the earliest history and tradition of the Chinese has its source, Dr. Chi Li was led to inspect certain old temples in the city of Yun-Chi'eng, a brief note on which appears in "The Explorations and Field Work of the Smithsonian Institution in 1926," accompanied by the photograph which the Institution has generously allowed me to reproduce here. Dr. Li's account is as follows:

In "Shansi-t'ung-chih" (Vol. 52, p. 2) it is recorded that the stone pillars of these temples were formerly the palace pillars of Wei Hui-wang (335-370 A.D.), recovered from the ruined city south of An-i Hsien. Some of them are now used as the entrance pillars in Ch'en-huang Miao and Hou-t'u Miao, and those of Ch'en-huang Miao certainly show peculiar features which are worth recording. Two pillars, hexagonal in section, and carved with dragons coiled around them, are found at the entrance. The left one is especially interesting because in the claws of the dragon are clasped two human heads with perfect Grecian features: curly hair, aquiline and finely chiselled nose, small mouth and receding cheeks. One head with the tongue sticking out is held at the mouth of the dragon, while the other is held in the talons of one hind leg. It is an unusually fine piece of sculpture in limestone. . . . I saw 28 of this kind of pillar in the succeeding two days; but most of them were imitations. It is possible, however, that some are of the ancient type and were made earlier than others. The whole subject is well worth more detailed study.

This brief account (which comes while the book is in the hands of the printer so that the facts may not be further elucidated here), is of particular interest as one of the earli-

DRAGONS AND UNICORNS—FACT? OR FICTION?

est representations of the creature we are studying after it had begun to take its modern shape. Here it has a more naturally crocodilian form, especially as to the head, which has not yet acquired the fantastically frightful shape and appendages given it by later artists. It is also notable that the precious flaming 'pearl,' so important a feature in all modern figures, is already associated with this statue of fifteen centuries ago.

A very ancient bit of folklore, which accounts for the birth of the dragon in the form in which we now know it, was found in the archives of Weihaiwei, in Shantung, by R. F. Johnston, and is recorded in his book as follows:

The legend current in Weihaiwei regarding the origin of the dragon-king (who may be compared with the naga-raja of the Indian Peninsula) runs somewhat as follows: His mother was an ordinary mortal, but gave birth to him in a manner that was not—to say the least—quite customary. Being in his dragonshape the lusty infant immediately flew away on a journey of exploration, but returned periodically for the purpose of being fed. As he grew larger and more terrifying day by day his mother grew much alarmed, and confided her woes to her husband, the dragon's father. The father after due consideration decided there was no help for it but to cut off his preposterous son's head: so next day he waited behind a curtain, sword in hand, for the dragon's arrival. The great creature flew into the house in his usual unceremonious manner, curled his tail around a beam below the roof, and hung head downwards in such a way that by swaying himself he could reach his mother's breast.

At this juncture his father came from behind the curtain, whirled his sword around his head, and brought it down on what ought to have been the dragon's neck. But whether it was that his hand shook or his prey was too quick for him the fact remains that the dragon's head remained where it was. . . . Before the sword could be whirled a second time the dragon seized his father round the waist, untwisted his tail from the beam in the roof, and flew away to the eastern seas. The dragon's father was never seen again, but the dragon and his mother were elevated to divine rank from which they have never since been displaced. The reasons for elevation to godhead are perhaps not quite apparant: but the popular saying that "the dragon's bounty is as profound as the ocean, and the mother-dragon's virtue is as lofty as the hills," has a reference to their functions as controllers of the rains and clouds.

Passing by various more or less fabulous sources of doubtful information, we come down to the time of the Chow dynasty in the twelfth century, B.C., where begins a fairly trustworthy account of imperial acts. Collections of songs and stories that are older remain, but the most important of ancient literary productions, the five great 'Classics,' were published during the early reigns of this period. "With the Chow founder, the great Wen Wang," writes Professor Ernest Fenollosa, "we are on pretty firm historic ground. This acute personage, whose name means 'king of literature,' was the first great Chinese author and philosopher. It was he who composed in prison the original score of the Yi King, or Book of Changes, which Confucius much later elaborated. In this work the symbolism of dragon categories is so bound up with imperial acts as to be the origin of all

DRAGONS AND UNICORNS—FACT? OR FICTION?

that is still implied in the terms 'dragon-throne,' 'dragon-face,' 'dragon-banner.' In a sense the dragon is the type of a man self-controlled and with powers that verge on the supernatural."

It must not be forgotten, meanwhile, that these notions are closely connected with that mysterious Chinese conception called feng-shui, which from time immemorial has been the ruling influence in determining a large part of personal and public affairs throughout the nation, especially with whatever has to do with disturbance of the ground, fixing a local position (as for a house or a grave), or the supposed celestial influences.

Feng-shui, literally translated, means nothing more than wind and (rain-)water,' but these words alone fail to convey Its full significance. "It originated," De Groot explains, "In ancient ages from the then prevailing conceptions . . . that the inhabitants of this world all live under the sway of the influences of heaven and earth, and that every one desirous of securing his own felicity must live in perfect harmony with those influences. . . . This reverential awe of the mysterious influences of nature is the fundamental principle of an ancient religious system usually styled by foreigners Taoism [Tao's Way, i.e., path]." Few Chinese even now are enlightened or brave enough to put up any sort of building except in accordance with the theories of feng-shui, which often require childish particulars. Most important is it, for instance, that a grave should have something symbolic of the tiger on its right, or theoretical west side, and of a dragon on the left (east) side, "for these animals represent all that is meant by the word Feng-shui, 'viz: both aeolian and aquatic influences." So writes De Groot. Anesaki explains further, in his book on Buddhist art, the reference to the association of dragon and tiger: "In this contending pair the Zenists, a sect of Buddhists, saw a graphic representation of the all-controlling forces which break down terrestrial distinctions and fuse together heaven and earth."

Ball quotes an example of how feng-shui may be troublesome to both European and native attempts at progress in Western fashion. He writes:

In the phraseology of this occult science, when two buildings are beside one another the one on the left is said to be built on the Green Dragon, and the one on the right on the White Tiger. Now the tiger must not be higher than the dragon, or death or bad luck will result. Supposing now a European or American gets a site for a residence next to and on the right-hand side of a native dwelling—here are all the elements ready for trouble, for, to begin with, the foreigner will naturally desire a house more suitable for habitation than the low abode of the average Chinaman.

Feng-shui has well been called China's curse!

In view of the association of dragons with this geomantic superstition it need not surprise us to find that divination and prophecy belong to their powers; but the portents and omens derived from this source depend so much on external conditions and the opinions of soothsayers that no satisfactory rules for consultation seem to exist. Visser

DRAGONS AND UNICORNS—FACT? OR FICTION?

learned that the appearance of a black dragon presaged destruction—but who knows a black dragon when he sees it? Traditions report that the advent of certain great men of the past was foretold by dragons. They say that in the night when Confucius was born two azure dragons came from the sky to his mother's house. A dragon appeared in a red vapour just before the birth of Hiao Wu, the famous man of the Han dynasty. The appearance of yellow or azure dragons was always in old times considered a very good omen, provided they did not present themselves at the wrong time or place. Lu Kwang, who lived in the fourth century B.C., saw one night a black horned dragon. "Its eyes illuminated the whole vicinity, so that the huge monster was visible until it was enveloped by the clouds which gathered from all sides. Next morning traces of its scales were to be seen over a distance of five miles, but soon were wiped out by heavy rains." Other ancients have seen similar nightmonsters, such as that which shone upon the palace of Shun-shuh, who, became emperor in A.D. 25.

This introduces the pseudo-science, geomancy, which is founded on the almost divine doctrine of feng-shui, and in which the dragon plays a most important part, because it represents the watershed-slopes and foothills as well as the streams that wind their way among them in any locality toward the general outlet. "In short," to quote again from De Groot, "geomancy comprises the high grounds in general: hence many geographical names, such, for example, as Nine Dragons (Kau Lung) given to the range of hills opposite Hong Kong known to the English as Kowloon. The apparent contradiction here seems to be adjusted by considering the hills as the source of the watercourses." This identification with water, an all-important element in feng-shui, classifies dragons with the spring, the season of fertilizing rains, and in southern China March is called dragon-month. The relations and symbolism of the seasons and the four quarters of the earth, etc., are as tabulated below:

Spring	**East**	**blue**	**azure dragon**
Summer	**South**	**red**	**phenix (feng)**
Autumn	**West**	**white**	**tiger**
Winter	**North**	**black**	**tortoise**

Here the dragon heads the list of the four 'celestial' or 'intelligent' animals that existed in and made possible the Golden Age.

I find in Dr. Laurence Binyon's delightful little book, *"The Flight of the Dragon,"* a comment illuminating this association of things and ideas:

In Chinese popular tradition there are five colours. These are blue, yellow, red, white, and black. Each of these are linked by tradition with certain associations. Thus blue is associated with the east, red with the south, white with the west, black with the north and yellow with the earth. . . . Blue appears originally not to have been distinguished from green—at least the same word was used for both—and it was associated with the east because of the coming of spring with its green. That black should be associated with the cold north seems more intelligible, and that to the black north would be opposed the red

DRAGONS AND UNICORNS—FACT? OR FICTION?

of the fiery south; but that white should belong to the west because autumn comes with the winds from that quarter, heralded by white frosts, seems a far-fetched explanation. And when we pursue the ulterior significance of the colours into still wider regions; when we find blue associated with wood, red with fire, white with metal, black with water; still more when we are told that the five colours have each correspondences with the emotions (white with mourning, for instance, and black with worry), and not only with these but with musical notes, with the senses and with flavours, I fear the august commonsense of the Occident becomes affronted and impatient.

Preeminent in all this plexus of faiths and fancies is the cardinal fact that the Oriental dragon stands for 'water.'

"If one represents water without representing dragons there is nothing to show the divinity of its phenomena," declared an ancient writer cited by Dr. Visser. Another antique script describes a divine being in the waters of the earth akin to the snake, which sleeps in pools during the winter, whence in spring it ascends to the sky. These mysticisms evidently refer to fresh waters alone (the salt seas are in another class), just as in Ur, Ea, the god of the rain-clouds, and of the streams and lakes they fed, was regarded as quite distinct from oceanic deities; and such reverential ideas must, it would seem, have had their genesis in the minds of people of an arid region whose thoughts were continually on their water-supply. But in the softer circumstances which resulted from their finding homes in the fertile valleys of China they felt the apprehension of drouth less severely, and began to ponder on the reasonableness of their ancient fears and present veneration. "Water," declared Lao Tzu, "is the weakest and softest of things, yet overcomes the strongest and the hardest." It penetrates everywhere subtly, without noise, without effort. "So it becomes typical of the spirit, which is able to pass out into all other existences of the world and resume its own form in man; and, associated with the power of fluidity, the dragon becomes the symbol of the infinite." Water-worship, indeed, is a widespread and very ancient cult, the central idea being that water is the source and means of fertility and also of purification in its higher senses. Hence great rivers have been invested with a sacred character, notably the Nile and the Ganges; even the Yangtse and Hoang rivers have inspired similar sentiments. Plutarch says that Nile water, which fecundated the earth, was carried in processions in honour of Isis as representing the seed of Osiris. The stark necessity of water in the plan of creation and the scheme of life seems to have impressed the primitive man of and Central Asia with amazing force.

A Chinese author of the third century B. C. assures his readers that mankind cannot see dragons rise, but that wind and rain assist them to attain a great height; another asserts that the dragon does not ascend if there is no wind. Whirlwinds that carry heavy objects aloft, and at sea cause waterspouts, have always been looked upon as dragons winging their way to the upper regions of the air; and smoking holes in the ground connected with volcanic action are said to be holes whence they emerge for their flights. In the beginning of summer, as we are informed by one commentator, the dragons of the world are divided, so that each has a separate territory whose limits he does not pass. This is the reason why in summer it may rain very much at one place and not at all at

DRAGONS AND UNICORNS—FACT? OR FICTION?

another not far away.

The dragon is also god of thunder, appearing in the sky as clouds (said by some to be formed of his breath) and in the rice-fields as rain, whence he is worthy of veneration as the power that produces good crops. Sometimes cloud-birds (or bird-clouds) are seen helping him.

Since early times high floods, tempests and ordinary thunderstorms have been attributed by rural Chinese to dragons fighting in the air or in rivers. This is not a blessing to humanity, such as they bestow by peacefully shedding rain on the planted fields, and therefore the threatening 'herds' of dragons advancing to combat were looked at with fright. An account of a dragon-fight in a pool in northern Liang, in 503 B.C., relates that vicious creatures "squirted fog over a distance of some miles." The only way to stop such dreadful duels is by the use of fire, which no water-spirit can endure; therefore heaven sends sacred fire (the lightnings) to compel angry demons to cease troubling the clouds or muindane waters and injuring poor farmers, as all-destroying deluges might result. Hence, occasional small or local damage to mankind, as innocent bystanders, from the vigorous quelling of draconic riots, is regarded as cheap payment for security against overwhelming floods. More dreadful however than immediate storm-damage was the presage in the sky-battles of possible harm to, or even the overthrow of, the reigning family, which almost certainly would follow were the yellow and the blue dragon-hosts, partisans of the Imperial House, to be defeated.

It is true that in primitive China as elsewhere serpents were regarded as the genii of lakes, springs and caves, and here and there the people paid them worship. The dragon, however, is not, nor ever was, an ordinary snake deified, but has been exalted, albeit rather uncertainly, into a true deity as a manifestation of a principle that underlies all Chinese philosophy, and is expressed in the contrasted and pregnant words yang and yin—fight versus darkness, the constructive as opposed to the destructive, goodwill contrasted with badheartedness.

In the Shan hai King, a very old Classic, is described a god seated at the foot of Mt. Chung. "He is called 'Enlightener of the Darkness.' By looking [i.e., opening the eyes; a popular belief is that a dragon's vital spirit lies in his eyes, also that he is deaf] he creates daylight, and by closing his eyes he creates night. By blowing he makes winter, by inhalation he makes summer. He neither eats nor drinks, nor does he rest. His breath causes wind. His length is a thousand miles. . . . As a living being he has a human face, the body of a snake, and a red colour."

The author assures us that this god is The Dragon, that he is full of yang (heavenly virtue), and that it is logical that he should diffuse light, overcoming the nine yin; wherefore he symbolizes great men (assumed to be full of yang) particularly the emperor and his sons ('dragon-seed') which is one of the many explanations of the association of the Thunder dragon, specifically the yellow one, with the imperial estate. If this be true— and the possession of yang by dragons is affirmed by sages again and again—the good

DRAGONS AND UNICORNS—FACT? OR FICTION?

nature of Chinese dragons in general is well accounted for. In China, at any rate, they have been on the whole benevolent and helpful when treated with respect and generously encouraged by sacrifices and gifts. Undoubtedly they have sometimes shown poor judgment in the matter of flooding rains and a careless use of lightning, yet in general they seem to mean well, and to be kind in answer to prayers for rain when the crops really need it. If not—well, the farmers know how to bring them to their sense of duty!

Such an abstraction, precious to devout minds in spite of puzzling characteristics and a vague aspect, must of course be visualized in some way if it is to hold heroic place and influence. "The dragon is the spirit of change," writes Okakoro-Kakuzo in his Book of Tea, "therefore of life itself . . . taking new forms according to its surroundings, yet never seen in final shape. It is the great mystery itself. Hidden in the caverns of inaccessible mountains, or coiled in the unfathomed depth of the sea, he awaits the time when he slowly arouses himself into activity. He unfolds himself in the storm-cloud, he washes his mane in the darkness of the seething whirlpools. His claws are the fork of the lightning. . . . His voice is heard in the hurricane. . . . The dragon reveals himself only to vanish."

DRAGONS AND UNICORNS—FACT? OR FICTION?

CHAPTER FIVE

DRACONIC GRANDPARENTS

AS SOON as men learn to form, by means of a drawing or an image, a representation of what is in their mind's eye, they apply their art to religion. The first attempts are often grotesquely rude and uninspiring, yet embody an idea; and if the people cherish this idea, and themselves grow in art-skill and refinement, a conventionalized figure will in time be evolved that will satisfy tradition, and thereafter no essential change will be made in it.

Fair progress toward this satisfactory representation of the (or a) dragon, now apparently realized, seems to have been reached by the Chinese at a time when the earliest existing, or at any rate oldest known, pictures and carvings of it were made, nor are any written descriptions much older, so that we may assume a long anterior period for the growth of the dragon-notion in public thought. A few years ago many large inscribed slabs of stone were found buried in Shantung, one of the most anciently occupied provinces of China. They bore engravings in an amazing mixture of more or less legendary incidents and worthies, and experts refer this work to the third century B.C. One of these slabs shows a silhouette-like drawing that we are told represents Fu hsi with a woman regarded as his consort. Both are crowned and fully dressed down to the waist, but the lower half of their bodies is serpent-like (in proportional length for legs) and the 'tails' are inter-twined. Attendant pairs of sprites of anomalous outline, with tail-like lower halves similarly twisted together, are supported by rolled clouds terminating in birds' heads; and the remaining space of the picture is crowded with figures of mythical creatures, some queer beyond description, many recognizable birds, fishes, or other animals, all with reptilian tails. Rubbings of these astonishing lithographs are before me as I write, and small reproductions of some of the figures may be seen in Bushell's Handbook of Chinese Art. They, as well as other relics from Han times (earlier than which no useful representations have been recovered), show clearly the ophidian origin of the dragon

DRAGONS AND UNICORNS—FACT? OR FICTION?

idea, and also indicate strongly its derivat from the West.

It is a curious circumstance that among remains of the earlier Gnostics, whose strange doctrines are credited with descent from Aryan (Persian) serpent-worship, are repre sentations of deities, half man, half snake, precisely similar in shape, save that they have two snake-legs instead of a single thickened tail, as was the case with some of the figures on the stone slabs of Shantung. With the overthrow of the Chow (or Chou) dynasty by the widely conquering 'General' Chin (so impressive were the extent and publicity of his enterprises that his domain came to be known to the commercial West as China) the enlightened and progressive Han period began; and in the general stimulus to art that followed, the dragon furnished to artists a motive constantly employed and ingeniously varied. No depiction in painting or on pottery as ancient as that has survived, if any such ever existed. It is surely an interesting fact, however, that the first Chinese painter on record, Ts-ao Fuh-king, who died in 250 A.D., was famous for his Buddhist pictures and sketches of dragons. An oft-told legend recounts that a certain painting by him which had been preserved until the advent of the Sung dynasty, then produced rain in a time of bitter drouth when appealed to by the desperate farmers.

As for Han carvings in this direction, the most striking and exceptional are those strange and beautiful 'girdle-buckles' which were almost unknown in the United States until Mr. Arthur D. Ficke brought a large collection of them to New York, where they were sold at the Anderson galleries in January, 1925. The work on them, in exquisite modelling, proper anatomy and fine sense of action, and in the glyptic skill involved, indicates a long-antecedent familiarity by artists with both the conception and render-ing of the mythical creature portrayed. Most of these articles were carved in jade, a few only in rock-crystal, agate or other hard stone. Mr. Ficke wrote of them in his Catalogue:

It would be impossible, in a brief catalogue such as this, to give any intimation of the wealth of symbolic meanings that have been carven into these buckles. The dragon, the hydra, the bat, the fungus, the horse, the mantis, the cicada, the monkey, and the ram, has each its significance in Chinese mythological legend. Some of these forms go hack at least two thousand years, repeated over and over again in bronzes and jades of cen-tury after century. These fantastic shapes are therefore racial rather than personal in-ventions: they are the creatures of prehistoric ritual—mythology turned to stone.

Few of these are as old as the Han period, but all remind a naturalist of a salamander by their flexible, soft-skinned bodies, limber legs usually with three toes, and their long, cleft tails. In every specimen the tail is branched. I write 'branched,' not 'forked,' be-cause the lobes are unequal, a shorter one curving out of the larger or main stem—as, by the way, sometimes happens in the case of real newts whose tails have been lost or dam-aged. This style of dragon is named ch'ih-lung, and is said to be pre-Buddhistic (also, according to Bushell, kut'ing-lung, or dragon of old bronzes); and he mentions that it appears on a Kuang Yao vase of the second century B.C., while another pair is to be seen on a more recent incense-burner "disporting in the midst of scrolled clouds and project-ing their heads to make two handles." It is very interesting to note that although many of

DRAGONS AND UNICORNS—FACT? OR FICTION?

the jade girdles are of comparatively recent manufacture, and vary in ornamental details, the newt-like character of the body and branched tail persists. It seems to me, indeed, that the ch'ih-lung represents, as nearly as we can reach it, the primitive dragon-notion that prevailed (at least in northern China) before the Buddhistic invasion from India became widespread and influential in the country, and that it came overland from the northwest.

Dr. Berthold Laufer describes an antique jade girdle-ornament which had "the figure of a phenix standing on clouds and looking toward the slender-bodied hydra (ch-ih), which has the bearded head of a bird with a pointed beak, very similar to that of the phenix. The left hind foot of the monster terminates in a bird's head, presumably symbolizing a cloud. It is rearing the left fore paw in the direction of the bird, supporting the right on the clouds below." Dr. Laufer supposes that this design (which is very like those of the Shantung slabs mentioned above) signifies that the dragon is assisted by birds in moving clouds and in sending down rain; and he mentions that when rain is to be expected dragons scream. "The dragon," Dr. Laufer continues, "in intimate connection with the growth of vegetation, appears as a deity . . . invoked in times of drouth with prayers for rain." The dictionary Shuo Wen, referring to a certain jade carving named 'lung,' placed on an altar as a prayer for rain, has the form and voice of a dragon. These Han jades were ring-shaped, but were soon superseded by engraved prayer-tablets. The Son of Heaven wore a robe embroidered with royal dragons when he sacrificed in the ancestral temple; his own memorial altar will have the dragon-tablet when he "has ascended upon the dragon to be a guest on high."

The dragon possesses the power of self-transformation, may make itself dark or luminous, or render itself invisible. A Chinese informed Mr. Ball that it becomes at will reduced to the size of a silkworm, or swollen till it fills the space of heaven and earth. When its breath escapes it forms clouds, sometimes changing into rain at other times into fire; and its voice is like the jingling of copper coins. Formerly, glass was thought to be its solidified breath. The creature may descend into the depths of the ocean, and rest in palaces of pearl.

In early days, if ancient books are trustworthy, there were tame dragons—they dragged the chariots of legendary kings; and Visser found a tradition of a family making it their business to breed them for the emperors—hence their family name Hwan-lung, 'dragonrearer.' Later it became the custom to ornament the prows of pleasure-junks with dragonheads, and certain kinds of long, slender boats are known as 'dragon-boats' to this day. A popular story relates the adventures of a sort of celestial Robin Hood, Feng Afoo-chow, who stole from the rich and gave to the poor. He rode about the country on a winged, fire-breathing dragon (precurser of the automobile?), righted wrongs and appropriated treasure, until at last he perpetrated a theft of such magnificence that he left it to be the crown of his career, and settled down to remain a law-abiding citizen until his tame dragon bore him to the heaven of the repentant rich.

The popular understanding is that dragons were supernaturally created but are of

33

DRAGONS AND UNICORNS—FACT? OR FICTION?

different sexes, and are able to reproduce their kind; and according to Visser the book Pei Ya supports the general opinion that they are born from eggs. When these are about to hatch the sound made by a male embryo makes the wind rise, whereas the cry of a female 'chick' causes the wind to abate and change its direction. One account of how the sexes differ explains that the male dragon's horn is "undulating, concave and steep"; it is strong on the top but very thin below. The female has a straight snout, a round mane, thin scales and a stout tall.

Dragons' eggs are the beautiful pebbles picked up beside mountain brooks; and they are preserved by nature until they split in a thunderstorm, releasing a young dragon which immediately goes up to the sky. An old woman who found such eggs had various adventures with them that children like to hear about. A dragon's egg much bigger than a hen's egg, light and apparently hollow, was found, history says, in the Great River in the tenth century; and to it, in the opinion of the local people, was due subsequent calamitous floods. Another egg found was very heavy, and when shaken rattled as if it contained water; perhaps it was a geode—at any rate it became an object of worship.

An interesting legend is appropriate here. The uppermost and worst cataract in the Yangtse gorges, known as the New or Glorious Rapid, was formed in 1896 by a landslip that filled three-fourths of the channel. The rivermen account for this mishap thus, as related by Dingle: "The ova of a dragon being deposited in the bowels of the earth at this particular spot in due course of time hatched out. . . . The baby dragon grew and grew, but remained in a dormant state until quite full-grown, when, as the habit of the dragon is, it became active, and at the first awakening shook down the hillside by a mighty effort, freed itself from the bowels of the earth, and made its way down to the sea."

A ford in the upper Hoang Ho is called Dragon-Gate. Fishes that pass above it become 'dragons'; those that fail remain simple fishes. Rapids and waterfalls in various parts of the country, and in Japan, have the same name and frequently a similar story.

DRAGONS AND UNICORNS—FACT? OR FICTION?

CHAPTER SIX

THE DRAGON AS A RAIN-GOD

I HAVE been speaking thus far of the Oriental dragon in a generic sense, trying to show the nature of a mythical, half-animal, semi-divine, wholly imaginary being, vague and intangible, swayed by human motives and emotions yet endowed with a demonic combination of ability and instability—a Chinese abstraction derived from a prehistorically antique awe of the serpent and clothed in the mystery of such a lineage; and most appropriate is it that such a quasi-deity should be worshipped at ancestral altars, for doubtless it is a relic of tribal, perhaps totemic, idolatry, an elaborate product of a long-forgotten animism.

"It is in China," wrote John Leyland a few years ago (Magazine of Art, Volume 14) "that the dragon reaches its highest pinnacle as an object of reverence . . . for it is markedly an object of propitiation, and festivals are held in its honour. Yet its connection with the root-ideas of the Hindoos is never lost, for it is a monster of mists and waters, and is painted issuing from clouds. There is evidence also of human sacrifice to the monster, for Hieun Tsang relates that one Wat-Youen, on the failure of a river, immolated himself in propitiation of the dragon; and at the dragon-boat festivals it is now believed that the boats intimidate the monster. Such ideas were probably carried to China and Japan with Buddhism, for Buddha himself was a dragon-slayer—a destroyer of savage demonism and cruel magic."

DRAGONS AND UNICORNS—FACT? OR FICTION?

The dragon of recent art, say since the time of the Mings, has lost, however, in the process of conventionalization, some of the characteristics that are needful to its complete composition, according to what may be designated as an official formula for making a perfect image of it. This is given by Joly as follows:

"The Chinese call the dragon 'lung' because it is deaf. It is the largest of scaly animals, and it has nine characteristics. Its head is like a camel's, its horns like a deer's, its eyes like a hare's, its ears like a bull's, its neck like an iguana's, its scales like those of a carp, its paws like a tiger's, and its claws like an eagle's. It has nine times nine scales, it being the extreme of a lucky number. On each side of its mouth are whiskers, under its chin a bright pearl, on the top of its head the 'poh shan' or foot-rule, without which it cannot ascend to heaven. The scales of its throat are reversed. Its breath changes into clouds from which come either fire or rain. The dragon is fond of the flesh of sparrows and swallows, it dreads the centipede and silk dyed of five colours. It is also afraid of iron. In front of its horns it carries a pearl of bluish colour striated with more or less symbolical lines."

Most of these features have been discussed elsewhere. The horns in many existing figures show plainly as two straight, smooth, level spikes from the back of the head, usually with one or more short, deer-like prongs and have no resemblance to the un-branched, curved, rugose horns of an antelope or goat; hence they do not suggest descent from those of the Babylonian 'goat-fish.' The scales, however, are regarded as piscine rather than ophidian; they seem to be related to those of the carp, with which the dragon in one of its aspects is closely connected. These scales, we learn, are properly eighty-one in number, that is nine times nine, which in mystical calculations represent yang, as the number six equals yin. Both golden and silver scales are spoken of in the Classics. The annals of Welhaiwei, studied by R. F. Johnston, contain a story on this point. "In the year 1732 there was a very heavy shower of rain [in Shantung]. In the sky, among the dark clouds, was espied a dragon. When the storm passed off a man named Chiang of the village of Ho Ch'ing or Huo Ch'ien picked up a thing that was as large as a sieve, round as the sun, thick as a coin, and lustrous as the finest jade. It reflected the sun's light and shone like a star, so that it dazzled the eyes. . . . The village soothsayer was appealed to for a decision. A single glance at the strange object was enough for the man of wisdom. 'This thing,' he said, 'is a scale that has fallen from the body of the dragon.'"

Chinese mythology and custom recognize (or used to) various separate kinds of dragons, species of the genus lung. The most ancient and highly respected of these are three: the Lung in the sky; the Li in the sea; and the Kiau in the marshes.

The first of this trio is properly styled t'ien lung, Celestial or Heavenly Dragon. It doubtless typifies and embodies the original object of veneration, and remains supreme and most sacred. It resides in the sky where it guards the mansions of the gods and sustains their power; as these powers are represented on earth by the sovereignty of the realm in the person of the emperor, it alone has the right to be attached to him and his affairs, and in that relation is designated Imperial Dragon. Hence it has long been recog-

DRAGONS AND UNICORNS—FACT? OR FICTION?

nized as the emblem of the Chinese empire, and was borne on its triangular flag and other appurtenances of government until the establishment of the present Republic; and it has well been remarked that nothing could express more forcibly the change of mind that has come over official China than the abandonment of this antique and venerated symbol.

The dragon in relation to the social constitution of the Chinese State falls into several classes or ranks, distinguished by the number of its claws. Thus representations of the imperial dragons proper, restricted to the emperor himself, should alone have five claws, while princes and nobles of lesser rank must be content with a less number. This sumptuary rule seems not to have been observed uniformly. We are told that on early coins and standards four-clawed dragons appeared as driven by prehistoric emperors. Chester Holcomb states in his Catalogue that the imperial badge used during the Sung (tenth century A.D.) and previous dynasties was represented with three claws only; during the subsequent Ming period by four; and only during the most recent (Ching) period by five claws. Mr. Ripley insists, on the contrary, that the five-clawed form was introduced by the Ming rulers, as he thinks is proved by the carving on tombs of the early Ming emperors at Mukden. J. F. Blacker gives the rule and practice in recent times thus: "The Imperial dragon is armed with five claws on each of its four members, and is used as an emblem by the emperor's family and by princes of the highest two ranks. The four-clawed dragon is used by princes of the third or fourth class. Mandarins and princes of the fifth rank have as an emblem the four-clawed serpent. The three-clawed dragon— the Imperial dragon of Japan—is in China the one commonly used for decoration." According to Albert J. Jacquemart, the mandarin four-clawed dragon became the conventionalized figure called mang; yet, despite their inferior rank, mangs adorn "many very superior articles of pottery and porcelain."

It appears, however, that it was not until the advent of the powerful and progressive Han dynasty began its enlightening and stimulating rule that dragons in various forms began to serve decorators. At first they seem to have been applied almost exclusively to royal robes and furnishings, but their use gradually broadened. Here first appeared winged dragons, the bird-like wings drawn indicating that the creature was to be regarded as a spring animal. Since that time, however, winged dragons have almost disappeared from both Chinese and Japanese art, as 'old-fashioned.' (In medieval Europe they were common, but the wings were more like those of bats.)

The second of the three 'great' dragons is the shen-lung, or 'spiritual' species, which may be called that of the common people, for it is the one that wafts the rain-cloud and sprinkles the farmers' fields. Hence its image decorates household altars and is worshipped, especially when prolonged drouth threatens loss of expected crops.

It is in this matter of prayers for rain that the people of China nowadays regard the dragon as divine—it is beyond all else a rain-god. In his philosophical treatise Kwan Tse, one of the early Classics, Kwang Chung declares a dragon to be a god (shen) because in the water he covers himself with five colours, "that is, with the cardinal virtues," and can

37

DRAGONS AND UNICORNS—FACT? OR FICTION?

change his shape to go where he pleases under or above the earth. "He whose transformations are not limited by days, and whose ascending and descending are not limited by time, is called a god (shen)." Another ancient sage asserts the yellow dragon to be the quintessence of shen as it exerts the most power and is of the highest rank, therefore it is called 'imperial.' Laufer considers the dragon the embodiment of the fertilizing power of water and a veritable deity when invoked for rain, and he thinks that if we look on it as a deity "we shall arrive at a better understanding of the various conceptions of the dragon in religion and art: the manifold types and variations of dragons met with in ancient Chinese art are representations of different forces of nature, or are, in other words, different deities."

I was long puzzled to account for the close connection that seems to exist between the doctrines and practice of worshipping ancestors and that directed toward the dragon as the controller of rainfall and of its often destructive concomitant, the lightning. Why were these religious notions so closely interrelated? The totemic theory is unsatisfactory; and I will confess that my cogitations were unproductive until I read a remarkable paper on serpent-worship by C. S. Wake," from which I will cite a paragraph that seems to give an enlightening explanation of the connection referred to:

The serpent-superstition is intimately connected [in China] with ancestor-worship, probably originating among uncultured tribes who, struck by the noiseless movement and the activity of the serpent, combined with its peculiar gaze and marvellous power of fascination, viewed it as a spirit-embodiment. As such it would appear to have the superior wisdom and power ascribed to the denizens of the spirit-world, and from this would originate also the ascription to it of the power over life and health, and over the moisture on which these benefits are dependent. Among ancestor-worshipping peoples, however, the serpent would be viewed as a good being who busied himself about the interests of the tribe to which he had once belonged. when the simple idea of a spirit-ancestor was transformed into that of a Great Spirit, the father of the race, the attributes of the serpent would he enlarged. The common ancestor would be relegated to the heavens, and that which was necessary to the life and well-being of his people would be supposed to be under his care. Hence the Great Serpent was thought to have power over the rains and the hurricane, with the latter of which it was probably often identified.

A writer of the second century before Christ, says Visser, explains that "clouds follow the dragon, winds follow the tiger." These cloud-dragons are invited to dispense rain by means of their likenesses, "wherefore when earthen [clay-made] dragons are set up, yin and yang follow their likenesses and clouds and rain arise." The making of such earthen images is of forgotten antiquity. Rules existed for moulding and ornamenting them according to varying circumstances, and an elaborate ritual and set of costumes was long ago prescribed for the priests and officials in the praying for rain. The dragon-boats, to be described, had the same character and purpose. These ceremonies may be described as sympathetic magic intended to force the dragons to follow their images and to ascend from their pools to the skies; but often scolding and even flogging of the images has been necessary to bring about the desired action.

38

DRAGONS AND UNICORNS—FACT? OR FICTION?

Dr. Visser found in a well-known old book, the Wah Tsah Tsu, dated near the end of the sixteenth century, information as to the significance of several different young dragons, whose shapes are used as ornaments, each according to its nature. Those that like to cry are represented on the tops of handles of bells; those that like music figure on musical instruments, and so forth. "The ch'i-wen, which like swallowing, are placed on both ends of the ridgepoles of roofs (to swallow all evil influences). The chao-fung, lion-like beasts which like precipices, are placed on the four corners of roofs." Sword-belts have as ornaments the murderous ai-hwa, and so on through a list of significant applications. Dragons are embroidered on the front curtains of catafalques and on grave-clothes, surrounded by many emblematic animals. It is not plain, however, that all these belong to the shen class. Laufer also mentions, in his paper on grave-sculptures, that in certain Han bas-reliefs on stone, dragons are "fettered by bands, i.e., do not send rain—are in a state of repose." These are surrounded by birdshaped clouds which he interprets as tranquil clouds yielding no rain.

Whether the metaphysics of this matter of the relation between dragons and rainfall is comprehended by ordinary folk in the Flowery Kingdom may well be doubted; but at any rate when dry weather prevails too long clay images of the shen-lung are likely to be carried about the district, accompanied by priestly ceremonials and incantations arranged with carefully suitable accessories and colourings, the ritual and colours varying with the season of the year. This has been a custom since remote ages, but in modern times prayers inscribed on tablets of jade and metal are much used, or the appeal is made in a more public and forcible way than formerly by means of large, image-bearing processions. "The Chinese are adepts in the art of taking the Kingdom of Heaven by storm," remarks the author of The Golden Bough!

These great processions have been frequently described by travellers. Mr. Ball says that in Canton, where he frequently witnessed them, the mock-rain-god is a serpentine creature of great girth and 150 to 200 feet long, made of lengths of gaily-coloured crepe, and sparkling with tiny, spangle-like mirrors. "Every yard or so a couple of human feet-those of the bearers —buskined in gorgeous silk, are visible. The whole is fronted by an enormous head of ferocious aspect, before the gaping jaws of which a man manoeuvres a large pearl, after which the dragon prances and wriggles." These figures are of two kinds (but on what ground is not stated by Mr. Ball), one sort having golden scales and the other silver scales. Such processions may occur whenever one seems called for, but are staged regularly about January 15 and June 5, dates representing the winter and summer solstices. The latter is the time of the dragon-boat festival; but before proceeding to that let me say that should no rain follow these ceremonial prayers the images are abused, even torn to pieces, to remind the god that he must do his duty or he will be similarly punished; furthermore he must do it properly and be watchful to stop the downpour when enough has fallen, or take the consequences. The story goes that once when the lung neglected to stop an immoderate storm the local mandarins put his image in jail, whereupon the downpour quickly ceased.

The famous Dragon-boat Festival of southern China is held on the fifth day of the fifth moon, which usually falls in our June. Tradition informs us that it began in commemoration of a virtuous minister of state, Chii Yuan, whose remonstrances against the unworthy acts of his sovereign were met by his dismissal and degradation. This happened some 450 years before Christ. He committed suicide, presumably by drowning, for on the first anniversary of his death began a search for his body in the water, which still continues in the form and meaning of this festival. More scientifically minded persons, however, such as Visser, De Groot, and Frazer, scout the pious tale, and regard this water-festival as in its origin an effort or supplication for rain. That it has become a time of feasting, fun and goodwill is doubtless owing to the sense of midsummer, celebrated by rejoicing in all parts of the world. In Burma and Siam, also, it is marked by three days of jollity when everybody plays with water, rowing, swimming, ducking one another, spraying the crowds in the streets from big syringes, and rollicking generally.

The principal feature in Southern China is a great number of boats and boat-races on the rearest river, with every gay, and amusing accessory that can be devised. The boats used are built for the purpose, and are from 50 to 100 feet long, but only just wide enough for two men to sit abreast—that is, as near like water-snakes as is feasible. They are propelled as rapidly as possible—a traditional requirement—and the rowers try to keep time with the drums and gongs with which each one is provided. Impromptu races are challenged, often resulting in accidents, as the boats are slight, and dangerous when paddled by perhaps a hundred Chinamen wild with enthusiasm and unsteady with liquor. Large crowds of spectators occupy the river-banks urging their favourite boats to win, and the excitement and fun are intense.

The third member of the first class of dragons is Li-lung to whom belongs the earth and its waters, who marks out the courses of rivers and who is the ruler of the ocean. When a waterspout is seen the people view it reverently, saying: "Li is going up to heaven." This dragon is described as yellow, and as having a lion's body with a human-faced, hornless, dragon's head. The monster's quadrupedal form and close relation to sea and inland waters, indicate perhaps that it was introduced to the people of the southern and eastern coasts by early voyagers from the west bringing stories of Babylonian Ea and Marduk, and their sea-goat; so that it may really be a different species of partly separate origin from those of the western and northern interior.

As the earth-dragon, Li is supposed to exist beneath the surface, and to cause earthquakes by uneasy movements of its gigantic frame; and in one case, as has been noted, these movements, the boatmen say, caused a great landslide, which partly dammed the Yangtse and formed the dread rapids in the gorge above Ichang, called the Dragon's Gate. The fossil bones of huge reptiles—of which I shall have more to say presently-occasionally exhumed in various parts of China are thought by the people to be its bones, attesting to its prodigious size; and these bones are naturally endowed with magically curative qualities, as we shall see. This subterranean dragon is reputed to guard heaps of gold and silver and gems, and it is the protector of the veins of precious minerals in the underlying rocks.

It should be needless for me to say that no real animal of the more or less distant past

DRAGONS AND UNICORNS—FACT? OR FICTION?

was the ancestor or originator of the object of our study; yet I find the is belief still held, vaguely, by even the most intelligent among my neighbours. Every fossil that has come to light, and formerly misled ignorant or unthinking men into supposing it a relic of a real ancestor, was buried and petrified millions of years before any human eyes to see, or minds to consider, it were in existence. The dragon is a pure figment of the human imagination.

As an oceanic divinity Li is believed to possess a great treasury under the sea in which he stores the wealth that comes to him from wrecked junks. Among his most precious possessions are the eyes of certain large fish, believed to be priceless gems; that is the reason, say the fisher-folk of Shantung, why big dead fish cast on the beaches are always eyeless—Lung Wang has added them to his hoard. So says St. Johnston, and then tells us that in the jung-ch'eng district is a pool of water which, though several miles in the interior from the Shantung coast, is said to taste of sea-salt, to be fathomless, and to remain always at sea-level; it is dedicated to the seadragon, locally known as Lung Wang. "One day an inquisitive villager tried to fathom its gloomy depths with his carrying-pole. Hardly had he immersed it in water when it was grasped by a mysterious force and wrenched out of his hand. It was immediately drawn below, and after waiting for its reappearance the villager went home. A few days later he was on the seacoast, gathering seaweed for roof-thatch, when suddenly he beheld his pien-tang floating in the water below the rocks on which he was standing. On the first available opportunity after this he burned three sticks of incense in Lung-Wang's temple, as an offering to the deity that had given him so striking a demonstration of its miraculous power."

This one may be the "coiled dragon" (Pan Lung) mentioned by some writers, which "hibernates in the watery depths and marshes, and is often met with in the form of medallions in porcelain bowls and dishes." It may also be the creature referred to in a little story by L. J. Vance (Open Court, 1892) of a small girl that fell into a Chinese river where boats and boatmen were numerous. "Nobody helped her, and when finally she caught at a rope and climbed on a boat, she was scolded, sent home and punished." The apathy exhibited was due to the belief that the river-dragon wanted that child and mysteriously caused her to fall overboard.

The account of the Golden Dragon Kings given by Dr. Du Bose perhaps belongs here. These 'kings' are said to be yellow (?) snakes that come floating down the Hoang Ho in times of great flood. One of them is recognized by the priestly authorities as the 'golden dragon.' It has a square head with horns, and is hailed with delight as it signifies that the waters are about to recede. "The governor," Du Bose tells us without geographical particulars, "receives the divine snake in a lacquered waiter, carries him in his sedan to the temple, and the mandarins all worship the heaven-sent messenger. Many courtesies are offered him until at last he takes his leave. . . . Mandarins who do not believe in idolatry are entirely satisfied with the divinity of this snake."

One phase, or avatar, of this dragon seems to be that named Yu Lung, the special model and emblem of perseverance and success to literary aspirants who are seeking

41

DRAGONS AND UNICORNS—FACT? OR FICTION?

public offices by way of the stipulated education in the Classics—the only way in old times. This is the 'fish-dragon' so well illustrated on blue-and-white commercial jars, where the metamorphosis that links together the dragon and carp is variously depicted. The legend is that when a carp has succeeded in climbing over the cataracts in the Dragon Gate of the Yangtse it finds its reward by being transformed into a dragon, with which goes a grant of immortality. Seizing on the apt imagery of this legend, the fish-dragon was adopted as their 'patron-saint' by the students who toiled in their cheerless cells over the still more cheerless lore of long-dead sages, whose star of hope was the prospect of a government office and a possible chance for immortal fame, if only they could surmount the rocky obstacle of the official examinations. The parallel is grimly humorous! But cells, and classics and students are gone—and perhaps their Patron-saint must go too.

DRAGONS AND UNICORNS—FACT? OR FICTION?

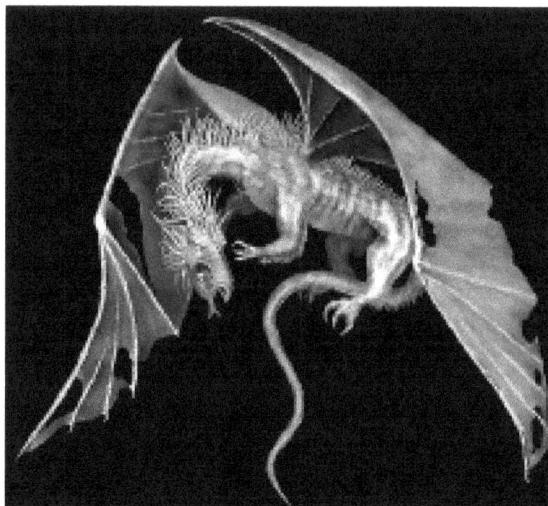

CHAPTER SEVEN

KOREAN WATER AND MOUNTAIN SPIRITS

KOREA CAME very early in Oriental history under the influence, if not under the domination, of China, and a cult of the Dragon has existed there since antiquity. Dr. William E. Griffis, in his valuable book Corea, the Hermit Nation, has this to say of its presence there under the local name riong; and some absurdly extravagant legends might be quoted.

"The riong [Li Lung?]," Dr. Griffis writes, "is one of the four supernatural or spiritually endowed creatures. He is an embodiment of all the forces of motion, change, and power for offence and defence in animal life, with the mysterious attributes of the serpent. There are many varieties of the genus Dragon. . . . In the spring it ascends to the sites, and in the autumn buries itself in the watery depths. It is this terrific manifestation of movement and power which the Corean artist loves to depict—always in connection with waters, clouds, or the sacred jewel of which it is the guardian."

There is also a terrestrial dragon, which presides over mines and gems; and the intense regard for it is perhaps the chief reason why mines have been so little worked in Chosen, the people superstitiously fearing that disasters may follow disturbance of the metals which they believe are peculiarly the treasure of this jealous earth-spirit.

"All mountains are personified in Korea," we are told by Angus Hamilton, and are "usually associated with dragons. In lakes there are dragons and lesser monsters. . . . The serpent is almost synonymous with the dragon. Certain fish in time become fish-dragons; snakes become elevated to the dignity and imbued with the ferocity of dragons when they have spent a thousand years in the captivity of the mountains and a thousand years in the water. All these apparitions may be propitiated with sacrifices and prayers."

43

DRAGONS AND UNICORNS—FACT? OR FICTION?

The most important of Korean heights are the Diamond Mountains, where the mines of the country are most extensively worked, to the trepidation of the populace who anticipate that some day a dreadful retribution will fall on the impious foreign exploiters of their mineral veins. "One dizzy height is named Yellow Dragon, a second the Flying Phenix; and a third, the Hidden Dragon, has reference to a demon who has not yet risen from the earth upon his ascent to the clouds."

Mr. Hamilton gives a description of the temples of Yu-chom-sa in the Diamond Mountains. Of one of them he says: "The altar of this temple is adorned by a singular piece of wood-carving. Upon the roots of an upturned tree sit or stand fifty-three diminutive figures of Buddha. The monks tell an old-world legend of this strange structure. Many centuries ago fifty-three priests, who had journeyed from far India to Korea to introduce the precepts of Buddha into this ancient land, sat down by a well beneath a spreading tree. Three dragons presently emerged from the depths of the well and attacked the fifty-three, calling to their aid the wind dragon, who thereupon uprooted the tree. As the fight proceeded the priests managed to place an image of Buddha on each root of the tree, converting the whole into an altar, under whose influence the dragons were forced back into their cavernous depths, when huge rocks were piled into the well to shut them up. The monks then founded the monastery, building the main temple above the remains of the vanquished dragons."

Apart from any historical suggestions which this interesting story may contain, one notes that the exorcism of the threatening demons was accomplished in just the same way as Christian monks did by a show of the Cross, as we shall see when we come to consider the dragon-lore of mediaeval Europe.

Whatever is most excellent the Koreans compare to the divinely virtuous Dragon. A 'dragon-child' is one that is a paragon of propriety; 'a dragon-horse,' one having great speed, and so on to indicate the superlative. A common proverb, "When the fish has been transformed into the dragon," means that a happy change has taken place. This embodiment of good nature and good luck is, of course, simply the Chinese lung, friendly and worthy of respect and worship.

It appears, however, that Buddhistic travellers and missionaries from cobra-worshipping India, corrupted this gentle faith long ago by the introduction of the Hindoo doctrines and practice of naga-worship, inculcating a system of diabolism that filled the land with fear and defensive magic: the cheerful old dragons of the past became horrid snakes, lurking in every pool, and filling the seas with terror. A Korean book describes an exorcist of nagas who went with his pitcher full of water to the pond inhabited by a naga, and by his magic formulae surrounded the reptile with a ring of fire. As the water in the pitcher was its only refuge the naga turned himself into a small snake and crept into the pitcher. Whether the exorcist then killed him the story does not reveal; but in the tale Visser finds evidence of the nagas "not only as rain-gods, but also as beings wholly dependent on the presence of water and much afraid of fire—just like the dragons in Chinese and Japanese legends."

DRAGONS AND UNICORNS—FACT? OR FICTION?

Hulbert, author of The Passing of Korea, describes things and ideas as they were before the modernization of the country by the Japanese. He informs us that every Korean river and stream, as well as the surrounding oceans, was formerly believed to be the abode of a dragon, and every village on the banks of a stream used to make periodic adoration to this power. The importance of paying so much formal respect to it lay in the fact that this aquatic dragon had control of the rainfall, and had to be kept in good humour lest the crops be endangered by insufficient showers; furthermore it was able to make great trouble for boatmen and deep-sea sailors unless properly appeased. Hence not only the villagers and farmers, but the owners and masters of ships desiring favourable weather for their voyaging, made propitiatory sacrifices—not alone the important war junks, but the freight-boats, fishermen, ferry-boats, etc., each conducting its own kind of ceremony to ensure safety. In all cases it was addressed as tribute to a water-spirit.

The ceremony, at least when held on land, was performed by a mudang (a professional female exorcist) in a boat, accompanied by as many of the leading persons of the village as were able to crowd in with her. "Her fee is about forty dollars. The most interesting part of the ceremony is the mudang's dance, which is performed on the edge of a knife-blade laid across the mouth of a jar that is filled to the brim with water." Even more elaborately nonsensical was the ceremony on a ferryboat—a great institution in a land without bridges, as Korea used to be.

Mr. Hulbert says that not until the beginning of the reign of the present dynasty was the horrible custom of throwing a young virgin into the sea at Py-ryung, as a propitiatory offering to the demon of the ocean-world, discontinued. "At that place the mudang held an annual seance in order to propitiate the sea-dragon and secure plenteous rains for the rice-crop and successful voyages for the mariners." With the change of the royal house a new prefect was appointed to the district, who had no faith or sympathy with either the theory or its frightful demands. He attended the next seance, where he found three mudangs dragging a screaming girl towards the seashore. Stopping them he asked whether it was really necessary that a human being be sacrificed. They answered that it was. "Very well," he said; "you will do as an offering." Signing to two policemen they tied and hurled one of the mudangs into the waves. The dragon gave no sign of displeasure, and a second, and after her the third, were 'sacrificed' without any visible response from the demon the people had been taught to fear. This demonstration ended the practice and the profession of the mudangs together.

DRAGONS AND UNICORNS—FACT? OR FICTION?

CHAPTER EIGHT

"THE MEN OF THE DRAGON BONES"

WHEN IN September, 1923, Dr. Henry Fairfield Osborn, President of the American Museum of Natural History in New York, was on his way to visit the camps of the Third Asiatic Exploring Expedition, conducted by Dr. Roy Chapman Andrews, aided by a staff of expert assistants, he halted for the night at a frontier Chinese village. Strolling about the station in the early evening, as he relates in the Museum's magazine Natural History (May-June, 1924):

I suddenly noticed a small group of men in the darkness pointing toward Andrews and myself. I asked Andrews to listen to what they were saying, and it was here that I learned the Chinese designation of our party, for the words were:

"There go the American men of the dragon bones!"

I was delighted with this Chinese christening, because it seemed to me both a tribute to the valour of our men and a wonderfully apt designation of the main objective of the Third Asiatic Expedition as it impressed itself upon the Chinese. For what purpose were we in Mongolia? Obviously enough to the Chinese mind to collect the bones of dragons-the dragons which for ages past had ruled the sky, the air, the earth, the waters of the earth, and which even today are believed in implicitly by the Chinese. Of course we should find small bones corresponding to small dragons, large bones corresponding to remains of large dragons—also of vast dragons, some of which, according to Chinese myth, leave their tails in the eastern part of the desert of Gobi while their heads rest on the slopes of the Altai Mountains, four hundred miles distant!

Here is the sum of the paleontology and zoology of the native Chinese—the dragon and the phenix.

The 'dragon bones' were the fossilized remains of prehistoric animals for which the men of science were searching the deserts of Mongolia, the discovery of which, then and since, have added vastly to the sum of paleontology and increased the world's knowledge of and interest in China and Central Asia, and in their inhabitants and history. Incidentally these explorations have illuminated certain obscurities in the broad and antique myth now engaging the reader's attention.

Fossil bones have long been known to the Chinese, although almost nobody, even the wisest, had any just notion of the sort of creatures they represented. One may find in every apothecary's shop their fragments, or the powder made by crushing them, but rarely can a druggist tell you whence they came, for the wholesale dealers are loath to reveal trade-secrets. They offer them as the bones of dragons which, when properly administered, must have strong curative virtues; the source of supply is, in their view, unimportant either for trade or healing the more mystery about it the better. As everybody believes this, not suspecting any magic in the matter, the demand is so extensive that an immense supply of bones is annually gathered and dispensed.

Various theories exist among the people, however, as to the nature of these bones. It was generally agreed in the past that they were the cast-off skeletons of living dragons which had sloughed away their bones as well as their hides—once in a thousand years according to one authority; but some persons, with less credulity even in those ancient days, pronounced them the bones of dead dragons. This was much nearer the truth, for we now know that they are the fossilized skulls and limbs of real animals of long-past eras; and in our own time it has been soberly argued that from these fossils has been built up the whole fabric of faith in the reality of dragons past and present.

From this universal faith has arisen the popular trust in the therapeutic value of these mid-Tertiary fossils. According to the Pen-ts'ao Kang-Muh, the best source of information as to medical practice among the ancients, and extensively quoted by Visser, from whom I borrow again, the best bones are those having five colours, corresponding to the five visceral parts of the human body, namely: liver, lungs, heart, kidneys and spleen. White and yellow specimens rank next in healing value, and black ones are poorest, while those gathered by women are useless. Thin, broad-veined bones are regarded as female; those coarse and with narrow veins as male.

The preparation of the bones for administration in medicine is described as follows by Lei Hiao: "For using dragon's bones first cook odorous plants; bathe the bones twice in hot water; pound them to powder, and put this in bags of gauze. Take a couple of young swallows, and after having taken out their intestines and stomach, put the bags in the swallows and hang them over a well. After one night take the bags out of the swal-

DRAGONS AND UNICORNS—FACT? OR FICTION?

lows, rub the powder, and mix it into medicines for strengthening the kidneys. The efficacy of such a medicine is as it were divine." An author of the Sung dynasty recommends that the bones are to be soaked in spirits for one night, then dried on the fire and rubbed to powder. Another authority warns the people that some bones are a little poisonous, and in preparing and using them iron instruments and utensils should be avoided, because, as is well known, dragons dislike iron.

The list of illnesses curable by means of dragon-bones is a long one. Their curative power is attributed to the strong yang virtue in the bone, which makes yin demons abandon those portions of the body in which they have been trying to establish themselves. The teeth and horns of dragons are especially good for diseases developing madness, or difficulty in breathing, or convulsions, also for liver diseases. A Sung physician explains that, because the dragon is the god of the Eastern Quarter, his bones, horns and teeth can conquer any disorganization of the liver.

A book of the ninth century carries the information that when dragon's blood enters the earth it becomes amber; and in the Pen-ts'ao Kang-Muh you may read: "Dragon saliva is seldom used as a medicine. . . . Last spring the saliva spit out by a herd of dragons appeared floating [on the sea]. The aborigines gathered, obtained and sold it, each time for 2000 copper coins." Another treatise, written in the Sung period, instructs us that the most precious of all perfumes is seadragon's spittle, which is hardened by the sun, floats, and is blown ashore by the wind in hard pieces. This may be amber, or ambergris. Another source of perfume is the froth produced by fighting dragons.

From the same book, says Visser, we learn that anciently, at least, dragons' blood, fat, brains, saliva, etc., were also deemed useful as medicines, but how obtained is not clear from the classics. "Perfumes were made from the spit; hence it was asserted that fighting dragons might be smelt. An old emperor used dragon's spittle for ink for writing on jade and gold. Having got a quantity of saliva he mixed it with the fruit of a herb which bore flowers in all four seasons. This produced a red liquid which penetrated into gold and jade."

Many more particulars as to this medicinal use of the bones are given by H. N. Moseley in his book Notes of a Naturalist on the Challenger.

When, early in the present century, the Geological Survey of China was organized, little more was known of the geology of that country than its broad outlines. Well aware that thousands of fossil skeletons of the utmost importance to science were being ground to powder and swallowed by millions of people daily, it was plain that the discovery of the sources of supply would lead to the paleontological knowledge so much desired; but between general ignorance and the jealousy of wholesale collectors and merchants of the bones it was difficult to learn where the fossils were found. Therefore when, in 1921, Professor Osborn and Mr. Walter Granger sought to co-operate with the China Survey, all the Director of the Survey could say was that he had been told that at a place in eastern Szechuan a short distance above I-chang, on the Yangtse River, many fossils had

DRAGONS AND UNICORNS—FACT? OR FICTION?

been excavated for the medicine dealers. Mr. Granger went there and finally learned that the spot was near a small village called Yin-ching-ao, twenty miles from the town of Wan Hsien, and there Granger made his residence. He described the situation in Natural History, for May-June, 1922, as follows:

The fossils at Yinchingkao occur in pits distributed along a great limestone ridge about thirty or forty miles in length and rising ibove our camp more than 200 feet. These pits are the result of the dissolving action of water on limestone, and some of them have a depth of one hundred feet or more. They are of varying sizes averaging say six feet in diameter, and are filled with a reddish and yellowish mud, which is, I take it, disintegrated limestone. The fossils are found imbedded in the mud at varying depths, usually below twenty feet. A crude windlass is rigged up over the pit, and the mud is dug out and hauled to the surface in scoop-shaped baskets. At fifty feet it is dark in the pit, and the work is done by the light of a tiny oil wick. . . . The excavation has been going on for a long time—possibly for several generations. Digging is done only in the winter months.

The excavation of the pits is opening up just now on a large scale, and in the coming month will probably give us about all we can take care of. The fauna is Stegodon, a primitive elephant, Bison, Bos, Cervus, Tapirus, Sus, Rhinoceros, besides many small ruminants, several carnivores, and many rodents; no horses, queerly enough.

The natives in taking out the bones used no care to preserve them whole; they knew they were destined to be pulverized for medicinal purpose, so why be careful. Each day's 'catch' was brought down to the village and piled up in a corner of the digger's house to await the coming of the buyers, who from time to time visited the village and collected the stock, paying about $20 a picul (133 lbs.). One can imagine the heartsick emotions of a paleontologist exploring an unknown fauna, as he viewed these local heaps of fragments of skulls and skeletons, or the many tons of them heaped in the warehouses at I-chang—how he would pick out teeth and recognizable pieces and attempt to interpret them. By careful watching, instruction and rewards to the diggers, however, many skulls and other parts were procured uninjured, and so on this and subsequent visits a valuable collection was gradually accumulated, and divided between the museums in Peking and New York. As the report of such operations rapidly spread, it is not surprising that the wondering Chinese dubbed the American scientific staff "Men of the Dragon Bones."

DRAGONS AND UNICORNS—FACT? OR FICTION?

CHAPTER NINE

THE DRAGON IN JAPANESE ART

"HAVE You seen the dragon?" asks Mr. Okakura in The Awakening of Japan. "Approach him cautiously, for no mortal can survive the sight of his entire body. The eastern dragon is not the gruesome monster of mediaeval imagination, but the genius of strength and goodness. He is the spirit of change, therefore of life itself. . . . Hidden in the caverns of inaccessible mountains, or coiled in the unfathomed depths of the sea, he awaits the time when he slowly arouses himself into activity. He unfolds himself in the storm-clouds; he washes his mane in the blackness of the seething whirlpools. His claws are in the fork of the lightning, his scales begin to glisten in the bark of rain-swept pine-trees. His voice is heard in the hurricane, which, scattering the withered leaves of the forest, quickens a new spring. The dragon reveals himself only to vanish."

Joly continues these impressions thus: "The dragon is full of remarkable powers, and seeing its body in its entirety means instant death; the monster never strikes without provocation, as, for instance, when its throat is touched. The Chinese emperor Yao was said to be the son of a dragon, and several of the other Chinese rulers were metamorphically called 'dragonfaced.' The emperor of Japan was described in the same way, and as such [in old times was] hidden by means of bamboo curtains from the gaze of persons to whom he granted audiences to save them from a terrible fate.

DRAGONS AND UNICORNS—FACT? OR FICTION?

Let me insert here two remarkable paragraphs from Dr. William E. Griffis's standard work on old Japan, say previous to fifty years ago:

Chief among ideal creatures in Japan is the dragon. The word 'dragon' stands for a genus of which there are several species and varieties. To describe them in full, and to recount minutely the ideas held by the Japanese rustics concerning them would be to compile an octavo work on dragonology. . . . In the carvings on tombs, temples, dwellings and shops—on the government documents—printed on the old and the new paper money, and stamped on the new coins—in pictures and books, on musical instruments, in high relief on bronzes, and cut in stone, metal and wood,—the dragon (tasu) everywhere "swinges the scaly horror of his folded tail," whisks his long moustaches, or glares with his terrible eyes. The dragon is the only animal in modern Japan that wears hairy ornaments on the upper lip. . . .

There are many kinds of dragons, such as the violet, the yellow, the green, the red, the white, the black and the flying-dragon. When the white dragon breathes the breath of its lungs goes into the earth and turns to gold. When the violet dragon spits, the spittle becomes balls of pure crystal, of which gems and caskets are made. One kind of dragon has nine colours on its body, and another can see everything within a hundred ri; another has immense treasures of every sort; another delights to kill human beings. The water-dragon causes floods of rain; when it is sick the rain has a fishy smell. The fire-dragon is only seven feet long, but its body is of flame. The dragons are all very lustful, and approach beasts of every sort. The fruit of a union of one of these monsters with a cow is the kirin; with a swine, an elephant; and with a mare a steed of the finest breed. The female dragon produces at every parturition nine young. The first young dragon sings, and likes all harmonious sounds, hence the tops of Japanese bells are cast in the form of this dragon; the second delights in the sound of musical instruments, hence the koto or horizontal harp, and suzumi, a girl's drum, struck by the fingers, are ornamented with the figure of this dragon; the third is fond of drinking, and likes all stimulating liquors, therefore goblets, and drinking-cups are adorned with representations of this creature; the fourth likes steep and dangerous places, hence gables, towers, and projecting beams of temples and pagodas have carved images of this dragon upon them; the fifth is a great destroyer of living things, fond of killing and bloodshed, therefore swords are decorated with golden figures of this dragon; the sixth loves learning, and delights in literature, hence on the covers and titles of books and literary works are pictures of this creature; the seventh is renowned for its power of hearing; the eighth enjoys sitting, hence the easy chairs are carved in its images; the ninth loves to bear weight, therefore the feet of tables and hibachi are shaped like this creature's feet,

Marcus Huish gives a description of the figure that has become conventionalized among the artists of Japan in the following terms, which show that it differs markedly from the Chinese convention: "A composite monster with scowling head, long straight horns, a scaly, serpentine body, a bristling row of dorsal spines, four limbs armed with claws, and curious flamelike appendages on its shoulders and hips. The claws are usually three on each foot, but are sometimes four or even five." A famous print by Ichiyusai

51

DRAGONS AND UNICORNS—FACT? OR FICTION?

Hiroshige shows a dragon in a cloud about Fuji, which has three bird-like toes and claws on every foot.

I have underscored the item of the row of spines along the ridge of the back, for that is a special characteristic (sometimes a double row, as in those turned about the bronze drum at Nara), and significant in relation to its history; and in general its figure is more distinctly that of a serpent than is the typical dragon of China. Its name in Japanese is Tatsu, the equivalent of the Chinese Lung; and in both countries it serves as one of the signs of the zodiac in the place occupied by Leo in the European symbols of the sun's stations in its apparent annual circuit of the heavens. It also represents the four seas which, as in the Chinese cosmogony, limit the habitable earth, and are ruled by four dragon kings. "The snake," says G. E. Smith, "takes a more obtrusive part in the Japanese than in the Chinese dragon, and it frequently manifests itself as a god of the sea. The old japanese sea-gods were often female watersnakes. The cultural influences which reached Japan from the south by way of Indonesia—many centuries before the coming of Buddhism-naturally emphasized the serpent form of the dragon and its connection with the ocean. But the river-gods, or 'water fathers,' were real four-footed dragons identified with the dragon-kings of Chinese myth, but at the same time were strictly homologous with the naga-rajas or cobra-kings of India."

Joly describes the four 'dragon kings' recognized in Japan as follows:

Sui Riu—a rain-dragon, which when in pain causes reddish rain, coloured by its blood.

Han-Riu—striped with nine different colours; forty feet long; can never reach heaven,

Ka Riu-scarlet; fiery; only seven feet long.

Ri Riu-has wonderful sight; can see more than 100 miles.

The dragon queen is occasionally shown in art dressed in shells, corals, and other marine attrihutes.

The Chinese winged dragon ying lung (rare in decorations) is the hai riu of the Japanese, and is shown with feathered wings, a bird's claws and tail, and a dragon's head; it is also called tobi tatsu and sachi hoko. Children are told of a dragon with a fish's body clothed in large scales; it is called maket-sugo, and may be a nursery version of the Chinese carp-and-dragon story. The dragon of good luck is fuku riu, contrasted with which is one of bad luck. It is popularly believed that dragons may breed by intercourse with earthly animals as a cow or mare, and in folklore a special name is given to each kind of hybrid so resulting. Joly, whose interest in this subject is in explaining its symbolism in art, says that a dragon ascending Fuji in a cloud is symbolic of success in life; that one issuing from a hibachi has the proverbial significance of "It is the unexpected that happens"; and that in connection with a tiger, usually drawn near a cave or some bamboos, the dragon in the sky above represents the power of the elements over the stron-

DRAGONS AND UNICORNS—FACT? OR FICTION?

gest animals. (We have seen hitherto that the tiger is the antithesis of the dragon in many situations.) Joly concludes: "As an emblem the dragon represents both the male and female principles, the continual changes and variations of life, as symbolized by its unlimited powers of adaptation, accommodating itself to all surroundings."

A Japanese myth represents Susan-o-no-o-no Mikoto as an 'impetuous' man who killed an eight-headed dragon, or snake, by making the brute drunk with eight cups of sake (one for each head), and then cutting off all the heads at once. (Eight is a number of great significance in Buddhistic mysticism.) From the tail he drew a marvellous sword, later consecrated to and preserved in the temple of Atsuta. A sword got from a dragon figures, by the way, in several other legends; and various dragons are common ornaments of sword-guards and netsukes, presumably with symbolic intent.

Another version of this story runs thus: A man came to a house where all were weeping, and learned that the last of eight daughters of the house was to be given to a dragon with seven (?) or eight heads, which came to the seashore yearly to claim a victim. He changed himself into the form of the girl, and induced the dragon to drink sake from eight pots set before it, and then slew the drunken monster. From the end of its tail he took out a sword which is supposed to be the Mikado's state sword. The hero married the maid and with her got a jewel or talisman, which is preserved with the royal regalia. Another prize so preserved is a mirror.

Commenting on these tales from Japanese folklore, Dr. G. Elliot Smith expresses the opinion that the appearance in them of a seven-headed monster adds to the probability of their importation from the West, and regards it as a reminiscence of the Egyptian Seven Hathors myth. "The seven-headed dragon is found also in the Scottish dragon-myth, and the legends of Cambodia, India, Persia, western Asia, East Africa, and the Mediterranean area. . . . In southern India the Dravidian people seem to have borrowed the Egyptian idea of the seven Hathors. . . . There is a close analogy between the Swahili and the Gaelic stories that reveals their ultimate derivation from Babylonia. In the Scottish story the seven-headed dragon comes in a storm of wind and spray. The East African serpent comes in a storm of wind and dust. In the Babylonian story seven winds destroy Tiamat. . . . But the Babylonians not only adopted the Egyptian conception of the power of evil as being seven demons, but they also seem to have fused these seven into one."

Foremost, however, among Japanese dragon-legends is that of Riujin and his submarine palace Ryugo-Jo. His messenger is Riuja (or Hakuja), a small white serpent with the face of an ancient man. To the anger of this dragon-king of the sea we owe the boisterous waves. Joly instructs us that he is usually represented by artists as a very old, long-bearded man with a dragon coiled on his head or back. Some say that a man named Hoori once visited the sea-god's palace and got a wife whom he brought ashore and married in earthly fashion; but as soon as the first baby came the wife became a dragon again and sank under the surface of the sea. Other tales are told of visits of this submarine ruler of storms, some of which deal with marvellous gems romantically recovered.

DRAGONS AND UNICORNS—FACT? OR FICTION?

This brief sketch indicates that the dragon is a different affair in Japan from what it is in China, despite a superficial similarity. In both countries the learned and more or less modernized top-crust of society is, or pretends to be, unaffected by this superstition—if it be permissible so to designate it—but this unbelieving class is far broader and deeper in Japan than in China, although still finding in the dragon of tradition an art-motive which is more than merely effective in decoration, for it is instinct with an antique sentiment which all cannot help feeling. This sympathy and sense of symbolism, fostered by the romantic wonder-tales of childhood, in which the dragon figured, is perhaps stronger in sensitive Japan than among the more matter-of-fact Chinese; while faith in the actuality of dragons and the reality of their powers and divine influence is much stronger among the latter people than in Japan.

I shall quote here a paragraph illustrating this point from that most delightful book, John La Farge's An Artist's Letters from Japan. The author is speaking of what he saw at Nikko when visiting the splendid temple built by the Tokugawa rulers in memory of the great shogun Iyeyasu, who died in 1616, and was buried and deified on the Holy Mountain of Nikko. It is entered by the gate called 'magnificent,' above which is an ornate balcony.

The balcony is one long set of panels—of little panels carved and painted on its white line with children playing among flowers. Above, again, as many white pillars as below; along their sides a wild fringe of ramping dragons and the pointed leaves of the bamboo. This time the pillars are crowned with the fabulous dragon-horse, with gilded hoofs dropping into air, and lengthy processes of horns receding far back into the upper bracketings of the roof. Upon the centre of the white-and-gold lintel, so delicately carved with waves as to seem smooth in this delirium of sculpture, is stretched between two of the monster capitals a great white dragon with gilded claws and gigantic protruding head. But all these beasts are tame if compared with the wild army of dragons that cover and people the innumerable brackets which make the cornice and support the complicated rafters under the roof. Tier upon tier hang farther and farther out, like some great mass of vampires about to fall. They are gilded; their jaws are lacquered red far down into their throats, against which their white teeth glitter. Far into the shade spreads a nightmare of frowning eyebrows, and pointed fangs and outstretched claws extended toward the intruder. It would he terrible did not one feel the coldness of the unbelieving imagination, which perhaps merely copied these duplicates of earlier terrors.

An interesting legend, which has been made the theme of a popular Japanese play, is related by Arthur D. Ficke in his Catalogue of colour-prints, 1920. In the tenth century the monk Anchin, having repulsed the amorous advances of an infatuated girl Kiyohime, fled from her wrath and hid in the shadows beneath the great bell that hung in the grounds of the temple at Dojoji, in the Province of Kii, near Kyoto. She, having procured the aid of evil spirits, pursued him; and transforming herself into a dragon she touched the enormous bell, which at once fell to the ground covering the unfortunate priest. Thereupon the revenged dragon-woman curled her fiery length about the bell and, lashing it into a white heat with her flaming body, she consumed her reverent lover and perished herself

54

as the bell collapsed in a molten flood.

The prevalence of the Shinto doctrines in Japan has weakened, no doubt, the more corrupt and superstitious features of mediaeval Buddhism, and the natural gentleness and sensitiveness to beauty in the Japanese have freed them from the grossness and terror belonging to such ideas and rites as came with the horrible naga-cult imparted to their ancestors by early travellers and emissaries from India. Relics of this ancient demonism remain, however, in both their literature and their antique art. The emphasis put in the legends on the sea-god in his submarine palace, and his attendants of both sexes, their ability to become humanized and to mate on shore with human beings, show distinctly an Indian origin.

Climate also has had an effect here as elsewhere on men's views of life. The dragon in northern and central China, at least, is primarily a rain-god, as it was in Mesopotamia and in the valley of the Indus, where drouths were dreaded. In Japan, on the contrary, rain was rarely lacking in agriculture, so that prayers for it were seldom necessary-often, rather, were petitions that its excess should cease. Hence among landsmen the principal motive for prayer and sacrifice to sky-dragons, at any rate, disappeared; while the scarcity of dangerous snakes destroyed the fear of and consequent veneration for serpents, so that actual naga-worship probably never took a strong hold of the people. What held most firmly and longest was the notion of a sea-god, for the Japanese have ever been mariners, and all seamen are inclined to love mysteries and to deify the wondrous phenomena of the ocean.

DRAGONS AND UNICORNS—FACT? OR FICTION?

CHAPTER TEN

THE DRAGON'S PRECIOUS PEARL

A MOST curious, interesting, and at the same time obscure feature of this whole baffling subject is that of the so-called Pearl which accompanies the dragon in pictures and legends from the earliest times, and is common to the religious traditions of the whole East—India, China and Japan. Necklaces of pearls are a regular part of the regalia of naga-queens in their submarine palaces; and we read often in the old Vedic books of a magical 'jewel of good luck,' which was in custody of the naga-maidens but was lost by them through terror of their monstrous enemy, the bird garuda. There are traces of it in early Taoism, but it is best preserved in Buddhism as the jewel in the lotus, the mani of the mystic, ecstatic, formula Om mani padme hum—the "Jewel that grants all desires," the 'divine pearl' of the Buddhists throughout the Orient. Koreans commonly believe that the yellow (chief) dragon carries on his forehead (as also in Japan) a pear-shaped pearl having supernatural properties and healing power. In China alone, however, is this mystical accessory of the dragon made a significant part of pictures and decorative designs. Some say that originally every proper dragon carried a pearl under his chin; others that it was a special mark of imperial rank. A sixth-century writer asserts that such pearls are "spit out of dragons like snake-pearls out of snakes," and have enormous value.

This extraordinary gem is represented as a spherical object, or 'ball,' half as big, or quite as large, as the head of the dragon with which it is associated, for it is never depicted quite by itself. The gem is white or bluish with a reddish or golden halo, and usually has an antler-shaped 'flame' rising from its surface. Almost invariably there hangs downward from the centre of the sphere a dark-coloured, comma-like appendage, frequently branched, wavering below the periphery. A biologist might easily at first glance conclude that the whole affair represented the entry of a spermatozoon into an ovum; and the Chinese commonly interpret the ball with its comma-mark as a symbol of yang and yin, male and female elements, combined in the earth—which seems pretty close to the biologist's view. Such is the Dragon-Pearl.

DRAGONS AND UNICORNS—FACT? OR FICTION?

In purely decorative work, where the figure of a dragon is writhing in clouds or adapting its lithe body under an artist's hand to the shape or purpose of a piece of porcelain, a bronze article, or a silken garment, the pearl may be drawn close to the dragon, or wherever convenient. When, however, it is desirable to express the significance of this sacred adjunct of dragonhood, it is treated with strict attention to reverence and tradition. Then are pictured celestial dragons ascending and descending through the upper air, tearing a path, perhaps, through swirling mists and shadows, "in pursuit of effulgent jewels or orbs that appear to be whirling in space, and that were supposed to be of magic efficiency, granting every wish." A passion for gems is a well-known characteristic of these beings, and that it has 'always' been so is shown by a fable recorded by Joly. T'an T'ai Mieh Ming, a disciple of Confucius, was attacked, at the instigation of the god of the Yellow River, by two dragons seeking to rob him of a valuable gem; but T'an T'ai slew the dragons and then, to show his contempt for worldly goods, threw the treasure into the river. Twice it leaped back into his boat, but at last he broke it in pieces and scattered the fragments.

Can these be the two dragons so often depicted facing one another in the air, and apparently rushing, as if in eager play, toward a pearl floating like an iridescent bubble between them? Nothing in the decorative art of China has occasioned more guessing and controversy than this. An eighteenth century vase described by Chait is "decorated with nine dragons (a mystic number) whirling through scrolled clouds enveloping parts of their serpentine bodies in pursuit of jewels of omnipotence, which appear in the midst of clouds as revolving disks emitting branched rays of effulgence." Ball points out that in books issued under imperial auspices "two dragons encircle the title, striving . . . for a pearl." Japanese designers like to form the handles of bells, whether big temple-bells or tiny ones, of two dragons affrontes, with the tama between them. One Japanese carving represents a snake-like dragon coiled tightly around a ball, marked with spiral lines, illustrating devotion to the tama. "A great ball of gilded glass," writes Visser, "is said to hang from the centre of the roof of the great hall of the Buddhist temple Fa(h)-yu-sze, or Temple of the Reign of Law, while eight dragons, curved around the 'hanging pillars,' eagerly stretch their claws towards the 'pearl of perfection.' . . . Dragons trying to seize a fiery 'pearl,' which is hanging in a gate, are represented twice in the same temple. . . . We may be sure that the Chinese Buddhists, identifying the Dragon with the Naga, also identified the ball with their cintamani or 'precious pearl which grants all desires.'"

In these and many similar examples we, as outsiders, may grasp little of the significance or symbolism in this conspicuous 'ball' or 'pearl,' but we may approach an understanding of it through Dr. De Groot's investigation of Chinese religion.' He describes the ceremonial dress of the Wuist priests as having a "broad border of blue silk around the neck stitched with two ascending dragons which are belching out a ball probably representing thunder." De Groot explains further that "the ball between two dragons is often delineated as a spiral," and adds that 'in an ancient charm . . . a spiral denotes the rolling of thunder from which issues a flash of lightning." In Japanese prints a dragon is frequently accompanied by a huge spiral indicating a thunderstorm caused by him. Are the antler-shaped appendages rising above the 'ball' intended to represent lightning-

DRAGONS AND UNICORNS—FACT? OR FICTION?

flames?

Dr. Visser discusses this hypothesis at length, pointing out that the whole attitude of the two dragons in such art-productions displays great eagerness to catch and swallow the gleaming sphere. This attitude and avidity become clear, Visser thinks, when one sees a Chinese picture like that in Blacker's Chats on Oriental China, of two dragons rushing at a fiery spiral ball above the legend: "Two Dragons Facing the Moon." Sometimes two dragons confront each other, each having a flaming pearl floating just in front of their faces.

There is nothing absurd about this suggestion of swallowing the moon. Celestial dragons are, in reality, personifications of clouds; and among the most primitive and widespread impressions respecting lunar eclipses is the notion that a monster is devouring the moon. Dark and writhing clouds advancing as if alive, and finally extinguishing its light, might easily suggest a similar thought; and it was a matter of early experience that after these hungry cloud-dragons had completed their feast, fertilizing rain usually blessed the thirsty fields and pastures, so that the dragons got the credit. Hence artists liked to represent these public benefactors playfully contending for the opportunity to devour the 'queen of night' and so produce a crop-saving fall of showers for which they (the dragons) would enjoy grateful appreciation. Incidentally, artists note that a pair of their graceful figures make a well-balanced composition. The moon and water are closely connected in all mythologies; hence the moon is closely linked with fertilizing agencies in general. Faith in the moon's influence on the weather lingers strongly in the mind of rural communities even in these progressive United States of America; and it is easy to believe that the dragon-thanking agriculturists and shepherds of China felt assured that the rain-giving will and power of their celestial friends were refreshed by frequently absorbing this bright and stimulating object in the sky.

That these reflections are not 'all moonshine' is shown by evidence in the writings of the old philosophers of the East, who assure us that the actual mundane pearl taken from the oyster in whose shell it is formed beneath the salt waters is the "concrete essence of the moon" distilled through the system of the mollusk—an emanation from the moon-goddess herself. "The pearls found in the oyster," as one student interprets it, "were supposed to be little moons, drops of the moon-substance (or dew) which fell from the sky into the gaping oyster. Hence pearls acquired the reputation of shining by night, like to the moon from which they were believed to have come." All this tends to demonstrate that the theory that the moon is the mani, the 'pearl of great price,' the divine essence of the gods, is not unreasonable; and its probability is reinforced by the stated fact that in both Chinese and Japanese dictionaries an ideograph combined of elements meaning respectively 'jewel' and 'moon' is defined as 'moon-pearl.'

I am inclined to regard this as a better explanation of the puzzling object so constantly associated with dragons in Chinese decorative art than is the 'thunder' hypothesis. At the same time it is to be noted that the spiral character of the 'pearl,' and of the 'tag' that springs from its centre, is the widely recognized symbol for thunder; while the

58

DRAGONS AND UNICORNS—FACT? OR FICTION?

antler-like appendages indicate accompanying lightnings; therefore the identification of the 'pearl' with the moon need not preclude its co-association with thunderstorms, for the dragon is a rain-controller, and in a fair sense is the deity heard and seen in thunder and lightning, who is in particular the storm-god of sailormen.

In Japan, whose dragon-mythology has been strongly tinctured with Indian notions, as we have seen, the pearl appears mainly in connection with mythical tales of the ocean- a very natural connection. In the Nihongi, an ancient Japanese historical work, it is related that in the second year of the Emperor Chaui's reign (A.D. 193) the Empress Jingo-Kogo found in the sea "a jewel which grants all desires," apparently the same lost by the frightened Naga Maidens. She also obtained from the submarine palace of the dragon king the ebb-jewel (kan-ja) and the flood-jewel (man-ja), by which she was able, on at least one important occasion, to control the tides; they are described in the Nihongi as about five sun long, the former white and the latter blue—the colour of the east, whence rain comes; and the moon is controller of the oceanic tides!

Japanese legends relating to this matter, as briefly given by Joly, in his elaborate work on the legendary art of Japan, are connected with the mythical character Riujin, the ruler of the waters of the globe, whose home is beneath the sea, or in deep lakes, and who is represented as a very old man bearing a coiled dragon on his head or back. Riujin carries the divine jewel tama, esteemed as a symbol of purity and usually shown in Japan on the forehead of the dragon; also the jewels of the flowing and the retreating tides, which he gave to Jingo-Kogo, Hikohodermi, and others.

In representations of Hendaka Sonja, one of the worshipful sixteen arhats, special disciples of Buddha, "he is generally shown," Joly tells us, "with a bowl from which issues a dragon or a rain-cloud. He holds the bowl aloft with his left hand and with his right carries the sacred gem. Sometimes he is shown seated on a rock, the dragon occasionally aside, and crouching to reach the tama."

Another legend relates that Riujin once captured from the Chinese queen, the daughter of Kamatari, a most precious jewel, which later was recovered from Riujin by a fisher-girl, wife of Kamatari, who went to the dragon's submarine palace and got possession of the gem. She immediately stabbed her breast and hid the jewel in the wound, then floated to the surface and was found by Kamatari, the jewel guiding him to her by the dazzling light it shed from the concealing wound that became fatal to the heroine. Such stories are logical if the 'jewel' (tama, pearl) is identified with the moon.

Now it may well be asked: how is it that, granting the fondness of dragons for gems and the identity of the several gems and jewels mentioned in myths and ceremonies, they all trace back in significance to the pearl? Well, the pearl is an excellent image in miniature of the full moon; it, like the moon, represents water, and is a part of the history of the sea and sea-wanderings. Hence pearls were regarded as in the special possession of the sea-gods and water-spirits; and these beings were often pictured in forms far more fishy, or crocodilian, or shark-like, than were the terrestrial, serpentine dragons.

DRAGONS AND UNICORNS—FACT? OR FICTION?

But Japanese mythology includes also an earthquake-fish (Namazu) like an eel, with a long, attenuated head and long feelers on both sides of the mouth, which stirs about underground, thus causing earthquakes.

"The cultural drift from West to East, along the south coast of India," Dr. Smith reminds us, "was effected mainly by sailors who were searching for pearls. Sharks constituted the special dangers the divers had to incur in exploiting pearlbeds to obtain the precious 'giver of life.' But at the time these great enterprises were undertaken in the Indian Ocean the people dwelling in the neighbourhood of the chief pearlbeds regarded the sea as the great source of all life-giving, and the god who exercised these powers was incarnated in a fish (ancestor of Dagon). The sharks therefore had to be brought into this scheme, and they were rationalized as the guardians of the storehouse of life-giving pearls at the bottom of the sea. . . . Out of these crude materials the imaginations of the early pearl-fishers created the picture of wonderful submarine palaces of Naga kings in which vast wealth, not merely of pearls but also of gold, precious stones, and beautiful maidens, were placed under the protection of shark-dragons."

DRAGONS AND UNICORNS—FACT? OR FICTION?

CHAPTER ELEVEN

THE DRAGON INVADES THE WEST

AN ENTIRELY new field of research lies before us in the West—in Europe. There the word 'dragon' is as familiar as in China, but its form and connotations are decidedly different. Certainly civilization began much farther back in time in Egypt and Iraq, India and China, and the object of our curiosity took form in the Orient long before its image appeared in the West, but was it invented anew in Europe, or was it brought in? If imported, whence? and how?

The earliest traces of European civilization belong to Greece, and the oldest indication of the Mediterranean man's thoughts about great mysteries is given in the hero-tales that have come down to us from that history-laden peninsula and its islands. These ancient and cloudy myths imply that "in those days" the earth was possessed by a race of Titans, giants huge and fierce, whose bodies below the waist were supported by a pair of thick serpent-tails instead of legs, reminding us of those pictures of mythical fore-runners of Chinese tribes engraved on the tombs of the ancestors of the Wu family in Shantung; and the Titans' wives were the Lamiae—abominable hags. The chief God of that time was Ophion, the Great Snake; and it is difficult in studying these primitive fables to distinguish between the 'giants' of some stories and the 'dragons' of others: they seem to be the same. It was the task of newcomers, heroes bringing foreign gods, to conquer the giants and to enthrone on Olympus wholly human figures of power in place of the monstrous Ophion and his reptilian hosts. Saturn and Neptune (himself half man, half fish), and after them Zeus the sky-god, struggled for mastery of the world, and famous deeds against giants and dragons were performed by the Olympian heroes before Greece was rid of them.

Now, if all this ophidian prehistory was an original conception of the primitive inhabitants of eastern Greece, where the incidents seem to have been laid, and was remembered in tradition and folklore down to the time of Homer, the fact is remarkable, be-

DRAGONS AND UNICORNS—FACT? OR FICTION?

cause no real serpent exists on the coasts or islands of the Agean Sea, or on the mainland of Greece, that has large size or would inspire either fear or respect worth mention. The only venomous snake thereabout is the small viper common all over the warmer half of Europe. Are we not, rather, considering dim, distorted recollections Of serpent-worshipping aborigines, for whom, if needed, there had been no lack of teachers during unnumbered previous centuries? Long before the days of Homer and Hesiod, or of the annalists and singers of Palestine, Egyptian and Syrian navigators were sailing about the Aegean Sea and between India and Egypt. They brought ideas from the East as well as goods. Nomadic 'Aryan' tribes were migrating with their flocks back and forth, as the seasons and pasturage changed, all over the plains between Thessaly and the highlands of Scythia and far Bactria. When they met other migrants and related tales of scenes and adventures in far countries, they told of strange gods and demons—half-human serpents often gigantic and terrible. With the dramatic sense strong in all primitive story-tellers, they garnished their reports with marvels undreamed-of by their listeners, and to be effectively enlarged when retold by the shepherds and fishermen of Macedonia, or among the Attic hills, or in the 'isles of Greece.' From such narratives, probably "all made out of the carver's brain," were developed the queer and often horrid conceptions that took shape in the mythology of almost prehistoric Greece, and afterward these were seized upon as 'material' in symbolic art and epic poetry.

The oldest definite traces of the dragon in Europe are in the Greek legend, preserved by Homer and Hesiod, of Cadmus and his band of adventurers—probably some long-remembered incursion of raiders from the eastward; and, judging by his fancied presentment on a vase exhumed at Palermo, he was a wholly human warrior, and not at all like Cecrops, the mythical founder of Athens, a being whose body terminated in the shape of a fat and scaly serpent. As Seiffert condenses the legend, Cadmus, having been led by a magic cow to a spot in Boeotia where he was thus impelled to plant his intended colony, proposed to dedicate the site at once by the sacrifice of a (or perhaps the) cow-a distinctly Aryan proceeding. Therefore he sent his companions for the necessary pure water to a near-by spring, where all were immediately slain by a huge serpent, the dragon-guard of the fountain. This incident is quite in accord with Asiatic ideas of the time regarding dragon-serpents' functions. As soon as Cadmus learned of the slaughter of his comrades he rushed to the spring and killed the dragon; then, at the command of an invisible voice (some say of Athene), he drew out its teeth and 'sowed' them over the adjacent ground. A host of armed men immediately sprang up, each from one of the broadcast teeth, who instantly began to fight and slay one another until only five remained alive. These survivors then quieted their fury and helped Cadmus build a stronghold, which finally developed into the city of Thebes. The five naturally became the ancestors of the Theban aristocracy, and one of them, Echion, called 'the serpent's son,' married Cadmus's daughter Agave. After many troubles King Cadmus retired to Illyria, where at last he and his wife Harmonia were changed into snakes, died, and were carried by the gods to the place of the blest. This denouement is very inconsistent, but it shows how the "trail of the serpent" lies over every incident and fancy in that fantastic infancy-story of Hellas.

DRAGONS AND UNICORNS—FACT? OR FICTION?

One cannot gather from the writings of the early poets and chroniclers any distinct idea of the traditional or supposed appearance of the monsters with which the sun-gods were incessantly battling, except that whenever a chance glimpse is permitted one sees the serpent-likeness. Such was Python, half man, half snake, as some say, which haunted the caves on Mt. Parnassus, particularly that cleft in the rocks, originally called Pytho, where afterward was established the Delphic oracle. Apollo seized the place just after his birth, slaying Python with the first arrows from his infant bow; and in later times a festival was held there every year at which the whole story was represented in pageantry—the prototype of similar historic festivals celebrated during the Middle Ages in Europe and not yet quite obsolete.

Python was one of the offspring of Typhoeus and Echidna, themselves apparently son and daughter of Tartarus (underworld) and Gaea (earth). Echidna was part woman and part snake, and her brother-husband is identified with the Typhon of Egyptian mythology, otherwise Apop, one of the forms of wicked Set and a sort of duplicate of the Persian Azhi-Zohak, since he also is a gigantic demon, and has snakes sprouting from his shoulders. This diabolical pair further afflicted the world by engendering, in addition to Python, the three-headed dogs Orthos and Cerberus, the lion of Namaea, the Lernean hydra, the guardians of the orchards of Hesperus and of the Golden Fleece in Colchis, and perhaps other monsters of fable.

The most notable, perhaps, of this horrid brood was Hydra, a water-fiend that infested the region about Lake Lerna, near Argos, where it devastated the country of cattle and sheep, and whose breath even was a deadly poison. All accounts agree that it was an enormous water-snake with many heads—a hundred according to Diodorus, fifty says Eumenides, but the accepted opinion is that its heads numbered nine, one of which was believed to be immortal. To destroy this dreadful creature was thought worthy to be one of a dozen or so 'labours' assigned to Heracles (as tests of manhood?) by the Delphic oracle; and it was the only feat of the lot that he could not accomplish without help, because whenever one of the hydra's heads had been amputated two new ones would sprout in its place unless the wound were scarified by fire. Having scared the hydra out of its lair among the reeds by shooting at it fiery arrows, Heracles hewed at its heads, and as fast as he cut them off his nephew and charioteer, Iolaus, seared the bleeding stumps with a burning-iron. The hydra having at last been totally decapitated, the heroes piled a huge stone on its 'immortal' head and so prevented resuscitation of the evil.

A later and lesser sort of hydra was the chimaera, of which we may read in the Iliad, and which appears on the monuments "with the body of a serpent terminating in a head, and having two other heads as well, one a lion's in the usual place, the other a goat's rising out of the centre of the body. No one could overcome the chimaera, and it caused the death of many men by the fire it exhaled, until at last Bellerophon slew it."

The hydra seems to me a mere extravagance of the serpent-cult, not at all different from the Hindoos' many-headed nagas, and probably akin to them in history. Again, is the chimaera anything but a caricature of Marduk's sea-goat? The inference seems irre-

63

DRAGONS AND UNICORNS—FACT? OR FICTION?

sistible that the religious notions of the aborigines of Macedonia and prehistoric Greece were derived from India, by way of the wandering 'Aryans' of Thrace and the northern plains, tinctured with somewhat of the mythology of Egypt and Chaldea.

It has been said that the hydra was copied from the poulpe, or octopus, which infests the rocky shores and shallows of the eastern Mediterranean, but this seems to me improbable, however much the octopus may be recognized in certain other aspects of the myths and conventional designs characteristic of the Mediterranean region. More logically this repulsive cephalopod might well be regarded as the parent of the marine monster Scylla, finally exterminated by Heracles. She is described by Homer as dwelling on a tall rock in the sea where the lower half of her body is concealed in a cavern, whence she reaches out six long necks, each bearing a horrid head with three rows of teeth closely set (like the suckers of the cuttle), by which she catches fishes and other marine creatures, and snatches men off passing ships. (In later times she personified one of the two great perils in the navigation of the Strait of Messina.)

It is needless to catalogue all the misshapen and fearful monsters recorded in the legends found in the writings of Homer and Hesiod, and revived by Ovid and the later poets and artists of Greece and Rome. Heracles, Perseus, Theseus and other heroes arose to kill them off when a developing civilization and humourous skepticism required their extinction. Meleager freed the peasantry from the ravages of a gigantic boar. Heracles slew the huge Nemaean lion, dispersed the man-eating Stymphalian birds, and overcame in amazing battles several giants, such as Cacus and the river-god Achelous, who nearly escaped by transforming himself into a snake; and captured the Island of the Hesperides from the hundred-headed serpent Ladon, protector of the golden apples that Gaea had cultivated as a wedding gift for Hera when Zeus should marry her in this garden of the gods. Ladon, expelled from earth, was set up in the sky by Juno as the constellation known to us as The Serpent. Extremely ancient is the tale of the Argonauts, which has so many features in common with that of Cadmus, and records Jason's final achievement of their purpose by vanquishing the dragon that held the post of custodian of the coveted golden fleece, and who was the last of the progeny of Echidna and Typhon. Finally Perseus, by conquering a prodigious sea-serpent, rescued the forlorn but interesting maid Andromeda, and thereby became the remotest ancestor of all the redoubtable 'Saint-Georees' whose adventures are in store for us. Trail of the serpent again!

Perseus became the son of Zeus and Danae, after Zeus had visited her in the guise of a shower of gold poured into her lap. He had many adventures, including the killing of Medusa, the chief of the snaky-locked Gorgons, but the heroic incident that interests us most is his saving of Andromeda. This unhappy maid was a daughter of Cepheus and Cassiopeia. Cassiopeia had boasted herself fairer than the Nereids, whereupon Poseidon, the sea-god, to punish this profanity, sent a flood to overwhelm the land and a sea-monster to consume the people. The oracle of Ammon promised riddance of the plague should Andromeda be thrown to the monster (represented in a sculpture of the classic period, preserved in the Capitoline Museum in Rome, as a big, pike-like fish); Cepheus therefore felt compelled to chain his daughter to a rock on the shore, convenient to the marine

64

DRAGONS AND UNICORNS—FACT? OR FICTION?

'dragon' when the tide rose. In this distressful situation Perseus appears, full of gallantry, destroys the approaching monster, and having thus rescued her and freed the threatened country, obtained the girl as his wife. The legend of Heracles and Hesione is virtually the same.

These 'snake-stories' and other figments of the imagination of a rude and adventurous people would have been forotten long, long ago, had not their dramatic possibilities been seen and utilized by the early bards to enrich the more or less rhythmical stories they chanted in village huts and by the shepherds' camp-fire, not to mention their use by the early vase-painters. Considering these matters in his valuable treatise on modern Greek folklore, Mr. John C . Lawson has distinguished several kinds or classes of genii visible in the fables and folk-tales of the Hellenic people past and present.

The third class of genii [he remarks], is terrestrial, inhabiting mountains, rocks, caves, and other grim and desolate places. These genii are the most frequent of all, and are known as dragons. Not, of course, that all dragons are terrestrial; the dragon form has already been mentioned as among the forms proper to the genii of springs and wells. . . . The term drakos or drakontas indicates to the Greek peasant a monster of no more determinate shape than does 'dragon' among ourselves. The Greek word, however, . . . is often employed in a strict and narrow sense to denote a 'serpent' as distinguished from a small snake (phodi). On the other hand a Greek 'dragon' in the widest sense of the word is sometimes distinctly anthropomorphic in popular stories, and is made to boil kettles and drink coffee without any sense of impropriety. It is in fact only from the context of the story that it is possible to tell in what shape the dragon is imagined; in general it is neither flesh, fowl nor good red devil; heads and tails, wings and legs, teeth and talons, are assigned to it in any number and variety; it sleeps with its eyes open, and sees with them shut; it makes war on men and love to women; it roars or it sings; . . . it is the dragon above all other supernatural heings, who provides the wandering hero of the fairy-tales with befitting adventures and tests of prowess.

Now, a striking feature of this whole race of prehistoric Greek 'dragons' is that they have no lizard-like, four-footed body, no kindliness of disposition, and nothing to do with rainfall or productivity of the soil. The exception to complete dissimilarity with the Chinese variety is that some of them have the office of guardians of women and treasure. On the other hand these fierce and horrid 'Pelasgian' creatures of a lively imagination portray, far more evidently than do the Oriental 'dragons,' the fears and emotions of a people half-savage, it is true, yet possessed of an alertness of mind very different from the rather bovine and 'single-track' mentality of the Hindoos and Chinese. The varied personages and adventures of the Greek hero-stories appeal in one way or another to us as they did to the men of antiquity (and as the Oriental ones do not); and this must account both for their seizure and preservation for us by the poets and artists between us and them in time, and for their present power to move us as symbols of things we feel and understand, though long disregarded as facts. A similar quality of dramatic reality belongs to much of the Persian mythology, and this strengthens the theory that Greece derived these notions from the prehistoric men of central Asia overland, rather than from

DRAGONS AND UNICORNS—FACT? OR FICTION?

Asia Minor by way of the Aegean islands, or to any great extent from Egypt by way of Crete—the latter in later times the channel of an invigorating influence.

Yet one cannot be sure that the Egyptian demonology did not tincture the superstition of the earliest Greeks, for prehistoric sculptures exhumed in Crete show water-demons of queerly changed crocodilian aspect with strange mammalian heads, and distinctly four-legged, which might have served as prototypes of the forms later developed in western Europe.

The Hittites and Phoenicians do not appear to have had in their history or religion any proper dragons, for their fiendish Moloch was certainly not of that (Chaldean) race; hence nothing of the sort has been revealed in Carthage or in the remains of other Phoenician settlements on the shores of the Mediterranean.

All the foregoing matter is mythical or legendary. We get upon fairly firm ground of fact about fifteen centuries before the Christian era, when invaders from the north penetrated the Epirus, expelled or subdued the barbarous 'Pelasgians,' and established themselves as settlers and rulers. These conquerors, known henceforth as Achaeans, were Nordic tribes of somewhat superior physique and culture, speaking an Aryan dialect out of which the Greek language developed. With their advent the history of the country begins, and the aboriginal stories of dragons, giants, and incredible heroes fade rapidly into folklore and become merely literary and artistic materials. Camps and caves are replaced by substantial buildings, and these become improved into the splendid edifices of the Golden Age of Greek art. It is noteworthy at this point to remark that from the very beginning in megalithic or 'Mycaenian' structures the ornamentation of neither temples, official buildings, nor private houses had any suggestion of the ancient serpent-cult, unlike what has happened in China and Japan, where images of dragons and snakes meet the eye in every city and village and keep alive their sacred and symbolic significance. Even statuary and decorative designing among the Greeks almost completely ignored this temptingly useful material, evidently rejected on grounds of good taste because of the unpleasant suggestions involved in everything reptilian. The horrifying figures of the Laocoon form a notable exception, but there the terrible serpent is an image of a real snake, not one derived from a myth.

When, in its decadence, Greece sank into the Roman empire, its legends were absorbed along with its lands, but the Romans were a very hard-headed people (apart from their day-by-day watching for omens), and having thrown away long before such antique lumber as dragon-tales—if ever they had any—they were not inclined to adopt any new ones from a neighhour's garret, save as here and there a small and picturesque bit might be worth saving as a 'museum-piece' of folklore or poetry. They still held to some relics of serpent worship, such as the attribution of snakes to Apollo and to Aesculapius, and their connection with the cult of the Lares, or household gods, under the impression that these house-haunting mouse-hunters were guardian spirits, whence images of them were hung up in shrines—for luck! But Lares were not dragons. The nearest approach to our subject appears to be the fable of the basilisk or cockatrice, and that I

DRAGONS AND UNICORNS—FACT? OR FICTION?

judge to be of Egyptian origin, and made up of travellers' tales about spitting vipers; at best this undesirable creature was nothing but a venomous serpent endowed with supernatural qualities.

That they knew in Rome what a proper dragon looked like is plain from the engravings that remain of the standard of one of the legions in the Roman army. The Rev. J. B. Deane, whose old book bears the appearance of patient care, assures his readers that at the time when Rome was growing up the warriors of the Persians, Scythians, Parthians, Assyrians, and even the Saxons, "had dragon standards"; he explains also, quoting Latin writers of the age of the Caesars, that in the army of Marcus Aurelius, and afterward, flag-like images woven into the shape of a traditional dragon, were carried by each of the ten companies (cohorts) in a regiment (legion), whose regimental standard represented an eagle. Later, the dragon emblem was taken from the regular army and, in its Parthian form, was adopted as the general standard for the Auxiliary Corps. Thus in time it became the ensign of the emperors of the West whose troops were wholly Auxiliaries; and in the painting in the Vatican depicting Constantine the Great announcing to his soldiers his conversion to Christianity, a buoyant image of a winged, four-footed, proper dragon is prominently displayed, floating from a lofty pike-head.

With the 'decline and fall' of Rome, then, knowledge of the dragon might have disappeared from the western world forever had it not been revived at the last gasp, as it were, in the interest of Christianity and in the person of His Eminence the Devil.

DRAGONS AND UNICORNS—FACT? OR FICTION?

CHAPTER TWELVE

THE 'OLD SERPENT' AND HIS PROGENY

IT is difficult to determine whether the Hebrews, as we know them in the Bible, believed in the actual existence of what we call a 'dragon,' at least as resident in Palestine. "Hebrew theology," Geiger concludes, "had no demonology or Satan until after the residence at Babylon. . . . The account of the Garden of Eden dates from a time subsequent to the captivity"; and this eminent expositor assumes that Satan came from the Zoroastrian conception of Arhiman, "the evil serpent bearing death."

The features of the original Sumerian, of pre-Sumerian, myth of the struggle of Marduk with Tiamat had become considerably modified by that time even in Babylonia. Dr. Ward mentions a cylinder on which Bel-Marduk is depicted as chasing and killing the Evil One—an unmistakable serpent. "This," Dr. Ward thought, "is convincing proof that in the region where it was made the spirit of evil was conceived as a serpent, as it is in Genesis, and also in Job 26:13 and Isaiah 27:1." Job calls it a 'crooked serpent,' and Isaiah declares that in due time the Lord of Israel "shall punish the leviathan, that crooked serpent; and he shall slay the leviathan that is in the sea."

Most of the allusions in the Old Testament appear to be allegorical or poetic, 'dragon' merely serving with the owl, raven, and other creatures of the Syrian wilderness as an expression for desert desolation. The prophets and bards, addressing a people fond of

DRAGONS AND UNICORNS—FACT? OR FICTION?

figurative speech, were no doubt confident their allusions and metaphors would be understood, even when a devouring, malignant, and unearthly agent of evil was meant, as in the frightful visions limned by the excited author of the Book of Revelations. Take, for example, John's vision in Patinos of dragon-horses (Rev. 9:17) whose heads "were as the heads of lions; and out of their mouths issued fire and smoke and brimstone . . . for their power is in their mouth and in their tails, for their tails are like unto serpents, and had heads, and with them they do hurt."

Then there is that powerful modern picture in enduring phrases: "There was war in heaven: Michael and his angels fought against the dragon; and the dragon fought and his angels, and prevailed not; neither was their place found any more in heaven. And the great dragon was cast out, that old serpent called the Devil and Satan, which deceiveth the whole world; he was cast out and his angels were cast with him." Milton in next describing Satan's return to Pandemonium, changed to a dragon, finely distinguishes this hellish monster from the snaky tribe out of which it has grown, in these verses from Paradise Lost (10: 519):

For now were all transformed

Alike, to serpents all, as accessories

To his bold riot. Dreadful was the din

Of hissing through the hall, thick-swarming now

With complicated monsters head and tail,

Scorpion, and asp, and imphishaena dire,

Cerastes horned, hydrus and ellops drear,

And dipsas (not so thick swarmed once the soil

Bedropt with blood of gorgon, or the isle

Ophiusa); but still greatest he the midst,

Now dragon grown, larger than whom the sun

Engendered in the Pythian vale on slim,

Huge Python; and his power no less he seemed

Above the rest still to retain.

DRAGONS AND UNICORNS—FACT? OR FICTION?

The figures of metaphor chosen by St. John show that he knew the traditionary characteristics (largely derived from India) of these reptilian ogres, and counted on the public's familiarity with them. No doubt he had often heard or read dozens of legends about them-such tales, for example, as the following one recounted in the long story about Job by Thal'labi, who died in 1035 A.D. It is a part of the Book of the Stories of the Poets, from which it was quoted into the American Journal of Semitic Languages (vol. 13, p. 145). God is haranguing the fretful job:

"Where wast thou in the day when I formed the dragon? His food is in the sea and his dwelling in the air; his eyes flash fire; his ears are like the bow of the clouds, there pours forth from them flame as though he were a whirling wind-column of dust; his belly burns and his breath flames forth in hot coals like unto rocks; it is as though the clash of his teeth were sounds of thunder and the glance of his eye were the flashing of lightning; armies pass him while he is lying; nothing terrifies him; in him there is no joint . . . he destroys all that by which he passes."

The rendering by the English word 'dragon' in the authorized version of the Bible of both the two similar words tan and thanin is explained by Canon Tristram in his authentic Natural History of the Bible. "Tan," he announces, "is always used in the plural for some creature inhabiting desert places, frequently coupled with the ostrich and wild beasts." The Prophets and Psalmist abound in such references, and hear their cries from the most desolate haunts they are able to picture to their minds. "I will make a wailing like the dragons, and mourning as the ostriches," exclaims Micah, remembering nocturnal voices that had echoed in the desert from ghostly ruins and perilous wastes—voices of real animals such as jackals, whose mournful howlings disturb the nervous and superstitious, or owls, always troublesome to timorous souls.

The writer of the article 'Dragon' in the Jewish Cyclopedia informs us that in the Septuagint version the word signifies a dangerous monster whose bite is poisonous. This accords with the Hindoo definition of a naga, which designates a venomous snake alone, a cobra. Such monsters must be imagined, says this Hebrew commentator, as of composite but snake-like form, and always as at home in water, even in the waves of the sea (Psalms 48: 7), where they were created by God with the fishes. "In the beginning of things YHWH overpowered them in creating the world. It is clear that this story, which is found only in fragments in the 0. T., was originally a myth representing God's victory over the seas."

The hot and arid country of the Holy Land was particularly favourable to serpent life. Several venomous species were present then as now, lurking not only in thickets and hedges (Eccl. 10: 8), and among rocks, but even in and about the rude, stone-built, dark houses of Judean villages, where they crept in search of mice, insects, etc. Amos alludes warningly to the danger in leaning against a house-wall lest an unseen serpent bite the lounger. Men saw the snake crawling in the dust, and held as a fact that it had been cursed in Eden (Genesis 3:14) to travel forever on its belly as a mark of degradation; only wondering why, instead, the good Lord had not removed altogether so dangerous a

DRAGONS AND UNICORNS—FACT? OR FICTION?

pest from his chosen people. Add to this power for harm its traditional history as something impious, and nothing seems more natural to a zoologist or an anthropologist than that this sly reptile should typify the unseen and dire influences that we name Eblis, Satan, the Devil, the Old Serpent, and so forth, and should become the prototype of the Dragon of Biblical and hence of modern legendary love, almost independently of Far Eastern notions.

Faiths, traditions, and figures of speech relating to these matters were an important element in the Christianity brought to Rome by early Jewish propagandists of the new religion, a striking novelty in which was the doctrine of punishment after death for wickedness wrought in life. No longer were men taught that when life ceased their spiritual selves were transported to another world more or less like this one; on the contrary they were sternly warned that if they died in their sins they went to a place of eternal suffering, in charge of a supreme torturer, who daily went roaming about on earth in ingenious and subtle disguises, tempting men to put themselves everlastingly in his power. He was called chiefly 'Satan' and 'Devil.' Both these names were terms taken from Oriental languages, and naturally soon came to be concretely represented by the figure of the Eastern dragon, with whom the populace, grown acquainted with Oriental things by the empire's conquests in Asia Minor and Persia, was vaguely familiar.

To fully identify this dragon of tradition with the Devil of the Bible, and so increase the terror of his power, was easy to the zealous, if not over-wise, ministers of Chistianity, and evidence of their success is found in the many representations in mediaeval religious art to be seen in ancient books and manuscripts, numerous examples of which have been copied into Carus's History of the Devil and other similar treatises.

"Set," remarks Dr. G. E. Smith, "the enemy of Osiris, who is the real prototype of the evil dragon, was the antithesis of the god of Justice; he was the father of falsehood and the symbol of chaos. He was the prototype of Satan, as Osiris was the first definite representative of the Deity of which any record has been preserved. . . .

"The history of the evil dragon is not merely the evolution of the Devil, but it also affords the explanation of his traditional peculiarities, his bird-like features, his horns, his red color, his wings and cloven hoofs, and his tail. They are all of them the dragon's distinctive features; and from time to time in the history of past ages we catch glimpses of the reality of these idetitifications. In one of the earliest woodcuts found in a printed book Satan is represented as a monk with the bird's feet of the dragon. A most interesting intermediate phase is seen in a Chinese watercolor in the John Rylands Library (at Manchester, England), in which the thunder-dragon is represented in a form almost exactly reproducing that of the Devil of European tradition."

Here we have the genesis of the figure of Mephistopheles! In the oldest version of the Faust legend (sixteenth century) Mephistopheles, the servant-devil, sends Faust through the air whithersoever he wishes to go, according to their compact, on a carriage drawn by dragons, not by wafting him on a magic cloak, as is the more modern rendering.

71

DRAGONS AND UNICORNS—FACT? OR FICTION?

Dr. Smith continues: "Early in the Christian era, when ancient beliefs in Egypt became disguised under a thin veneer of Christianity, the story of the conflict between Horus and Set was converted into a conflict between Christ and Satan. M. Clermont Ganneau has described an interesting bas-relief in the Louvre in which a hawk-headed St. George, clad in Roman military uniform and mounted on a horse, is slaying a dragon which is represented by Set's crocodile. But the Biblical references to Satan leave no doubt as to his identity with the dragon, who is specifically mentioned in the Book of Revelations as 'the Old Serpent, which is the devil and Satan.'"

As Greco-Roman-born civilization gradually displaced savagery and barbarism throughout Europe, the idea expressed by the modern term 'dragon' spread with it in two streams and with two meanings, but lost much of its religious significance.

The eldest of these streams, derived from a prehistoric Asiatic source, was carried westward in that steady movement of eastern tribes which began to be felt along the Danube about ten thousand years ago, and slowly pressed forward to the Atlantic coast. This Neolithic current of rude, yet superior men and women, brought with it, along with certain arts and customs of a settled life, faith in and awe of a more or less demonic serpent connected with the guardianship of springs, rivers, and waters generally, but which was not much concerned with rainfall, for these early invaders of central Europe had little reason for anxiety as to sufficient rain for their simple gardening or pasturage. Later came invasions of Europe by ruder migrants from Scythia. Sarmatia, and other oriental tribes and regions.

The other stream of ideas proceeded at a later time from Christianized Italy by means of Roman soldiers (who carried an image of the dragon on their lances), or by wandering missionaries of the Church inculcating among the peoples north of the Alps religious creeds and allegories in which the dragon became a symbol and representative of the Biblical devil, and hence of all enemies of 'the true faith,' especially heresy and heathenism. Archaeologists find that all over eastern Europe, even to within historic times, reverence was paid to serpents, partly in a worshipful way, partly with superstitious dread- a universal characteristic of primitive religions which reached its highest development in the tropics, where great and formidable snakes inspired just respect. This prevailed, as we know, among the plainsmen of southeastern Asia and on the Russian steppes, but affected very little the tribes of the forested country west of Russia.

Hence in Europe the presentation of the dragon as the Spirit of Evil and Anti-Christ, in a garb borrowed from Hebrew imagery and the visions of the Book of Revelations, easily superseded aboriginal notions yet, especially in the north and in the mountainous eastern borderland, was never wholly freed from them.

In his Zoological Mythology Angelo de Gubernatis presents many facts of modern Balkan and Russian folklore showing coordination with Hindoo theology. A story from Serbian folktales quoted in Frazer's Folklore in the Old Testament tells how a human giant of great ferocity, the owner of a mill, was wheedled by a woman until he revealed where his strength lay—as follows:

Far in another kingdom, under the king's city, is a lake; in the lake is a dragon; in the dragon is a boar; in the boar is a pigeon, and in the pigeon is my strength." A prince, whose two brothers the ogre had killed, learned this fact from the woman and made his way to the lake, where, after a terrible tussle, he slew the water-dragon and extracted the pigeon. Having questioned the pigeon, and ascertained from it how to restore his two murdered brothers, to life, the prince wrung the bird's neck, and no doubt the wicked dragon [of the mill] perished miserably at the same moment.

Craigie, writing of Scandinavian folklore, says that stories of dragons that fly through the air by night and vomit fire are fairly common in Norway and Denmark, and are not unknown in England. "In various places all over the country there are still shown holes in the earth out of which they are seen to come flying like blazing fire when wars or other troubles are to be expected. When they return to their dwellings, where they brood over immense treasures (which they, as some say, have gathered by night in the depths of the sea), there can be heard the clang of the great iron doors that close behind them."

Not only do these fiery, long-tailed dragons fly about, but terrestrial ones still brood over piles of gold coins in mounds and beneath churches. When they appear, as they sometimes do, various recipes exist for forcing them to reveal or even to shower down their gold, but the conditions accompanying these instructions are usually impossible to fulfil. The 'lindorms' and 'king-vipers' mentioned by Craigie are said to be serpents, usually of great size, that do various sorts of mischief, one kind having ghoulish habits; and these malicious beings are almost always connected in some way with imaginary bulls-an association constantly observed in serpent-myths, and undoubtedly indicating a phallic significance.

Frazer quotes (Balder, Vol. 1) a mediaeval writer who recorded that in some parts of Europe on Midsummer Night it was the custom to burn bones and filth to make a foul smudge, because this smoke drove away "certain noxious dragons which at this time, excited by the summer heat, copulated in the air and poisoned the wells and rivers by dropping their seed into them."

Grimm adds such items of Teutonic lore as follow. The dragon lives 90 years in the ground, 90 in the lime-tree, and 90 more in the desert, sunning his gold in fine weather. Heimo finds a dragon in the Alps of Carneola, kills it and cuts out its tongue, and with the tongue in hand finds a rich hoard. The swords of Sigurd and of Alexander (the Great?) were tempered in dragon's blood, which when eaten confers a knowledge of the language of birds, which are messengers of the gods. Dragons are hated; but it is a German saying that a venom-spitting dragon can blow its poison through seven church-walls but not through knitted stockings.

Such are dozens of living northern stories and fancies, traceable back into an almost forgotten antiquity.

DRAGONS AND UNICORNS—FACT? OR FICTION?

Very old and primitive is the Teutonic tale of the dragons of the Underworld which come flying toward the shades of the dead, trying to obstruct their advance when on their way to the realm of a blissful eternity. There were also dragons on earth as well as beneath it; and one of these has survived to serve on the operatic stage wherever Wagner's Nibelungen series is produced. This is the story as recited in the Saga of Volsung—a German epic of unknown authorship produced about the end of the 12th century: The great god Wotan (or Odin) is possessed of a vast treasure which is committed by the gods into the keeping of two giants. One of them, Fafnir, kills his brother in order to get possession of all the wealth, and then transforms himself into a dragon to guard it. Wotan wants to recover his treasure. A knight, Siegfried (Norse, Sigurd) forges a magical sword out of the pieces of his father's sword 'Nothing.' Wotan and his brother Alberich come to where the dragon Fafnir is watching over the stolen money and jewels, including a magic ring belonging to Alberich to which a curse is attached. Siegfried approaches the horrid lair, whereupon Fafnir comes out, and in the fight that ensues Siegfried slays the beast by aid of his magic sword. The king tells the hero about the ring, and Siegfried goes and gets it, but its possession insures him constant trouble and unhappiness. Everyone regards this 'dragon' as a demon in serpent form, and he is always so represented on the operatic stage, and in the illustrations accompanying the tale in the many books in which it has been recounted in prose and verse, for it is the favourite hero-myth of the Germans.

In the Norse saga of King Olaf the hero ploughs the northern seas in his viking boat and surprises and seizes the great freebooter Raud, who has been ravaging the shores of Norway in his 'dragon-boat.' That craft is destroyed, and Olaf then instructs the shipwrights to construct for his majesty a 'serpentboat' twice as big. These were Norse seaboats having tall figureheads of serpent-dragon form, in regard to which much that is entertaining is written in old books.

DRAGONS AND UNICORNS—FACT? OR FICTION?

CHAPTER THIRTEEN

WELSH ROMANCES AND ENGLISH LEGENDS

SUPERNATURAL BEASTS abound in the traditions and early records of the British Isles, and stand as ominous shades in the background of modern rural folklore, especially where the population is predominantly of Celtic descent. Celtic invaders from the continent possessed themselves of Ireland, Cornwall, Wales and western Scotland, even before the beginning of the Christian era, expelling or absorbing the previous native occupants, also many savage notions. They brought with them, and all sections share the substructure of, a body of faiths and fancies, poetic and superstitious, engaging demonic creatures, supermen and personifications of nature, that form a more or less unified mythology known to antiquarians as the great Celtic dragon-myth. Its stories, in which prehistoric fiction and legendary or real incidents and personages are inextricably mingled, abound in giants, semi-human ogres, serpents and dragons of land, water and air, sea-monsters, mermaids and fairies. J. F. Cambell has devoted a whole book to this matter, and an awesome belief in much of its mystery still lingers among the peasantry about the Irish lakes, in the glens of wilder Wales, and among the lochs and sea-isles of Scotland. Dreadful 'warrums,' half fish, half dragon, still inhabit some Irish lakes, while on others the boatmen will speak with bated breath of monstrous beasts that formerly lurked in their depths; and the 'water-horses' of certain Scottish lochs are near cousins to them.

Dragon or demon, raven or serpent, eagle or sleeping warriors, Mr. Wirt Sikes declares in his British Goblins, the guardian of the underground vaults in Wales where treasures lie is a personification of the baleful influences which reside in caverns, graves and subterraneous regions generally. It is something more than this when traced hack to its source in the primeval mythology; the dragon which watched the golden apples of Hesperides, and the Payshthamore, or great worm, which in Ireland guards the riches of O'Rourke, is the same malarious creature which St. Samson drove out of Wales. According to the monkish legend this pestiferous beast was of vast size, and by its deadly breath

DRAGONS AND UNICORNS—FACT? OR FICTION?

had destroyed two cities. It lay hid in a cave near the river. Thither went St. Samson accompanied only by a boy, and tied a linen girdle about the creature's neck, and drew it out and threw it headlong from a certain high eminence into the sea. This dreadful dragon became mild and gentle when addressed by the saint. . . . The mysterious beast of the boy Taliesin's song in the marvelous legend of Gwion Bach, told in the The Mabinogion, is a dragon worthy to be classed with the gigantic conceptions of primeval imagination, which sought by these prodigious figures to explain all the phenomena of nature. "A noxious creature from the ramparts of Santanas," sings Taliesin, "with jaws as wide as mountains; in the hair of its two paws there is the load of 900 wagons, and in the nape of its neck three springs arise, through which the sea-roughs swim."

Cuchulain, the supreme Irish hero, who had to undergo Herculean tests of fortitude, was once attacked by such a beast of magic, which flew on horrible wings from a lake. Cuchulain sprang up to inect it, giving his wonderful hero-leap, thrust his arm into the dragon's mouth and down its throat and tore out its heart. With figures from such legends as these Spenser embellished his Faery Queene, picturing an

". . . ugly monster plaine,

Half like a serpent horribly displaide

But th' other half did woman's shape retaine,

Most lothsom, filthie, foule, and full of vile disdaine."

A very ancient fragment of the Celtic myth still remembered among Scottish Gaels is the tale of Froach and the Rowan Tree, preserved in the Book of Linsmore, a Gaelic text of the sixteenth century. There was a king in the land whose wife was named Meve, and they had a marriageable daughter, the princess. The rowan (our mountain ash) stood among the ancient Celts as 'the tree of life' because wondrous medicinal virtues were believed to reside in its red berries; and the lesson of the tale exhibits the sin and dire consequences of disturbing its growth. The king with Queen Meve and their daughter lived near a lake in the midst of which was an island on which stood a rowan-tree guarded by a dragon, as is told in Henderson's translation in verse of the old 'grete':

A rowan tree grew on Loch Meve-

Southwards is seen the shore-

Every fourth and every month

Ripe fruit the rowan bore:

Fruit more sweet than honeycomb,

DRAGONS AND UNICORNS—FACT? OR FICTION?

Its clusters virtues strong,

Its berries red could one but taste

Hunger they stand off long.

Its berries' juice and fruit when red

For you would life prolong:

From dread disease it gave relief

If what is told be our belief.

Yet though it proved a means of life

Peril lay closely nigh;

Coiled by its root a dragon lay,

Forbidding passing by.

In the neighbourhood dwelt a young nobleman named Froach, the suitor of the king's daughter, who tells him that her mother, the queen, is ill, and that her only cure is in the berries of the rowan growing on the island as gathered by Froach's hands. Froach protested a little at the extreme peril of the task given him, but bravely agreed to try, and stripping off his clothes plunged in. Swimming to the island he gathered and brought back a goodly quantity of the ripe berries, unnoticed by the dragon. But Meve declared that they were useless—to cure her she must have a branch of the tree bearing fruit.

Froach gave consent; no fear he knew

But swam the lake once more;

But hero never yet did pass

The fate for him in store.

The rowan by the top he seized,

From root he pulled the tree;

And the monster of the lake perceived

As Froach from the land made free.

DRAGONS AND UNICORNS—FACT? OR FICTION?

The dragon then attacked the hero, who had no weapon, "and shore away his arm." The princess seeing his plight, ran into the water and gave the man a sword, with which he ultimately killed the brute; but his wounds were fatal, and he reached the shore only to deliver the tree and the dragon's head to the women, and to die at their feet. In another version, however, Froach is nursed in the palace to recovery, outwits a rival, and obtains the princess despite Queen Meve's illwill.

Very similar and more famous is the romance of Tristan and Iseult, which was written out by Gottfried Strasburger, a German poet who lived early in the thirteenth century. In Ireland, his poem tells us, was once a dreadful dragon wasting the land. The king swore a solemn oath that he would give his daughter, Princess Iseult, to whatever man should slay it. Many knights tried the feat, but lost their lives: always with the candidate rode the seneschal of the palace, but always at sight of the beast he ran away to safety. At last the knight Tristan offered himself, and rode toward the dragon's den, accompanied by the seneschal, who turned back the moment danger appeared, but Tristan rode on steadily. "Ere long he saw the monster coming towards him breathing out smoke and flame from its open jaws. The knight laid his spear in rest and rode so swiftly, and smote so strongly that the spear . . . pierced through the throat into the dragon's heart." The beast was not yet quite killed, however, and fled with Tristan's spear sticking in its vitals. The knight followed fast, overtook the brute, and a long and terrific fight ensued, "so fierce that the shield he held in his hand was burnt well-nigh to a coal" by the flames from the dragon's nostrils. Struggling painfully back to the king's city, the exhausted hero fell into a pond and would have drowned had not Iseult and her mother come by and dragged him out. Then the cowardly seneschat asserted he had done the glorious deed, whereupon Tristan shows the tongue of the dragon as evidence of his own claim to the reward. This is an example of the many mediaeval stories of later birth (progeny of Perseus), in which some untoward circumstance prevents the hero establishing his claim before an impostor has run before him to the court, yet wins in the end by means of concealed evidence.

The terms dragon, drake, serpent, worm, were more or less interchangeable in northern Europe, where even now you may hear described to you a fabulous wurm-bett, or serpent's bed, as the place of gold with a dragon-guardian. So it was in Britain, where this creature was associated with the exploits of the Round Table; for we find the following among the Arthurian legends which are more particularly Welsh: Merlin, the magician, was asked by King Vortigern (fifth century), how to render stable a tower of his castle which thrice had tumbled down. Merlin explained that the trouble lay in the fact that the tower had been built over the den of two immense dragons, whose combats shook the foundations above them. "The king ordered his workmen to dig," as Bulfinch tells it, "and when they had done so they discovered two enormous serpents, the one white as milk, the other red as fire. The multitude looked on with amazement till the serpents, slowly rising from their den, and expanding their enormous folds, began the combat, when every one fled in terror except Merlin, who stood by, clapping his hands and cheering on the conflict. The red dragon was slain, and the white one, gliding through a cleft in the rock, disappeared."

DRAGONS AND UNICORNS—FACT? OR FICTION?

This incident is reputed to have taken place on an isolated rocky eminence in Carnarvonshire, where remains of extensive prehistoric stone-works are still to be seen, says Rhys; in truth it is, of course, purely mythical.

"Whence came the red dragon of Cadwaladar? Why was the Welsh dragon in fables of Merddin (Merlin), Wennius, and Geofrey described as red, while the Saxon 'fenris' was white?" asks Mr. Sikes. He expresses his belief that there is no answer outside the realm of fancy, but notes that in the Welsh language draig means 'lightning,' while the Welsh-English Dictionary asserts that it symbolizes the sun. These might account for the ruddiness, but the facts are needless, for blood-red is the natural choice of warriors, and these fiery Welshmen seem to have preempted it in Britain. The dragon itself was perhaps that of Froach, the great Celtic hero—at any rate it was the device on the banners of the old Welsh kings, legendary and real, and was carried by Cadwaladar (or (Caedwalla), king of North Wales, in his battles with Northumberland in the seventh century A.D. Those old warrior-kings had the title Pendragon, as Tennyson knew when in Guinevere he referred to the royal headquarters in the field-

They saw

The dragon of the great Pendragon

That crowned the state pavilion of the king.

And Shakespeare writes: "Peace, Kent. Come not between the Dragon and his wrath."

This is the red, or sometimes golden, dragon that has been so closely associated with British royalty. The Black Prince flourished it over the heads of his soldiers at Crecy, and so it came to be recognized for many years as the badge of the Principality. New honours for the historic symbol naturally followed the accession of the Welsh Tudors to the English throne, for Henry VII, on his entry into London after his victory on Bosworth Field, offered at the altar in St. Paul's cathedral a standard with the fiery dragon of Wales "beaten upon white and green sarcener." This king then granted formally to King George, then Prince of Wales, and to his successors, a second badge, namely: "A red dragon with elevated wings, passant thereon, for difference a silver label of three points." This grant was continued by Henry VIII, Edward VI, Mary, and Elizabeth—the last named preferring as the supporter of her arms a golden figure with a narrow red back.

But the device on the Welsh flag was not invariably red—or perhaps the variation to be mentioned designated the South Welsh as distinct from those of the North; at any rate we read among the Arthurian legends that in the time of Arthur's father, Uther, there appeared a star at Winchester of wonderful-magnitude brightness, "darting forth a ray at the end of which was a flame in form of a dragon." Uther then ordered two golden dragons to be made, one of which he presented to Winchester, and the other he carried with him as a royal standard. Arthur himself, it is stated, wore a dragon on the crest of his helmet—a tradition Spenser knew:

DRAGONS AND UNICORNS—FACT? OR FICTION?

His haughty helmet, horrid all with gold,

Both glorious brightness and great terror bred,

For all the crest a dragon did enfold,

With greedy paws.

In historic times, the Roman soldiers in England carried images or pictures of dragons as ensigns in their wars with the native Britons. If these were mainly white that fact might account for the whiteness of the emblems used by the 'Saxon' armies of the South (Sussex), with which, after the Roman troops had quit England, the west-central kingdom, Wessex, was incessantly in conflict. Wessex, supported by the southern Welsh, fought under a 'golden' banner, and the adoption of a white-dragon flag by the Sussex men may have been merely a matter of useful distinction between the opposing forces.

It was the Wessex men under Harold that finally expelled the Norsemen by the victory gained at Stamford Bridge, Yorkshire, in September, 1066. Hardly had the young king of the united English accomplished this momentous task when he was called upon to defend his country against the invasion of a new foe—the Normans led by that William who so soon was to become 'the Conqueror.' Harold had been preparing to resist William's threatened landing. The time had arrived, and when ready to march towards Hastings, he enters the headquarters of the army, where his officers are assembled, and issues the orders so picturesquely phrased by Tennyson (Harold, Act iv, Sc. 1)-

Set forth our golden Dragon, let him flap

The wings that beat down Wales!

Advance our standard of the Warrior,

Dark among gems and gold; and thou, brave banner,

Blaze like a night of fatal stars on those

Who read their doom and die.

Alas for the outcome of this brave boast!

But we have run somewhat ahead of the historic march of events. Long before the rise of Wessex to the control of all England, the 'Anglo-Saxon' settlers from northern parts of the continent had begun to cross the channel and recover from the barbarous Britons the fertile fields abandoned by the Romans. They brought with them many a wonder-story and superstition to add to the native stock and Celtic accretions, among them the narra-

DRAGONS AND UNICORNS—FACT? OR FICTION?

tive of the exploits of that noble and romantic Jutish hero Beowulf, who thus became an English hero by adoption; but of him I shall speak more fully in the next chapter. Hardly emerging from the legendary obscurity of Beowulf and his time—say in the fifth century-one finds traces of several other imported dragon-tales inherited from remote Teutonic sources and more and more tinctured as the centuries advanced with the theological notions and interpretations brought by early Christian missionaries to the British people. Thus in The Antiquary (vol. 38, 1902) I find an account by E. Sidney Hartland of such a trace in Gloucestershire.

The church at Deerhurst in that county, he informs us, is one of the oldest in western England; its tall square tower may have "witnessed the Norman conquest, is it unquestionably heard the clash of arms . . . on that bloody field by Tewkesbury." Two stories in the tower still bear some uncouth resemblance to the head of a mythical monster, and may be connected with a legend of a local dragon— "a serpent of prodigious bigness" that plagued the neighbourhood, poisoned the inhabitants and slew their cattle. The people petitioned the king, who offered a crown estate to anyone who should kill the beast. This was achieved by John Smith, a blacksmith. He put a large quantity of milk in a place frequented by the monster; and the 'snake' having swallowed the whole "lay down in the sun with his scales ruffled up," whereupon John advanced and, by striking it between its scales with an ax, chopped off its head. Mr. Hartland "believes that the protruding, jaw-like figures set in the tower of this Deerhurst church have reference to this legend; he refers to several similar carvings in continental- churches that are known to commemorate the local deliverance of communities from dragon-rage. "One of the most ordinary Anglo-Saxon sculptures," he remarks, "is that of a dragon. All sorts of Anglo-Celtic work bear this figure."

Scandinavians strengthened the general belief in reptiles as demons by inventing the theory of a great world-serpent, stories of which abound in the Edda and the sagas of old Norseland, and many evidences remain that this notion was well domesticated in Britain during the long domination of the 'Danes' in the north and east of that island. The 'Pollard Worm,' described so fully by Henderson is an example, although this demon was a wild boar—all such pests in the 'north countree' were 'worms'!—killed by a member of the Pollard family. A similar tradition belongs to Sockburn, and here the offender had the form of a serpent. Galloway has a legend of a snake which was accustomed to lie coiled around Mote Hill at Dalry—probably the site of an early Norman palisaded fort— a folktale outlined by Andrew Lang (Academy, Oct. 17, 1885) as follows:

The lord of Galloway offered a reward for its destruction; but one of his knights was swallowed up by the monster, horse and armor and all, and another was deterred by evil omens. The adventure was then attempted, as at Deerhurst, by a blacksmith, who devised a suit of armor for himself covered with long, sharp spikes, which could be drawn in or thrust out at the wearer's will. The snake of course swallowed him whole, like his predecessor, but as the smith slipped down his throat he suddenly shot out his spikes, and rolled about violently; nor did he cease until he had torn his way out through the monster's carcass!

DRAGONS AND UNICORNS—FACT? OR FICTION?

This is not the only nor the earliest example of conquering the dragon from the inside: it was thought of hundreds of centuries before that. When Heracles undertook the deliverance of Hesione, daughter of Laomedon, king of Troy, from the sea-monster to which her father had exposed her, he sprang full-armed down the creature's gullet and hacked his way out of its maw. A similar folk-tale is related by Rumanian gypsies. One such story, indeed, has received ecclesiastical sanction to the extent, at least, of being incorporated in The Golden Legend and represented in stone among the sculptures adorning many European sacred edifices. The heroine here is that St. Margaret who was thrown into a dungeon after tortures of the kind that churchmen ascribe to their martyrs and have with equal piety and relish inflicted upon their opponents. "And whilst she was in prison she prayed our Lord," as Caxton recounts in his translation of The Golden Legend, "that the fiend that had fought with her He would visibly show unto her. And then appeared a horrible dragon and assailed her, and would have devoured her, but she made the sign of the cross and anon he vanished away. And in another place it is said that he swallowed her into his belly . . . and the belly broke asunder so she issued out all whole."

This miracle was denounced as apocryphal by critics centuries ago, yet the same set of adventures are related of Saints Martha, Veneranda, and Radegund. What troubled the minds of the monks was the difficulty of believing that the Devil had ever been killed! A ridiculous, but celebrated yarn of this class is that of the Lambton Worm, which I quote from the concise narrative by Hartland:

This was a creature caught by the heir of Lambton (in England on the banks of the Weir) one Sunday morning when fishing, and, to add to its iniquity, using very bad language. He threw it into a well, where it grew and grew until it outgrew the well and resorted to the river, lying coiled by night thrice around a neighbouring hill. Meantime, the heir of Lambton, having repented of his evil life and spent seven years in the wars, returned, and determined to rid the land of the curse his wickedness had inflicted upon it. A wise woman whom he consulted advised him to get his suit of mail studded thickly with spearheads, and required him before going forth to the encounter to vow to slay the first living thing that met him on his way homeward, warning him that if he failed to perform the vow, no lord of Lambton for nine generations would die in his bed.

He met the worm and challenged it to the conflict by striking a blow on its head as it passed. It turned upon him and, winding its body around him, tried to crush him in its folds; but the spikes pierced it, and the closer its embrace the more deadly were the wounds it received, until with the flowing blood its strength ebbed away, and the knight with his sword cut it in two.

The knight failed to fulfil his vow because his eager old father was the "first living thing met," and he could not bear to strike him down, so the curse remained on the Lambton family until worked out nine generations later by the death of Henry Lambton, M.P., in 1761.

DRAGONS AND UNICORNS—FACT? OR FICTION?

Another and more burlesque comedy identified with a place and local families in England, and frequently spoken of, is that of The Dragon of Wantley. Its history is preserved in Bishop Percy's Reliques under the title—An Excellent Ballad of that most Dreadful COMBATE FOUGHT Between Moore of Moore Hall, and the Dragon of Wantley.

This title-page bore also a picture of a scaly, lion-bodied monster "sharp, fierce and hungry-looking, with wings at his sides, an enormous tail, and two of his feet are hoofed, while the other two are strongly 'clawed'!" When the ballad was written is not known, but it refers to Sir Thomas Whortley, who aroused the hatred of the people by destroying a village on a hill at Wharncliffe in Yorkshire. He was a great aristocrat, serving as 'bodynight' to Edward IV, Richard III, Henry VII, and Henry VIII, and died in 1514. He was vastly wealthy, jovial and hospitable, and was extravagantly fond of stag-hunting for which he kept a pack of hounds widely admired. Among his possessions was the village of Wantley, which gave him only partial satisfaction, for, as we read: "There were some freeholders within it with whom he wrangled and sued until he had beggared them and cast them out of their inheritance, and so the town was wholly his, which he pulled quite down and laid the buildings and town fields even as a common, wherein his main design was to keep deer, and make a lodge, to which he came at the time of the yere and lay there, taking great delight to hear the deer bell." Remains of this destroyed town were said to be visible not long ago on a lofty moor between Sheffield and Peristone, including the romantic cavity still known as the 'dragon's den,' and near it are a 'dragon's well' and a 'dragon's cellar.' The cruel and highhanded ejection of farmers, and destruction of good houses, just for sport, so disgusted and angered the people that they cast about for some means of redress. Near the castle of the wicked Whortley was Moore Hall (still standing), whose owner was far from friendly with the Whortleys. To the head of the Moore family, therefore, the distressed people went for a champion —

Sighing and sobbing, came to his lodging

And made a hideous noise,

Oh, save us all,

Moore of Moore Hall,

Thou peerless knight of the woods!

Do but slay this dragon-

He won't leave us a rag on-

We will give thee all our goods.

Thee champion refused the goods, but asked for

DRAGONS AND UNICORNS—FACT? OR FICTION?

A fair maid of sixteen, that's brisk

And smiles about the mouth,

. . . .

To 'noint me o'er night ere I go to fight

And to dress me in the morning.

This is rather a reversal of the rescuing of maids customary in dragon-stories! The ballad—which is given in full in The Reliquary (vol. 18, London, 1878), and is discussed in Yorkshire local histories—relates the amazing combat in which the dragon was killed. Briefly, Moore, the doughty knight, clad in a suit of armour studded with long, sharp spikes, hid in a well to which the dragon was wont to come when thirsty; and when the beast arrived, and lowered its head into the well, Moore kicked it in the mouth, where alone it was vulnerable, and so accomplished its death. This method reminds us how, according to one account, Siegfried managed to kill the Nibelungen serpent Fafnir by hiding in a pit over which it must pass, and stabbing its belly as it crawled across the trench over the hero's head. In all these stories the dragon appears to be a wofully stupid and defenceless beast, agreeing with the foolish Devil of folklore.

It is probable that this Wantley ballad is founded on some incident of long-past feudal oppression, vengefully perpetuated by the Yorkshire peasantry by aid of this allegorical narrative —safer as a form of publication than would be an accusing statement in bald prose. Evictions of that sort have occurred far more recently than in the reputed era of the master of Wantley; and disagreements between neighbours still arise, leading third persons to take up arms in behalf of the oppressed, especially when the oppressor happens to be a rival or enemy of their own. So here was a nice dramatic situation ready to be turned into a pathetic (and saleable) ballad by some would-be historical verse-maker clever enough to invent a 'dragon' to carry the somewhat dangerous burden of his song.

But the best of these legends, and one which carried nothing burlesque in the estimation of its hearers, or to the minds of those who now read its 'saga,' is the story of Beowulf. It is true that its scenes have not the background of British landscape or habits; yet, as Bulfinch has said, "The splendid feat of Beowulf appeals to all English-speaking people in a very special way, since he is the one hero in whose story we may see the ideals of our English forefathers before they left their continental home."

Beowulf, a prince of the Greatas (probably a Swedish coast tribe, but possibly Jutes) gathered a band of dauntless vikings and sailed away to offer aid to Hrothgar, king of the Western Danes, who was in great distress because of the long-continued ravages of an unconquerable dragon—an allegory that seems to refer to certain historical happenings on the lower Rhine in the sixth century, A.D.

DRAGONS AND UNICORNS—FACT? OR FICTION?

Grendel this monster grim was called,

match-reiver mighty, in moorland living,

in fen and fastness; fief of the giants

the hapless wight a while had kept

since the Creator his exile doomed.

On kin of Cain was the killing avenged

by sovran God for slaughtered Abel. . . .

Of Cain awoke all that woful breed,

etins and elves and evil spirits,

as well as the giants that warred with God

weary while.

The 'etins' mentioned here (Norse, jotuns) were giants, or ogres; and ancient tradition says they descended from the murderous Cain, whose progeny were thus cursed for his sin. This Grendel, whose home was in a great morass, is imagined as a nocturnal, man-eating monster in human form, with diabolical strength and ferocity. At frequent intervals he came in the night to Hrothgar's palace-hall, 'gold-bright Hereot,' where his Danish warriors slept, and seized, killed, and carried away as many men as he pleased as food for himself and his even more savage mother.

The Danes were cowed to powerlessness, and welcomed Beowulf and his band with a royal feast, where Beowulf declared his purpose to kill the giant, and to do it unarmed by wrestling-strength alone, boasting of past deeds of victory so obtained. The feast over, Hrothgar and his gracious queen retired to safer quarters, and the wine-bemused courtiers lay down to sleep on the benches and floor of the great hall. Grendel had knowledge of these doings, and gloating over the increased food supply, came that very night on one of his raids. Bursting the 'forge-bolts' of the door with a blow of his fist, he seized, tore to pieces and devoured the first man he came to, then advanced upon another victim—the watchful Beowulf, who sprang up and clutched the cannibal's arm. Grendel tried to escape, but Beowulf held on:

The house resounded,

Wonder it was the wine-hall firm

DRAGONS AND UNICORNS—FACT? OR FICTION?

in the strain of their struggle stood, to earth

the fair house fell not.

A hundred lines of the saga scarce suffice to tell of that prodigious, weaponless, struggle of hero against fiend; but at last Beowulf tears the giant's arm from its shoulder, and Grendel creeps away to die in the noisome fen. Great rejoicings and rewards follow, but the glorification is short-lived, for a few nights later Grendel's mother, burning with ferocious vengeance, murders in the midst of the slumbering Danes the King's favourite sage and warrior, and terror returns to the kingdom. Thereupon Beowulf prepares to finish the job by extinguishing this dam of a hellish brood. Sword in hand, this time, he marches to the 'horrid mere' where she hides, walks alone into its loathsome depths, and in a magical, submarine hall finds and destroys in a magical combat the last of the murderous tribe.

As this adventure was not the first so it was not to be the last of this righteous hero's battles with supernatural foes. Fifty years later Beowulf, now become a king in his own land, learns that in a certain part of his realm a fiery dragon—now not an anthropomorphic cannibal but an enormous serpenth—has gone on the rampage. For three hundred years it had lain quiet in an antique stone grave, protecting there an immense treasure of heirlooms and coin "which some earl forgotten in ancient years, left the last of his lofty race, heedfully there had hidden away, dearest treasure." In hundreds of vivid verses we read what the old king was told, and how he goes forth to free his land from the rage of the fire-breathing dragon—majestic verse recounting an age-old legend of the guardian-dragon and utilizing it in a drama of heroism as Noldic bards conceived it in the height of its glory. One of the latest editors of this stirring epic summarizes and interprets this part of the narrative thus:

We have the old myth of a dragon who guards hidden treasure. But with this runs the story of some noble, last of his race, who hides all his wealth within this barrow and there chants his farewell to life's glories. After his death the dragon takes possession of the hoard and watches over it. A condemned or banished man, desperate, hides in the barrow, discovers the treasure, and while the dragon sleeps makes off with a golden beaker or the like, and carries it for propitiation to his master. The dragon discovers the loss and exacts fearful penalty from the people round about.

These burial-places of the inhabitants of western Europe, or of their chiefs, at least, known in Britain as barrows, and on the continent as dolmens, are small grave-chambers sunk in the ground and walled and roofed with stones; or, as in many cases, built on the surface of huge stone-slabs, the whole structure finally concealed beneath a mound of earth. Hundreds of such interments have been exposed by the washing away of the soft or by the sacrilege of robbers, as in the famous necropolis of Karnac in Brittany; and it is plain that many of them had a secret entrance into the tomb, as intimated in the poem. It was customary to bury with a great man not only his arms and accoutrements of

DRAGONS AND UNICORNS—FACT? OR FICTION?

war but often much or all of his wealth, and to try to render the sepulchre and its contents safe from molestation by publishing fearful curses and fictions about guardian spirits of frightful mien, usually clothed in dragon shape.

The fiery dragon fearful fiend, with flame was scorched. Reckoned by feet, it was fifty measures in length as it lay. Aloft erewhile it had revelled by night, and anon came back, seeking its den; now in death's sure clutch it had come to the end of its earth-hall joys. By it there stood the stoups and jars; dishes lay there, and dear-decked swords eaten with rust, as, on earth's lap resting, a thousand winters they had waited there. For all that heritage huge, that gold of bygone, was bound by a spell, so the treasure-hall could be touched by none of human kind.

The robbery of graves filled with such treasures must have offered a strong temptation, and superstition surrounded the crime with every sort of danger. Lifting buried gold is still an uncanny business, and everywhere folklore teaches that its possession brings the worst of luck.

Old though he was, and feeble as compared with the strength that had torn Grendel's arm from its socket, King Beowulf, despite the remonstrances of his court, goes against the poison-breathing, fire-belching 'worm'—that mighty serpent who nightly 'rages' through the burning grain-fields and at dawn retreats to his castle-like den in the barrow. There Beowulf attacked the beast alone, bidding his followers stand away. The battle was long and terrific, until finally one warrior, Wiglaf, could stand it no longer, but rushed to his sovereign's side, for Beowulf's sword had been broken by a too mighty stroke.

Then for the third time, thought on its feud, that folk-destroyer, fire-dread dragon, and rushed on the hero, where room allowed, battle-grim, burning; its hitter teeth closed on his neck, and covered him with waves of blood from his breast that welled. It was then Wiglaf reached the midst of the fray-Heedless of harm, though his hand was burned, hardy-hearted, he helped his kinsman. A little lower the loathsome beast he smote with sword; his steel drove in bright and burnished; that blaze began to lose and lessen. At last the king

wielded his wits again, war-knife drew,

a hiting blade by his breastplate hanging,

and the Weders'-helm smote that worm asunder,

felled the foe, flung forth its life.

Here, as in many another tale of the period, where the dragon has the form of a serpent, victory is gained by the hero only when he is able with dagger or short sword to pierce the under side of the beast, where the belly and throat are unprotected by the

DRAGONS AND UNICORNS—FACT? OR FICTION?

tough scales that make its back and head invulnerable.

Beowulf's noble and unselfish fight for his people is his last. His wounds are fatal, and he dies; and the glittering wealth of gold and polished steel, so hardly won, are buried with him in that royal tomb whose site no man knows.

DRAGONS AND UNICORNS—FACT? OR FICTION?

CHAPTER FOURTEEN

THE DRAGON AND THE HOLY CROSS

IT IS noticeable in scanning the legends thus far recited, as purposely grouped, that the supernatural apparitions described, requiring superhuman feats for their extermination, were killed off because they were destroying human life and property, particularly cattle, or possessed desired treasures; not, as in the East, because they were maliciously withholding rain or other needed waters; and nowhere in Britain or northern Europe have we encountered a captive maiden or one about to be sacrificed to a dragon, which is the ruling feature in another and more recent group of tales. This, it seems to me, betokens a distinctly northern attitude of mind, and indicates legendary descent through a history of migrations from Scythia (to go no farther east for origins), where women were little regarded as compared with property, and chivalric sentiment all but absent from men's minds.

The type of stories, on the other hand, which was derived from aboriginal Greek imaginings, more or less tinctured with Hebrew and Egyptian teaching, and which filtered westward along the European shore of the Mediterranean, south of the great mountains dividing that sea from the basin of the Baltic, included almost always the idea of rescuing a woman in danger, and represent a southern as distinct from a northern inspiration and dramatic sense. Dr. Spence has remarked that the mediaeval dragon was a story teller's, or literary, subterfuge to give the hero an opportunity to be heroic. This latter style in dragon-stories remains to be treated; but before proceeding to that I want to say something about those tales current in Roman times and for centuries afterward on the continent of Europe, as recorded with pious credulity in the biographies of Catholic saints. These zealous missionaries, who went forth from Rome to spread the gospel of Christ beyond the Alps, often at the risk of life (the hardships endured by missionary priests among Canadian Indians in the eighteenth century make us understand what must have been the experience of many a would-be teacher among the wild tribes of northern Europe), were men who believed in a real, and at will corporeal, Satan and his

DRAGONS AND UNICORNS—FACT? OR FICTION?

imps; and they felt themselves obstructed by powers of darkness quite as much as by the natural reluctance of the 'savages' to abandon their ancestral gods and fetishes—in fact the apostles regarded such reluctance as due to past instruction as well as to present advice by the Devil. From the serpent who tempted Eve in the Garden of Eden, down to the fire-breathing all-devastating dragon (Greek drako, English 'drake,' literally 'big snake') of Revelation, the missionaries had the authority of the Scriptures to make it the image and synonym of Satan; and it was easy to impress this image upon the minds of pupils of the new faith, terrified by pictures of the tortures awaiting their souls at the hands of this same clawed and horned devil-dragon unless they came into the Roman religious fold. Remembering these threats, and recalling the clerical faith of the time in the divinely endowed virtue of the Cross or its symbols, and the miracle-working powers imparted by its aid to 'holy men,' there need be no wonder at the monkish legends recorded with such sincerity by the early chroniclers.

The industry of Dr. E. Cobham Brewer has brought together, in his Dictionary of Miracles, a large number of such records, culled from the authentic writings of St. Jerome, Gregory of Tours, and other fathers of the Church, among which is the following characteristic example indited by Richard de la Val d'Isere, the successor of the 'great' St. Bernard of Menthon (993-1008), who declares he was an eye-witness of the incident. "Saint Bernard left at the bottom of the Alps," as Dr. Brewer repeats the story, "the bishop, clergy and procession, which had followed him thither; and with nine pilgrims ascended the mountain where was the brigand Procus, called 'the giant,' and worshipped as a god. Saint Bernard and his companions came up to the giant and saw hard by a huge dragon ready to devour them. Bernard made the sign of the Cross, and then threw his stole over the monster's neck. The stole instantly changed itself into an iron chain, except the two ends held in the saint's hands." The nine pilgrims thereupon killed the dragon, and the two silken ends of the stole were long preserved in the abbey of St. Maurice-en-Valais.

This method of subduing Satanic demons which, owing to the ancient curse (Genesis 3:14) were obliged to assume a form that compelled them to crawl on their bellies, was a favourite one—we have already seen it used by St. Samson in Ireland. St. Germanus (fifth century) marched boldly into the dark cavern in Scotland inhabited by a prodigious dragon, threw his handkerchief around its neck, and led it forth to a deep pit into which he cast it, and so relieved the district of a mankilling nuisance. Paris was freed from a dreadful dragon of goulish habits in A.D. 136, by St. Marcel, who knocked it on the head three times with his cross. This done he wrapped his cloak about the creature's neck and led it four miles beyond the city's gates, where it was set free after it had promised to remain in a certain wood to the end of time—at any rate it has never reappeared. This is told by Gregory of Tours. After Ste. Marthe had quieted the frightful dragon of the Rhone, she conducted it by her girdle (Maury describes it more piquantly as her garter) to Tarascon, where the people put it to death; and they have been celebrating this deliverance ever since. Several other saintly heroes made captives of cave-dwelling monsters by similarly sanctified leading-strings.

DRAGONS AND UNICORNS—FACT? OR FICTION?

In another class of cases evil beasts, and particularly serpents, are subjugated by holy men by the exhibition of a crucifix or some sign representing it. A terrorized community would summon a saint, sometimes from abroad, to deliver it from a despoiling monster (in one instance with a penchant for devouring children—possibly a reminiscence of child sacrifice to bloody deities) just as villagers in India or Africa now seek the help of sportsmen to kill for them a man-eating lion or tiger.

Out of these stories and faiths came the ascription to many of the religious worthies of the Middle Ages of a dragon in some form as a badge of distinction—needful when the mass of the people could not read, and must have some means of identifying the 'saints' one from another, just as they had to have a bush to tell them where wine was sold and a bloody pole instead of a written sign to indicate the barber's shop. In his book, Saints and Their Emblems, M. M. Drake shows that dragons appear thirty-five times attached to thirty martyrs and other persons, for some exhibit more than one, perhaps having more than a single experience with the fearsome beast. The artist depicting the saint in statue, painting or decorated glass, tries also to tell the story attached to his or her name. Thus in the case of Martha of Bethany she is shown in a sixteenth century window at St. Mary's in Shrewsbury, England, holding an asperge and holy water vessel with a dragon behind her; but elsewhere you may see her more often in the attitude of vanquishing a dragon by presenting her crucifix to his gaze. Instances might be multiplied, but the reader may find them in the Catalogues and descriptive Lives of mediaeval celebrities of the Church.

Maury connects the many tales of the freeing of various districts of serpents with the Biblical promise: "They shall take up serpents . . . and it shall not hurt them" (Mark 16: 18). Thus is explained St. Paul's escape from harm by the adder which he flung into the fire in Malta. Hence arose the popular belief that the ministers of the gospel were immune from poisoning by the venom of serpents and might safely attack them. "In Brittany," Maury reminds us, "the apostles who reached the faith are regarded as having destroyed serpents that ravaged the country. Thus did St. Cadon [at Karnacl, St. Naudet and St. Pol de Leon [at Batz]. In Gaul in the fifth century St. Keyna the Virgin destroyed the snakes that ravaged the country in the vicinity of Keysham. In Pomerania were expelled serpents that vomited flames." St. Radegond fought in Poictiers the dragon called Grand Gueule; St. Clement did a like service at Metz; St. Saturnin at Bernay; St. Armond at Maestricht, etc.; and some of these Christians are reported to have been snake-bitten without injury to their health. The most famous, however, of all these exploits is that by St. Patrick in Ireland, and it is more manifestly mythical than any of the others because there never were any snakes in Erin's Isle! A sequel to this beloved tradition is less familiar than the main facts, and is told by Dr. Brewer as follows:

When St. Patrick ordered the serpents of Ireland into the sea one of the older reptiles refused to obey; but the saint overmastered it by stratagem. He made a box and invited the serpent to enter in, pretending it would be a nice place for it to sleep in. The serpent said the box was too small, but St. Patrick maintained it was quite large enough. So high at length rose the argument that the serpent got into the box to prove it too small; where-

DRAGONS AND UNICORNS—FACT? OR FICTION?

upon St. Patrick clapped down the lid and threw the box into the sea.

Critics justly regard most of these tales as allegories of the success had by various missionary priests in staying the 'devils' of paganism or of false doctrine in their several fields of labour, and in converting local groups of people to Christianity. Some such expulsion of native rites and idols from one or another district probably indicates the reality behind the many legends of serpent clearance. Several of these tales, nevertheless, seem to me based upon actual feats of heroism, as, for example, that exploit of Bishop Romanus, annually celebrated at Rouen, which may not be wholly mythical, since the 'horrible dragon' in this case might well be a bad man instead of a false doctrine. The adventure of that soldier-general of the army of Licerius in Thrace of the fourth century, who fought and slaughtered a dragon with his sword, and afterward canonized as St. Theodorus of Heraclea, furnishes another case. The Thracians would probably insist, could they return to tell us about it, that Licenus and his officers had put something to the sword more strategic than dragons, and more substantial than heresy.

These few typical examples out of many may suffice to show the way in which the general belief in supernatural and more or less harmful beings was utilized by the early Christian missionaries in Europe, to impress the sanctions of the new religion upon both the heathen and the indifferent or hostile men and women to whom they preached. Some of the best remembered of these legendary incidents, involving acts of extraordinary heroism or religious significance, have been periodically celebrated by quasi-religious ceremonies in Europe until recent times.

The most serious, elaborate, and picturesque of these festivals is that which, until lately, was annually celebrated at the ancient town of Tarascon, in Provence. It commemorated the taming of a singularly horrible and ravenous demon-beast by Ste. Marthe; but just who she was no one knows. Some say her name is a Christianized form of that of the Phoenician goddess Martis, patroness of sailors, whose symbols were a ship and a dragon; others recall classic reminiscences of Hercules and his battling with local giants, one of which was named Taras or Tariskos. Baring-Gould investigated the matter at length, and concluded that a Christian woman-missionary called Martha, who, soon after the death of Jesus, came with others to this part of Gaul, has become strangely confused with a Syrian prophetess named Martha, who accompanied the Roman general Gaius Marius, and aided him greatly by her magic and inspiration, during the two years of hard fighting by which he beat back the ravaging hordes of northern barbarians who invaded southern Gaul at the end of the second century, B.C. He regards the 'dragon' in this case as an image of the undying recollection of the appalling terror, devastation and suffering wrought by that invasion, and the ceremony as a grateful acknowledgment of the deliverance. The citizens generally, however, know little and care less about these explanations, for their minds are fixed on the miracle by which their forefathers were rescued. Roman monuments remaining at or near Tarascon, which represent Marius, Julia his wife, and the Syrian woman, the people have interpreted for centuries past as figures of Lazarus, Mary Magdalen, and Martha the hostess of Jesus. The legendary incident celebrated is this:

DRAGONS AND UNICORNS—FACT? OR FICTION?

While Martha was preaching Christianity to the pagan people at Arles an urgent message was sent to her from Tarascon, reciting that an awful dragon called the Tarasque, whose lair was in the neighbouring desert of Crau, was killing the Tarasconais, and they begged her to come and destroy it. She gladly complied, and going to his cave was able, by sheer force of lovingness (and a sprinkler of holy water), to subdue and regenerate the ravaging Tarasque, so that he meekly followed her into the midst of the astonished populace. "Along the bright ways of the city," as the legend goes, "the procession moved: a crowd of excited people, a beautiful woman with the light playing round her head, leading by a silken cord a reformed monster who ambles after her as quietly as if he were a pet lamb. . . . And never again did he ravage the country or carry off so much as a single babe after Ste. Marthe had pointed out to him, with her usual sweet reasonableness, how wrong-headed and how essentially immoral such conduct had been." So Mona Caird pictures the scene of the deliverance from a devouring creature more dreadful, if we can credit mediaeval descriptions, than anything we have thus far discovered in this history of beastly demons—a figure worthy to represent the hellish character of the Teutonic invasion of this fair land 2000 years ago.

Toward the end of the fifteenth century, the kindly and artistic king Rene, desiring to gratify and amuse his favourite subjects, the Tarasconais, instituted a fete, the central feature to be a representation of the legendary miracle for the glory of Ste. Marthe. It was appointed for April 14, 1474, and proved a lasting success, for it was repeated annually up to the beginning of this the twentieth century. "A grotesquely terrible monster, red and black, of the pantomime type, made of wood, paraded the streets on the second Sunday after Pentecost. Enormous red-rimmed eyes stared out of a round, catlike countenance fringed with bristling white whiskers. The men inside who carried him, and whose legs were his, danced and capered about, so as to make the huge wooden tail wag and upset any spectator whose curiosity prompted him to come too near. For it was the monster's day out. His ferocity was as yet untamed. Then the Tarasque was taken back to the stable, where he is still to be seen, to await the day of his doom, St. Martha's day, 29th July. Tamed now, and gentle as a sucking dove, he was led forth once more, but this time by a ribbon held by a young girl, as a lamb to the slaughter."

Although this pantomime was attended by clergy who endeavoured to make it impressive, the day was one of hilarity and fun of every sort; and the gay crowd sang as they followed the lumbering figure through the streets the chant that they say King Rene himself wrote—

Lagadigaddeu!

La Tarasco!

Lagadigaddeu!

La Tarasco!

93

DRAGONS AND UNICORNS—FACT? OR FICTION?

De casteu!

Leissas-la passa

La vieio masco!

Leissas-la passa

Que vai dansa!, etc.

Another long-lived fete sanctioned by the Church is that of the 'Privilege' in Rouen. In that historic city on the Seine a narrow street leads down from the cathedral to the river, crossing on its way a large open space where stands the Chapelle de la Fierte Saint-Romain. With this ancient chapel is connected a curious custom, which was exercised for more than 750 years. The charter establishing it was granted to the Chapter of Rouen Cathedral by King Dagobert in the eighth century, and empowered the archbishop to release, once every year on Ascension Day, a chosen criminal from among those in the city condemned to death. On every Ascension Day, therefore, the people of Rouen flocked into the streets to witness the ceremonies with which this behest was carried out—the Procession of the Privilege of Saint Remain. First came the solemn visit of the Church to the Civic authorities, carrying the annual formal proclamation of the privilege (fierte). "Then every prison in the city must be searched, and every prisoner put on oath and examined as to the cause of his imprisonment. Finally the election of the favoured prisoner was put to vote of the Chapter. . . . He then confessed to the Chapter of Saint Romain, his fetters were removed, and he followed the archbishop to the Place Haute-Vielle Tour, where, in the Chapelle de la Fierte, a solemn service made him a free man. A solemn and magnificent procession then bore him, crowned with flowers, to the great thanksgiving Mass, after which he was free to go whither he would."

So the Marshalls describe the ceremony in their volume on the cathedral cities of France; and they give in the subjoined paragraph the legend that accounts for its origin, explaining that this legend appears to be of later date than the festival, which is mentioned "certainly as late as the twelfth century, and continued to delight the Rouennais as late as 1790." It looks to me as if it originated as an ingenious method by some kindly Church authority, in a time when tyranny ruled rather than law and justice, and innocent men, or personal enemies, might be immured in dungeons and forgotten, to make an annual survey and clearance of the prisons, freeing persons unjustly confined. This is the legend:

While Romain was bishop of Rouen a terrible dragon laid waste all the land and devoured the inhabitants. No one dared approach the monster, who was known as the Gargoyle [gargouille] until Saint Romain, armed only with his sanctity, set out to subdue it, accompanied by a condemned criminal—the prototype of those who were released on Holy Thursday—when the Gargoyle at once submitted and, with the episcopal stole around its neck, was led by the prisoner to the water's edge. It was then pushed in and

94

DRAGONS AND UNICORNS—FACT? OR FICTION?

drowned, whereupon the 'condemned criminal' was presumably rewarded for his courage by being given his freedom. At the head of the Portail de la Calende, the north porch of the cathedral, stands the figure of Saint Romain, and under his feet, with the stole around his neck, is the Gargoyle, craning its head around to look into the face of the bishop with the expression of a very hideous but very faithful dog. . . . In memory of the occurrence the standard of the dragon was borne in the processions at the Privilege—banners similar to those of the dragons of Bayeux and Salisbury.

Similar festivals and processions in which the dragon, as a symbol of wickedness, heresy, and so forth, took place in old days in many European communities. We read of them at Metz, where the evil beast was dubbed Grauly, at Bergerac (the dragon of St. Front), at the abbey of Fleury, and even in Paris. "The images are made of silk, very large, and are manoeuvred by children hidden in the interior." The celebrations were commonly identified with the Rogation days, and some have continued up to fairly modern times. Rogation days, as set apart by the Catholic Church, are the three days preceding Ascension Day, which is the fortieth day after Easter; and they are observed with prescribed litanies or liturgical prayers, and in some places with public processions, all the ceremonies combining to make a supplication for God's blessing on the crops. In view of this purpose, and the spring season, it is very significant that the dragon should be associated with this particular celebration—a prayer for rain! Mr. J. W. Legg contributed some statements as to these ceremonies to Notes and Queries for October, 1857, which are condensed below:

In the thirteenth century inventory of 'ornaments' of Old Sarum cathedral banners called Leo and Draco are specified. Documents state that at that epoch the use of these banners was ordained in certain rubrics, e.g., for Rogation processions. The custom of carrying images of the dragon is spoken of by many liturgical writers. Besides the figure in the Old Sarum Processionale, Barrault and Martin give a drawing of a processional dragon preserved at Metz at page 44 of their Baton Pastoral (Paris, 1856). Sometimes the dragon was carried on Palm Sunday, as at Orleans, when both a dragon and a cock, as well as these banners, were borne. I think these banners must be separated from the Easter dragon. The latter was a serpent-shaped candlestick for the triple candle, which was carried at Rouen on Easter Eve until the end of the seventeenth century. The processional dragon is not peculiar to either Sarum or the Celtic church. What its source is, whether a figure of the noisome beasts to which St. Mamertus began the Rogations, or whether it has come from the labarum of Constantine, or is of Pagan origin, I must leave others to determine.

Maury records that at Provins, in France, the bell-ringers of the churches formerly bore in Rogations processions, in advance of the Cross, an image of a winged dragon, and also an image of a lizard, garnished with flowers, in memory of ravenous beasts. At Paris the dragon always carried at Rogations was regarded as the image of the monster exterminated by Saint Marcel. At Aix-en-Provence, the marchers saw arranged upon an eminence called Dragon Rock, near a chapel dedicated to St. Andrew, the figure of a dragon in imitation of the one tradition sad that apostle had killed.

DRAGONS AND UNICORNS—FACT? OR FICTION?

A curious survival of these mediaeval combinations of piety and pranks was the 'snap-dragon' as a feature in the festive procession accompanying the induction of every new mayor in Norwich, England, up to 1832. Here the image was small enough to be managed by one man inside; it had a distensible neck so that the head could be wagged about, short, batlike wings, and a pig's tall. As described and pictured in an old number of Harper's Magazine, the head had its lower jaw furnished with a plate of iron "garnished with enormous nails which produced a terrible clatter." The jaws were made to open and shut by means of strings, and as the creature marched along, its head turning to right and left, the children amused themselves by throwing halfpence into the gaping jaws.

It must be borne in mind, of course, that the word 'dragon' in these mediaeval narratives does not necessarily imply that the creature for which it stands had a snake-like or crocodilian form, for the ghost-haunted minds of the people of that era readily conjured up marvellous and abominable shapes and combinations of animals with which no legitimate and self-respecting dragon would consent to associate, even in the limbo betwixt fable and allegory. Fine examples of the weird and unholy extravagances possible to a brisk imagination set at work to devise vivid caricatures of beastly demons may be found in Albrecht Durer's etched illustrations for the Faust legend, the temptation of St. Anthony, etc.; but three thousand years before him similar monstrosities were cut in miniature by the gem-engravers of Crete on seals and ornaments. Durer never saw these little horrors, which perhaps were intended to be talismans to ward off evil glances; but when he was bidden to depict the grizzly terrors that seemed to swarm about the sorely abused mind and body of the half-starved eremite in his chilly cell, his fancy could reach no other result than that found by the AEgean artist so long ago. "The Dream," painted by Raphael, is another collection of horrors of unnatural history. It is in and by art, indeed, that the fiction we are considering has been preserved to us; and artists now tell us that the survival and extensive use of the dragon in art is accounted for by its 'manageability' as an element in a decorative composition. All the multitude of dragon-forms, diverse as they are in reflecting the fears or the fancies of widely differing races of men, agree in fulfilling certain conditions that make them exceedingly useful in ornamentation. It is of course always possible to put some animal figure in place of a dragon, but the real creature is not nearly so manageable as the imaginary one. "The actual creature, whatever it may be," explains the English artist Lewis F. Day, "must be considered to some extent from the point of view of nature; but the monster leaves the artist free. . . . This is an incalculable convenience in design, and enables the artist to arrive with certainty at the effect at which he alms. There is a kind of keeping, too, between the ideal creature and the ideal ornament. The natural birds and other living creatures that occur at intervals among the purely ornamental arabesques of the cinque-cento always seem to me out of place. They suggest that the artist was not quite content with his art of ornament, and must needs relieve himself at intervals by indulging in a bit of naturalism. . . . If, then, the dragon has lingered in art long past the time when we have any faith in him, it will be seen that there is a reason for his prolonged existence."

Since the blazonry of more or less boastful badges on knights' shields and family

DRAGONS AND UNICORNS—FACT? OR FICTION?

possessions began, the dragon, as 'wivern,' has been a favourite device in European heraldry, and possibly the most antique one. Long before any College of Heralds was instituted we learn by tradition of the helmet-crests of the heroes of Romance. Tennyson sings of the 'great Pendragonship' and that sightly helm of Arthur, "to which for crest the golden dragon clung."

Let me quote another pertinent paragraph from Mr. Day's fine article in the third volume (1880) of the Magazine of Art:

The heraldic dragon conforms, after the manner of its kind, to decorative necessities. His business is to look full of energy and angry power. His jaws are wide; his claws are sharp; wings add to his speed and to his terrors; he is clothed with scaly and impenetrable armour, and he lashes his tail in fury; and all the while he is careful to spread himself out on shield or banner that all his powers may be displayed. In the days before the invention of the term 'fine art' the dragon was frequently introduced into pictures of sacred and legendary subjects, and it invariably formed an ornamental feature in the composition. St. Michael and St. George were habitually triumphant over the evil thing; and . . . if the rigid virtues were sometimes insipid, it must be allowed that the demons were usually grotesquely characteristic and often delightful in colour. The grim humour of the medieval Germans found its latest exponent in Albert Durer, some of whose imaginary creations are very remarkable. . . . They belong half to Gothic tradition and half to Renaissance influence, but yet they are wholly German and wholly Dureresque. The creatures of the Italian cinque-cento partook for the most part of the grace of the ornaments of which they were a part, though occasionally there lurks among the beautiful and fanciful foliation a monster that is inexpressibly loathsome. Art might well dispense with such imaginings. If the fabled creature is to live in ornament—and why should it not?—let it be on the supposition that it is a thing of beauty.

DRAGONS AND UNICORNS—FACT? OR FICTION?

CHAPTER FIFTEEN

**TO THE GLORY
OF SAINT GEORGE**

THE WESTERN half of our history is closing true to form—a history that originated in myth and resulted in the loftiest reality. It began in the romantic fable of Perseus and Andromeda, and it ends on the shore of the Western Ocean to the glory of Saint George and Merrie England!

The connecting lineage and record are clear. The Hero family has been a prolific one, and widely spread, with a history full of noble diversity, but its temper has held true, and its mission of the rescue of maidens in peril, or, more largely, of distressed and wrong-headed peoples, has never been neglected: its career is a continuous picture of the ideal of the West-knightly valour in service, the duty of the strong to aid the weak. From Persia to Italy, from cultured Greece to the barbarous shore of the Atlantic, the tale of noble deeds was told, the fame of one and another brave soul was celebrated, and so Chivalry was born of Romance, and the Renaissance arose to rejuvenate a benighted old world.

Whether or not the names we read were ever or never those of actual men; whether or not anything like a dragon ever threatened forlorn princesses or devastated a smiling countryside, is of no consequence. As history, and its record may be as unsubstantial as the quickly dissolving clouds that reflected a rosy light upon the towers of a mythical Ilium—doubtless it is, for the most part, only an immortal legend repeating itself as do human generations, but it portrays, century after century, the highest virtue in the manly soul.

It is needless to spend time over the variants in what we may style the Perseus legend as written in classic and mediaeval books and poems. Stories identical in substance with that of the rescue of Andromeda from the jaws of a monster were widely related in antiq-

98

DRAGONS AND UNICORNS—FACT? OR FICTION?

uity and have not yet been forgotten. They form a class by themselves, differentiated from the traditions and fables that have heretofore been related, by the fact that always a young virgin, usually of royal birth, is delivered from impending death by a bold and ardent youth; and that in most cases there is the attendant, but less important, fact that the hero is nearly robbed of his just reward (the maiden's hand and heart) by the evil machinations of a rival who never quite succeeds. A typical example is found in far Arabia. One day, as we are told, a dragon comes to a city in Yemen and demands a beautiful virgin. The lot falls on the king's daughter, but a young knight kills the monster, and the brave adventurer gets the girl. Another very old example is that attached to the most precious relic in the storied island of Rhodes. Luke the Evangelist, the islanders say, desired to move the body of John the Baptist from its burial-place in Caesarea to Antioch, but was able to transfer only the saint's right hand, with which Jesus had been baptized. "Subsequently it was deposited in the new Hagia Sophia at Constantinople, and after further adventures reached security in Rhodes. While it yet remained in Antioch a dragon haunted the country about that city, and the people appeased the monster yearly with the sacrifice of one of their number, chosen by lot. At last the lot fell on a maid whose father greatly venerated the holy relic. Making as though he would kiss the hand, he bit off a fragment from the thumb: and when his daughter was led out to sacrifice he cast this fragment into the dragon's jaws and the monster quickly choked and perished."

A widely familiar 'St. George' legend is that belonging to Mansfield, in Germany, over whose church-door is a statue commemorating the incident. The great man of the place at the time was Count Mansfield, and near the town is a hill still called Lindberg because in former days it was the abode of a lindwurm, or dragon, to which the towns-people were obliged to give a young woman every day. Soon no more maidens were to be found except the knight's own daughter. Whereupon Count Mansfield rode forth and slew the beast, and the citizens made him a 'saint' and gave him (or somebody else!) a statue, in spite of his previous indifference as to the fate of their daughters. Mansfield is one of the many places believed locally to be the site of the famous combat of that 'St. George' whose exploits were as numerous and widespread as were those of Hercules-in each case probably a misplaced tradition of some dimly remembered fight between local barons or bullies.

A still closer approximation to the Perseus type was taken down a few years ago from the lips of an illiterate peasant woman of the Val d'Arno, Italy, and is quoted by Hartland. A part of it describes the hero finding in a seaside chapel a lovely maiden, who urges him to hasten on his way lest he suffer the fate to which she is doomed, namely, to be eaten by a seven-headed dragon. Instead of obeying her he dismounts, attacks the dragon on its rising from the sea, and cuts out its seven tongues which he carries away—these trophies proving his claim, a few months later, to the credit of the feat and the hand of the willing girl.

This seven-headed, seven-tongued hydra-dragon of fiction appears all down the ages, at least since the days of Hercules. Such a brute, to which a king's daughter is to be offered, figures in Grimm's tale of The Two Brothers, and variants may be found in folk-

DRAGONS AND UNICORNS—FACT? OR FICTION?

legends everywhere in Europe. That within comparatively recent times it was popularly believed to be a reality is shown by serious accounts of its doings in books regarded as sensible and authoritative. Conrad Gesner gives a picture in his Historia Animalium of a hydra in the form of a serpent, "the heads like those of lions and as it were ornamented with crowns, two feet in the front of the body, the tail twisted inwards." He relates that this hideous, aquatic creature was brought from Turkey to Venice in the year 1530, exposed to public view, and afterward sent to the king of France. The Italian compiler Aldrovandus, a contemporary, illustrates in his book about serpents a seven-headed dragon; and in the Encyclopaedia Londonensis, issued in 1755, may be seen a large coloured plate of a dreadful, seven-headed creature credited to Seba, an author who published a Thesaurus of natural history about 1750, with an extensive account of it.

And so at last we come to our own Saint George! Who was this patron of the valorous, this model of devotion to an ideal of duty, this indomitable George? Nobody knows. He has been relegated to the sun-myths, and declared a mere relic of Mithraism. Gibbon and others identified him with the author of Arianism, but Eastern churches were named for the martyr before that prelate existed. It has also been said that he was that nameless Christian who tore down the edict of persecution in Nicomedia. These and other identifications have been discarded. The nearest approach to probability that any distinct personality is at the root of this heroic development of a noble idealism lies in a tradition that a Christian man named George (or its equivalent) was martyred in Palestine before the era of Constantine the Great; that he became the object of a religious cult (said to be referred to in an inscription dated A.D. 367); and that in 1868 his sepulchre was discovered at Lydda (or Diospolis) near Jerusalem, where his martyrdom is alleged to have occurred. Tradition has expanded these facts (if they be facts) into a story in many varying versions, the most acceptable summary of which appears to be the following:

"According to legend [this Christian George] was born, about A.D. 285, of noble parents in Cappadocia, eastern Anatolia. As he grew to manhood he became a soldier; his courage in battle soon won him promotion, and he was attached to the personal staff of the emperor Diocletian. When this ruler decided to enter on his campaign of persecution, George resigned his commission and bitterly complained to the emperor. He was immediately arrested, and when promises failed to make him change his mind he was tortured with great cruelty. . . . At last he was taken to the outskirts of the city and beheaded [April 23, A.D. 303]. . . . The earliest narrative of his martyrdom known to us is full of the most extravagant marvels: three times George is put to death, chopped into small pieces, buried deep in the earth, and consumed by fire, but each time he is resuscitated by God. Besides this we have dead men brought to life to be baptized, wholesale conversions, including that of the 'Empress Alexandra,' armies and idols destroyed simultaneously, beams of timber suddenly bursting into leaf, and finally milk flowing instead of blood from the martyr's severed head."

This and several other more or less extravagant, and equally, legendary accounts derived from old manuscripts and books, are related and discussed extensively in Mrs. Cornelia S. Hulst's admirable history of this essentially mythical saint or hero, and his veneration in Europe.

This was a remarkable man, whoever and whatever he was, and it is not surprising that, probably stimulated by some shining circumstance unknown to us, he became so distinguished in the religious world of his time. Besides St. Stephen, he is the only martyr venerated by the entire Church; is one of the fourteen 'great martyrs' and 'trophy-bearers' of the Greek Church, and is honoured by special masses and ceremonies in the Latin, Syrian, and Coptic communions. All over the Orient, in Greece, Italy and Sicily, many churches were dedicated to him in the sixth century, and since. His relics are scattered over the entire Church, Santo Georgio in Velabro, at Rome, possessing the head. Holweck catalogues this saint's ecclesiastical distinctions thus: "S. George is principal patron of England, Catalaunia (Spain), Liguria (Italy), Aragon, Georgia, Modena, Farrara (24 April), of the isle of Syros, dioceses of Wilna, Limburg, Regio de Calabria, and other dioceses, also of the Teutonic Knights, minor patron of Portugal, Lithuania, Constantinople. He is protector of soldiers, archers, knights, saddlers, sword-cutlers, and of horses, against fever, etc. He is mentioned daily in the Greek mass." Moslems, in fact, reverence Saint George, identifying him with the Prophet Elijah, and have long allowed Christians to celebrate a mass once a year at the tomb of the martyr at Lydda, in Palestine, now a mosque; and the first church dedicated to St. George (at Zarava, in Hauran, A.D. 514) was a re-consecrated mosque.

That the fame of this martyr had spread in very early times to Britain is shown by references to him in the writings of the Venerable Bede and in other chronicles. Ashmole says, in his history of the Order of the Garter, that King Arthur placed a picture of St. George on his banners, and Selden states that he was regarded as the patron-saint of England in Saxon times. It was not, however, until after the great Third Crusade, in which the English played the leading part, led by their magnificent prince, Richard the Lion-hearted, that George, as warrior rather than as martyr, became noticeable in that national dignity. It was believed among the disheartened crusaders before Acre that St. George had appeared to Richard in a vision and had encouraged him to continue the long and dreadful siege; and afterward the story spread that the troops themselves had beheld him, on a white horse, fighting for them above their heads in the drifting smoke of battle, as did the angel who was "captain of the hosts of the Lord" when Joshua was battling against the walls of Jericho. Even the French soldiers under Robert, son of William the Conqueror, accepted him as their patron and defender.

It is perhaps to this figure that Dr. Hanauer refers in relating this bit of folklore current in Palestine. A fountain (Gihon?) in the outskirts of Jerusalem was formerly a part of the water-supply of the city, but a big dragon took possession of it and demanded a youth or maid every time anyone came for water; until at last, as usual, only the king's daughter was left. When she was about to be sent, Mar Jirys appeared in golden panoply mounted on a white steed, and riding full tilt at the dragon, he pierced it dead between the eyes. This is probably the same spring which is noted for its intermittent flow, which the people explain by saying that the dragon drinks the water low whenever it wakes, and when the beast sleeps the water rises. The Tyrolese speak of a dragon that "eats its way out of the

DRAGONS AND UNICORNS—FACT? OR FICTION?

rock" when the intermittent spring at Bella, in Krains, begins to flow. The Maltese also have a dragon's spring which issues from a cavern with noises said to be the snorts of the monster within its source.

The returning crusaders, reporting this supernatural assistance in full faith, made a very deep impression on the credulous populace of England, who at once proclaimed this White Knight military protector of the kingdom; and in 1222 the Council of Oxford ordained that the feast day of St. George (April 23) should be observed as a minor holy day in the English Church. In 1330 he was formally adopted as the patron-saint of the Order of the Garter just then instituted by Edward III, which was equivalent to an ascription for the whole country, and he became that indeed when the Royal Chapel at Windsor was dedicated to him in 1348. He was invoked by Henry V at Agincourt (1415), where the English swept forward to victory with the inspiring battle-cry of his name.

Saint George he was for England,

Saint Denis was for France,

rings out the old song!

Thus this hero of the Middle Ages became in England more than elsewhere the favourite of the people and the principal figure of the time in mystic plays, mummeries, and religious dramas and processions, especially on Corpus Christi Day. Until recent times one of the diversions in Wiltshire and other English counties was the play "St. George and Turkey-Snipe" (a corruption of Turkish Knight), wherein a Christian knight overcomes a Saracen. The opening words of this pious drama are quoted by Miss Urlin as follows:

I am King George, the noble champion bold,

And with my trusty sword I won ten thousand pounds in gold.

It was I that fought the fiery Dragon, and brought him to the slaughter,-

And by these means I won the king of Egypt's daughter.

It is not surprising that mistakes and legends early began to cluster around this notable character all over the continent.

Legends are the weeds of history. They are sown by winds of gossip, and bear fruits of the imagination which sometimes are sweet and wholesome but are more often ugly and baneful. They take deep root and flourish prodigiously, overshadowing the less interesting growths of fact and voucher, and obscuring, by a sort of protective mimicry, the truths in tradition. For example: where, if anywhere, among the many places, do the red flowers growing year by year on this and that meadow or hilltop, indicate the true

102

DRAGONS AND UNICORNS—FACT? OR FICTION?

spot "where the Dragon was killed"? Here and there we may say—as at Coventry—that is the field of the battle of so-and-so, a thousand years ago; but to get proof of it we must search among the roots of hardy fictions as botanists do for stifled native plants among the weeds of an abandoned field.

The eminent French antiquarian, Louis F. A. Maury, points out that many local dragon stories probably originated in or have been kept alive by mistaken interpretations by the unlearned of relics, pictures, and votive offerings in churches—the last-named including specimens of skeletons or bones of serpents, whales and so forth, stuffed crocodiles, big fishes and other strange animals, deposited by persons who had escaped perils by one or another exotic beast. Formerly, at least, there hung in the church of Mont St. Michel pieces of armour which the peasantry held in awe as that worn by the angel Michael when he drove that old serpent, the Devil, out of heaven. At Milan, where now stands the ancient church of St. Denis, was previously a profound cavern, in which, we are told, once dwelt a dragon, always hungry, whose breath caused speedy death to any person receiving it. The Milanese hero, Viscount Uberto, killed it, according to a local legend-the basis of which is a figure, named Givre, of a heraldic dragon on the armour of an early viscount of that city. Count Aymer, of Asti, in Savoy, owes his high place in the list of dragon-slayers, says Maury, to a heraldic dragon carved at the foot of his effigy on his monumental tomb at St. Spire de Corbil. The identification of Gozon with the myth of the destruction of the dragon of Rhodes, was owing to the accidental presence near Gozon's tomb of a commonplace picture of St. George in his famous act.

How a name may serve as a punning-peg on which to hang a courtier's story or a minstrel's ballad, which later may become an element in dubious history, is shown in a saga of King Regnor Lodbrog, a famous pirate chief of the Viking era, who, when a young man, about the year 800, showed his mettle in an exploit of gallantry of which his companions loved to sing when the drinks went round. A Swedish prince had a beautiful daughter whom he entrusted (probably when he was sailing away on some freebooting expedition) to the care of one of his officers in a strong castle. This officer fell in love with his ward, and seizing the castle, defied the world to take her away from him. Upon this the father proclaimed abroad that whoever would conquer the ravisher and rescue the lady might have her in marriage. Of all the bold fellows who undertook the adventure Regnor alone achieved success and obtained the prize. Now, it happened that the name of the faithless guardian was Orme, which in Icelandic means 'serpent'; wherefore the first minstrel who seized upon the incident to glorify the valour and renown of his prince (and retrieve the lady's reputation?) represented the girl as detained in the castle by a dreadful dragon!

It is a striking fact that, although dragons and dragon-killers were commonplaces of both ancient and mediaeval storymaking (someone has wittily said that the dragon itself was brought into being merely as a much-needed device to exhibit the valour of more or less fictitious knights) the association of this fearsome beast with George the venerated martyr-saint, is a comparatively modern addition to his history. The oldest written account of him, that by Pasicrates, does not mention a dragon. "The Greek Church, which

103

DRAGONS AND UNICORNS—FACT? OR FICTION?

was naturally the first to render St. George honour," as Mrs. Hulst points out, "from very early times represented him with a dragon under his feet and a crowned virgin at his side, a symbolical way of saying that he overcame Sin, for the dragon represents the Devil . . . and the crowned maiden represents the Church."

This religious feeling characterized legends of such a combat found in Greek and Russian verses, and tales of a somewhat later period, but nowhere is this worshipful hero of the Church represented as fighting on horseback. The first account of a combat between St. George and a dragon that reached western Europe was in the thirteenth century in the Latin of The Golden Legend, where a distinctly romantic flavour tinctured the holy narrative. This epic poem became popular and spread the heroic legend, which was recited in many versions, used in dramatic representations, and led to the localizing of the adventure in many different places. Where and when this poem originated remains a mystery.

In the early part of the fifteenth century The Golden Legend was paraphrased by Lydgate and introduced to a few scholarly English readers in a manuscript preserved in the Bodleian Library in Oxford. It was more widely spread by Caxton, the publisher, in the translation made by him and printed in 1483. His second edition was illustrated by woodcuts borrowed from a Dutch edition of the tale, and these publications not only informed England as to the tale brought from the East, but settled the version which has been the adopted faith of our British forefathers ever since. The crabbed old English and print of Caxton's book (William Morris issued a delightful facsimile from the Kelmscott Press) are so difficult to read now that many modern renderings in both verse and prose have been produced, of which I have chosen the authentic one by Baring-Gould given below.

And so, finally, we have come to the legend of the proper, most eminent Saint George, and his most celebrated and distinguished of all Dragons-possessions peculiarly our own as Englishmen and by inheritance; and here is the creed of it for your worshipful instruction:

George, then a tribune in the Roman army, while travelling, came to Silene, a town in Libya, near which was a pond inhabited by a loathsome monster that had many times driven back an armed host sent to destroy it. It even approached the walls of the city, and with the exhalations of its breath poisoned all who came near. To prevent such visits it was given every day two sheep to satisfy its voracity. This continued until the flocks of the region were exhausted. Then the citizens held counsel and decreed that each day a man and a beast should be supplied, and at the last they had to give up their sons and daughters—none were exempted. The lot fell finally on the king's only daughter; and those who tell the story describe with vivid rhetoric the heartrending struggle of the royal father to submit to the decree, and his final victory in favour of duty to his people over his affection. So, dressed in her best, and nerved by high resolve, the princess leaves the city alone and walks toward the lake.

George, who opportunely met her on the way and saw her weeping, asked the cause

DRAGONS AND UNICORNS—FACT? OR FICTION?

of her tears. "Good youth," she exclaimed, "quickly mount your horse and fly less you perish with me." He asked her to explain the reason for so dire a prediction; and she had hardly ceased telling him when the monster lifted its head above the surface of the dark water, and the maiden, all trembling, cried again—"Fly! fly! Sir knight." His only answer was the sign of the Cross. Then he advanced to meet the horrible fiend, recommending himself to God; and brandishing his lance he transfixed the beast and cast it to the ground. Turning to the princess he bade her pass her girdle about the creature's prostrate body and to fear nothing. When this had been done the monster followed her like a docile hound. When they together had led it into the town the people fled before them, but George recalled them, bidding them put aside their fear, for the Lord had sent him to deliver them from their danger. Then the king and all his people, twenty thousand men with all their women and children, were baptized, and George smote off the head of the dragon.

Somehow, centuries ago, the people of Britain came to believe that this happened in England at Coventry; and it is no wonder that they learned and sang a Paean of victory over it, comparing George's superlative bravery with the great deeds of bygone heroes. You may find it in Bishop Percy's Reliques, and one stanza will give you the spirit of it:

Baris conquered Ascapart, and after slew the boare,

And then he crossed the seas beyond to combat with the Moore.

Sir Isenbras and Eglamore, they were knights most bold,

And good Sir John Mandeville of travel much hath told.

There were many English knights that Pagans did convert,

But St. George, St. George, pluckt out the Dragon's heart!

St. George he was for England; St. Dennis was for France,

Sing: Honi soit qui mal y pense!

I have traced the dragon in time from the birth of light out of darkness to the present, and in space from the Garden of Eden eastward to farthest Cathay, and westward to the crags that withstand the Atlantic's fury. I go out where I came in: There is no dragon-there never was a dragon; but wherever in the West there appeared to be one there was always a St. George.

DRAGONS AND UNICORNS—FACT? OR FICTION?

Saint George And The Dragon

THE LORE OF THE UNICORN

by ODELL SHEPARD

REVISED EDITION
by
Inner Light Publications

DRAGONS AND UNICORNS—FACT? OR FICTION?

UNICORN ELF AND FAIRY
by
Carol Ann Rodriguez

DRAGONS AND UNICORNS—FACT? OR FICTION?

THE LORE OF THE UNICORN
BY ODELL SHEPARD
(b. 1884—d.1967) London: George Allen & Unwin;
Boston: Houghton Mifflin [1930]

DRAGONS AND UNICORNS—FACT? OR FICTION?

CONTENTS
INTRODUCTION

DRAGONS AND UNICORNS—FACT? OR FICTION?

THE LORE OF THE UNICORN

INTRODUCTION

ON the table before me there lies a long straight wand of ivory. Cut to the length of a walking-stick, it is somewhat more than two inches in diameter at the top and it tapers evenly to a blunt point. Smooth-backed ridges, not more than a quarter of an inch in height, spiral round it counter-clockwise, making about two turns and a half between one end and the other. As a whole, it is a twisted spear. One can fancy that it has been taken in powerful hands and wrung, as one wrings a wet cloth. Thomas Fuller, having seen another such ivory wand as this, said excellently that to his dim eyes and at some distance it seemed "like a taper of wreathed waxe".

This walking-stick has been fitted at the upper end with a gilded silver cap which bears the arms of a certain noble house and a motto in Welsh. Four inches below the cap a hole has been bored through the stick—one would say, at first, to receive the cord to which some gentleman of the grand old days attached the silken tassel that adorned his cane. I scarcely think, however, that this particular stick ever tapped its way along Bird-cage Walk or through the gardens of Versailles, partly because there are no signs of wear on its point and partly because it weighs something like three pounds. More probably, the cord that went through this hole was used not to carry a tassel but to hang the stick against the wall in some great house of three or four centuries ago.

And yet I do not doubt that some of the former owners of this wand carried it about with them, but when they did so they carried it neither for comfort nor display; rather, it was their companion on dark nights and in perilous places, and they held it near their hearts, handling it tenderly, as they would a treasure. For indeed it was exactly that. It preserved a man from the arrow that flieth by day and the pestilence that walketh in darkness, from the craft of the poisoner, from epilepsy, and from several less dignified ills of the flesh not to be named in so distinguished a connection. In short, it was an amulet, a talisman, a weapon, and a medicine-chest all in one. Small wonder that such a wand as this, in the days when such things were appreciated, sold for twenty times its weight in gold, and that one alone, as Thomas Dekker said, was "worth a city". Small wonder

DRAGONS AND UNICORNS—FACT? OR FICTION?

that perfect sticks like this were to be seen only in the treasure-chambers of popes and emperors and kings, or, when some opulent church like St. Mark's of Venice did manage to acquire one, that it should be shown to the public only on gala days and beneath a pall of purple velvet. The stick before me, although of ivory, was not cut from an elephant's tusk or even from the tusk of a mammoth or mastodon. It grew as it is, and according to the most learned. opinion of many generations it grew single on the brow of a beast so glorious, so virtuous, so beautiful, that heaven vouchsafed the earth, as in the case of the phoenix, only one specimen at a time. For this is the horn of the unicorn.

To retrace the devious ways by which this piece of ivory, so reverently handled, has come to lie here on my writing-desk, I shall have to tell a story that ranges back through more "wild centuries" than we can count—a story that begins with a time before cities or agriculture, when barbarous tribes wandered with their herds from summer to winter pasturage and back again, a tale that includes at one end the most primitive myths and the first stirrings of the moral sense and at the other the trickery of the charlatan and the mountebank. Into the web of this tale I shall have to catch up many strands of the history of exploration, of medicine, of art, of commerce, and of scientific thought. The fact is that I cannot explain how this ivory wand came to lie before me—I purchased it not long ago from a London dealer in antiques for about three guineas—without indicating, in one vivid example, the ways by which magic rose into religious dogma and this gradually succumbed, or is succumbing, under the attrition of modern science. But even then, of course, I shall fall short of a full explanation, and any reader of these words who cherishes the few relics of superstition that we have left to us may be assured that this book will not "murder to dissect", will not substitute a dull explanation for one of the most beautiful legends in the world. The remote and solitary strangeness of the unicorn is perfectly safe from me, and I think from any one; for even if I did not prefer to do so I should have to let him stalk away, at the end, into the mystery out of which he comes.

The lore of the unicorn is enormous in range and variety, not only because of the great expanse of time it covers but because it involves so many different departments of knowledge, and the literature dealing specifically with the topic is surprisingly extensive. Like most of my predecessors, I have hunted the unicorn chiefly in libraries, realizing the delightful absurdity of the task quite as fully as any one could point it out to me. A zoologist would have written on my topic a different and probably a shorter book, but for me the unicorn is interesting almost entirely as a denizen of "the Monarch Thought's dominions". Whether there is or is not an actual unicorn—and this is one of the questions upon which I shall merely quote the opinions of others—he cannot possibly be so fascinating or so important as the things men have dreamed and thought and written about him. A dream, if it is no more than that, of such great age and beauty as this of the unicorn, is far more worthy of consideration than the question whether we shall have one species more or less in the earth's fauna. And the dream, at any rate, is an unquestionable fact, a phenomenon of the mind; it has grown like a tree, striking deep roots in thought and spreading huge boughs against our mental sky. This book about the unicorn is a minute contribution to the study of the only subject that deeply and permanently concerns us—human nature and the ways of human thought.

DRAGONS AND UNICORNS—FACT? OR FICTION?

In view of the fact that I am tracing what has been thought and said about the unicorn and that most of the literature concerned is found in rare and forgotten books, it has seemed necessary to quote more freely than would otherwise have been desirable. After reading hundreds of pages of unfounded and ignorant recent writing on my topic I have no apology to make for the care I have taken to prove my points by exact citation of authority. The lore of the unicorn owes much to the work of accurate scholars, and I have tried to present their opinions with an accuracy they would have approved; but the mere apparatus of scholarship is a scaffolding that should always be kept as much as possible out of sight, and my notes will be found at the back of the book, where they will trouble no one for whom they are not intended.

Perhaps it would not be inappropriate to explain how I first struck into a footpath so far, at least in appearance, from any of the highways of contemporary research. Some time ago, while reading Petrarch's treatise De Vita Solitaria, I came upon a vivid description of the noon-day meal in the house of an Italian tyrant in the fourteenth century. Like most things in Petrarch's Latin prose, this description is derivative, its main source being St. Ambrose's De Abstinentia, but a sentence or two in the middle of it stood out as a rather startling bit of personal observation. "Among all these yellow and black and livid lumps of flesh", says Petrarch, who was himself a vegetarian, "the diligent taster goes exploring for the suspected and not undeserved bit of poison. But another kind of precaution has been taken against secret plots: between the wines and the viands project the livid horns of serpents skilfully fastened to little gilded trees, so that it is a wonder to see how Death himself stands guard, as it were in the very stronghold of pleasure, against the death of this miserable man."

What the horns of serpents might be doing on a rich man's dinner table I had no idea, and I determined to find out. A few hours of excavation in the pages of Pietro de Abano, Ardoynus, and Cardinal Ponzetto taught me all that I cared to know about the devices once used in Italy for detecting poison at the table—devices such as that of the cerastes's horn which Petrarch mentions, the vulture's claw, the "sealed earth", the crystal goblet, the eagle-stone, the snake's tongue, and others of the same sort. But while I read, the terror of those evil times when death might lie at the bottom of any cup took hold of me, and, still more powerfully, a sense of pity for the wild and ignorant ways in which the danger was encountered. Gradually, however, I found myself moving out into a purer air along a path not entirely strange even then, for the unicorn's horn was long the chief defence against poison of those who could pay the huge prices at which it was held. And then several other questions arose: How did this horn acquire its great reputation? How was it supposed to act in detecting poison? How could it maintain its prestige while the princes and dukes of Italy who owned it were dying on every hand suddenly and from no apparent cause? Where did these horns come from, and what was the nature of the traffic that purveyed them? Was the belief in their powers a vulgar superstition only or was it held by learned men and perhaps even by physicians? How old was this belief, and what was its origin? These are some of the questions I asked myself and shall try in this book to answer.

DRAGONS AND UNICORNS—FACT? OR FICTION?

CHAPTER I

THE GORGEOUS EAST

WE may never know precisely when or where or how the legend of the unicorn began. It pervades recorded time and may be dimly visible even in the clouds that hover just above history's sunrise. The mystery of its origin, leaving a wide field for speculation and surrounding even the facts of which we are certain with bands of twilight, is one of the legend's most evident charms, but it precludes the possibility of tracing that legend from its beginnings. We can best take up the tale of the unicorn at the point where it first emerges into the literature of the western world, early in the fourth century before Christ.

Few need to be reminded that at just this time Mediterranean civilization was sweeping rapidly up to one of the summits, perhaps the highest, of human achievement. In structures of stone and of words and of pure thought the Greek world was then creating marvels which compel us to accept the assurance with which the men of that world ruled out all who did not belong to it as "barbarians". There are two aspects of that Greek civilization, however, from which we barbarians of the modern world are accustomed to draw a little comfort: in the first place, it was an affair of a few small cities and, even in these, of few individuals; in the second place, it was achieved in spite of what we must regard as an abysmal ignorance. Greece in the Age of Pericles was like the hand's-breadth of lighted country, surrounded by shadow, that may be seen from a hill-top on a lowering day. The best minds in the Hellenic world knew little—and, with a few exceptions, they cared less—about what lay beyond the circle of their light, and even of what lay within it their ignorance is likely to seem to us pathetic. This may well remind us to what a slight extent deep wisdom and high intellectual attainment depend upon mere information, but the interesting fact remains. Greek notions of geography, with regard to every part of the earth's surface remote from the Mediterranean, were grotesquely few and wrong; in the field of zoology there were no clear ideas about species, and,

DRAGONS AND UNICORNS—FACT? OR FICTION?

before Aristotle, no ideas whatever about orders and genera; with regard to the animals of distant lands where no Greek had ever been men were completely at the mercy of travellers' tales.

It was from this civilization and this intermingling of intellectual brilliancy and ignorance that the physician Ctesias went out in the year 416 B.C., going eastward from his native town of Cnidus to accept an appointment at the court of Darius II, King of Persia. This appointment he owed partly to the already great prestige of Greek medicine and partly, perhaps, to the fact that he was a member of the priestly caste of the Asclepiadai in which medicine was a hereditary profession. He remained in Persia for some seventeen years, serving both Darius and Artaxerxes. For a single instant he appears in familiar history, for Xenophon tells us that when Cyrus broke through the bodyguard of the Great King at Cunaxa and struck him through his breastplate, it was Ctesias, one of those fighting near at hand, who healed the wound. About the year 398 he returned to Cnidus and there wrote his two works, a History of Persia in twenty-three books, now largely lost, and his Indica, preserved in a fragmentary abstract made in the ninth century by one Photius, Patriarch of Constantinople.

There is reason to suspect that Photios subordinated the more commonplace passages of his original and stressed the marvels, yet that original work was the Mandeville's Travels of its time and even the Greeks who knew the text of Ctesias regarded him as a romancer. It is fair to remember, however, that he wrote, confessedly, about a district which he had never seen, so that he had to depend upon the tales of travellers and the reports of Persian officials, and that his most remarkable stories have usually some discernible foundation in fact. In justice to him we may ask ourselves what would be the present reputation of Herodotus, his great contemporary, if the History had been preserved only in a few selections chosen by a credulous cleric of the Dark Ages. In the thirty-third and final fragment of the Indica Ctesias asserts roundly—or perhaps it is Photius who does it for him—that his book is all perfectly true, that he has set down nothing which he has not either seen himself or else heard from the mouths of credible witnesses. Indeed, says he, many more wonderful things than he has put into his book have been left out simply because he does not wish to be thought a liar. We do well to keep this assurance in mind when we come to consider his twenty-fifth fragment, the earliest and one of the most important of European documents relating to the unicorn:-

"There are in India certain wild asses which are as large as horses, and larger. Their bodies are white, their heads dark red, and their eyes dark blue. They have a horn on the forehead which is about a foot and a half in length. The dust filed from this horn is administered in a potion as a protection against deadly drugs. The base of this horn, for some two hands'-breadth above the brow, is pure white; the upper part is sharp and of a vivid crimson; and the remainder, or middle portion, is black. Those who drink out of these horns, made into drinking vessels, are not subject, they say, to convulsions or to the holy disease [epilepsy]. Indeed, they are immune even to poisons if, either before or after swallowing such, they drink wine, water, or anything else from these beakers. Other asses, both the tame and the wild, and in fact all animals with solid hoofs, are without the

DRAGONS AND UNICORNS—FACT? OR FICTION?

ankle-bone and have no gall in the liver, but these have both the ankle-bone and the gall. This ankle-bone, the most beautiful I have ever seen, is like that of an ox in general appearance and in size, but it is as heavy as lead and its colour is that of cinnabar through and through. The animal is exceedingly swift and powerful, so that no creature, neither the horse nor any other, can overtake it."

Whatever else we may think of this passage, we cannot call it a baseless fabrication.

We can believe that Ctesias added to it nothing whatever out of his own fancy, but recorded what he had heard from men who, in their turn, spoke quite honestly and even accurately of what they had seen and heard. Considered from the zoologist's point of view, the fault of the passage is that the facts it contains are strangely combined, but for our present purposes this is just its charm and value. Evidently, Ctesias is describing at least two different animals at once, and it is as though a child, having read descriptions of the lion and the camel, should combine them into a tertium quid vaguely like both but exactly similar to neither.

A main ingredient of this compound beast is almost certainly the Indian rhinoceros. The evidence for this lies in what is said of the horn's alexipharmic virtue, that those who drink from beakers made of it are free from certain diseases and from poisons. This belief about rhinoceros horn, still widely current in the Orient, was already old, apparently, in the time of Ctesias, and underneath it there lies a welter of symbolism and superstition exceedingly difficult to comprehend. Without attempting to explain it at present, we may accept it as an important datum of our study.

Thinking, then, of the rhinoceros horn, what explanation can be made of the remark about its colours, white and black and red? The actual horns of the rhinoceros vary somewhat widely in hue, and the colour of a carved specimen is really a strange dull red in the thinner parts, deepening toward reddish black where it is thick. At first thought, therefore, it seems possible that Ctesias described the natural colours of the horn by his words xxxxx and xxxxxxx xxxx, although both epithets are much too strong. This interpretation makes no account, however, of the pure white that is said to extend upward from the brow for two hand's-breadths, for there is no hint of white in the natural horn. The words suggest, by their precision, that Ctesias imagined the horn as having three broad bands of sharply distinct and vivid hues, and this is an effect not of nature but of art. It seems possible that he got his idea of the horn's colouration, not necessarily at first hand, either from some representation of it or else from a horn artificially decorated.

Support for one of these suggestions is given by Manuel Philes, a Greek poet who, although he lived in the thirteenth century, is a mere echo of the ancients. Seeing in the hands of an Indian king a drinking vessel adorned with three bands of colour, white and black and red, Philes asks what this cup is made of, and is told that it is the horn of the ovdypos or wild ass. The ultimate source of this passage is Ctesias himself, so that the story in Philes amounts not to a discovery but to an interpretation; yet, considered as such it is both shrewd and plausible. The rhinoceros cups of India may well have been

116

DRAGONS AND UNICORNS—FACT? OR FICTION?

painted with these three colours for symbolic or magical reasons now lost, and the mistaking of such an artificial for a natural colouring would have been only one of several such confusions that we shall meet in unicorn lore.

Yet even this interpretation is not wholly satisfying, for it leaves out of account the remarkable colours of the animal's body. No matter how feeble the colour-sense of the ancients may be thought, no matter how different it may have been from our own or how widely the meanings of colour words may have changed, it seems incredible that any man who had ever seen a rhinoceros could call its body white, its head dark red or purple, and its eyes blue. Taking these hues together with those of the horn, we have a beast coloured like the peacock—and one so gaudy, indeed, that here again we suspect the intervention of art. The splash of vivid dye at the end of the horn holds special attention.

It recalls a passage in the twenty-first fragment of Ctesias in which we are told that near the sources of the Hyparkhos "there is found a certain flower used for dyeing purposes and not inferior to the Greek purple, giving in fact a far more vivid hue even than that. In the same district there is an animal about as large as a beetle, with very long legs and as red as cinnabar, which the Indians grind into a powder and so use for dyeing the robes and tunics to which they wish to give a purple colour. Their dye-stuffs are better than those of the Persians."

This means, almost certainly, that the Persians of the time of Ctesias imported dyed fabrics from the regions of northern India over which they ruled-fabrics in which a vivid purple was a prominent hue. May it not be that they sometimes found the rhinoceros, a beast unknown to them but familiar to the manufacturers, represented upon these fabrics, and in the strong hues made possible by the native dyes? We know that the animal was so represented, in colours that made no attempt at verisimilitude, by Scythian and Chinese embroiderers of later centuries. The colours of Ctesias's unicorn may, just possibly, have had some such origin.

Undoubtedly there is an appearance of the fantastic in this theory, but we are moving here in a world of fantasy. Ctesias never saw any part of the vast romantic region comprising the Himalaya mountains and Tibet which is what he means by "India", but he heard it talked about for seventeen years, for the most part in languages that he understood imperfectly, by men to whom it was a Land of Cockayne lying many caravan-journeys deep in the gorgeous East. Their gold and ivory and spices and woven fabrics came from there, and concerning the beasts said to inhabit its forests they believed what they were told. Ctesias must have been told something, for his idea about the properties of the onager's horn were not derived from plastic or tectile representation; the suggestion is only that he may have filled in his description with details of an artistic origin. He was not well equipped for criticism of his sources of information, and if it had occurred to him that his unicorned wild ass had an odd look, in particular that it was remarkably polychromatic, he would have quieted his doubts by recalling that it was a native of India.

It may be objected that even in the fourth century before Christ no intelligent man

117

DRAGONS AND UNICORNS—FACT? OR FICTION?

could have assumed the actual existence of a beast such as this on no better evidence than that of a rude representation. Against this objection one may bring forward the exactly similar assumption made by a scientifically trained traveller of the nineteenth century who was converted to belief in the existence of unicorns by the discovery of a primitive picture of what he took for one in a South African cave.

But thus far we have ignored the fact that Ctesias calls his unicorns wild asses, and even with such an absurd name as that of the hippopotamus—"river horse"—before us it seems unlikely that either he or his informants could ever have seen anything asinine in the rhinoceros. The wild ass, a native of Persia, as well as of India, should have been familiar to Ctesias by personal observation. It was vividly described by Xenophon and was a favourite quarry of Mesopotamian kings, its great speed and ferocity making the chase of it indeed a royal sport. Ctesias could scarcely have spent seventeen years in Persia without knowing rather definitely what he meant when he referred to the wild ass, and it seems probable that this animal contributed something to his description of the unicorn. In a part of that description which I have not translated above he says that the unicorn fights "with horn, teeth, and heels". This, and what is said of the beast's great speed, suggests the wild ass; but in saying that the unicorn increases its speed as it runs he gives us a closely observed trait of the rhinoceros. Xenophon tells us that the flesh of the wild asses killed by the soldiers of Cyrus in the Arabian Desert was "like the flesh of deer, although more tender", but Ctesias, with obvious reference to the rhinoceros, says that the flesh of his unicorn is too bitter to be eaten. There is even a possibility that the colouration of the real wild ass, which is described as "reddish above" and "silvery grey" on the belly and hinder parts, may have suggested the white body and red head of the one-horned onager.

For a moment, all difficulties seem to be solved, and one is ready to believe that Ctesias or his informants confused and combined the rhinoceros with the wild ass, clapping the artificially decorated horn of the one upon the brow of the other. When this solution is closely examined, however, its plausibility vanishes, for common sense demands a reason why a known animal should have been thus violently transmogrified. Gross inaccuracy with regard to the rhinoceros is what we should expect, but the addition of a horn to a beast that Ctesias must have seen many times, and always hornless, calls for explanation. Common sense asks how it happened that the horn of the rhinoceros, so obviously on the nose that its position there gave the beast its very name, was transferred to a totally different position, so as to stand xx xx xxxxxx. What is needed, apparently, is some intermediary between the rhinoceros and the wild ass, to ease the transference of shape and characteristics from the one to the other.

A vigorous and widespread belief in a unicorn inhabiting the table-lands of Tibet—a region included within the "India" of Ctesias—can be traced in existing documents as far back as the time of Genghis Khan, and there is good reason for supposing that it is much older still. This Tibetan "unicorn", undoubtedly, is the Antbolos Hodgsoni, a large and fleet antelope the nearly straight horns of which, seen from one side, give the effect of a single horn. It is certain that the natives, who see these animals frequently, have long

DRAGONS AND UNICORNS—FACT? OR FICTION?

believed that some individuals in almost every herd—those individuals, naturally, which they have seen in profile and at a distance—are unicorns. May it be that some vague report of these antelopes helped to set the single horn of the Indian rhinoceros upon the brow of the Mesopotamian wild ass? The conjecture looks hazardous at first, and too complex, but it gathers credibility as we consider the evidence bit by bit and as we find much the same sort of thing happening elsewhere. Such a confusion, instead of being unique, might rather be called typical, and typical not of the ancient world alone but of far more recent times. Compared with the juggling of species and the transferences of animal attributes to be found in the mediaeval bestiaries, it approaches scientific exactness.

This confusion, rolling three different beasts into one, need not be attributed to Ctesias. The rumour of the unicorn came up to him over the long trails running westward from a land as strange, as replete with incredible possibilities, as America was to the Spanish conquistadors. His unicorn, like the far less probable beasts of the Arabian Nights, was pieced together by travel-weary men sitting about many a camp-fire, drowsy, uncritical, pooling all that they had seen and heard. We may believe that every contributor meant and tried to tell the exact truth—just as each of the blind men in the proverb intended to give an honest report about the elephant, the discrepancies in their results being due to the fact that one of them had hold of the animal's trunk, another grasped a tusk, and a third was pulling at the tail. Some of these scientists of the camp-fire had seen the rhinoceros, perhaps, or had talked with men who had seen him; others had handled the painted horn and had heard report of its occult virtues; still others, hearing talk about a beast with a single horn, and that a horn of magic properties, would recall the apparently unicorned animals they had seen feeding at a distance with a herd of antelopes, and they might even know that the apparently single horns of these animals were objects of veneration in Tibet and were sold to pilgrims at high prices; finally, the merchants and tax-gatherers of Persia, returning from the lands where such tales were told and trying to make clear what they had heard, might say that the beast with the precious vari-coloured horn standing in the middle of its forehead was a good deal like a wildass—a statement practically equivalent to the declaration that it was a wild-ass. For all these earnest, far-travelled, and well-intentioned men Ctesias, the court physician, acted merely as amanuensis, freshening and defining his impressions somewhat, perhaps, by means of any figures and images of the unicorn there may have been available.

Or so, at any rate, I make it out. Besides these three actual animals, towering above them all, there may have been a guiding and shaping conception of a celestial and purely symbolical unicorn of which the beast thus compounded was only a feeble earthly representative. Of that I shall have something to say in the proper place. For the present it is enough to have shown how the unicorn of Ctesias may have been constructed out of mundane materials.

The close attention we have paid to one brief passage in an unimportant book is justified by the fact that this passage is one of the two main sources from which the Western legend of the unicorn comes down to us. It was written far back in the Ages of Authority,

119

DRAGONS AND UNICORNS—FACT? OR FICTION?

during which men seldom thought of acquiring opinions of their own by independent investigation and when scholarship consisted largely in the discovery, balancing, and recording of what others had said. This habit of mind made it possible for the passage just considered to reverberate through twenty centuries.

Shortly after the time of Ctesias there arose one supreme authority, "il maestro di color che sanno", who might have given the legend of the unicorn its quietus by a single blow. The animal had a narrow escape when Aristotle passed it by with a few scant references merely sufficient to show that he believed in its existence. Why he should have believed in it at all, considering that he thought Ctesias untrustworthy, and what other evidence he may have had, we shall probably never know. He even makes a slight addition to the unicorn lore handed on by Ctesias, for he says: "We have never seen an animal with a solid hoof and with two horns, and there are only a few that have a solid hoof and one horn, as the Indian ass and the oryx. Of all animals with a solid hoof, the Indian ass alone has a talus." Aristotle, then, not only believed in the existence of a one-horned Indian ass but he thought also that the oryx has only one horn and a solid hoof. He was a man whose very errors were to be far more fruitful than most men's correct opinions.— Already there are two different species of unicorns for the echoers of authority to describe.

The unicorn has no place in the classic literature of Greece and Rome, yet during the five hundred years between Aristotle and Aelian its legend somehow made progress. Aristotle knew of only two unicorns, but Aelian and Pliny between them muster seven: the rhinoceros, the Indian ass, the oryx, the Indian ox, the Indian horse, the bison, and the unicorn proper and par excellence. Aelian's acquaintance with two or three of these, moreover, is far more extended than that shown by Aristotle or even by Ctesias, but there is no way of discovering how his increments of knowledge came to him. His book about animals, composed in a florid Greek, although he was a Roman and spent his life in Italy, exerted an influence upon later writers on zoology inferior only to that of Aristotle and of Pliny. Every phrase of his three considerable passages about the unicorn was conned and reiterated many times during the following fifteen hunched years and for this reason they deserve careful attention.

In the first of these passages Aelian adds nothing to the statement of Ctesias. In the second he says: "I have found that wild asses as large as horses are to be seen in India. The body of this animal is white, except on the head, which is red, while the eyes are azure. It has a horn on the brow, about one cubit and a half in length, which is white at the base, crimson at the top, and black between. These variegated horns, I learn, are used as drinking-cups by the Indians—although not, to be sure, by all of the people. Only the great men use them, after having them ringed about with hoops of gold exactly as they would put bracelets on some beautiful statue. And it is said that whosoever drinks from this kind of horn is safe from all incurable diseases such as convulsions and the so-called holy disease, and that he cannot be killed by poison. In the rest of the chapter Aelian speaks of the black ankle-bone, of the onager's way of fighting with horn and teeth and heels, and of its bitter flesh.

DRAGONS AND UNICORNS—FACT? OR FICTION?

The foundation of this passage, obviously, is that of Ctesias, but there are significant additions and variations. Aeian adds that the beakers are used only by the great men of India and that they are adorned with gold rings. He diverges from Ctesias in saying that the horn is about a cubit and a half in length instead of only one cubit, and also in asserting that the astragalus or ankle-bone is black. Ctesias, who affirms that he has seen this ankle-bone, declares that it is red like cinnabar. Shall we infer that Aelian had some source of information about unicorns other than the book of the court physician? He might well have increased the length of the horn without authority, as several others were to do after him, but his remark about the gold rings and about the use of the cups by great men alone is hardly of the sort that even a naturally inaccurate man like Aeian evolves from his own mind. His disagreement with Ctesias about the colour of the ankle-bone raises a curious problem. Ctesias gives us the impression that this bone was important by saying in the first place, quite wrongly, that among solid-hoofed animals only the wild ass has it, and secondly that the unicorned onager is hunted in India for the horn and the ankle-bone only. What could have given it this importance? Possibly the use of it as a charm or talisman, for we know that every part of the body of the rhinoceros was thought to have magical virtues; and it may be that the specimen seen by Ctesias had been painted or dyed so as to make it both an ornament and an amulet. The common use of these ankle-bones in the ancient world, however, was for the making of dice, as one is reminded by the Latin word talus, which means both "an astragalus" and "a die". There is a bare possibility that Aeian was thinking of the black dice of Italy.

The third passage in Aelian about the unicorn is the most important. "They say", he writes, "that there are mountains in the interior regions of India which are inaccessible to men and therefore full of wild beasts. Among these is the unicorn, which they call the 'cartazon'. This animal is as large as a full-grown horse, and it has a mane, tawny hair, feet like those of the elephant, and the tail of a goat. It is exceedingly swift of foot. Between its brows there stands a single black horn, not smooth but with certain natural rings, and tapering to a very sharp point. Of all animals, this one has the most dissonant voice. With beasts of other species that approach it the 'cartazon' is gentle, but it fights with those of its own kind, and not only do the males fight naturally among themselves but they contend even against the females and push the contest to the death. The animal has great strength of body, and it is armed besides with an unconquerable horn. It seeks out the most deserted places and wanders there alone. In the season of rut it grows gentle towards the chosen female and they pasture side by side, but when this time is over he becomes wild again and wanders alone. They say that the young ones are sometimes taken to the king to be exhibited in contests on days of festival, because of their strength, but no one remembers the capture of a single specimen of mature age."

In this passage we part company with Ctesias. Aelian is here describing the rhinoceros and getting much closer to the real animal than Ctesias did, even giving it a name, "cartazon," which is apparently connected with the Sanscrit kartayan, lord of the desert. His account is correct with regard to the beast's habitat, size, feet, tail, voice, strength, and solitary habits, although he is wrong in what he says of its mane, its tawny hair, its

121

DRAGONS AND UNICORNS—FACT? OR FICTION?

pugnacity, and its great swiftness. These errors are of little importance, however, in comparison with his assertion that the horn stands between the brows. This horn is black, and it is not smooth but has certain natural rings. It is about a cubit and a half, that is to say about twentyseven inches, in length. Almost certainly, this is the horn of an antelope. The suggestion made above that the Ctesian unicorn owes something to the antelope is corroborated by Aelian's independent and unconscious recourse to the same animal.

The most influential of Aelian's remarks about the unicorn were those concerning its indomitability, its solitude, its habit of fighting with others of its own species except with females during the season of rut, and the custom of taking such specimens as were captured when young to the king, who exhibited them on public holidays.

By this last touch one is inevitably reminded again of the rhinoceros, which Aelian, as a Roman of the third century A.D., must have seen frequently at the Circus. He had not the slightest suspicion, however, that his "cartazon" of India and the well-known rhinoceros were identical. The one, as he tells us here, has a horn between the eyebrows; in XVII, 40, he discusses the other briefly, saying that it, would be ridiculous for him to describe its appearance, because it is familiar to all Greeks and Romans; but he does say that it has a horn on its nose. Thus we see that he describes the rhinoceros, rather accurately in most respects, without knowing that he is doing so, and that in another place he refuses to describe the rhinoceros because it is too familiar. The strange confusion had strange results, lasting on into the nineteenth century. One of the more amusing phases of it is the fact that when Aeian is speaking of the wild ass he makes much of the magical properties of its horn, but when he comes to speak of the "cartazon," or rhinoceros, to which alone those properties were originally attributed, he has not a word to say of them.

Among the several passages in which the elder Pliny mentions unicorned animals, the only one of present importance is that in which he says: "The Orsan Indians hunt an exceedingly wild beast called the monoceros, which has a stag's head, elephant's feet, and a boar's tail, the rest of its body being like that of a horse. It makes a deep lowing noise, and one black horn two cubits long projects from the middle of its forehead. This animal, they say, cannot be taken alive."

Here, one observes, is a sober account written by a serious-minded man. We may be sure that Pliny had read stories of the horn's prophylactic powers because Pliny read everything, but he does not speak of them, contenting himself with adding another half-cubit to the horn's length and then passing on to other matters. His brief reference to the unicorn is important chiefly because for more than a thousand years his beliefs about animals were the beliefs of almost every reader of Latin in Europe. If he had enlarged, like his Greek authorities, upon the horn's medical values, the western legend of the unicorn, with a full millennium added for the development of its more interesting elements, would have attained an even richer and stranger complexity than it did. Pliny might have transplanted the fascinating Oriental idea of the horn's prophylactic virtues into the hotbeds of western folklore and magic, where it would have flourished mightily, but, having to do without his assistance, that idea came into the popular legend of the West only a few centuries before the awakening science of Europe was ready to cope with it.

The docility with which later writers accepted the opinions of Pliny was shown almost at once by Julius Solinus, whose description of the unicorn has a sonority that makes it worthy of direct quotation: "Atrocissimum est Monoceros, monstrum mugitu horrendo, equino corpore, elphanti pedibus, cauda suilla, cepite cervino, cornu ? media fronte protenditur splendore mirifico ad longitudinem pedum quatuor, ita tamen, ut quidquid impetat, facile ictu ejus perforetur. Vivus non venit in hominum potestatem, et interimi quidem potest, capi non potest." Whatever rhetoric can do to make the unicorn impressive Solinus has done. In this passage not even Arthur Golding can improve upon his original, for he translates: "But the cruellest is the Unicorne, a Monster that belloweth horriblie, bodyed like a horse, footed like an Eliphant, tayled like a Swyne, and headed like a Stagge. His home sticketh out of the midds of hys forehead, of a wonderful brightness about foure foote long, so sharp, that whatsoever he pusheth at, he striketh it through easily. He is never caught alive; kylled he may be, but taken he cannot bee."

We observe, to be sure, that Solinus has added another foot to the length of the horn and that he calls the monoceros a "monster"—an epithet vehemently exclaimed against by the pious of later ages, who considered it both sacrilegious and bad zoology to call any beast monstrous that was mentioned in the Bible. Otherwise, there is nothing new in Solinus, and nothing not to be found in Pliny except the vivid touch of colour on the horn which, as we have seen, may come from the indelible dyes of Upper India.

One really learned and thoughtful man of the ancient world seems to have been confronted with the rhinoceros and with the Indian superstition concerning it at the same time. This was the enigmatic seer, traveller, and rhetorician Apollonius of Tyana, whose life and sayings, as they have come down to us, form the strangest tissue of idle nonsense and lofty wisdom. During his travels in India, says his biographer, Apollonius saw the wild asses that were captured near the Hyphasis and was told that cups made from their horns-single horns, which grew from the brow—were used by the kings of India in the belief that those who drank from them were free for that day from sickness and poison. When Damis, one of the philosopher's companions, asked what he thought of this story, he said: "I should have believed it if I had found that the kings of this country were immortal." these words the man who has usually been regarded as a mystagogue and a liar, partly because of the attacks of his Christian enemies, takes high rank among the commentators upon the unicorn. He is the first man of whom it is asserted—he does not make the assertion himself—that he actually saw the unicorn, but even this was not sufficient to induce a perfect faith.

Only two further references to the unicorn in ancient literature are worthy of attention. In his long poem on the art of hunting Oppian speaks of certain Aonian (Boeotian) oxen as having solid hoofs and one heavy horn protruding from the middle of the brow. Of these we can only say that if they really did inhabit Boeotia in his time it is strange that

DRAGONS AND UNICORNS—FACT? OR FICTION?

we hear nothing of them from Aristotle or Pausanias or even Plutarch, who would scarcely have left such remarkable denizens of his district unheralded. We suspect that Oppian erred about the habitat and even the species of these bulls when we read that their horns are coloured white and black and red, for we seem to remember having heard of this colouration elsewhere.

The other reference occurs in the writings of a man often regarded as the greatest figure of the ancient world. Julius Caesar tells us that in his time there was to be found in the Hercynian Forest—where wonders have always abounded—a huge beast with the form of a stag, from the middle of whose brow and between the ears there stood forth one horn, longer and straighter than the horns known to the Romans. The words are impressive by their precision and directness, and they convince us at least of this, that one of the keenest minds recorded in history believed in the unicorn.

And yet it is clear that the unicorn legend did not really flourish in the ancient Western world. It lived merely from book to book, a literary life, taking no hold and showing no vitality in the popular imagination. It found no place in creative literature or in plastic art; religious symbolism and mythology knew nothing of it; if it ever appeared in the ancient folklore of the Mediterranean it seems to have left no trace; Galen, Hippocrates, Dioscorides even, never mention the prophylactic and therapeutic values of the horn. A thousand such merely literary references as those we have considered, most of them borrowed and reflecting a belief which had vitality only in a distant land, would never, unless by lucky chance, have given the unicorn an important position in true legend. To gain such standing, together with the complexity and strangeness and human significance that would accrue, it had to be brought closer home to the erring, dreamful, devoted hearts of men than the books of the most learned zoologists and the most honey-tongued rhetoricians could ever bring it. The legend had to be helped out of the library into the world.

Such assistance was close at hand.

DRAGONS AND UNICORNS—FACT? OR FICTION?

CHAPTER II

THE HOLY HUNT

IN the King James Version of the Bible there are seven clear references to the unicorn, all of which occur in the Old Testament. The animal is mentioned twice in the Pentateuch, once in job, once in Isaiah, and three times in the Psalms. These passages read as follows:-

"God brought them out of Egypt; he hath as it were the strength of the unicorn."-Numbers xxiii. 22.

"His glory is like the firstling of his bullock, and his horns are like the horns of unicorns: with them he shall push the people together to the ends of the earth."—Deuteronomy

xxxiii. 17. "Save me from the lion's mouth; for thou hast heard me from the horns of unicorns."-Psalm xxii. 21. "He maketh them [the cedars of Lebanon] also to skip like a calf; Lebanon and Sirion like a young unicorn."—Psalm xxix. 6. "But my horn shalt thou exalt like the horn of the unicorn: I shall be anointed with fresh oil."—Psalm xcii. 10. "And the unicorns shall come down with them, and the bullocks with their bulls; and their land shall be soaked with blood, and their dust made fat with fatness."—Isaiah xxxiv.

7. "Will the unicorn be willing to serve thee, or abide in thy crib? "Canst thou bind the unicorn with his band in the furrow? or will he harrow the valleys after thee?

"Wilt thou trust him because his strength is great? or wilt thou leave thy labour to him?

"Wilt thou believe him, that he will bring home thy seed, and gather it into thy barn?"

125

DRAGONS AND UNICORNS—FACT? OR FICTION?

-Job xxxix. 9-12.

One thing is evident in these passages: they refer to some actual animal of which the several writers had vivid if not clear impressions. Although the allusions were made at widely different times, the characterization is consistent, bringing before us a beast remarkable for strength, ferocity, wildness, and unconquerable spirit. Nothing suggests that it was supernatural, a creature of fancy, for it is linked with the lion, the bullock and the calf; yet it was mysterious enough to inspire a sense of awe, and powerful enough to provide a vigorous metaphor.

Much patient toil has been expended in the effort to identify the Biblical unicorn. At the outset of such an inquiry one finds that we owe the word "unicorn" in the King James Version 2 to the xxxxxx everywhere used by the Septuagint to translate the Hebrew Re'em, a bit of translation, interesting in itself, which had enduring results. So far as the western development of the unicorn legend is concerned, this translation is like the main jewel of a watch, holding the intricate structure together. One does not like to see it set down, therefore, as a mere blunder, and when we think of the problem with only such light as the Seventy had we are inclined to call it a minor stroke of genius. They did not know what animal the Hebrew seers and poets had in mind when speaking of the Re'em, but they found that it was characterized as fleet, fierce, indomitable, and especially distinguished by the armour of its brow. Dim recollections were awakened by these traits, and so the Seventy called the one unknown animal by the name of another. Even from our point of vantage it seems doubtful whether they could have found a closer equivalent for a beast which had been mysterious and awful to the Hebrews than this monoceros or unicorn which was to themselves still strange, remote, and conjectural.

Apart from such appropriateness, we discover another value of a different kind in this translation. For the greater part of their course, and until the scholarship of the late Renaissance brought them together, what may be called the Hellenic and the Hebraic branches of the unicorn legend ran separately, with a cleanness of division that would have satisfied Matthew Arnold himself. This one word xxxxxxxx, however, with its already accumulated overtones, was a connecting channel between the two, more important in fact than in appearance. For a long time it maintained belief in the Greek tradition by seeming to imply that whatever Ctesias and his successors had said about the unicorn had the sanction of divine authority. The Septuagint translation of Re'em by xxxxxxxxxx, a translation which meant hardly more than that X = X, was accepted, as the inspired word of God. Ctesias, Aelian, Pliny, and Solinus seemed to be corroborated by Jehovah.

In several passages of the Vulgate the Re'em becomes a rhinoceros, losing as much in imaginative value as it gains in clarity of outline. We are hardly to suppose, however, that Jerome derived this translation directly from the Hebrew text in complete independence of the Septuagint version; it is more likely that he, like St. Ambrose, held the xxxxxxx of the Greeks to be identical with the rhinoceros—a view in which he was to have many followers and as many ardent antagonists. His word amounts, therefore, to an interpretation of the Septuagint's word, and one feels that it is less good largely because it is more precise. How often Jerome may have attended the Circus during those unregenerate days in Rome which he so bitterly repented we cannot be sure, but if he went at all he probably saw there the animal that he later identified with the Biblical Re'em. In superficial appearance it would seem to correspond closely enough.

An attempt to trace the devious and learned arguments by which Biblical scholars have tried to establish the identity of the Re'em would lead us too far afield, considering that there is no reason to believe that the Hebrews themselves thought of this animal as onehorned. None of the passages cited above forces such an interpretation, and only one of them, that from the ninety-second Psalm, even suggests it. Elsewhere, as in Deuteronomy xxxiii. 17 and Psalms xxii. 21, the word for "horns" is used in the plural while "Re'em" is singular. Clearly, therefore, this deep and dark little pocket of erudition need not be explored at present, and we may be content with seeing what has been brought out of it.

After the general abandonment of belief in the unicorn during the eighteenth century there was a return to Jerome's view that the Re'em was the rhinoceros; but as this animal became better known it was felt that he was not fierce and swift enough, and there was doubt whether the Hebrews were likely to have known him. Another view attributed the whole belief in the Re'em to the bas-reliefs of huge mythological beasts seen by the Jews in Egypt and Mesopotamia. Under the leadership of Samuel Bochart, the profoundest scholar who has ever waded these deep waters, a considerable company once contended for the oryx, pointing out that the Arabic name of this animal is still rim; but the value of this discovery was soon destroyed by the announcement of another school that rimu was the Assyrian name of the gigantic aurochs or Bos Primigenius, a species of wild buffalo which became extinct in the sixteenth century. Cuvier, basing his measurement upon remains of the aurochs much smaller than others since discovered, estimated that this animal was twelve feet long and almost seven feet high; its teeth have been found in a cave on Mount Lebanon; Julius Caesar describes it as indigenous to his prolific Hercynian Forest, and in terms fitting all that is said in the Bible about the Re'em; Layard identified the animal with the majestic sculptured bulls of Nineveh. The Bos Primigenius now holds the field. Its bulk, speed, and savage ferocity are described by Caesar in words that make it clear why the Hebrews always spoke of the Re'em with bated breath. So much, then, for the source of the Septuagint xxxxxx—a word inspired by Apollo if not by Jehovah—and therefore of the Biblical unicorn. One is glad to have found the Re'em worthy of his descendant.

Although it seems clear that the writers of the Old Testament did not think of the Re'em as one-horned, there is a possibility that the Talmudic writers did come to consider it so. Any horned animal remembered chiefly by its representations in the sculptures of Egypt, Babylon, Nineveh, and Persepolis, was likely, as we shall see, to be regarded sooner or later as a unicorn, and there came a time when Hebrew writers, with no native sculpture to guide them, were dependent upon just such representations. The Talmudic interpreters, it is certain, had never seen the Re'em, for they exaggerate its size "out of all reason-

DRAGONS AND UNICORNS—FACT? OR FICTION?

able compass", asserting in one passage that it is so tall as to touch the clouds and in another that it was too large to be got into the ark and so had to be towed along behind by a cord tied to its horn. Obviously, the Re'em is here seen fading into myth, and so it may have been the original of the wonderful ox three times mentioned in the Talmud as the victim of Adam's first sacrifice—an ox with the interesting peculiarity that it had only one horn on its brow.

The unicorn legend gained valuable and lasting corroboration from the brilliant error of the Septuagint, but this alone would not have won for it anything like its later prestige; another influence was required to carry the unicorn into the centre of Christian myth and symbolism. Fully to understand the second influence that was brought into play we should need to know more than we do about that agglomeration of vice and virtue, wealth and poverty, ignorance and erudition, wisdom and folly, which we call Alexandria. In that city, during the third century after Christ and under Christian influence, there were brought together a number of animal stories, some of them drawn from the wide-spread "Beast Epic" of the world and others apparently concocted to serve the immediate need, each of them fitted with a "moral" somewhat after the fashion of Aesop's Fables. It seems unnecessary to assume that any single individual was responsible for the collection as a whole or that a single original text ever existed.

Readers of Tertullian, Cassiodorus, and even Origen, will not need to be told that the habit of allegorizing not merely everything in the Scriptures but everything outside of them was at this time fastening upon the Christian mind. The world of nature, seldom valued for its own sake by the typical Christian, was more and more regarded as a mere storehouse of edifying metaphors. What we should call facts were felt to be of little worth in comparison with the moral truths that alleged facts could be supposed to signify and it was considered that God had created the lower animals, particularly those that seemed to have no other use, solely for the moral and spiritual instruction of mankind. Very little of Aristotle's objective spirit and method was carried over into the Christian thought centring at Alexandria, disabled as that was from the start by a puerile moral-hunting and phrase-making, by the determination to make facts bend to the uses of edification and to see, almost literally, books in the running brooks, sermons in stones, and good—or, what was considered the same thing, moral significance—in everything.

These were some of the conditions surrounding the haphazard selection, fabrication, and welding together of the stories composing the Christian Beast Epic. In the primitive forms of that body of fable, apparently, each article began with a quotation from Scripture followed by the formula: "But the physiologus [i.e. the naturalist] says . . . " and then came a description of the major traits, real or fancied, of some animal, capped by the moral deduction, the lesson to be learned therefrom. Later copyists seem to have separated the animal descriptions and the morals from the texts they were intended to illustrate, so that each article began with the words: "The Physiologus says." Thus the whole collection, naturally regarded as the work of one author called Physiologus, came to be called by that supposed author's name. In later centuries it was called, in Europe, the "Bestiary".

DRAGONS AND UNICORNS—FACT? OR FICTION?

What sort of thing we may expect from this treasury of animal lore is indicated by its account of the ant-lion: "Physiologus says that the ant-lion's father has the shape of a lion and his mother that of an ant. His father feeds on flesh and his mother on herbs. These two bring forth the ant-lion, which is a mixture of both, for his fore part is that of a lion and his hind part that of an ant. Being thus composed, he can eat neither flesh like his father nor herbs like his mother, and so he starves to death."

Official Christianity did what it could to repudiate this collection, for a synod of Pope Gelasius in 496 condemned it as the work of "heretics", although it had been falsely ascribed to Saint Ambrose. In spite of this and other attacks it remained familiar and influential throughout Christendom for over a thousand years, and there are extant texts in Greek, Arabic, Syriac, Latin, Armenian, Old High German, Icelandic, Old French, Provençal, Ethiopic, Italian, and Anglo-Saxon. It was chiefly by means of these Bestiaries that the popular as distinguished from the learned tradition of the unicorn was disseminated. Not Ctesias and not Aelian but this grist of old wives' tales fathered upon an imaginary "Physiologus" was responsible for scattering the image of the unicorn throughout Europe, making him familiar where books were never read, contorting his shapely limbs on corbels and cornices and miserere seats, depicting him in stained glass and on tapestry, lifting him finally to the British Royal Coat of Arms.

Existing texts of the Physiolous vary considerably in minor details, but this is the substance of what they have to relate about the unicorn: He is a small animal, like a kid, but surprisingly fierce for his size, with one very sharp horn on his head, and no hunter is able to catch him by force. Yet there is a trick by which he is taken. Men lead a virgin to the place where he most resorts and leave her there alone. As soon as he sees this virgin he runs and lays his head in her lap. She fondles him and he falls asleep. The hunters then approach and capture him and lead him to the palace of the king.

One may have known this story for years and may have seen it represented a hundred times in Christian art, yet if he has any gift for stubborn wonder he will be surprised at each return by its strangeness, and curious to know by what queer twist of thought or accident of transmission it has taken on its present form. For this tale, absurd though it may be, is not childishly and feebly absurd like that of the ant-lion; there is a suggestion of age about it and a hint of symbolism not wholly due to the fact that it has served for centuries as a Christian symbol. What affinity did the makers of the tale imagine between the unicorn and the virgin? Why should this animal be thought worth so elaborate a ruse? Why is he led "to the palace of the king"? These questions have puzzled a good many acute and learned minds, and they have never been answered.

But these questions arise out of the Physiologus story by itself, without reference to the fact that another unicorn legend was already current in the Mediterranean world. The moment we recall that fact, another set of questions comes into view. What strands of connection can be discerned between the two legends? Instead of the proud beast of Ctesias and Aelian—fierce, shaped like an ass or horse, solid-hoofed, dangerous, indomitable—we have here an animal so small that it is likened to a kid, with a divided

129

DRAGONS AND UNICORNS—FACT? OR FICTION?

hoof and a beard as seen in later Christian art, and chiefly characterized by a propensity to fall asleep in virgins' laps. The only discernible likenesses are that in both legends the animal is said to be fierce and not to be taken by the ordinary arts of the hunter, and that the quarry in both belongs to the king; but these similarities are so slight as to seem hardly worth mentioning. Apparently we must conclude that the unicorn legend has had two independent origins, or, in stronger terms, that there are two legends of the unicorn, one of which we may call the Ctesian and the other that of Physiologus.

With this not very satisfactory conclusion in mind we may leave, for the present, the larger question of inter-relationship, turning back to the Physiologus account for a closer examination. Some light may be thrown upon that account by the allegorical interpretation that usually follows, though in varying forms, the story itself. In its simpler versions this interpretation likens the unicorn directly to Christ: its one horn is said to signify the unity of Christ and the Father; its fierceness and defiance of the hunter are to remind us that neither Principalities nor Powers nor Thrones were able to control the Messiah against His will; its small stature is a symbol of Christ's humility and its likeness to a kid of His association with sinful men. The virgin is held to represent the Virgin Mary and the huntsman is the Holy Spirit acting through the Angel Gabriel. Taken as a whole, then, the story of the unicorn's capture typifies the Incarnation of Christ.

Thus we see the unicorn caught up into the fervours and ecstasies of Christian symbolism and into the very worship of the Virgin. There could be no limit, once this had happened, to the glory of his career. For this reason one is all the more eager to discover, if possible, the origin of the remarkable story upon which the symbolism is based.

The widest variations from the typical unicorn story to be found in what may be called, with caution, the primitive texts of Physiologus, are those to be seen in the Syriac and Provençal versions. In the Provençal Bestiary, composed under Waldensian influences, the "properties" of many of the beasts are changed, and the unicorn is made to represent the Devil, the signification of the virgin-capture being that evil can be overcome only by virtue. The Syriac version is so interesting as to deserve quotation:-

"There is an animal called dajja, extremely gentle, which the hunters are unable to capture because of its great strength. It has in the middle of its brow a single horn. But observe the ruse by which the huntsmen take it. They lead forth a young virgin, pure and chaste, to whom, when the animal sees her, he approaches, throwing himself upon her. Then the girl offers him her breasts, and the animal begins to suck the breasts of the maiden and to conduct himself familiarly with her. Then the girl, while sitting quietly, reaches forth her hand and grasps the horn on the animal's brow, and at this point the huntsmen come up and take the beast and go away with him to the king.—Likewise the Lord Christ has raised up for us a horn of salvation in the midst of Jerusalem, in the house of God, by the intercession of the Mother of God, a virgin pure, chaste, full of mercy, immaculate, inviolate."

Little assistance in one's search for the origin of the virgin-capture story would seem to be obtainable from this wild tale, which looks like confusion worse confounded, but at least it precludes all possibility that that story was invented ad hoe by Christian allegorizers. One is convinced of this partly by the fact that the signifiatio does not here fit the story as told but is forced upon it in accordance with a custom known to be followed elsewhere. More conclusive is the emphasis upon sexual attraction as the source of the power exercised by the "virgin" over the unicorn. If the virgin-capture story had been deliberately composed as a symbol of Christ's incarnation—such a supposition implying, of course, that the virgin was always and from the start understood to represent the Virgin Mary—it would scarcely have been corrupted by Christians in just this way. In this version the Christian interpretation is forced upon a tale not fully prepared to receive it; old and incongruous elements—or so one might say if disposed to beg the question—have not been deleted here as they have in the other versions. The Syriac version seems to represent an idea about the right method of capturing unicorns which is older than Physiologus; it suggests a possibility that the origin of the virgin-capture story, if it can be found, will turn out to be non-Christian and will rest more heavily, or at least more obviously, upon sexual attraction than the Christianized form of the story usually does.

This element was not entirely ignored in later Christian writing about the unicorn. Hildegarde of Bingen and Thomas of Cantipré, among others, enlarge upon the animal's skill in detecting a virgin at sight, and in some stories we are told that when the huntress is not really a virgin she is killed by the beast—a fairly obvious intrusion of the virginity-test theme. Furthermore, it was held by some that the hunt was more likely to succeed if the virgin was naked, and several insist that she must be beautiful. Alanus de Insulis, who flourished at the end of the twelfth century, gives a curious explanation of the story in which the sexual interpretation is made in terms of mediaeval science. He concludes that the virgin's power is due to a radical difference in "humours", the calidissima natura of the unicorn being drawn irresistibly to its opposite, the femina frigida et humida. The unicorn, he says, has an excess of fervent spirits or humours which dilate his heart, and when he comes into the pure moist air surrounding the virgin he feels such relief and is so delighted by that feminine atmosphere that he lies down in her lap. In several early versions, moreover, and notably in the Ethiopic Bestiary, the virgin is not wholly passive but adds certain calculated blandishments to the natural attraction of her charms.

The connotations of the virgin-capture story are in fact definitely erotic, and the Christian interpretation put upon it does not harmonize with the tale exactly but seems to wrench it out of its natural course of development. In saying that the interpretation does not harmonize I refer to the difficulty of imagining the Virgin Mary as lending herself to a deliberate deception of her Son, the omniscient God. In saying that the story seems to have been wrenched out of its natural course I am thinking of what would probably have been done with it elsewhere. The Greeks, if they had been at all interested in animal allegories, might have made it a symbol of the overmastering power of erotic emotion, leading to the ruin of a strong, proud nature; the Hebrew poets might have used it somewhat as they did the great legend of Samson which it so curiously and perhaps significantly resembles—although Delilah is not a good surrogate for the virgin; but in Christian legend

DRAGONS AND UNICORNS—FACT? OR FICTION?

the story's original intention has been thwarted, I believe, to serve the purposes of edification. The attempt to point out what that original intention was, and so to solve, in some sense, the long-standing mystery of the virgin-capture story, may be postponed until we have followed the development of the story during the Christian ages.

Probably the earliest narration of the tale in literature outside of the Physiologus itself is that in the Commentary on Saint Basil's Hexaemeron, long attributed to Saint Eustathius of Antioch, who died about A.D. 330. This curious work weaves about Basil's poetic account of creation a tissue of popular legend which makes it good hunting-ground for the student of folklore. In most of its discussions of animals it drags a wide net through the sea of Levantine superstition, but the unicorn passage follows Physiologus in every detail, its only importance for our purpose consisting in the fact that here we see the virgin-capture story moving out into literature under its own sail, without assistance from allegory.

The next mention of the tale was far more influential, for it occurred in a work that was read, copied, imitated, and learned almost by heart for centuries, a work used as quarry and foundation by most of the "encyclopaedists" of the Middle Ages—writers who tried, not so unsuccessfully as might be supposed, to compress all human knowledge within a single book. Isidore of Seville, who died in 636, was one of the men who have exerted an influence upon human thought out of all proportion to their powers chiefly because of their strategic positions in time or place. Played upon by many forces, which he is incapable of criticizing or relating, his tendency is to shovel together rather helplessly all that he has read and heard. This tendency is evident in his important account of the unicorn, which I give myself the pleasure of quoting in John of Trevisa's English:-

"Rynoceron in grewe [i.e. in Greek] is to meanynge an Home in the nose. & Monoceros is an Unycorne: and is a ryght cruell beast. And hath that name for he hath in the mydull of the forehed an home of foure fote long. And that home is so sharpe & so stronge that he throwyth downe al or thyrleth al that he resyth on . . . . And this beest fyghtyth ofte wyth the Elyphaunt and woundyth & stycketh hym in the wombe, and throwyth hym downe to the grounde: And the Unycorn is so stronge that he is not take with myghte of hunters. But men that wryte of kynde of thinges meane that a mayde is sette there he shall come: And she openyth her lappe and the Unycorne layeth theron his heed, and levyth all his fyerinesse & slepyth in that wyse: And is taken as a beest wythout wepen & slayne wyth dartys of hunters."

It is sometimes said that Isidore took the unicorn to be the rhinoceros, but this statement is due to a careless reading of his two first sentences; the fact is that he confused the two animals, which is a quite different thing, as we have seen in considering the third passage from Aelian. In what is said of the unicorn's fight with the elephant and of the great strength of its horn he is dependent upon one or more of the several accounts of the rhinoceros to be found in late classical writers, and especially in Pliny. Unlike Aelian, he had probably never seen a rhinoceros; he had no means of knowing that this animal supplied most of the details of his description of the unicorn, and so he is not entirely responsible for the ridiculous picture he gives us of a rhinoceros slumbering in the lap of a virgin. That picture, in all its gay absurdity, we owe to his mingling of two diverse traditions.

Isidore's account of the unicorn is important, as I have said, because of its influence on later writers, and it was copied, usually with slavish exactness, by most of his successors in the long line of mediaeval encyclopaedists. His passage, indeed, may almost be said to have established a third tradition in which what I have called the Hellenic and Hebraic branches come together; one not confined to the learned like that emanating from Ctesias, nor yet to the ignorant like that of Physiologus, but familiar to the many persons, mostly monks, who could read Latin but had little power of discrimination in what they read. A few of the encyclopaedists, such as Vincent of Beauvais, showed greater independence, but in general it may be said that Isidore determined middle-class opinion about the unicorn, giving the animal an authenticity it could not have won from Physiologus and a vogue it would not have gained from Ctesias, Aelian, or even Pliny.

Intimately associated by the Bestiaries with the central mystery of the Christian faith, and corroborated by a document which even the semi-learned regarded as authoritative, the unicorn was at length firmly fixed in the popular imagination of Europe. The fact that no one ever saw a unicorn did not disturb belief in the slightest degree. No one in mediaeval Europe ever saw a lion or an elephant or a panther, yet these beasts were accepted without question upon evidence in no way better or worse than that which vouched for the unicorn. The stories everywhere told and believed about these three actual animals were not at all less marvellous than those that recommended the unicorn to popular attention; all were upon exactly the same footing so far as credibility was concerned, and side by side with them stood the griffin, the dragon, the amphisboena-a snake with a head at either end—the basilisk, the salamander that lives in fire, and a score of other beasts similarly spawned in the fertile fancy of man and swept together out of all past time. By virtue of his beauty and beneficence, but chiefly because he had the holiest associations, the unicorn was probably the most important of these, yet he was only primus inter pares. He was not regarded as in any sense or degree a mythical, legendary, or supernatural animal—any more than the horse or cat or cow, the hydra or kraken or were-wolf was so regarded; neither was he thought of as a symbol in any degree in which any other animal might not be symbolic. The peculiarity or weakness, call it which one will, which made him so susceptible to the wiles of virgins was merely his "property" or "natura", his idiosyncrasy, exactly analagous to the "property" attributed by mediaeval science to every other creature.

And yet it is probably true that the unicorn attracted more attention during the Middle Ages than any other single beast except the ass. He is the only imaginary animal of Physiologus that passed over into the Renaissance and the most important figure in those menageries of the fancy, gathered for the most part out of Physiologus, that began to swarm in the Cathedrals of Europe during the thirteenth century. From the time of Isidore to the present day he has been more significant to the imagination, and more prominent therefore in literature and art, than any other beast that man has made more or less "in

DRAGONS AND UNICORNS—FACT? OR FICTION?

his own image".

Anything like a full presentation of the literature devoted to the virgin-capture story would involve an intolerable amount of repetition, for all this writing was done when it was still sound doctrine that

Who-so shal telle a tale after a man,

He moot reherce, as ny as evere he can,

Everich a word.

To take a few examples: the versified Bestiary of Philippe de Thaun tells the tale rather feebly in perfect accord with Isidore and develops the allegory at considerable length; that of William, Clerk of Normandy, carries the significatio to great length and complexity; and Richard de Fournival in his Bestiaire d'Amour manages to inject some novelty into the theme by using it as a symbol of the courtly instead of the celestial love—an audacious thing to have attempted in the middle of the thirteenth century. Richard's poem is a protracted wooing in terms of animal symbolisms, and the lady, quite as learned in the lore of beasts as the lover himself, replies in kind. The lover says in the unicorn passage: "I have been drawn to you by your sweet odour alone, as the unicorn falls asleep under the influence of a maiden's fragrance. For this is the nature of the unicorn, that no other beast is so hard to capture, and he has one horn on his nose which no armour can withstand, so that no one dares to go forth against him except a virgin girl. And as soon as he is made aware of her presence by the scent of her, he kneels humbly before her and humiliates himself as though to signify that he would serve her. Therefore wise huntsmen who know his nature set a virgin in his way; he falls asleep in her lap; and while he sleeps the hunters, who would not dare to approach him when awake, come up and kill him. Even so has Love dealt cruelly with me; for I have been the proudest man alive with regard to love, and I have thought never to see the woman whom I should care to possess . . . . But Love, the skilful huntsman, has set in my path a maiden in the odour of whose sweetness I have fallen asleep, and I die the death to which I was doomed."

In this charming passage one sees that Isidore's confusion of the rhinoceros and the unicorn has done its work: the horn of Richard de Fournival's unicorn is en la narine. Rudolf von Ems places the horn on the brow—

Emmiten an der stirnin sin

hat er ein horn reht als ein glas,

vier fuze lanc, als ich ez las-

but in other details he depicts the rhinoceros. Thus it happens again and again, as though by a fatality, that the unicorn slips back, as it were, into the rhinoceros; and even

DRAGONS AND UNICORNS—FACT? OR FICTION?

the virgin-capture story, violently incongruous as it is with that huge and ugly beast, is often involved in the confusion. It was not that these writers thought the two animals identical, for most of them were almost passionately convinced that the two were different; but no sooner have they finished insisting upon the differences than they describe the one in terms that apply only to the other. Thus the nose-horned beast of India, lumpish and gross and mud-wallowing, looms always just behind the delicate unicorn, related to it as fact to dream, as actuality to the ideal, as Sancho Panza to Don Quixote.

Rudolf von Ems makes as clear a statement as any one of the belief that the ruse of the hunters can succeed only when the girl chosen for the decoy is really a virgin. If she is not, the unicorn shows great anger and runs her through with his horn to punish her deceit. A similar power of distinguishing at sight between the true and the pretended virgin is attributed in folklore to several other animals such as the stag and elephant and lion, and among the many "virginity-tests", all supposed to be unerring, one of the simplest was that of setting the woman in the way of one of these beasts: if she was killed, then she deserved her death; if she lived, overcoming the animal's natural ferocity, it could be only through chastity's magic power. Such ideas, so pervasive and enduring as to have had echoes even in Milton's Comus, were widely current during the centuries when the virgin-capture story was growing, and it would have been strange if they had not found expression there; but one cannot believe that they had a shaping, not to say an originating, influence upon that story. Suggestions of the virginity test are rare in unicorn literature, and they are late; any argument based upon them would be strongly countered by the frequently seductive conduct of the woman herself. In the Syriac Bestiary, as we have seen, the decoy is so obviously not a virgin that no unicorn with the slightest discernment in such matters should have been deceived by her, and we learn, also, from a Greek grammarian of the twelfth century, that the animal can be taken as well by a young man dressed in a maiden's garments as by the maiden herself.

The feminine garments of this youth, we are told, must be heavily perfumed, and this reminds one that in fully half of the virgin-capture narratives in which any explanation is vouchsafed of the virgin's powers of fascination she is said to attract her victim by what may be called the odour of chastity—a scent which could be purchased, apparently, like feminine beauty in our own time, of any good chemist. This idea appears subordinately in the elaborate explanation already cited from Alanus de Insulis. John of San Geminiano says that the unicorn, while stepping along through the forest, "smells the odour of a virgin". Philippe de Thaun remarks that the animal is attracted by the odour of the maiden's breast. Richard de Fournival makes his unicorn aware of the maiden "au flair". The list is a long one, extending from Albertus Magnus, who ascribes the whole phenomenon to the unicorn's keen sense of smell—and here again one is reminded of the rhinoceros—to a learned pharmacist of the seventeenth century, Laurens Catelan who decides, after deep thought and expenditure of much erudition, that the maiden can attract her prey only by the odour which is peculiar to virgins.

Laurens Catelan, however, had not the strange mediaeval belief—a belief which endures to-day in some districts—in the attractive and holding power of the eye. The Ab-

DRAGONS AND UNICORNS—FACT? OR FICTION?

bess Hildegarde of Bingen felt quite at home in mysteries such as this, and her explanation is therefore more confident than most. She believes that several virgins wandering together in a wood are much more attractive to unicorns than a single virgin can be. (Considering that almost all other authorities say that the virgin must be left alone, some even asserting that she must be naked and bound to a tree, is it permissible to suggest that the Abbess may have been led to take this view by her responsibilities as head of a houseful of nuns?) Hildegarde makes it clear that these virgins should be no mere rustics but well born, and neither too old nor too young. When the unicorn sees a bevy of such damsels wandering about, gathering flowers or engaged in some other such maidenly pursuit, he stops at once in his tracks and eyes them; they eye him; then he advances very slowly, crouches on his hind legs and looks at them for a long time from a distance. He is surprised at the fact that although they have in general the appearance of human beings yet they have no beards; he loves them because he sees, forsooth, that they are gentle and kind; and while he is gazing at them, all his wild and innocent heart drawn forth in adoration, the hunters steal up behind and slay him and cut off his horn.

Hildegarde's naive remark that the unicorn loves the maidens because they are gentle and kind, so charmingly oblivious of the purpose of those maidens, recalls the fact that not once in all the hundreds of references to the virgin-capture story is there dropped the slightest hint that this device of venery is somewhat lacking in "sportsmanship". The girl always plays her detestable role, drawing the unicorn to his death by acting upon his highest nature, without the slightest compunction, and in the faces of the virgins that were painted in this tableau during the Middle Ages there is always an expression of profound serenity. One feels that some of the supernal charm of chastity might be dispensed with if we could have a little more of the sense of fair play in its place.

The force of this feeling is increased when we turn to consider the use to which the virgin-capture story was put in Christian symbolism. To secure clarity of presentation, I have thus far ignored as much as possible the allegorical meanings put upon the story even in Physiologus and this separation is justified by the fact that the story is sometimes told without any reference to those meanings; yet the vogue of the unicorn legend was largely due to its symbolism, and the efflorescence of the story in the thirteenth and fourteenth centuries synchronized significantly with the increase of devotion to the Virgin Mary. During those centuries the story that I have called the Virgin-Capture was elaborated swiftly, in the fervid devotional spirit of the time, into a form which, though the same in origin, seems to deserve another name, and which I shall call the Holy Hunt. Beginning in Physiologus as an allegory of the Annunciation alone, the story came to comprehend in one rich and compact symbol the total life and death of Christ and to shadow forth the whole divine plan of redemption. In its final form it is one of the strangest and one of the most compressed symbols or allegories ever devised—and it sprang, as we shall see, from a strange seed.

The scope of the Holy Hunt allegory may be shown most readily by a paraphrase of an extended passage in an old German book written in honour of the Virgin. A very great king, it is said, had two noble sons. One of them wilfully stabbed himself to death, and the other brought himself so near to death by his misconduct that his life was despaired of. The father, though angry with this second son, was determined to do all that was possible for him, and so sent abroad for the advice of physicians. The wisest of these counselled that no medicine would avail except the blood of a unicorn poured upon the wound.

The King therefore inquired how a unicorn might be captured, and he was advised to seek out the most beautiful maiden in his dominions and to seat her in a garden with six other maidens about her; then he should find four swift dogs, set a huntsman over them, bind them two and two together, and cause them to drive the unicorn toward the maiden. This device was successful. In the geistliche auszlegong or spiritual interpretation of this story we are told that the King is God the Father, the first son Lucifer, the second son Adam and his seed; the chief maiden is Mary and those about her are the personifications of her virtues; the huntsman is the Holy Ghost, represented by the Angel Gabriel; the four dogs are strangely identified with the four winds of heaven. In other narrations and frequently in the numerous Holy Hunt tapestries and stained glass windows these dogs are called Veritas, Justitia, Pax, and Misericordia—strange names indeed, considering the purpose the animals serve. The coupling of the dogs, which usually takes place after the unicorn's death, signifies that whereas Mercy and Truth, Justice and Peace, were formerly foes they are now united.

When once the story of the Holy Hunt had attained such complexity as this it was likely to occur anywhere in the vast literature written in praise of the Virgin and of chastity in general. We find it, for example, in a thoroughly detestable book celebrating virginity written by one Heinrich Kornemann early in the seventeenth century. Here the huntsmen who slay the unicorn are called Jews and the "palace of the king" to which the animal is taken after its death is identified with heaven where, "ante conspectum paterni vultus et civium supernorum", it is greeted with appropriate ceremonies like a returning Roman general. The story was never questioned or criticized in any way, for it had been sanctified, and any suggestion that the Virgin acted deceitfully in ensnaring her own Son would perhaps have been regarded as impious. How engaging is the picture of the Angel Gabriel driving the beast into her embraces, with God looking on benignly over the garden wall! And then how ingenious, when the creature has been soothed to rest and slaughtered, to blame its death, which all three of the holy Persons concerned had foreseen and planned and brought about, upon the Jews! The idea suggested by Kornemann that the Son of God, transformed into a unicorn, is harried and hunted through the forests of this world in order to be brought back as a "spectacle" for the citizens of heaven—a faint memory of the Roman Circus—is not so much "quaint" as it is degraded and brutal. Furthermore, the story as told by Kornemann and many others is soaked in a peculiarly foul praise of sexual asceticism which is more base, to all clear and clean thinking, than honest pornography.

The virgin-capture story is not, for all its interest, a pleasing one, and in its later ramifications it becomes positively painful. When he strayed into Physiologus the unicorn entered a region not worthy of him. A creature imagined nobly as terrible, solitary, with

DRAGONS AND UNICORNS—FACT? OR FICTION?

the beauty of power, was transformed under Christian influence into a little goat-like animal eating out of the hand, going to sleep in maidens' laps, and serving as a symbol of virginity. Nietzsche could not have asked for a more brilliant illustration of "slave morality."

The Greek version of Pysiologus brings before us a trait of the unicorn which is quite as strange as its weakness for virgins and which had a development in Europe quite as extensive and bewildering. The statement of this trait is brief and simple, but we shall find that the explanation of it, in so far as it can be explained, is neither simple nor brief but will lead us up and down over great stretches of time and into some of the darkest places of the mind. The Greek Bestiary says that when the animals assemble at evening beside the great water to drink they find that a serpent has left its venom floating upon the surface—a characteristic trick of serpents which is elsewhere vouched for. They see or smell this venom and dare not drink,but wait for the unicorn. At last he comes, steps into the water, makes the sign of the cross over it with his horn and thereby renders the poison harmless. The significance of this trait is elsewhere explained by saying that the animal's single horn represents the Holy Cross, that the serpent stands for the Devil, and that the poisoned waters are the sins of the world.

It is remarkable that this trait—which I shall call, somewhat arbitrarily, the water-conning—exactly suited as it was to the uses of Christian allegory, was not reported in the Bestiaries of western Europe. To be sure it was known in the West, but not until late, and then chiefly in learned circles. Isidore of Seville and his followers seem never to have heard of it, and it was almost certainly unknown to Hildegarde of Bingen, who would have delighted in its magical connotations. We may be fairly certain, therefore, that the trait was not mentioned in the primitive versions of Physiologus and that it entered the Greek version from a source to which the other Bestiaries had not access.

The two themes of the water-conning and the virgin-capture were seldom brought together in a single account except in contexts professedly erudite, but a remarkable exception to this rule is found in a rather famous poem on hunting written by Natalis Comes in Latin hexameter about the middle of the sixteenth century. Here a large amount of unicorn lore is packed into little space:-

Far on the edge of the world and beyond the banks of the Ganges,

Savage and lone, is a place in the realm of the King of the Hindus.

Where there is born a beast as large as a stag in stature,

Dark on the back, solid-hoofed, very fierce, and shaped like a bullock.

Mighty and black is the horn that springs from the animal's forehead,

Terrible unto his foe, a defence and a weapon of onslaught.

138

DRAGONS AND UNICORNS—FACT? OR FICTION?

Often the poisoners steal to the banks of that swift-flowing river,

Fouling the waves with disease by their secret insidious poisons;

After them comes this beast and dips his horn in the water,

Cleansing the venom away and leaving the stream to flow purely

So that the forest-dwellers may drink once more by the margin.

Also men say that the beast delights in the embrace of a virgin,

Falling asleep in her arms and taking sweet rest on her bosom.

Ah! but, awaking, he finds he is bound by ropes and by shackles.

Strange is the tale, indeed, yet so, they say, he is taken,

Whether it be that the seeds of love have been sown by great Nature

Deep in his blood or for some more hidden mysterious reason.

Having seen in some detail the development of the unicorn legend during the Middle Ages, we may now turn to the difficult question regarding the origin of that part of the legend, the Virgin-Capture and the Holy Hunt, which is the special topic of the present chapter. Speculation about that origin has engaged a good many pens since the time when men began once more to ask questions about things instead of taking them on trust, for every thoughtful writer about the unicorn has been perplexed by the story and has wanted to know whence it came. The result of all this speculation may be summed up in the words of one of the most learned men who have ever touched the problem: "unde nostra fabella orta sit, ignoro"—whence our fable comes I know not. There are two attempts at a solution, however, to be recorded—one of them puerile, but the other, to say the least, highly ingenious.

The statement of Aelian will be recalled that the unicorn lives at strife with animals of its own species except during the season of rut, when the males make a temporary truce with the females. This is not a surprising or even a peculiar trait, but it has caught the attention of a number of scholars as a possible explanation, in default of a better, of the virgin-capture story. Such explanation may have been vaguely suggested by Manuel Philes in the thirteenth century; it was accepted by Andrea Bacci and by Conrad Gesner the zoologist; Samuel Bochart, the greatest scholar who has ever discussed the unicorn legend, added the weight of his name; even Dr. Friedrich Lauchert, a trained literary student of our own time, adopts it without hesitation. In spite of this impressive array of names, however, the theory is too absurd to be seriously entertained, and even if it were

DRAGONS AND UNICORNS—FACT? OR FICTION?

credible in other respects, we should reject it on the ground that Aelian came too late into the world to affect the fundamental stories of the Physiologus, and also on the ground that his influence was primarily rhetorical. There is hardly any likeness between the kid-like unicorn of Physiologus and the "cartazon" of Aeian, and it is to the last degree improbable that a single minor trait was adopted from Aeian's unicorn and given such extensive and surprising development while major differences were neglected. Finally, the distinction between the taming of an animal during the season of rut by the females of his own species and the taming of him by a human virgin is a difference "of all the sky".

The second attempt to account for the virgin-capture story requires more respectful attention. Professor Leo Wiener of Harvard University points out the striking similarity between the Physiologus account of the antholops or antelope and that of the unicorn. The former, as told in a Latin manuscript of the eleventh century, runs thus: There is an animal called antholops which is so exceedingly fierce that none of the hunters is able to approach him. He has long horns in the shape of a saw with which he can cut down the largest oaks . . . . When he is thirsty he goes to the great river Euphrates and drinks. Now there grow in that place certain soft and pliable branches of the vine [sunt autem ibi virgae viticeae subtiles et molles], and while he is playing about he entangles himself in them by the horn. When he is firmly caught by both horns he cries out with a great voice, because he is unable to escape from the slender branches [virgulis]; and then the hunter, hearing his voice, runs up, finds him bound, and kills him.

The analogies between this story and that of the unicorn are obvious. The antholops is very fierce and defies the hunters; he is remarkable for the armour of his brow, and this brings about his death; the hunters wait until he is hors de combat before advancing to dispatch him; furthermore, he is caught and held, according to this Latin text of Physiologus, by virgae—in the spelling common in old manuscripts, virge. Professor Wiener believes, if I understand him correctly, that the story of the virgin-capture arose from a misreading, or perhaps a scribe's error, which substituted for virge, "twigs" or "slender branches", the word Virgo, "a virgin". He also thinks that the antholops story itself is a retelling of Aesop's story of the Stag Caught by its Horns in the Forest, and that certain minor details of the unicorn story as told in Physiologus, are of Arabic origin. He sums up thus: "The autalops, after drinking from the Euphrates, goes into the woods and there plays with the branches, virgae . . . . The Physiologus or its source read Virgo instead of virgae, and thus produced the story of the unicorn which plays with its horn in the bosom of the virgo, maiden, and thus is caught. This, then, shows beyond a chance of doubt that the unicorn story arose only after the Arabs came in contact with Latin, which was after 711, and thus the earliest date of the Pbysiologus is established."

I have spared the reader as much as possible of the amazing involution in Professor Wiener's argument, but I cannot mitigate the surprise he will feel at seeing the virgin disappear, like Daphne, into a tree; I can only ask him to share my own disappointment that after such gigantic labours the mountain of scholarship should bring forth only this ridiculous mouse of an alleged mistranslation. Convinced that the Physiolous as we know it cannot be of earlier date than AD. 711, Professor Wiener is constrained to argue that

DRAGONS AND UNICORNS—FACT? OR FICTION?

the narrations of the virgin-capture story in Gregory's Moralia and in Isidore's Etymologiae are interpolations made after that date. He does not mention the fact that the story was told by Saint Eustathius of Antioch almost four hundred years before, nor does he explain how Pope Gelasius could have condemned in the fifth century a work that was not produced until the eighth. The words upon which his argument chiefly rests—"sunt autem ibi virgae viticeae"—are found only in a manuscript of the eleventh century, and this seems to me much too late for our present purposes. I do not believe, therefore, that the Latin phrasing of the antholops story gave the original suggestion for the story of the virgin-capture. There is a considerable difference between a unicorned animal and one with two horns fitted with saw-tooth edges, and Professor Wiener's explanation that the antholops may break off one of his horns in his struggle with the virgae, thereby making himself an artificial unicorn, does not seem to meet the needs of the case. We shall do well to look farther.

In considering the Syriac version of Physiolous we have found reason to suspect that the emphasis there laid upon sexual attraction indicates some non-Christian influence. A story similar to that in Syriac is found in Arabic literature of the fourteenth century. Al Damiri says that "a virgin or a beautiful girl" is put in the way of the unicorn, and that as soon as he sees her he leaps into her lap making signs for milk, of which he is naturally very fond. After he has been suckled he lies down drunk, as though with wine, and at this moment the hunters rush in and bind him without resistance. This Arabian unicorn has fallen even below the poor creature of Physiologus, for he is captured because he is drunk, and on milk! Equally interesting is the implication that if no virgin is available any beautiful girl will do as well. Now it seems remotely possible that this Arabian version is a degraded form of the Christian story, and that virginity has been subordinated because the Mohammedans are not Mariolaters and have never laid quite the Christian emphasis upon chastity; but it is certainly far more probable that we have here and in the Syriac version the relics of an older story which the Christians of Alexandria shaped to their purpose. The mention of the virgin in the Arabic tale is due, no doubt, to Christian influence, but her presence is so incongruous with the tale itself as to suggest that she has been imported from another form of the story.

In that case, we must abandon all effort to explain the virgin-capture story in terms of itself and its variants, and we are driven back into the sea of the world's folklore without compass or chart, there to make what accidental landfalls we may. We are seeking an explanation of the elective affinity between virgins and beasts with single horns, or, if virginity is not a primary notion, of the attraction, whether sexual or of some other sort, between women and horned beasts. Virgins undergoing sundry tests, beautiful girls seated lonely and receptive under trees, unicorns, rhinoceroses, faithful lions, elephants, appear and disappear in the mists. Bartholomew Anglicus says that "Elephants be hunted in this wise: there go in the desert two maidens all naked and bare, and these maidens begin to sing alone; and the beast hath liking when he heareth their song, and cometh to them and licketh their teats and falleth asleep anon for liking of the song; and then one maiden sticketh him in the throat and the other taketh his blood in a vessel, and with that blood the people dye cloth. This is useful information, but it is not directly to the purpose

DRAGONS AND UNICORNS—FACT? OR FICTION?

and the fog closes in again. We learn that the horn of the young female rhinoceros, taken before she has mated, sells both in Siam and in South Africa at a price at least ten times as great as that given for the horns of mated animals of either sex, on the ground that they are much more powerfully prophylactic. We delve into the myth of Diana the virgin huntress and ponder her connection with the horned moon which has had control over poisons since the beginnings of superstition. In all this rather aimless beating up and down one may learn much about the mental habits out of which the virgin-capture story arose, but the actual source of it eludes one. The suspicion grows upon the seeker that he is looking for the origin of a belief which has never had any single beginning and that all the success he can hope for will be like that of one who looks for the source of a great river—and finds it in half a dozen different springs separated, it may be, by hundreds of miles, or in the rainwind, or in the wandering cloud. And just as it is a hazardous thing to say that the Nile or the Mississippi or the Amazon springs out of precisely this or that hillside, so it would be rash to assert that the virgin-capture story must have had just this or that origin and no other. Such confident assertions are seldom made by those who have looked long into the mists of the primitive imagination where vague shapes are constantly forming and dissolving again.

And yet, though the ultimate origin of the story remains hidden, we have already traced that story somewhat behind the form it took on in Physiologus. It is possible to take one long step farther still, and then we shall have done what we can.

The sudden expansion of the known world during the sixteenth century and the consequent opening of new lands to exploration and conquest, gave to the imagination of Europe an impetus which had among its many results a sort of modern mythology. We are accustomed to think of this expansion in connection with the western hemisphere alone, but the sea route to India and the Far East contributed quite as much as America to European fancy. India, which had been a land of chimera to Ctesias and had remained such during all the intervening centuries, was no less marvellous now that the Portuguese were bringing back a cargo of wonders in every ship that rounded the Cape. By one of the stranger accidents in the history of legend, some of the tales that had once been told of India were transferred to a nearer land, Ethiopia, which had been confused with the great peninsula even in Virgil's time. Most of these tales moved westward with the fabulous Court of Prester John, which had originally been located somewhat vaguely in "India". Ever since the forged letter describing this Christian court had been received, and answered, by Pope Alexander III, Christian missionaries had been much interested in it, and they were none the less so in the early seventeenth century when there seemed to be grave danger that Prester John—at that time approximately five hundred years of age—would fall into heresy. These are the circumstances surrounding the several accounts of Ethiopia that we owe to Jesuits of the period, the best known of which is that of Jeronimo Lobo. Most of the Jesuit travellers to the Court of Prester John have something to say about the Abyssinian unicorn, and Father Lobo has a great deal. From one of them, Fray Luis de Urreta, we get an unmistakable clue to the original nature of the virgin-capture story.

DRAGONS AND UNICORNS—FACT? OR FICTION?

This clue is found in a book packed with unheard-of matters and quite worthy of its noble title: Historia de los Grandes y Remotos Reynos de la Etiopia, Monarchia del Emperador llamado Preste Juan. Well beyond the middle of it there is a clear description of the rhinoceros, which Fray Luis says has been made familiar to Europe by many pictures. He describes it as an extremely wild animal, very fierce and brave and proud, and so powerful that it can be killed only by one ruse or trick. The way of killing it is this: The hunters go into the province of Goyame, which is at the base of the Mountains of the Moon whence the Nile springs, for there alone, in all Africa, are these beasts to be found. When they learn that one is near at hand they load their muskets and they take a female monkey which they have trained for this kind of hunting, and they bring her to the place. She begins at once to run about looking for the rhinoceros, and when she sees him she leaps here and there and dances as she goes toward him, playing a thousand monkey-tricks. He is much delighted in watching this entertainment, so that she is able to approach until she can throw one leg over his back. Then she begins scratching and rubbing his hide, and this gives him keen pleasure. At last, jumping to the ground again, she starts to rub his belly, and then the rhinoceros is so overcome with ecstasy that he stretches himself out at length upon the ground. At this point the hunters, who have been hidden all the while in some safe place, come up with their cross-bows or muskets and shoot him.

Here is such a tale as hunters may have told round the camp-fire, time out of mind, as a matter-of-fact statement of the method by which a valuable animal, too tough for darts and arrows, might be killed. One who lays the two side by side will have little doubt, I think, that the tale reported by Fray Luis springs from the same root as the virgin-capture story, for they correspond not merely here and there but at every point. With regard to the question as to which of the two is probably the older, one sees that Fray Luis's relation, as compared with the other, verges everywhere toward the probable, even the realistic. Instead of the unicorn we have here the rhinoceros, his grossly actual doppelganger. In place of the virgin we are given a monkey—a female monkey, be it observed, and one specially trained in the appropriate feminine blandishments. Instead of depending upon such vague lures as the odour of chastity or the power of the eye, this decoy sets to work with seduction of the most physical kind. Instead of the sleep of the unicorn, which is usually left unexplained by the narrators of the other tale, we have here the natural stretching-out of the beast to enjoy itself to the fullest extent.

Now it seems unlikely that this account is a degraded or brokendown version of the virgin-capture story. Usually, when a myth or legend has reached such an elevation of the supernatural as that attained by the virgin-capture tale, it maintains itself at that level, if only because simple minds find it easier to remember and perhaps easier to believe. This rule—which has, of course, many exceptions—holds particularly for myths and legends that have become entangled with religious beliefs. Numerous written texts of the virgin-capture story, and very numerous representations of it, have existed for a long time to preserve it from corrupting influences. The variations from that story in the account of the rhinoceros hunt, moreover, are not of a sort to be accounted for by assuming a gradual decomposition of the Christian tale as it was tossed from tongue to tongue during the centuries. The two stories answer to each other point for point, so that one who tried to prove that the monkey-capture is a debased version of the virgin-capture story would be obliged to assume a conscious act of euhemerization for which he could scarcely assign a sufficient motive. But the most cogent argument against such a theory is the vaguest and the hardest to state: such a patient unravelling of a developed legend and the substitution, strand by strand, of baser materials, is simply foreign to the thought-habits of the times and the minds concerned. Such cynical performances are amusing to a Lucian or an Anatole France, but we cannot attribute them to African hunters of the seventeenth or of any earlier century. And this tale of the rhinoceros hunt is a hunter's tale. As such, it is probably ancient, for during historic times the rhinoceros of India-where the story first was told—was captured chiefly by great drives, such as that organized by Tamerlane in the fourteenth century, in which hundreds of men took part on foot and horseback.

We must conclude, then, that the tale told by Fray Luis is not derived from the account of the unicorn in Physiologus. But the two stories are related to each other, and closely related. Either they spring separately from a single root or else the Christian legend is the product of a more or less deliberate allegorizing of the heathen belief. The second of these possibilities seems to me to harmonize with the little we can safely surmise about the methods and purposes of the shapers of Physialogus. There may have been some intermediary forms of the story that are now lost, and there were probably some forms of the monkey-capture story more primitive and even less pleasing than that related by Fray Luis, for early Arabian tales about the monkey were often obscene. To pursue the story into the jungles of Siam would be an absorbing adventure, no doubt, but it would not advance our knowledge of unicorn lore. We have traced the Christian legend of the unicorn back, if not to its source, at any rate to a form as primitive, in all likelihood, as that in which the early Christians found it, and this should be sufficient.

The conclusion at which we arrive is a surprising one. On the one hand we have the rich and mystical beauty of the Holy Hunt comprising in one packed symbol the conception, life, and death of Christ—a symbol branching out into literature, flowering profusely in the arts, entangled with the central religious passion of the Middle Ages. On the other hand we have a ludicrous tale about the antics of a she-monkey trained to decoy the rhinoceros by scratching his belly and back. Our inference that the religious symbol is derived from the gross hunter's tale may be repugnant to some sensibilities, but the apparent contrast is exactly of the kind that confronts us everywhere in our probing toward the bases of life, of beauty, even of love. Ultimately we have to decide whether we shall think less highly of the flower or contrive to think somewhat better of the earth from which it grows.

DRAGONS AND UNICORNS—FACT? OR FICTION?

CHAPTER III

SHAPING FANTASIES

THE unicorn is one of the most beautiful of the "shapes that haunt thought's wildernesses", but he did not attain his beauty all at once. As soon as we begin to inquire how he looked to the imagination of the Ages of Faith we are reminded that his ancestry is mixed, that he descends from the horse and the ass on the side of the Greeks and from the goat on that of Physiologus. The results of this miscegenation were a series of hybrid variations as perplexing as those governed by the Mendelian law. Aristotle had said that the unicorn's hoof is solid, on the excellent ground that animals with divided hoofs have two horns when they have any horns at all; but on the other hand, Physiologus declared that the unicorn resembles a little goat, and the goat has a divided hoof. The faithful did not know what to think, and in default of a Thomas Aquinas to resolve the apparent discrepancies between Aristotle and Physiologus they tried to believe in a unicorn somewhat like a goat and somewhat like a horse at the same time. Early representations of the animal show cloven hoofs on the fore feet and solid hoofs behind, or vice versa; they show a goat's beard on a horse's head or even the body of a goat with the head of a horse. A more perfect example of the divided allegiance of the Renaissance could hardly be imagined; yet, in spite of these difficulties, the artists of the time made the unicorn at least as credible as the animals they had before their eyes, and usually far more graceful.

From the thirteenth century to the sixteenth, representation of the unicorn in ecclesiastic decoration was continuous and widespread. Formerly he had been depicted chiefly in manuscripts and it is clear that his increased popularity was due in some degree to the rapid intensification of Mariolatry. Although the animal's figure was not so much used in England as in Europe, I have seen him represented on misericords in Lincoln Cathedral, in St. George's of Windsor, in the chapel of Durham Castle, in St. Botolph's of Boston, and

DRAGONS AND UNICORNS—FACT? OR FICTION?

in at least half a dozen parish churches. Mrs. Jameson describes an elaborate representation of the Holy Hunt which stands over the altar in Breslau Cathedral, and the same subject is treated in stained glass at Bourges, Erfurt, Caen, Lyons, and many other places. Representations of the unicorn on old altarcloths, corbels, and capitals are almost numberless.

A subject so popular as this was certain to be adopted by secular art, as the Physiologus story was used by Richard de Fournival and others in erotic poetry, for it was only necessary to lay a slightly additional emphasis upon the theme of the hunt and to subordinate the holy symbolism in order to make the transition from sacred to profane. Perhaps the most sumptuous representations of the unicorn ever made are those in the "Millefleur tapestries" produced about the year 1480 for François de la Rochefoucauld. Here we are shown a pure white animal, vaguely equine but smaller than a horse, with goat's beard and cloven hoofs and the spiralled horn. Although the monogram "A.M."—Ave Maria-appears in each scene, the atmosphere of the whole series is not devotional but that of an elaborate hunt in the French manner. The death of the unicorn is shown, but we do not find the Virgin in her conventional position, and there are other indications that the theme is tending toward a purely secular treatment. The same tendency is observable in the superb Flemish tapestry, based probably upon an Italian cartoon and now in the Academy of Fine Arts at Florence, which shows the naming of the animals by Adam—most of the beasts trooping by in pairs, but the unicorn, significantly leading the procession, without a mate. The unicorn is singled out for such special honour in many other representation, as, for example, in the large picture by Tintoretto in the Church of San Rocco at Venice, which shows the Saint healing animals in the desert. Here the unicorn stands at the forefront of the group, very shaggy about the head but horse-like and with a striated horn. A purely secular treatment is seen in the familiar and beautiful d'Aubusson tapestries known as La Dame a la Licorne, probably intended to illustrate the metrical romance of that title, which is now in the Musée de Cluny, for in these the animal is scarcely more than ornamental.

Most influential in this secularizing of the unicorn were the numerous illustrations made, from the second quarterof the fifteenth century onward, for Petrarch's Trionfi. In only one of the divisions of his poem does Petrarch mention a triumphal car, but his illustrators-probably because a "triumph" necessarily meant for them a chariot with allegorical figures—provided such cars for each of the divisions. The chariots depicted by them to illustrate the "Triumph of Chastity" are always drawn by unicorns—two, four, or six in number—and these unicorns, if I may judge from the scores of examples that I have seen in woodcuts and on canvas, are always equine, cloven-footed, bearded, and with striated horns. Copies and editions of Petrarch's Trionfi were to be found in every European language during the Renaissance, and wherever they went some engraving on wood or metal of the Chariot of Chastity drawn by unicorns went with them. Many of the foremost painters of the age tried their hands at a subject which for several decades was second in popularity only to the well-worn Biblical themes. These allegorical Triumphs are to be found not in painting and engraving only but on tapestry, pottery, bas-reliefs in bronze and wood and ivory, marriage chests and birth-trays. Splendid and

DRAGONS AND UNICORNS—FACT? OR FICTION?

familiar examples of them are to be seen at the Victoria and Albert Museum in the two great tapestries—Flemish, of the sixteenth century—from a set illustrating Petrarch's poem. Other tapestries from the same design, once the property of Cardinal Wolsey, are at Hampton Court. Eugene Muntz, the historian of art, has collected over a thousand examples of them in the volume he has devoted to the subject, and in each of these examples the figure of the unicorn is necessarily prominent. Obviously, the influence of all this work would be to withdraw the unicorn from his exclusive association with sacred themes and history. The illustrators of the Trionfi, furthermore, developed and fixed the equine shape of the unicorn as we see it to-day in heraldic insignia.

For beauty of the higher sort I know of nothing in the artistic representation of the unicorn superior to the famous Santa Justina of Moretto, painted about 1530 and now in the Belvidere Gallery at Vienna. In this serene and noble picture the animal is again depicted as white, equine, and with cloven hoofs, but the horn is for once the black horn described by Pliny.

The unicorn of heraldry was devised by men who had rather more confidence in the classic writers of antiquity than they had in the Bestiaries, and therefore their animal has more of the horse than of the goat in his composition; yet the prominent position of the unicorn in heraldry is primarily due, of course, to the moral attributes that he acquired from the Physiologus tradition. Primarily, but not entirely. Several streams of influence converged to make him the chief emblem of purity: the identification with Christ and association with the Virgin first of all, but, in addition, the waterconning trait and the world-wide reputation of the horn as a drug and a magical prophylactic. Considering that chastity was one of the foremost chivalric virtues, we are not surprised to find the unicorn figured on many knightly seals and coats of arms. There was something essentially aristocratic about him. His kinship to the horse, always associated with knighthood, was suggestive, but more important was the headlong enthusiasm of his devotion to beautiful women. He was fierce and proud and dangerous to his foes, as a knight should be, and he was also gentle; he had the dignity of solitude; he was beautiful and strong; most significant of all, he was a protector and champion of other beasts against the wiles of their enemies. In all the range of animal lore there is no other story conceived so completely in the aristocratic spirit as that of the unicorn stepping down to the poisoned water while the other beasts wait patiently for his coming, and making it safe for them by dipping his magic horn. Here was a perfect emblem of the ideal that European chivalry held before itself in its great periods—the ideal according to which exceptional power and privilege were balanced and justified by exceptional responsibility. The lion, for all the heroic courage falsely attributed to him, the panther with his sweet breath, the bear with his mighty strength, had no such chivalric significance as the unicorn, which might almost seem to have been imagined precisely to serve as an emblem of the "verray parfit gentil knight".

John Guillim, who wrote his famous book on heraldry at a time when his subject had chiefly antiquarian interest, makes clear his own feeling that the unicorn is aristocratic and a fit subject, therefore, for a gentleman's crest. "Some," he admits, "have made doubt

DRAGONS AND UNICORNS—FACT? OR FICTION?

whether there be any such beast as this or no, but the great esteem of his horn (in many places to be seen) may take away that needless scruple." The animal's invincibility and virtue are praised, and then Guillim writes: "The greatness of his mind is such that he rather chooseth to die than to be taken alive: wherein the unicorn and the valiant-minded soldier are alike, which both contemn death, and rather than they will be compelled to undergo any base servitude or bondage they will lose their lives."

Later heraldic writers rival even the historians of art in the extent and variety of their misinformation about unicorns, perhaps because they are so accustomed to discussing creatures of which almost anything may be asserted that they do not know how to respect a beast with a definite legend. We are gravely told, for example, by a writer of the nineteenth century, that the whole notion of the unicorn was derived from the spike in the middle of the "tester" or head-armour of the horse, although this spike was not regularly used in Europe until late in the fifteenth century. It is true that the "panache" has been used since ancient times as a decoration of the war-horse's head, but one would prefer to believe that if there is any connection this was suggested by the unicorn. For dense and audacious error, however, the palm should be awarded to John Brand, who says of the unicorn: "This fabulous animal of heraldry . . . is nothing more than a horse with the horn of the pristis, or sword-fish, stuck in his forehead."

Before the accession of James I to the throne of England a great variety of "supporters" had been used for the Royal Arms, but a lion had for several generations been one of the two. Henry VI used the lion and the antelope; Edward IV the lion and bull; Richard III the lion and boar; Henry VII and Henry VIII the lion and dragon; Mary and Elizabeth the lion and greyhound. On the Royal Arms of Scotland the unicorn had been employed as consistently as the lion in England. It is often said that the lion and unicorn were chosen as supporters of the British Arms because of the belief in the natural animosity of these two beasts and as a symbol of the reconciliation between England and Scotland. James I was a learned man to whom such a symbol might well have been interesting, but the presence of these two historic foes in the British Royal Arms is really no more than a fortunate accident. James kept his Scottish unicorn and he chose the English lion merely because it had been the most persistent supporter of the English Arms before his time. He kept the lion dexter as it had been on Elizabeth's Arms, and he retained all its heraldic insignia. His unicorn remained, as it had been in Scotland, argent, armed, crined, unguled, gorged with a coronet of crosses patécs and fleur-de-lis, with a chain extending from the crown between the forelegs and reflexed over the back, all or. Since their adoption by James the British supporters have been used continuously, except that the seal of the Exchequer in the time of Charles I shows as supporters a stag and an antelope, chained and ducally collared.

No small amount of lore is implicit, to the pausing eye, in this heraldic unicorn as one may see him to-day on the first page of an English newspaper or rampant over the Old State House in Boston, Massachusetts. He owes his horse's head and neck and mane to Pliny and to certain artists of the Italian Renaissance, his graceful legs to a series of mediaeval writers who will be named in due course, his beard and divided hoofs in part to

DRAGONS AND UNICORNS—FACT? OR FICTION?

Physiologus, his tail either to the oryx or else to the aesthetic taste of the College of Heralds, and the spiral twistings of his horn to a marine mammal of the northern seas. Here is a creature fearfully and wonderfully made, and yet, in spite of his compound ancestry, one more than a match in beauty for the megalocephalic lion, and one so credible, or rather so probable, in appearance as to make the hardiest doubter feel that if there is no such animal then an excellent opportunity was overlooked in the process of creation. He seems to fill a gap in nature.

One can readily understand that during the Middle Ages, when coats of arms were not confined to stationery and table-silver but were pictures in vivid hues that went everywhere in the world—flaunting in state processions, resplendent at Court, rallying soldiers about their lords in battle—the frequent use of the unicorn upon heraldic crests would do much to increase the animal's vogue and to make it seem certain, if there had ever been any doubt, that he was as real as any beast of field or forest. It is certain that the presence of the unicorn on the British Royal Arms, reproduced as they are millions of times in every year and scattered throughout the world, has tended to maintain interest in the animal and to develop a curiosity about its tradition even in our time.

One of the fundamental facts concerning lions and unicorns is that they hate each other by instinct, as Englishman and Scot once did, and that they never meet without fatal consequences. This is matter for later discussion, but in the meantime we may pause to wonder at the chance that brought such deadly opposites into accord, uniting majesty with gentleness and beauty with strength. To the adult observer they seem to be now at peace, but the familiar nursery rhyme will not have it so, for there, until recently,

The lion and the unicorn

Were fighting for the crown;

The lion chased the unicorn

All round the town.

I should never have doubted for a moment that this bit of doggerel was suggested by the British Royal Arms if I had not come upon the following remarkable passage: "In one of the rooms of the Borromeo Palace on the Isola Bella in Lago Maggiore are two large tapestries—say fifteen feet by twelve feet—apparently of the sixteenth century or earlier. The first represents a lion and a unicorn engaged in combat for a crown lying between them. The second shows the lion chasing the unicorn round a mediaeval walled town drawn quite small in the centre of the tapestry, the lion and the unicorn being on a much larger scale." These assertions are so surprising and indeed inexplicable that I have gone many miles out of my way on a journey through northern Italy in order to verify them—only to find them false. The Borromean Palace does contain two excellent Flemish tapestries in which the lion and the unicorn are prominently figured, but in neither of them can I find either a crown or a pursuit round a walled town. Both tapestries

149

DRAGONS AND UNICORNS—FACT? OR FICTION?

show the two animals fighting: in one the unicorn has gored the lion and is lifting him off his feet, and in the second the unicorn is attacked from behind by two lions while goring a third. The tapestries may have been intended to bear some symbolic significance, for the unicorn is prominent in the Borromean arms—a huge unicorn of stone stands on the summit of the palace gardens—but there can be no connection between them and the English nursery rhyme.

There is much to be surmised, but little that a cautious investigator would care to affirm positively, about the symbolic meanings ascribed to the unicorn in pre-Christian times. Several bits of evidence concur, however, in the suggestion that for a very long time one-horned animals have been regarded as emblematic of unlimited or undivided sovereign power. We have made nothing as yet of the curious statement which occurs in nearly all the older texts of Physiologus that when the unicorn is captured he is "taken to the palace of the king"—a remark which, as I have said, is one of the few traces of a connection between the Physiologus unicorn and that of the Greeks. Philostratus makes it clear in the passage cited above from the life of Apollonius that only the kings of India hunt the unicorn and only they possess the beakers made from its horn. Aelian also tells us that only the potentates own these beakers, and he says in another place that the young of the "cartazon" are taken to the king. Of course there is abundant evidence that the larger animals of the chase are regarded in many parts of the world as belonging to the king," but the rule seems to apply with special force to unicorns as it does also to the rhinoceros. On his voyage to the East Indies in 1592 James Lancaster sent commodities to the King of Junsaloam, off the Straits of Malacca, "to barter for Ambergriese and for the homes of Abath [rhinoceros] whereof the king only hath the traffique in his hands." In South Africa the so-called "kerry", a sort of wand or sceptre made from the horn of the white rhinoceros—which, however, has two horns—is so well recognized a symbol of sovereignty that quarrels arising from disputes over the ownership of it have led to more than one Kaffir war in recent times. In China, again, the unicorn, or Ki-lin, has been associated for ages with emperors, the appearance of one of these animals being accepted as a certain prophecy of a beneficent reign. Plutarch tells us of a ram's head with only one horn that was brought to Pericles from his farm as a sign that he would become the single ruler of the Athenian state.

But the most remarkable and conclusive evidence for this ancient symbolism is to be found in the Bible. In the Book of Daniel (chapter viii) there is recorded this strange vision: "And behold, an he goat came from the West on the face of the whole earth, and touched not the ground; and the goat had a notable horn between his eyes. And he came to the ram that had two horns . . . and ran unto him in the fury of his power. And I saw him come close unto the ram, and he was moved with choler against him, and smote the ram, and brake his two horns: and there was no power in the ram to stand before him, but he cast him down to the ground and stamped upon him." Later in the same chapter we are given an interpretation of this vision: "And the rough goat is the king of Grecia, and the great horn that is between his eyes is the first king."

The one-horned goat of Daniel's vision, in other words, stands for Alexander the Great,

150

DRAGONS AND UNICORNS—FACT? OR FICTION?

and the whole allegory depicts his triumph over the hosts of the Persians, represented by the two-horned ram. The interesting thing is that the one horn should be chosen as a symbol of superior power. One can readily understand it as a symbol of single and supreme sovereignty, and it is permissible to paraphrase the sentence quoted above so as to make it read: "The great horn that is between his eyes signifies that he is the supreme king." Exactly the same symbolism is found in the pseudepigraphic first book of Enoch, in the ninetieth chapter: "And I saw till horns grew upon these lambs, and the rams cast down their horns; and I saw till there sprouted a great horn of one of these sheep, and their eyes were opened. And it looked at them and it cried to the sheep, and the rams saw it and all ran to it." The one-horned sheep of this passage, according to the notes of

R. H. Charles, must be Judas Maccabaeus. One recalls in this connection several Biblical references to horns, apparently single, which make it clear that they were symbols of power. In I Samuel ii. I are the words "By Jehovah my horn is exalted," and in Psalms lxxxix. "By thy favour our horn is exalted." "Lift not up your horn," says David again as a caution of humility, and in Jeremiah we read: "The horn of Moab is cut off." In these passages the horns concerned, whether actual or metaphorical, were those not of animals but of men. Frequently, no doubt, they were actual; that is to say, they were high headdresses of some sort related to the tall peaked caps worn by Persian and Assyrian kings and by the members of their households. Such symbolic adornments for the head were used by the flamines martiales of Rome, and they seem to have consisted of single horns. Bishop Taylor, writing at the end of the eighteenth century, says that he saw Sepoys in India who wore single spikes or horns on their foreheads attached to flat leather helmets. Perhaps the most familiar example of this symbolic head-dress is the peaked cap of the Doges of Venice, which seems to have been derived from the Orient.

"No one", says Coleridge, "has yet discovered even a plausible origin for this symbolism as to horns", but the problem is not quite so difficult as he suggests, now that we know a little more about the habits of primitive minds. Very simple men think of the power of a horned beast as residing in the horns with which it defends itself and attacks its enemies; to such men, therefore, horns are a natural symbol of vigour, power, strength of any kind, and they have been used as such a symbol for ages. Homer makes Achilles push the Trojans with his horns. Horace says that wine adds horns to a man of lowly condition; the Lamb of the Apocalypse is equipped with seven horns, the perfect number, to signify omnipotence; the famous horns of Moses, whatever they were originally intended to signify, have usually been interpreted as symbols of power. All these horns are double, but it will be readily understood that when the strength of two horns is concentrated in one that one is very strong indeed and a perfect emblem of strength.

We may take it as highly probable, then, that one-horned animals were regarded in the pre-Christian world, in many widely distant places, as symbols of sovereignty. Turning to the symbolism of the unicorn in Christendom we are on firmer ground. Partly because of its association with the Virgin, partly because of its service as a purifier of poisoned waters, and to some extent on account of the reputation of its horn, it came to be regarded as an emblem of purity. An instance of this is seen in its association with Saint

DRAGONS AND UNICORNS—FACT? OR FICTION?

Justina, and even clearer examples are found in the numerous illustrations of Petrarch's Triumph of Chastity and in the remarkable engraving made by an unknown artist for the Hypnerotomachia of Poliphilo in which the triumphal chariot of Diana is drawn by eight unicorns. So widely variable is symbolism of this kind, however, that Leonardo da Vinci makes the animal a type of incontinence, or what he calls Intemperana. Still another symbolic significance of the Christian unicorn is that of solitude—a significance derived not from Physiologus but from Pliny and Aelian, and one, therefore, which is found only in the more learned tradition. Several of the early Fathers and of their followers drew the unicorn into their praise of solitude, and in later centuries the animal was generally understood to be an emblem of the monastic life. There is still preserved at St. Fulda a pastoral staff supposed to have belonged to Saint Boniface, and, if genuine, dating therefore from the seventh century, on which the unicorn is shown kneeling at the foot of the Cross. Many monastic seals are still to be seen on which the animal is the central figure. I have already referred to the strange metaphor connecting the unicorn's horn with the central beam of the Holy Cross—a metaphor struck out, probably, in the disordered African fancy of Tertullian but used also by Irenaeus and by Justinus, to mention only two of many.

By far the most important emblematic significance of the unicorn, however, was that in which he stood for Christ. This signification is stated in Physiologus and in most of the passages derived therefrom, it is implicit in the pictorial allegory of the Holy Hunt, and the Church Fathers, with their enormous influence upon a millennium of thought and life, spread it broadcast. "Who is this Unicorn," says Saint Ambrose, "but the only-begotten Son of God." "The unconquerable nature of God is likened to that of a unicorn," writes Saint Basil. More extended interpretations were not uncommon, such as that in which we are told that the unicorn represents the Hebrew people as a whole, its one horn standing for their single law wherewith they are to toss aside all other nations. Speaking in general, however, one may say that from the third century of our era to the period of the Reformation the unicorn represented the person of Christ. Whether the pre-Christian symbol had any direct influence upon the Christian allegory one hesitates to say.

Only in recent years has the legend of the unicorn been turned over to avowed and professional dreamers; throughout the greater part of its history it has been shaped chiefly by practical menhunters, physicians, explorers, and merchant—adventurers—who regarded mere poetry with the healthy contempt shown by Shakespeare's Theseus. Yet the literary allusions to the animal are of course very numerous. I can choose only such examples as seem typical or otherwise important, and these may be arranged in an approximately chronological order.

Several of the earlier references to the unicorn occurring in what we may call imaginative literature—although it seemed no such thing to its authors—appear in the numerous mediaeval stories of Alexander. In one of these we hear that among the gifts sent by Queen Candace to the Conqueror there was a unicorn, valued not so much for itself as for the precious stone growing at the base of its horn. No translation can rival the rudeness of the original, but this is the sense of the lines:-

152

DRAGONS AND UNICORNS—FACT? OR FICTION?

I had from this rich queen

A beast of proud and noble mien

That bears in his brow the ruby-stone

And yields himself to maids alone.

But few such unicorns are found

On this or any other ground,

And only such are ever captured

As stainless virgins have enraptured.

No man of woman born

Endures the terror of his horn.

The ruby or "carbuncle" in the brow of Queen Candace's unicorn is an adornment which seems to have been of Levantine origin, and it reminds us that Pfaffen Lamprecht, the author of the poem, was a contemporary of the Crusaders, who brought back many such exotic marvels. For the rest, the meagre lines follow Physiologus except for the na·ve admission that the unicorn is scarce in this land (der ist luzzil in diz lant), which may possibly be a reminiscence of Aelian.

In Wolfram von Eschenbach's Parfal there is another reference to the unicorn's ruby (karfunkelstein), here used as one of the several medicines, including also the animal's heart, employed to cure the wound of Anfortas, King of the Grail:-

We caught the beast called Unicorn

That knows and loves a maiden best

And falls asleep upon her breast;

We took from underneath his horn

The splendid male carbuncle-stone

Sparkling against the white skull-bone.

DRAGONS AND UNICORNS—FACT? OR FICTION?

The unicorn story found expression even in a poem called, by one who should have known the word's precise meaning, a Volkslied. Although this poem does not seem to me to bear the marks of the popular ballad, it has beauty and a definite value for the present purpose, so that it seems worth while to attempt a translation:-

I stood in the Maytime meadows By roses circled round, Where many a fragile blossom Was bright upon the ground; And as though the roses called them And their wild hearts understood, The little birds were singing In the shadows of the wood. The nightingale among them Sang sweet and loud and long, Until a greater voice than hers Rang out above her song; For suddenly, between the crags, Along the narrow vale,

The echoes of a hunting horn Came clear upon the gale. The hunter stood beside me

Who blew that mighty horn; I saw that he was hunting The gentle unicorn

But the unicorn is noble, He knows his gentle birth, He knows that God has chosen him Above all beasts of earth.

The unicorn is noble; He keeps him safe and high Upon a narrow path and steep Climbing to the sky;

And there no man can take him, He scorns the hunter's dart,

And only a virgin's magic power Shall tame his haughty heart.

What would be now the state of us But for this Unicorn,

And what would be the fate of us, Poor sinners, lost, forlorn?

Oh, may He lead us on and up, Unworthy though we be,

Into His Father's kingdom, To dwell eternally!

The most interesting feature of this poem is the drawing of the unicorn into a local mise-en-scéne. The landscape is that of Switzerland or Upper Germany, the opening stanzas are those of a secular poem dealing with a hunt, and the unicorn is visualized by the writer as a chamois. In spite of its conventional prettiness, the poem gains from these peculiarities a certain freshness and charm.

As I have already pointed out, the unicorn provided a useful metaphor to the erotic verse of the later Middle Ages and the early Renaissance. Burkhardt von Hohenfels calls himself a unicorn because a woman has lured him to his doom, Guido Cavalcanti says the same thing in a sonnet addressed to Guido Orlandi, and Thibaut, Count of Champagne, writes:-

DRAGONS AND UNICORNS—FACT? OR FICTION?

The unicorn and I are one:

He also pauses in amaze

Before some maiden's magic gaze,

And, while he wonders, is undone.

On some dear breast he slumbers deep,

And Treason slays him in that sleep.

Just so have ended my life's days;

So Love and my Lady lay me low.

My heart will not survive this blow.

One of the most familiar literary allusions to the unicorn is that in Rabelais. Pantagruel says, in narrating his adventures in the Land of Satin: "I saw there two-and-thirty unicorns. They are a cursed sort of creature, much resembling a fine horse, unless it be that their heads are like a stag's, their feet like an elephant's, their tails like a wild boar's, and out of each of their foreheads sprouts a sharp black horn, some six or seven feet long. [Pliny, whom Rabelais follows in most other particulars, had made the horn only three feet in length.] Commonly it dangles down like a turkeycock's comb, but when a unicorn has a mind to fight or put it to any other use, what does he do but make it stand, and then it is as straight as an arrow."

The unicorn has a less prominent role in the romances of the Middle Ages than one might expect, considering his potentialities, but this fact merely reminds one again that he was not regarded as exceptionally romantic or wonderful. The title of Le Romans de la Dame a la Lycorne et du Biau Chevalier au Lyon arouses expectations which are not fulfilled, for here the animal's function is largely symbolic. He is given to the heroine by Li Diex d'Amours in recognition of her tres grant purté, and all that he has to do in the course of eighty-five hundred lines is to swim the moat surrounding the Castle of Chief d'Or with his mistress on his back—the lion belonging to the hero, similarly mounted, paddling proudly beside him.

Far more interesting than this merely ornamental beast is the unicorn we meet towards the end of the charming Old French prose romance called Le Chevalier du Papegau. King Arthur, wandering on his maiden adventure, has been stranded on a strange coast, and there he finds a square red tower, without door or window, in which a dwarf is living. The dwarf tells Arthur that he and his wife had been set on shore there many years before by the Lord of Northumbria, and that his wife had died shortly after giving birth to a son. "When my wife was dead and I had buried her," says he, "I put my

DRAGONS AND UNICORNS—FACT? OR FICTION?

food into my overcoat, wrapped up my child as best I could, and then went through the forest looking for a hollow tree where I might rest and find shelter from the rain and the night and the wild beasts. At last I found one with a hollow large enough for six knights to lie in, and within the hollow there were new-born fawns, each one with a little horn in the middle of its brow. And when I saw these fawns I went inside and looked at them for a long time with wonder, and I sat down among them. While I was sitting there the mother came—a huge beast, as large as a large horse, with a horn in her brow as sharp as any razor in the world and with fourteen great udders of which the smallest was as large as the bag of a cow, and when this beast saw me she looked at me so terribly that I leaped up and dropped my child and fled. The child began to cry bitterly—and you are to know that it was the finest and fairest infant that ever was seen—so that the beast was touched with pity and she came into the hollow, while I lay hidden behind a root looking to see what she would do to the child. She lay down before him and put the nipple of her udder in his mouth and nursed him until he fell asleep. All that night I lay there without sleep and without daring to move for fear that the beast might kill me, and the child lay sleeping among the fawns. In the morning the unicorn went out to feed and I arose and took up the child, but while I was swaddling him she returned again. This time, however, she showed me such affection that I stayed with her; and when my son and the fawns had been suckled, the beast, who saw that I was little—for I am a dwarf—seemed to think that I must be young, and she made a motion with her head toward one of her udders that was still quite full. Being very thirsty, I did as she wished, and I found she had the best milk and the sweetest that ever I had drunk. Sire, I lived thus while my food lasted, and my son was so well fed that he shows it still, I thank God. But when my food was gone I grew weak, and one day as I was looking out of the hole in our tree I saw a great stag going by, and I was so hungry, after living a long while on milk, that I cried out: '0 Lord God, how I wish that I had a steak from that stag, well cooked!' The unicorn overheard me; she dashed out of the hollow tree, made after the stag, and cut him in two with a single blow of her horn."

To make this delightful but rambling story as short as possible, the unicorn helped the dwarf gather firewood for cooking the stag, she helped him build a hut of boughs, she slew for him many other beasts as the needs of his larder required them. The child throve mightily on unicorn milk, and when he was weaned the dwarf fed him on the flesh of bears. Before long he had grown into a giant, able to uproot huge trees at a single jerk, and finally he built the square red tower, making it very tall and without doors or windows so that wild beasts would not eat the father while the giant boy was off at play. And everywhere he went the mother unicorn went with him.

While Arthur stands at the foot of the tower talking up to the dwarf, this son arrives, carrying a freshly killed bear in one hand and his club in the other. Introductions are made, the giant lifts Arthur to the top of the tower, and the three dine off the bear, the giant standing on the ground alongside. Next morning the giant and the unicorn drag Arthur's ship off the sands and the whole company sets sail for Windsor Castle.—*Cy finit le conte du papegaulx.*

156

DRAGONS AND UNICORNS—FACT? OR FICTION?

The unicorn is mentioned several times by Luigi Pulci in Il Morgante Maggiore, but no accurate treatment of the legend is to be expected from this burlesque upon romance. In one passage a strange combination is made of the water-conning trait with the ideas underlying the use of the horn at table, for we are told that the animal watches its own horn after dipping it to see whether it perspires:-

Ma non si fidi all' acqua, e non gli creda Se non vi mette il corno prima drento, E se quel suda sta a vedere attento.

Elsewhere we see Morgante and Margutte shoot and cook and eat a unicorn, taking advantage of the poor beast just as he is dipping his horn, in defiance of all the best authorities. The remarks of Luca Pulci, Luigi's brother, concerning unicorns are equally inaccurate, for he tells us that one of his characters by the name of Severe was turned into a unicorn by Diana to punish him for falling in love with a nymph; he ran straightway to a river's brink to look at his own reflection and while standing there was pierced by an arrow from the nymph's own bow which transformed him into the River Sieve.

Turning now to English literature, we come to the characteristically elaborate simile of Spenser:-

Like as a Lyon whose imperial powre A proud rebellious Unicorn defyes, T'avoid the rash assault and wrathful stowre Of his fiers foe, him to a tree applyes, And when him ronning in full course he spyes He slips aside: the whiles that furious beast

His precious home, sought of his enemyes, Strikes in the stocke, ne thence can be releast, But to the mighty victor yields a bounteous feast.

George Chapman provides an interesting variant of this lion-capture story by substituting a man for the lion:-

I once did see In my young travels through Armenia, An angrie Unicorne in his full carier Charge with too swift a foot a Jeweller, That watcht him for the Treasure of his browe; And ere he could get shelter of a tree, Naile him with his rich Antler to the Earth.

Shakespeare is obviously referring to this same story in the words: "Wert thou the unicorn, pride and wrath would confound thee, and make thine own self the conquest of thy fury." In the two other references to the animal to be found in Shakespeare's plays the speakers express disbelief. We may safely infer that Shakespeare himself did not believe in the existence of unicorns, and this is an interesting fact when one considers that thousands of his contemporaries, as well educated and as well read as he, accepted the animal apparently without a doubt. The shallower critics of Shakespeare have entertained us for many decades with speculations as to whether he did or did not believe in witches, fairies, ghosts, and other "night fears", some of them contending that so wise a man could not have entertained such childish superstitions, and others, more plausibly, that he was a man of his times with all that fact implies. Sound criticism will of course

DRAGONS AND UNICORNS—FACT? OR FICTION?

point out that he believed in these things at least imaginatively with an intensity adequate to his artistic needs. If an imaginative faith in the unicorn had been required of him by the day's work, such a faith would have been forthcoming, much as Milton's belief in the Ptolemaic system stood forth bold and clear when he saw that it would serve his purpose. As matters turned out, however, Shakespeare never had to write a play involving a "temporary suspension of disbelief" in the unicorn, and so he lets us see that belief in the animal is to his thinking a minor mark of easy credulity. Thus Decius Brutus, showing how easily Caesar may be swayed by old wives' tales, says:-

He loves to hear

That unicorns may be betrayed with trees.

A more revealing passage is that in which Alonso and his followers are entertained by Prospero with strange music and a phantom banquet, after which the irreverent Sebastian remarks, in the tone of a worldling whose scepticism is shaken:-

Now I will believe

That there are unicorns.

Little would be gained by an attempt to trace the later history of the legend in literature. It is true that a group of poets has recently pushed the hunt of the unicorn so actively that one critic has felt obliged to advocate a closed season, but most of this writing has been done in ignorance or neglect of the earlier legend. One reference to recent writing must suffice, and I make this chiefly because it suggests an aspect of the subject, never clearly expressed but often implied, which I do not care to consider extensively. Readers of Aubrey Beardsley's prose will recall that the Abbe Fanfreluche found in Queen Helen's library a pamphlet entitled "A Plea for the Domestication of the Unicorn," and that at the end of the story Helen goes out to feed her pet unicorn Adolphe—"milk-white all over except his nose, mouth, and nostrils". This is about all, but, as in nearly every other detail of the morbidly lascivious story, more is meant than meets the eye.

DRAGONS AND UNICORNS—FACT? OR FICTION?

CHAPTER IV

EAST AND WEST

IN the scientific discussion of any animal one of the prime essentials is the determination of its habitat, and we must not proceed farther with the study of the unicorn without naming the places where he has been supposed to be found.

Ctesias placed the unicorn, as we have seen, in "India", then as for long after a very inclusive term, and this location sufficed for his Greek and Roman followers. The Physiologus does not commit itself on this question, but when we consider that all the other animals it mentions—or all, at any rate, not concocted in libraries, like the ant-lion—were thought to belong to Egypt, we may infer that the unicorn also was regarded as a local species. Few of the Christian echoers of Physiologus have any notion of animal habitat, so that they give us little help.

Ethiopia had been confused with India even by Virgil, and therefore, if for no other reason, it was so confused during the Middle Ages. The bewildering transfer of "Prester John's Court" from India to Ethiopia, already referred to, helped on this confusion, and the transfer had a definite influence, as it happened, upon the legend of the unicorn. In the first letter supposed to have been addressed by him to one or other of the potentates of Europe, Prester John is made to describe himself as an Indian monarch, and in this letter, furthermore, he mentions the unicorns to be found in his realm. Fifty years later, that is to say about A.D. 1200, we find him established as a king and priest in Ethiopia, and it was naturally assumed that he had taken his unicorns with him—all the more because later versions of his letter, dated from Ethiopia, continued to mention these animals as prominent in the local fauna. But there were other influences at work to draw the unicorn into North Africa. For one thing, the people of Abyssinia had their own version of Physiologus; for another, the Arabs among them had a well-developed unicorn legend; finally, the Portuguese missionaries and merchants of a later time went into Ethiopia with

159

unicorn lore gathered from India itself, and when they found in this new land much the same legends and beliefs as those with which they had become familiar at Goa it is not strange that they were convinced.

Fray Luis de Urreta, whose account of rhinoceros hunting in Abyssinia we have already considered, places the unicorn—which he insists is an entirely different animal—in the Mountains of the Moon. He was by no means the first to hold this view. Cosmas Indicopleustes saw four brazen figures of the unicorn at the court of the King of Ethiopia in the sixth century of our era. A Mappa Mundi, made in the fifteenth century and now hanging on the wall of Hereford Cathedral, shows the unicorn, with a horn almost as long as its body, standing in the region of the Upper Nile. The Arabian zoologist Al Damiri testified to the same effect. John Bermudez reported unicorns in Abyssinia. Marmol Caravaial found them "en las sierras de Beht, o de la Lune". An English traveller of the sixteenth century asserts: "I have seen in a place like a Park adjoyning unto prester Johns Court, three score and seven-teene Vnicornes and eliphants all alive at one time, and they were so tame that I have played with them as one would play with young Lambes." Father Lobo handed on an extended account of the Abyssinian unicorn. Job Ludoiphus accepts these earlier declarations. We shall see also that a French consular officer of the nineteenth century corroborates them by a long and judicious letter about the unicorn of Central Africa addressed to a learned society.

Quite apart from this abundance of testimony, there is a fitness in the association of the unicorn with the enormous mountain ranges of Abyssinia. The Queen of Sheba is supposed to have hidden her treasure somewhere in those terrifying gorges, and they are a good place in which to hide any precious thing. The very name "Mountains of the Moon", which they owe to Ptolemy, makes them seem a proper home for wonderful beasts. If the unicorn does live among the snows held up for ever on the line of the Equator then it is clear why the world should know so little about him. An Arabian writer says that a great king once sent out a host of men to discover the sources of the Nile, but that they brought back no report because when they reached these mountains the heat reflected from their snows was so great that every man was reduced to ashes.

No sooner has one accustomed himself to think of the Mountains of the Moon as the unicorn's native place, however, than he finds that a case at least equally good may be made out for Tibet. An unknown Chinese traveller of the eleventh or twelfth century informs us that about eighty li from H'lari there is a lake in the vicinity of which unicorns are found in great abundance. Again, we are told by several Eastern historians that when the conqueror Genghis Khan set forth in 1224 to invade Hindustan he was met at the top of Mount Djadanaring by a beast with but one horn which knelt thrice at his feet as though in token of respect. The conqueror fell to brooding over this strange event, and he concluded that the beast was an incarnation of his father's spirit come to warn him against the expedition; therefore he turned his army about and marched down the mountain, leaving Hindustan unharmed. Centuries after this, Captain Samuel Turner, one of the most dependable of the earlier authorities upon Tibet, was solemnly told by the Rajah of Bootan that he had once owned a horse-like creature with a single horn in the middle of its forehead. The most famous of all travellers in Tibet, a learned man of the nineteenth century, was entirely convinced that the unicorn is to be found there. A certain Major Latter of the British Army wrote home in 1820 that he had found the unicorn beyond a doubt in Tibet.

Next one comes to the numerous reports of the unicorn in South Africa, where Garcias ab Horto heard it described—equipped with a single horn which it could raise and lower at will—on his voyage round the Cape in the middle of the sixteenth century. Somewhat over a century later Father Jerom Merolla da Sorrento, a Capuchin missionary, saw it in the region mentioned by Garcias. Baron von Wurmb writes from the Cape of Good Hope toward the end of the eighteenth century that he expects to see a unicorn any day, as the reports of it are all about him. Sir John Barrow, a well. trained observer, found so universal a belief in the animal among the natives of South Africa that he himself was inclined to believe, and his faith was rewarded by the discovery of a cave-painting, which he reproduced, of a beast with a single horn. Sir Francis Galton is half-convinced by the persistent reports he hears in Africa, and Dr. William Balfour Baikie finds his former scepticism "partly shaken".

Returning to the Near East, one finds a similar abundance of unicorns, either seen or surmised. One John of Hesse, a priest who visited the Holy Land in 1389, had the good fortune not only to see one but to witness the water-conning performance in actual operation. Felix Fabri, who made pilgrimage to the Holy Land a century later saw, on September 20, 1483, with his own eyes—as did all the members of his company—a unicorn standing on a hill near Mount Sinai, and he observed it carefully for a long time. Lewis Vartoman, regarded for centuries as an exceptionally veracious traveller, gives a careful description of two unicorns that he says he saw at Mecca about the middle of the sixteenth century—but it is to be observed that these two had been sent to the Sultan as a present by the King of Abyssinia. Vincent Le Blanc, who set out on his travels in 1567—at the age of fourteen—saw only one unicorn at Mecca, the other one mentioned by Vartoman having died, but by way of atonement he saw two at the Court of Pegu.

Not to make too intolerably long a list, there is the unicorn of Tartary reported by a British traveller of the eighteenth century and explained one hundred and fifty years later by Lieutenant-Colonel Prejevalsky. There is the unicorn of Persia, said to have been kept as a pet by the Sophy in his private gardens at Samarkand. There is the unicorn of the Carpathians made known by Antony Scheneberger in a letter quoted by Conrad Gesner. There is the unicorn of India, distinct from the rhinoceros, clearly depicted on a map of the Orient published with the English translation of Linschoeten's Voyages. There is the unicorn of Poland reported by Aldrovandus, the unicorn of Scandinavia of which we learn in the Historia Naturalis of Johnston, the unicorn of Florida made known to Europe by the Spanish conquistadors, the unicorn of the Canadian border described by Olfert Dapper, and finally there is the unicorn of China.

Chinese writers do not assert that the unicorn or ki-lin is a native of their land; on the contrary, they say that it comes from afar, presumably from heaven, and only at long intervals of time. They regard it, so to speak, as an intermittent animal, and its appearance on earth is considered a certain omen of a beneficent reign or of the birth of some great man comparable with a good emperor in importance. According to the testimony of Tse-Tche-t'ong-kien-kang-mou, the ki-lin was first seen in the year 2697 B.C., in the palace of the Emperor Hoang-ti, on which occasion it was a truthful prophet of national felicity. Another appeared to the mother of Confucius just before the sage's birth, holding in its mouth a great tablet of jade on which there was engraven a dithyramb in praise of the man her son was to become. Events of this sort have occurred so many times and the prophecy has always been so unerring that pictures of the unicorn are now pinned or pasted in the women's quarters of millions of Chinese houses in the hope that they may exert pre-natal influence and induce the birth of great men, or at least of boys rather than of girls. They are also affixed to the red chair in which the bride is borne to her husband's house, and the gods that oversee the distribution of desirable babies are often depicted riding upon the ki-lin. To say of any man that a ki-lin appeared at the time of his birth is the highest form of flattery.

The question is asked in the Li-Ki: "What were the four intelligent creatures?" and the answer is given: "They were the Phoenix, the Tortoise, the Dragon, and the Ki-lin." The last, though not so popular as the dragon, is commonly regarded as the king of beasts. No hunter has ever killed one; and it is seldom captured or even wounded, although we are told that one was injured by a hunter just before the death of Confucius. Like an exceptionally good Buddhist, the ki-lin eats no living thing, either animal or vegetable, so that its diet is severely restricted. It will not even tread upon an insect or a living blade of grass. It has the body of a stag, the hoof of a horse—conforming in these respects to the European tradition—the tail of an ox, and a single horn twelve feet long springing from the middle of its brow, which has at the end a fleshy growth. The most significant thing about the ki-lin's physical appearance, however, is the fact that he is resplendent in the five sacred colours, which are the symbols of his perfection.

The ki-lin is supposed to spring from the centre of the earth, and perhaps he was originally a representative of the earthy element as the phoenix represents fire, the dragon air, and the tortoise water. All commentators enlarge upon the excellence of his character. He knows good from evil, is reverential towards his parents and piously attached to the memory of all his ancestors; he is harmless, beneficent, and gentle, the fleshy tip of his horn indicating clearly that that otherwise formidable member has only symbolic and aesthetic uses. Like the Western unicorn, he keeps the dignity and the mystery of solitude, never mingling promiscuously even with those of his own kind and never treading upon soil tainted by the human foot unless he comes on a mission. He is not violently haled by hunters into the court of the sovereign, but arrives as one king visiting another. Unlike the Western unicorn, the ki-lin has never had commercial value; no drug is made of any part of his body; he exists for his own sake and not for the medication, enrichment, entertainment, or even edification of mankind.

We must infer that this Oriental unicorn was conceived on a higher plane of civilization than that which produced the European legend. Our Western unicorn does us credit

DRAGONS AND UNICORNS—FACT? OR FICTION?

in many ways, but when we compare him with the ki-lin we see that there is after all a good deal of violence and deceit and calculation implicit in the stories we have told of him. The ki-lin legend was developed by men who had got beyond fear and calculation in their attitude toward wild nature—by men not unlike those who painted the pictures and wrote the poetry of the Sung period in which Nature is loved for her own sufficient self almost a thousand years before the West learned to look at her without terror.

While speaking of the ki-lin's beneficence I may mention a detail of his legend which, although less firmly authenticated than one could wish, presents a surprising parallel with the legend of the West. The Chinese, we are told, preserve a tradition to the effect that the ki-lin "is to come in the shape of an incomparable man, a revealer of mysteries, supernatural and divine, and a great lover of all mankind. He is expected to come at about the time of a particular constellation in the heavens, on a special mission for their benefit." If this belief really exists—and it corresponds exactly with what we learn from better sources of the ki-lin's nature—then two apparently quite separate unicorn legends have worked out, in regions far apart, the same ultimate symbolism. Both in the East and in the West the unicorn comes to typify a Messiah. Shall we call this an accident, or shall we attribute it to the infiltration of Christian influence? A third possibility, one to which some slight support will be given in later pages, is that the two legends came to similar fruition because they sprang from a single root. It may appear that from the very beginning the unicorn has been conceived as beneficent, holy, in some sense divine, always striving for the healing of the nations.

Distinct as the ki-lin seems at first to be from the Western unicorn, and especially from the unicorn of Physiologus, it is hardly possible to think of him at last as an entirely independent creation. His different colouring, his more actively humane disposition, even the subtle but significant change in his horn—difficult to reconcile with our notions of physiology, but clear enough in allegorical intent—all these are due to his Chinese environment. On the other hand, he has the body of a stag and the solid hoof of a horse, like the unicorn of Aelian and Pliny and Solinus. Like all Western unicorns, he is solitary, and he cannot be captured. The Chinese are so certain of this last characteristic, indeed, that they never go forth against him even with virgins for bait. It seems likely, therefore, that the ki-lin and the unicorn of the West have a common ancestor.

Chinese writers enumerate six different sorts of unicorns: the King, the Kioh Twan, the Poh, the Hiai Chai, the Too Jon Sheu, and the Ki-lin; but it seems probable that all six are derived from a single original. The great age of some of the classics in which these animals are described proves that the unicorn legend is old in China, and this fact alone accounts for the existing discrepancies. In spite of these, the ki-lin is more consistent than the Western unicorn; it varies little in appearance and not at all in habits or temperament, being always gentle, beneficent, delicate in diet, regular and stately in pace, and with a call "which in the middle part thereof is like a monastery bell".

The ki-lin, moreover, does not show the tendency to sink down and fade away into the rhinoceros which is so deplorable in the Western unicorn, for the Chinese know the

163

DRAGONS AND UNICORNS—FACT? OR FICTION?

rhinoceros perfectly well and describe it accurately as a totally different species. From the time of the Han dynasty to our own day they have been the carvers of the rhinoceros horn, and old Chinese writers have much to say of the prophylactic value of this horn. During the T'ang dynasty (A.D. 618-905) the official girdles of mandarins were studded with pieces of it, used as charms somewhat in the way of the Japanese natsuke. Through all the many centuries that the commerce in rhinoceros horns has been going on, however, those who have had to do with it have known that the horns came from the rhinoceros, and the ki-lin has been kept apart from such associations. Uncontaminated by trade, never regarded as a drug or as an emblem of moral virtue, he has moved serenely all this while in the central recesses of the Oriental imagination.

One of the rarer titles in the "Americana" that have so strongly attracted the cupidity of book-collectors in recent decades is a wellprinted and brilliantly illustrated volume called Die Unbekante Neue Welt, by Dr. Olfert Dapper. The most accurate pages in this entertaining book are those that deal with New Amsterdam and the present site of New York City, so that a casual reader is the more surprised when he finds, immediately after those pages, a lively representation of the American unicorn in its native haunts—the suggestion is that they must have been in the general region of the Bronx—with an unmistakable American eagle upon its back. In the accompanying letterpress, however, and under the appropriate rubric Seltsame Tiere, the Doctor places this unicorn somewhat farther afield. "On the Canadian border", he says, "there are sometimes seen animals resembling horses, but with cloven roofs, rough manes, a long straight horn upon the forehead, a curled tail like that of the wild boar, black eyes, and a neck like that of the stag. They live in the loneliest wildernesses and are so shy that the males do not even pasture with the females except in the season of rut, when they are not so wild. As soon as this season is past, however, they fight not only with other beasts but even with those of their own kind."

While one reads this fairly accurate paraphrase of Aelian one's thoughts slip back more than two thousand years behind Dr. Dapper to another physician sitting in his library at the court of Darius and describing as accurately as he could the animals of another distant and wonderful land. (Without the medical profession the lore of the unicorn would have been far less rich than it is.) Here we see the animal's range enormously extended at a single leap, so that we may think of the unicorn as roaming, if not Manhattan Island, at any rate the woods of Maine and the Canadian border—that is to say, the region of the moose.

But it had not been reserved for Dr. Dapper to discover the American unicorn. His account is more than a hundred years too late for that, in addition to the fact that it has a strong smell of the lamp. We are told in the legends of the conquistadors that Friar Marcus of Nizza set out from Mexico in 1539 with Stephen the Negro to find the "Seven Cities of Cibola", and that when he got there the inhabitants showed him, among other wonders, "an hide halfe as big againe as the hide of an Oxe, and said it was the skinne of a beast which had but one home upon his forehead, bending toward his breast, and that out of the same goeth a point forward with which he breakes any thing that he runneth against."

DRAGONS AND UNICORNS—FACT? OR FICTION?

Furthermore, Sir John Hawkins writes in his account of his voyage of 1564: "The Floridians have pieces of unicornes homes which they wear about their necks, whereof the Frenchmen obtained many pieces. Of those unicornes they have many; for that they doe affirme it to be a beast with one home, which comming to the river to drinke, putteth the same into the water before he drinketh. Of this unicornes home there are of our company, that having gotten the same of the Frenchmen, brought home thereof to shew . . . . It is thought that there are lions and tygres as well as unicornes; lions especially; if it be true that is sayd, of the enmity betweene them and the unicornes: for there is no beast but hath his enemy insomuch that whereas the one is the other cannot be missing."

This passage helps one to see how notions of a new country's fauna developed even in the minds of intelligent men less than four centuries ago. Objects of horn or bone worn on necklaces by the natives of "Florida" proved that there were unicorns in that region, and in that case there must be lions too, for a beast cannot be left without its natural enemy. No man endowed with the divine faculty of reason required, or even wished, to see an actual American lion in order to be convinced; the bits of bone strung round the necks of the Floridians were a sufficient proof of lions to satisfy him. And if any one should be inclined to doubt the veracity of Captain Hawkins, now that his sword is rust, he has left a remarkable bit of "convincing detail" in a marginal rubric accompanying the text just quoted: "Unicornes homes, which ye inhabitants call Souanamma." He brought home, then, one hard bit of fact—a name. We see how he read what he thought he knew into the unknown, but that unknown belief of the Floridians may after all have been something worth finding out.

Twenty-three years after the voyage of Sir John Hawkins, John Davis, seeking a northwest passage to India, found a "unicorn's horn" in the hands of a savage on the coast of North America, in latitude 67 degrees. "Of them," he says, "I had a darte with a bone in it, or a piece of Unicornes home, as I did judge. This dart he [the savage owner] made store of, but when he saw a knife, he let it go, being more desirous of the knife than of his dart."

So much, then, for written records, by means of which we have traced the unicorn legend through the greater part of the world. And now, if one might shake off for a moment the necessity of finding definite authority for every opinion, if one might indulge his own fancy on this topic as thousands of others have done, and if it were not for the fear of being taken quite seriously, one would like to toy with the notion that the original home of the unicorn was the Lost Atlantis. Let us consider what may be said for this. Here we have a very ancient and persistent legend concerning a beast that seems to have vanished from the earth. The belief is of long standing that this beast, although as actual as the mammoth or the sabre-tooth tiger, was destroyed by the flood. Now it is generally agreed among Atlanteans that the world-wide tradition of the Flood—which Hebraizers will persist in calling "Noah's Flood"—is a racial memory of the submergence of the Atlantic Continent. Most significant are the few but startling evidences that the aborigines of the Western Hemisphere had their own legend of the unicorn, and that they actually used its supposed horn for magical ends. Legends so similar and so peculiar, found

DRAGONS AND UNICORNS—FACT? OR FICTION?

in both hemispheres, must have spread East and West from a common distributing centre, and that centre may well have been the vast region that has been covered for at least ten thousand years by the Atlantic waves. The Sargasso Sea has been for time out of mind the port of missing ships. Why may it not cover the primeval habitat of missing animals?

Here is an argument in support of Plato's theory about the Lost Atlantis that would have commended itself to the enthusiastic genius of Ignatius Donnelly; but one of the several objections to it is that we cannot really prove the existence of a unicorn legend among the American aborigines. One is sorry for this, feeling that Atlantis would have been as appropriate a habitat for the unicorn as even the Mountains of the Moon. We should solve several difficult problems if we could place him there with assurance.

DRAGONS AND UNICORNS—FACT? OR FICTION?

CHAPTER V

THE TREASURE OF HIS BROW

ALTHOUGH men have often been uncertain where unicorns were to be found, there has never been the same difficulty with regard to unicorns' horns. These have never been plentiful and they have usually been very dear, but they have been known. Almost any well-read or widely travelled European of the sixteenth century would have been able to name eight or ten whole horns kept in cathedrals, monastic houses, or kings' treasuries, not to mention the innumerable smaller pieces to be found in the hands of the wealthy. The study of these horns, of their distribution, origin, and use, leads into the centre of unicorn lore.

"Come we now", in the words of Thomas Fuller, "to the fashion and colour of the Horn, conceiving it no considerable controversy concerning the length and bignesse thereof, quantity not varying the kind in such cases." It is hard to know just what Thomas Fuller, who lived victoriously and contentiously through the English Civil Wars, may have understood by a "considerable controversy", but this one has been long and earnestly waged. Ctesias gives the length of the horn as one cubit or eighteen inches, Aelian as a cubit and a half, Pliny as two cubits, Solinus and Isidore as four feet, Cardan as three cubits, Rabelais as six or seven feet, and Albertus Magnus as ten feet. At this point the growth of the horn was checked, for the animal that bore it was obviously becoming top-heavy and needed, as several sceptics pointed out, to be "as big as a ship" merely to carry such a formidable bow-sprit. Arabian writers showed less retraint, for Al Damiri, among others, asserts that the unicorn, for all its great strength, is unable to lift its head because of the great weight of its horn. Other Arabian authorities inform us that he often carries about on this horn the bodies of several elephants which he has "perforated".

167

DRAGONS AND UNICORNS—FACT? OR FICTION?

Although the spoils went to the victor in these contests, they were frequently—as in human affairs—quite as lethal as defeat, for Alkazuwin says that when once the unicorn has gored the elephant he is unable to remove the corpse from his horn, so that he either starves to death or else dies of the putrefaction. (Here was material for a powerful pacifistic allegory, if the Arabs had been given to such things.) The end comes when the roc, seeing the unicorn with one or more elephants impaled upon his horn, swoops down and bears the whole mass of flesh away as a titbit for its young.

Concerning the length of the alicorn, then, one could think almost whatever one liked. The time was to come when specimens almost if not quite as long as that described by Albertus Magnus were to be seen in Europe, and undoubtedly the respect in which the unicorn was everywhere held was maintained by the effort to imagine a beast to which a horn ten feet in length would be proportionate.

Before the sixteenth century there was general agreement among the learned that the true horn was black, as Aelian had said, but after a long period of vacillation the opinion that it was white or of the colour of old ivory definitely triumphed. Less bookish persons had thought of it as white for a long time, if we may judge from the numerous pictures of the unicorn to be seen in mediaeval manuscripts. Andrea Bacci recalled the assertion of Aelian and Pliny, but had to admit that all the specimens he had seen were not black but more nearly white. His dilemma was really distressing, for he had, on the one hand, the Renaissance scholar's profound respect for ancient authority and, on the other, he felt obliged to avoid saying anything that would cast a doubt upon the genuineness of the horn, a white one, belonging to his patron, Don Francesco di Medici. He does the best he can in saying that "niger" does not necessarily mean pure black, but with all his learning he cannot make the word mean anything like white. Thomas Fuller suggests that the differences in colour may be due to age—"white when newly taken from his head; yellow like that lately in the Tower, of some hundred years seniority; but whether or no it will ever turn black, as that of Aelian's and Pliny's description, let others decide." But the most ingenious solution of these discrepancies was the view that the true horn is white within and black outside, on account of the "bark" that covers it, so that the same horn may be described as either black or white according as the bark has been left on or stripped off.

By far the strangest thing in the history of opinion about the alicorn's appearance is the age and persistence of the belief in the natural spiral twistings or striae. These are clearly delineated in every picture of the unicorn that I have seen in mediaeval manuscripts, some of which were drawn in the twelfth century. It is possible that Aelian meant to describe them in his phrase xxxxxx xxx Kai xxxx xxxxx for the word xxxxx may mean either "rings" or "spirals". Even the horns of the unicorned animals shown in bas-relief on the walls of Persepolis seem to show these twistings. There is nothing said about them, however, in Ctesias, Pliny, Solinus, Isidore, or Physiologus; aside from the mysterious passage in Aelian, there seems to be no ancient authority for them whatever, and learned writers do not mention them until after the close of the Middle Ages. Erudite Europeans were converted to the "anfractuous spires and cochicary turnings"—to adopt Fuller's

DRAGONS AND UNICORNS—FACT? OR FICTION?

charmingly pedantic phrase—at about the time when they admitted a possibility that the horn might sometimes be white, but Arabian writers had accepted them somewhat earlier. Alkazuwin says, for example, that the unicorn has one horn on its head, sharp at the top and thick below, with raised or convex striae outside and hollow or concave striae within.

Arabian notions of the inside of the alicorn are highly interesting. Ibn Khord‰dhbeh asserts that when the horn is split longitudinally one finds inside of it, on a black background, the white figures of a man, a fish, and a peacock or some other bird. Algiahid, in his Book of Holy Things, makes much the same remark, and Al Damiri affirms in more detail that when one cuts the alicorn lengthwise there are found in it various figures in white on black, as of peacocks, goats, birds, certain kinds of trees, men, and other things wonderfully depicted. Horns with such remarkable interior decorations were more prized, of course, than those without them, and the Arabs tell us that a good one was worth over four thousand shekels of gold and that they were used by the Chinese mandarins on their girdles.

This whole belief is certainly one of the most curious confusions of art with nature. Michelangelo seems to have found it helpful to imagine that his statue already existed in the stone block before him, so that his task was merely to strip away the superfluous material. Arabian travellers in the Orient could understand the work of the Chinese ivory carvers in no other way.

While considering the physical characteristics of alicorns we should not neglect the abundant testimony that they are not always fixed solidly in the skull, but that some unicorns have them "plyable", as Arthur Golding says in speaking of the one-horned bulls of Inde, "to what purpose they liste". There was the best authority for movable horns in general, Aristotle having ascribed them to the Indian bull and Solinus asserting that the Erythian ox could raise and lower its horns at will. The same advantage was enjoyed by the Yale, whose horns normally projected one forward and one backward, but who could switch them about to suit the exigencies of the moment in fighting. Cosmas Indicopleustes informs us that the rhinoceros's horn is normally so loose that it shakes and rattles when he walks, but that when he is in a rage it is suddenly tightened to such a degree that he can tear up rocks and trees.

The unicorn does not suffer in this comparison. Garcias ab Horto, rounding the Cape of Good Hope about the year 1550, heard of an amphibian on the eastern coast of Africa that could raise and lower its single horn and swing it to right or left as caprice or necessity dictated, and some years later André Thevet reported another amphibian unicorn-it had webbed feet behind and cloven hoofs before and lived on fish—from the Island of Molucca, with a three-foot horn that waved about like the crest of a cock. In this connection we must not forget the mobile horns observed by Pantagruel upon the unicorns of the Land of Satin. Finally, a consular agent of France writes a long letter in the middle of the nineteenth century to prove that the unicorn of the ancients has been discovered in Central Africa, and that it has a movable horn—"une corne unique, mobile, susceptible

DRAGONS AND UNICORNS—FACT? OR FICTION?

d'erection en ce sense qu'elle peut recevoir de la volonté de l'animal une position variable relativement a la surface du front".

There is one more thing, perhaps the most instructive of all, to be said about the physical characteristics of the alicorn. For two or three centuries many learned men, quite as intelligent as those of their kind to-day, measured and weighed and tasted these objects, speculated about them, subjected them to various tests, bought and sold them for great sums, wrote astonishingly erudite books about them—all the while calling them "horns". Not one of these men guessed, until the seventeenth century brought in new habits of thought, that the objects they had before them, ninety-nine times in the hundred, were not composed of horn at all but of ivory.

By the year 1600 Europe and England contained at least a dozen famous alicorns that were known to all travellers, were frequently exhibited on state occasions to the people, and were carefully described again and again. Most of these were kept in great churches or monasteries. They were regarded as sacred objects, and were sometimes used as pontifical staffs.

Best known of all was the horn of St. Denis, near Paris, seven feet long and weighing over thirteen pounds. This was included in the monastery's inventory of its treasures, together with other sacred relics, and was one of the "worthies" of Europe. Even John Evelyn speaks of seeing it—"a faire unicorne's horn, sent by a K. of Persia, about 7 foote long". The popular belief was that it had been presented to the monastery by André Thevet, the famous traveller, who was thought to have had it from the King of Monomotapa with whom he was said to have gone unicorn hunting; but this opinion was groundless, for Thevet speaks of having seen the horn of St. Denis "en ma grand' jeunesse", he never went unicorn hunting with the King of Monomotapa, and in fact he did not much believe in unicorns. How this alicorn was acquired we do not know, but it was lost during the general looting of old treasures, particularly those of the Church, during the Revolution of 1793. It was kept in a dark vault of the sanctuary, one end of it resting in water. We hear that "this water is given to drink to those that go under the hollow arch; and so soon as they have drunk they suddenly fall into a great sweat".

Cardan has left a careful description of the St. Denis alicorn which he saw during a visit paid to the monastery in company with the monks' physician. "After we had seen the sepulchres of the kings", he writes, "and the statues and other marble ornaments, I studied very closely the unicorn's horn hanging in the sanctuary. It was so long that I could not touch the top of it with my hand, but its thickness was slight in proportion to its length, for it was easily possible to surround it with the thumb and first finger . . . . It was smooth all over, but was marked by bands running from end to end as on a snail-shell . . . . Nature makes nothing else that I know of like this."

Almost equally celebrated were the two horns of St. Mark's in Venice, said to have been taken at the fall of Constantinople in 1204 as part of the Venetian share in the spoil. It is true that many of the treasures of St. Mark's were thus acquired, and the two horns

DRAGONS AND UNICORNS—FACT? OR FICTION?

have long been associated by tradition with the blind Doge Enrico Dandolo who, although ninety-seven years of age when Constantinople was taken, is said to have been the first man over the wall; but against this romantic and persistent tradition stand certain awkward facts. On the silver-gilt handle of one of these alicorns is the inscription: xxxxxx xxx xxxx xxxxx xxxxxx. (John Palaeologus, Emperor. Alicorn good against poison.) Now the first Emperor of the East named John in the Palaeologus dynasty was John V, who ruled 1341-1391; the only other, ignoring the non-dynastic John Cantacuzenus, was John VI, 1425-1448, and there are several reasons for believing that the alicorn in question belonged to him. For one thing, the Greek inscription upon it, although crude in several ways, is comparatively modern in lettering. It bears on the handle the familiar design of the double-headed eagle—probably Hittite in origin and perhaps brought into Europe by the Crusaders—which was adopted in the arms of the Emperor of the Romans not earlier than 1414. Finally, this John VI made a famous visit to the West, and especially to Venice, to seek aid for his crumbling empire, and we are told by the chronicler Phrantzes that when he appeared in St. Mark's Basin the Venetian galleys went out to meet him adorned with the design of the double-headed eagle—a gracious courtesy on the part of the city that had caused most of his distress. It seems to me more than possible that the alicorn bearing his name was brought to Venice by him on this occasion, although it is hard to see how it could have fallen, as it must have done, into the hands of the wealthy jewel merchant Giorgio Belbava. At any rate, St. Mark's Library contains a record that in 1488 this alicorn was given by the son of Belbava to Doge Barbarigo, and that the Doge at once handed it over to the Procurators of the Cathedral, "ut illud in Thesauris Sanctuarii in Celebritatibus portandum curarent".

The second alicorn of St. Mark's, like the first about one metre in length, is made of three pieces joined together. This also has a Greek inscription, but one that gives no hint of the horn's origin, so that one can believe, if one likes, that it was brought back by Doge Dandolo in 1204. Both of these alicorns have been coloured with vermilion for several inches from the points, and on this colour have been written various devotional ejaculations in Arabic, of no present interest except as they serve to indicate once more that the objects were regarded as sacred. Clearly, however, the Greek and Arabic inscriptions alike would be felt to increase the alicorn's magic power, and the phrases xxxx xxxxx xxxxxx xxxx xxxxxx on one of them were probably intended as a charm.

These two alicorns are still shown to visitors as they were when the hero of The Cloister and the Hearth saw them centuries ago, and when properly understood they are among the most interesting relics of the past to be seen in Europe. One's guide asserts that they were formerly used by admirals of the Venetian fleet as batons of office, and this, whether true or not, shows that they have long been popularly regarded as symbols of supreme power and leadership. The spiral ridges of both have been smoothed away to such an extent that Andrea Marini thought them not genuine, but the grain of the ivory may still be seen to run in counter-clockwise spirals, leaving one in no doubt as to their nature. This smoothing was not done, as some have surmised, to improve their appearance, but to get medicinal powder, and there exists a highly interesting, not to say amusing, decree of the august Council of Ten: "That the Procurators are to have the Alicorns decorated with silver from the points to the silver-gilt handles so that the marks of former scrapings may be concealed, and they are to prohibit any further scrapings except in cases allowed by unanimous vote of the Council of Ten."

There is in the St. Mark's Treasury still another alicorn, more than twice as long as the other two, unscraped, and without inscriptions. The history of this one can be traced accurately for a long period, although it is probably not so old as the others. In the year 1597 Francesco Contarini, ambassador from Venice to the Court of France, wrote to the Council of Ten advising the purchase from the Maréchal de Brissac of his alicorn, held at thirty thousand ducats. Francesco argued, like a Venetian, that in this way the Republic could get back some part of the debt owed to it by France. Venice seems to have offered the sum demanded, but for some reason did not get the alicorn until 1668, when it was sold to a descendant of Francesco Contarini by the Brissac family. In his will, dated 1684, Alessandro Contarini left it to the Treasury of St. Mark's, adding the information that it had been taken by the French in the sack of Turin. When given to the Treasury this alicorn stood on a pedestal of wrought silver, which gave it the appearance of a gigantic candle, but about the middle of the nineteenth century the pedestal was put to other uses.

Milan Cathedral also had its famous alicorn; the church at Raskeld somehow acquired several; St. Paul's in London and Westminster Abbey each had one or more before the Dissolution, when they were probably either taken into the royal treasury or else sold to the highest bidders. The inventory taken by order of Cromwell in 1536 of the property owned by the tiny Church of St. Swithun at Winchester shows: "One Rectors staf of Unicorns horn"—a proud possession indeed for one of the smallest churches in England at a time when the alicorn was still "worth a city". Chester Cathedral still keeps its alicorn, but I am told by the Dean that it has been in the Chapter's possession only since the eighteenth century.

The long association of the unicorn with Christianity and the Church is amusingly illustrated by an attempted act of vandalism in which the beast fully justified the ancient belief that he could not be captured. In a forgotten book of travels I find this passage: "Our leader having taken a great fancy to the unicorn which stands on one side of the great entrance to the Church of Saint John in Malta, wishing to place it as a figure-head to his brother's yacht, he resolved to have the animal, and his refractory crew were desired to be in attendance the next night . . . . The rope was placed round the unicorn's neck, and all of us began, with a true sailor-like 'one, two, three, haul!' to dislodge our victim. It was, however, so well fastened on its pedestal that we did not succeed."

A feeling that the horn had some vague sanctity, due perhaps to the symbolism of the unicorn, must certainly be assumed to explain the possession of these objects by so many churches and monasteries and the veneration in which they were held; but a quite different feeling lay behind the eager quest of them by popes and kings and emperors during the Renaissance. Andrea Bacci says that in his time—the second half of the sixteenth century—there was not a prince in Italy, to say nothing of those outside of it, who had not at least a piece of the horn in his possession. He describes in detail the alicorn belonging

DRAGONS AND UNICORNS—FACT? OR FICTION?

to the Grand Duke Francesco Medici, which he seems to have had before him while writing his book, and others belonging to the Pope, to the Duke of Mantua, to Ruberto Ricci of Florence, and to the King of Poland—this last a very famous specimen. Echoing Bacci, J. F. Hubrigk asks rhetorically: "Is there any Prince, Duke, or King in the world who has not either seen or possessed, and regarded as among the most precious of his possessions, a unicorn's horn?" Such men there may have been, but if so it was not for lack of desire but of funds.

Among the earliest references to the alicorns of kings' treasuries are those in the royal accounts of France. There we find recorded, for the year 1388, the sum paid to a goldsmith "pour avoir atachie une espreuve de lincorne et mise sur une chayenne d'argent doré et enchaconée." This was early indeed, for the alicorn was not to reach the height of its reputation for more than a century to come. Just eighty years after the King of France paid for the decoration of his horn, Edward IV of England gave a sumptuous dinner to his sister, the Princess Margaret, on the occasion of her wedding to the Duke of Burgundy, and in the contemporary description of the furniture prepared for the dinner we read: "In the myddis a copeborde, in triangle of IX stagis hight. On every corner unnycorns horns, the poyntes garnysshid, and othe thre in other places, accomplissinge the coopborde." One of the most amusing glimpses into remote history afforded us by unicorn lore is the possibility that at least one of the numerous alicorns at this wedding dinner was brought over from France by the bridegroom himself. This we may perhaps infer from the inventory of the Dukes of Burgundy made in 1467, the year before the wedding, for there we find described: "Une licorne garnye autour du bout, par dessoubz, d'or, a la devise de MS., et a la pointe garnie d'argent doré et depuis l'un des boutz jusques a l'autre garnye de plusieurs filetz d'or." Perhaps the Duke felt even on his wedding journey and while sitting beside his bride that he preferred to trust his own horn, for the times were troubled and one did not know how English alicorns might act. However this may have been, these people were certainly much interested in the alicorn. In September of 1472 Louis de la Grantehuse came to England as ambassador to Edward IV from the Duke of Burgundy. The highly interesting account of this visit records that "When the masse was doon, the Kinge gave the sayde Lorde Granthuse a Cuppe of Golde, garnished wt Perle. In the myddes of the Cuppe ys a greate Pece of Vnicornes horne, to my estimacyon, VII ynches compas." Somewhat after this, Commines relates that de Ballassat, plundering the palace of Pietro de' Medici in 1495 "took, among other things, a whole unicorn's horn worth six or seven thousand ducats, and two large pieces of another". D'Aubigne, also, narrating the exploits of one of his noble ruffians, says that he found in a villa he was plundering "pour butin principal une licorne estimée a quatrevingt mille escus".

These, however, were the alicorns of subjects, and comparatively humble things. The gorgeous popes of the Renaissance acquired a number of horns by one means and another, descending when necessary even to outright purchase, and they were accustomed to have them set with appropriate splendour in silver and gold. In his account of how he worsted his rival Tobbia, Benvenuto Cellini enables us to see how carefully this work of the goldsmith was done. He says that Pope Clement VII commanded him and

173

DRAGONS AND UNICORNS—FACT? OR FICTION?

Tobbia "to draw a design for setting an unicorn's horn, the most beautiful that ever was seen, and which had cost him seventeen thousand ducats: and as the Pope proposed making a present of it to King Francis, he chose to have it first richly adorned with gold: so he employed us both to draw the designs. When we had finished them we carried them to the Pope. Tobbia's design was in the form of a candlestick: the horn was to enter it like a candle, and at the bottom of the candlestick he represented four little unicorn's heads—a most simple invention. As soon as I saw it I could not contain myself so as to avoid smiling at the oddity of the conceit. The Pope perceiving this, said, 'Let me see that design of yours.' It was a single head of an unicorn fitted to receive the horn. I had made the most beautiful sort of head conceivable, for I in part drew it in the form of a horse's head and partly in that of a hart's, adorned with the finest sort of wreaths and other devices; insomuch that no sooner was my design seen but the whole court gave it the preference. However, as some Milanese gentlemen of great authority were witnesses of this contest, they said: 'Most Holy Father, if you propose sending this noble present to France, you should take it into consideration that the French are an undiscriminating tasteless people and will not be sensible of the excellence of this masterly piece of Benvenuto's. But they will be pleased with these grotesque figures of Tobbia's, which will be sooner executed; and Benvenuto will in the meantime finish your chalice.'" Whether for the reasons given or not, this advice was accepted: in 1553 Pope Clement met François I at Marseilles and there gave him the horn which had been decorated by Tobbia, the occasion being the wedding of the Pope's niece, Catharine de Medici, to the son of François, the later Henry II of France.

Temporal princes were not less eager purchasers than Pope Julius III, who bought a horn for ninety thousand écus for the Vatican museum. At the coronation of the Emperor Theodore Ivanovitch in Moscow, 1584, he wore "a bejewelled robe—worth two hundred pounds, his staff imperial in his right hand of an unicorn's horn of three and one half feet in length beset with rich stones bought of merchants of Augsburg by the old Emperor in 1581, and cost him seven thousand marks sterling." We hear also that the Sultan of Turkey sent twelve alicorns as a gift to Philip II of Spain, feeling, no doubt, that Philip needed them as much as any man in Europe. (This story was doubted by Caspar Bartholinus, who could not believe that even the Sultan was rich enough to own twelve horns at a time.)

One might write an entire book, and not a dull one, about the alicorns of kings' treasuries; but the present book has a longer road to travel, and I can only mention a few of the horns that have been owned by British sovereigns.

In 1303, while King Edward I of England was fighting far in the North, he learned that a large part of the immense treasure which he had hidden, before setting out, under the Chapter House at Westminster, had been stolen. As soon as he could return to London he set on foot a strict investigation, and the trial that followed proved the guilt of some of the Westminster monks. Under the bed of one of the chief culprits, the keeper of the palace gate, there was discovered a unicorn's horn which had been stolen from the treasury, and for centuries thereafter the skin of a fair-haired and light-complexioned man was to

DRAGONS AND UNICORNS—FACT? OR FICTION?

be seen nailed to the place in the wall where the entrance had been made—intended, no doubt, "to encourage the others".

An inventory taken in 1497 of the possessions of James III of Scotland shows: "In unicornis [i.e. in the coins of that name] nyne hundreth and four score. Item a serpent toung and ane unicorne home, set in gold. Item a covering of variand purpir taster, browdin with thressilis and a unicorne."

But by far the most famous of all British alicorns was the great "Horn of Windsor" which the German traveller Hentzner saw in 1598 and valued, if his Latin text is to be trusted, at one hundred thousand pounds. We know exactly when and where this horn was discovered; it was picked up on the twenty-second of July, 1577, on an island in Frobisher's Strait, and we are told that when it reached England it was "reserved as a jewell by the Queen's Majesty's commandment, in her wardrobe of robes." We have also a dark hint as to what became of it, for Thomas Fuller, speaking of it and of the Tower Horn, both of which he had seen in his youth, remarks: "It belongs not to me to inquire what became of them", and then somewhat later he says that a unicorn's horn has been presented to his Majesty "to supply the place of that in the Tower which our Civil wars have embeseled". We may infer that the Horn of Windsor was "embeseled" at the same time.

Fuller's words imply that the Tower Horn also belonged among the Crown jewels, and it deserved a place there if contemporary estimates of its value were not exaggerated. "In 1641 the Marquis de la Ferte Imbaut, Marshal of France, saw in the Tower of London a unicorn's horn covered with plates of silver and estimated at the enormous sum of forty thousand pounds." Such an estimate as this, at so late a date, must have been due largely to the goldsmith's work, for the value of alicorns fell away rapidly after 1625. The one belonging to Charles I and kept by him at Somerset House was valued at only five hundred pounds, although it was an exceptionally fine specimen. Pierre Pomet tells us that it was seven feet long and weighed thirteen pounds, so that it equalled the famous horn of St. Denis.

The cost of "true unicorn's horn" (verum cornu monocerotis) in its best period was a little over ten times its weight in gold when sold in small pieces or in powder, but whole alicorns sometimes brought twice as much as this. The inventory of Lorenzo the Magnificent, recently opened to the public in the new Medici Museum at Florence, shows that the most precious of his possessions after the famous Tazza Farnese was his alicorn, three and one-half braccia in length and valued by him—probably on the basis of what it cost him—at six thousand gold florins. About the year 1560 a group of German merchants offered an alicorn for sale in Rome and other Italian cities for ninety thousand scudi—the scudo being then worth about four shillings—and finally sold it to the Pope. We are told that the King of France refused one hundred thousand icus for the horn of St. Denis, although we are not told how it came to be in his control. A horn picked up on the coast of Wales in 1588 by a poor woman was sold for a great but unspecified sum. Edward Topsell could say in 1607 that "the price of that which is true is reported at this day to be of no

DRAGONS AND UNICORNS—FACT? OR FICTION?

less value than gold". The famous alicorn belonging to the city of Dresden was valued at seventy-five thousand thalers. Ordinarily it was kept on display, strongly protected, in the museum which was known to the more leisured classes as the:

exotikothaumatourgematatameion, and there was a strict municipal regulation that whenever raspings were taken from it for medicinal uses two persons of princely rank should be present in the room. Pierre Pomet tells us that a horn given to the King of France in 1553 was said to be worth twenty thousand pounds sterling. The Republic of Venice in 1597 offered for a whole horn the sum of thirty thousand ducats—ten times the price of Shylock's pound of flesh—and did not get it.

Many things in the history of commerce are less interesting than the curve of market quotations on unicorns' horns. The means that were taken to increase and then to maintain the price of them we can only infer from a number of minute details, but the reasons why that price rather swiftly declined are more open to examination. By 1734 a well-informed writer could say that horns which formerly brought many thousands of dollars could then be had for twenty-five; yet this same writer makes it clear that even in his time there was still an active sale, and it is certain that long after the wealthy had lost all interest in alicorns the poor continued to buy them. Something of this commercial history is indicated by the fact that the Book of Rates for the first year of Queen Mary, 1531, gives the import duty as "cornu unicorni ye ounce 20 shillings", and that in 1664 the French duty on unicorn's horn was fifty sous per pound.

There is something delightfully humorous, to the modern view, in the idea of adulterating and "faking" the unicorn's horn. The rewards of success were enormous, and human nature was almost as prevalent in the sixteenth century as it is to-day, so that one finds in all the more responsible and socially minded writers upon our topic bitter complaints about the frequency of counterfeiting, warnings that purchasers must be constantly suspicious, and tests by which the true horn may be known from the false. Andrea Bacci makes it clear that fraud was very common in his time, though he thinks it can only be practised in the sale of powdered horn and of fragments, for which, he says, various kinds of horn and pounded stone were sold; but even this would be impossible, he reminds his readers, if only the public would realize that the true horn is rarer than precious stones, so that none but great princes can hope to possess even a large piece. Bacci does not show his usual knowledge and acumen, however, in saying that the horn cannot be imitated in the whole piece, for there is evidence that the wicked knowledge of how this could be done was possessed and used in his time all over Europe. Amatus Lusitanus, following Dioscorides, says that if ivory is boiled for six hours in a decoction of mandragora it becomes soft so that one can bend and work it as he likes, and Cardan tells us that elephants' tusks were often so treated. One source of the supply of alicorns is revealed by Hector Bothius in his Histoty of Scotland, where he asserts, after a grotesque account of walrus hunting, that the tusks of the beasts are straightened artificially and sold in Europe as unicorns' horns. André Thevet affirms that he has actually seen this artificial straightening performed by clever Levantine artisans on an island in the Red Sea, a distributing station for both East and West. Antony Deussing admits that such fraud

DRAGONS AND UNICORNS—FACT? OR FICTION?

is possible, and he suspects that it is a good deal practised. Andrea Marini, always a sceptic, goes so far as to imply that even the sacred horns of St. Mark's, in his own city, are not above suspicion. For powdered alicorn the common substitutes seem to have been burnt horn, whalebone, various kinds of clay, the bones of dogs and of pigs, limestone, and, most important of all during the later history, stalactites and the bones of fossil animals. Edward Topsell, with all these facts in mind, advises that alicorn be bought "out of the whole horn if it may be done, or of greater crums, and which may describe the figure of the home".

Under these deplorable circumstances there was an obvious need of tests by which the true horn might be known and counterfeits detected. The scientist set himself once more to his ancient and endless task of outwitting and exposing the charlatan, with the result that we may study the nascent "experimental method", as applied to the alicomn, in examples much earlier than Francis Bacon. In these tests we see the fumblings of infant science: it does not ask what seem to us the fundamental questions; for a long time the effort was not to find out whether unicorns existed, nor yet, supposing that they did, whether the magical properties attributed to their horns really belonged to them. Unicorns and magical properties were assumed, so that the only question for scientific investigation was the practical one: is this particular horn genuine cornu monocerotis? Nevertheless, groping and childish as these experiments seem to us, it is with them that the unicorn legend enters its final phase. It had come through the "theological" period, to adopt Comte's famous generalization, and through another which we may perhaps call, by a somewhat violent wrenching of the term, the "metaphysical"; now it slowly emerges into the "positivistic" period, into the modern scientific world in which, after a long time and many hesitations, it was to be forgotten. Thus the history of human thought, so far as we have yet gone, is implicit and epitomized in the lore of the unicorn.

A full account of the alicorn tests would fill many pages, and I must choose a few examples that seem typical of their respective periods. One of the most curious passages concerning them is that given by one David de Pomis, who describes himself with no false modesty as "a Hebrew physician and philosopher of the Tribe of Juda, and a member of the noble family of Pomaria which the Emperor Titus led captive from Jerusalem to Rome." His book is at first sight somewhat bewildering. The fact that it is written in three languages—Hebrew, Latin, and Italian—contributes something to this effect; it is paged backward, the indexes run backward, and the title-page stands at the end; David uses the full-stop only when he is quite through with a topic, to mark a period in the exact sense, and he employs the comma for all other punctuation. All this is darkened rather than illumined for me, in the only copy I have seen, by the numberless marginalia in the hand of Isaac Casaubon, who improves upon his polyglot author by adding a vocabulary in Arabic. But it is precisely in such "quaint and curious volumes of forgotten lore" as this-how Edgar Allan Poe would have loved it!—that we have to delve for unicorn lore, and David of the Tribe of Juda does not disappoint one.

"The unicorn", says he, "is a beast that has one horn in its brow, and this horn is good against poison and pestilential fevers. But one is to observe that there is very little of the

DRAGONS AND UNICORNS—FACT? OR FICTION?

true horn to be found, most of that which is sold as such being either stag's horn or elephant's tusk. The common test which consists in placing the object in water to see whether bubbles will rise is not at all to be trusted, and therefore, wishing to benefit the world and to expose the wicked persons who sell worthless things at great prices, I take this occasion to describe a true test by which one may know the genuine horn from the false. The test is this: place the horn in a vessel of any sort of material you like, and with it three or four live and large scorpions, keeping the vessel covered. If you find four hours later that the scorpions are dead, or almost lifeless, the alicorn is a good one, and there is not money enough in the world to pay for it. Otherwise, it is false."

A series of alicorn tests is given by Laurens Catelan: the true horn, when thrown into water, sends up little bubbles, "like a pearl"; the water seems to boil, though cold, and one can hear the boiling; the horn gives out a sweet odour when burned; poisonous plants and animals, when brought near it, burst and die; it sweats in the presence of poison. This Catelan, we are to remember, was an eminent pharmacist of the seventeenth century, and he had a whole "true horn" of his own, yet he names these five tests in apparent good faith. The physician Jordanus in his book De Pe.cte speaks of seeing a Jew enclose a spider in a circle drawn on the floor with an alicorn, and he says that the spider could not cross the line, and starved to death inside it. Basil Valentine, in his Triumphal Chariot of Alchemy, specifies that the circle should be drawn, not with the horn, but with the flesh of the animal; and Ambroise Pare relates that the test was sometimes made by soaking the horn in water, dipping a finger in this water, and then drawing a circle with it on a table. This was something like the test that John Webster had in mind in the lines:-

As men, to try the precious unicorn's horn,

Make of the powder a preservative circle,

And in it put a spider.

These tests were not always accepted, however, by more thoughtful writers. Atnbroise Pare, like Andrea Marini, says that he has tried all of them and that those that cannot be explained on natural grounds do not work. Cardan gives his own set of tests, according to which the true horn is always striated, is extremely hard, very heavy, of the colour of boxwood, and able to save the life of a pigeon poisoned with arsenic. In the last of these tests we approach modern methods. It was used more and more frequently as time went by and gradually supplanted all rivals. Thus Andrea Bacci tells us that the Cardinal of Trent had an alicorn richly adorned with gold and gems which he used very generously-"and I am able to affirm that on one occasion, several signors being present, he put it to this test: he gave arsenic to two pigeons, and then to one of them he fed as much as it would take of powder scraped from the horn. This one, after a few symptoms of sickness, revived and lived; the other died in two hours." And again we read that on the 3rd of October, 1636, the Professors and College of Physicians of Copenhagen were present at an experiment made by a pharmacist of that city named John Woldenberg. He gave ar-

DRAGONS AND UNICORNS—FACT? OR FICTION?

senic to two doves and two kittens, and then administered scrapings of alicorn to one of the doves and one of the kittens. According to Ole Wurm, who was present, the test was "not entirely unsuccessful", for the dove to which the alicorn was given survived, but both kittens died.

This brings us to the most interesting, the strangest, and the central belief about the unicorn—that its horn has a mysterious alexipharmical or prophylactic "virtue". It was supposed to be a detector of the presence of poison. Opinions varied concerning the mode of its operation and the causes of its power, but that power itself was seldom questioned or subjected to intelligent investigation. The faith in it rested upon authority, tradition, and common consent, which have always been and are still the strongest influences governing belief; destruction of this faith took a century and a half of time and the gradual substitution of new habits of thought for old.

For a clear English statement of this faith we may go to John Swan, an unquestioning though late believer. "Monoceros", he writes, "is a beast with one horne, called therefore by the name of an unicorne . . . which hath naturally but one horne, and that a very rich one, which groweth out of the middle of his forehead, being a horne of such virtue as is in no beast's horne besides; which, while some have gone about to deny, they have secretly blinded the eyes of the world from their full view of the greatness of God's works. . . This horne hath many sovereign virtues, insomuch that being put upon a table furnished with many junkets and banqueting dishes, it will quickly descrie whether there be any poyson or venime among them, for if there be the horne is presently covered with a kind of sweat or dew."

For two full centuries at least, roughly speaking from the final decades of the fourteenth century to those of the sixteenth, this belief was almost universal and unchallenged throughout Europe; but even in the fourteenth century it was already ages old, for one sees at a glance that it must be closely related to the belief reported by Aelian about the beakers used by Indian potentates. After the sixteenth century it lingered on, in spite of repeated attacks, almost into our own time. At present we may focus attention upon the period of its undisputed sway.

As one would expect, considering the constant search of mediaeval medicine for a panacea, so remarkable an object as the alicorn was not allowed to remain a mere detector of poisons. To the basic faith in its supernatural properties there was added the belief that it had a more general prophylactic power, and at length, invading the other great department of medicine, it was widely accepted as a powerful therapeutic agent. Before the sixteenth century closed the alicorn had an important place in materia medica, for we learn from an accurate and scholarly physician of the time that it was then prescribed as a cure for all poisons, for fevers, for bites of mad dogs and scorpions, for falling sickness, worms, fluxes, loss of memory, the plague, and prolongation of youth. Charlatans were even known to assert that it could raise the dead.

One of the earliest indications that this superstition was beginning to form in Europe

179

DRAGONS AND UNICORNS—FACT? OR FICTION?

is to be found in the writings of Hildegarde of Bingen (1098-1179). A most remarkable woman—by no means a saint, though often called so, and scarcely a "mystic", proper regard being had to her pathological condition—Hildegarde lays strong claim to the respect of those who can be just to brilliant reasoning based upon false premises. The centre of her encyclopaedic interests was medicine, so that she could scarcely have ignored the alleged virtues of the alicorn if she had ever heard of them. I find no mention of them in her works, but I do find discussion of other matters closely allied. Hildegarde believed that not the horn alone of the unicorn, but the whole animal was medicinal: under its horn, she says, it has a piece of metal as transparent as glass in which a man may see his face; she tells us how to make an unguent of the yolks of eggs and powdered unicorn's liver, which unguent is a sovereign cure for leprosy—"unless the leper in question happens to be one whom Death is determined to have or else one whom God will not allow to be cured". (As Hildegarde is the only woman who has ever written anything important about the unicorn, the suggestion of the cook-book in her "yolks of eggs and powdered unicorn's liver" is the more welcome.) A belt made of unicorn's skin, she says, will preserve one from fevers, and boots of the same material assure one of sound legs and immunity from plague. All this is good to know, and it comes with the authority of one who, as head of a large religious house, had the health of a whole community in her keeping.

Albertus Magnus (1193-1280), as mighty in his influence as in learning, a cautious and even thoughtful writer considering his times, makes little of the horn's magical virtues and thinks they should be investigated further. Peter of Abano (c. 1250-1318), who carried on the work of Albertus in "conciliating" the remains of Aristotelianism with Aristotle's Arabic commentators, was a man of different stamp. Generally regarded as a magician, he seems to have saved himself from the stake only by an opportune death. During his exploration of Arabic lore he acquired a firm faith in the alicorn which he transmitted to many others, and indeed if one were asked to name a single writer to whom the European belief might be attributed with least exaggeration, one could not do better than to choose this Peter. The fact is, of course, that no single writer was even largely responsible, for the belief grew up at a time when no scholar ever expressed an original idea if he knew what he was doing. It may well be that the Crusaders returning from the East did more to spread the faith in the alicorn through Europe than all the books put together, but at any rate that faith was well established among the learned before 1350, and by the end of the same century it was accepted by the wealthier classes of Europe and Great Britain. The poor and ignorant were to have no practical interest in it for at least two centuries to come.

Detached expressions and indications of the belief are almost innumerable. The writer known as "Dame Juliana Berners" says that "venym is defended by the home of the Unycorne", and James I of Scotland speaks of

the lufare unicorne That voidis venym with his evoure horne.

We hear that the inquisitor Torquemada always kept a piece of alicorn on his table as

DRAGONS AND UNICORNS—FACT? OR FICTION?

a precaution against the wiles of his numerous enemies; it was carried by Spanish and English explorers of America as conscientiously as quinine is carried to-day by travellers in tropical countries; Cabeza de Vaca writes that during his journey down the Paraguay River in 1543 there were three attempts made to poison him with arsenic, but that he foiled them all with a bottle of oil and a piece of alicorn. When the Elizabethan adventurer, Edward Webbe, was at the point of death from poison administered to him by "some lewd gunners"—one sympathizes with those gunners, for they were probably worn out by the man's outrageous lies.—"his phisitian gave him speedily Unicorne's home to drinke", with the deplorable result that he lived on. A whole ship's company of Englishmen was poisoned in Elizabethan days "by the roots of Mandioca, but by a piece of Unicornes home they were preserved". It seems probable that even Francis Bacon, reputed "father of the experimental method", shared the belief of his time in the alicorn, although he admits that the general confidence in it was in his day declining. When the Apothecaries' Society of London was founded in 1617 two unicorns were chosen as the supporters of its arms, and the common sign of the apothecary's shop, both in England and in Europe, during the seventeenth century was the figure of a unicorn or that of its head and horn. Laurens Catelan lists the names of a dozen foremost medical authorities who had not only used the alicorn in their practice but had praised it in their writings. Conrad Gesner, a zoologist of great influence, says that the horn, especially that "ex novis insulis allatum", works miracles against poison. Even at Venice and in the middle of the seventeenth century there was a general belief that the remarkable sweetness of the water in a certain well was due to bits of alicorn that had been thrown into it years before. In 1639 James Primerose of Hull said that the horn was still more trusted than the bezoar-stone, although less common. But there is no need to extend this catalogue farther in order to show that the belief in the alicorn's magical properties was at least as general as the contemporary belief in witchcraft. I may end it by quoting the words of one of the most learned and witty of Englishmen. Thomas Fuller, having at one time doubted the stories of the horn's virtue, reconsiders his doubts, and concludes delightfully: "It is improbable that the vigour of Nature should extrude that so specious to sight which is not also sovereign to service."

Long before Fuller's time there were of course disbelievers abroad, as the Reverend Edward Topsell makes clear—"A vulgar sort of Infidels who scarcely believe any herb but such as they see in their own gardens, or any beast but such as is in their own flocks, or any knowledge but such as is bred in their own brains . . . so that of the true Unicorn, because of the nobleness of his horn, they have ever been in doubt: by which distraction it appeareth unto me that there is some secret enemy in the inward degenerate nature of man which continually blindeth the eyes of God his people from beholding the greatness of God his works." We shall have to hear from several base heretics of this kidney in their turn, but in the meantime there is no doubt what was the orthodox belief.

The rapid development and spread of this belief and the correspondingly rapid increase in the prices paid for alicorns synchronize curiously—one cannot help thinking, significantly—with another equally swift development, that in the art or profession of poisoning. Working upon the few poor hints left them by ancient writers, and urged on

181

DRAGONS AND UNICORNS—FACT? OR FICTION?

by the peculiar needs created by their political institutions, the Italians of the Renaissance carried this art and profession to wonderful heights. When every possible allowance has been made for the exaggeration caused by contemporary fear and by the romantic fancies of a later age, it remains clear that, during just those two centuries in which the interest in alicorns culminated, poison was a tool of social and political ambition very commonly used in Italy, always to be considered and provided against, never to be ignored. We need not believe in all the alleged crimes of the Borgias in order to recognize in the very nature of the Italian tyrannies a direct incitement to this basest and most cowardly form of murder, for the violence and crime and subterfuge by which the tyrant frequently gained his power often gave the suggestion, sometimes almost the excuse, for the insidious violence of his taking off, and there can be no doubt whatever that many of the noblemen of Italy lived in constant fear. The "poison-rings", the amulets and charms against poison, the crystal cups and the goblets of Venetian glass that have come down to us would alone show that. Between the early years of the fourteenth century, when Peter of Abano wrote his treatise De Venenis, and the appearance in 1586 of Andrea Bacci's book of similar title, scores of Italian scholars and physicians, most of them in the pay of great lords, pitted their learning and wits against the secret skill of the poisoner. The pharmacopceia was ransacked, ancient texts were searched, superstitions older than civilization were revived—but nothing would serve; the dukes and counts and captains and cardinals of Italy continued to die suddenly, mysteriously, and, at least in one sense, prematurely. Medical science could not then detect the nature of the poison by which a man had died, and could not even make certain that he had been poisoned at all; but this uncertainty did not mitigate the fear. If suspicion outran the facts, this did not slow down the search for antidotes and precautions.

Francis Petrarch, who lived for many years in the palaces of cardinals and dukes and who knew their hunted lives at first hand, left a vivid picture of one of them at his noonday meal to which I have already referred. There is exaggeration in that picture, but the facts were terrible enough. Those who think that our northern ideas of Italian poisoning are chiefly due to misinterpretation of Machiavelli and to diseased fancies, such as those of Webster, Tourneur, and Beddoes, may be recommended to study the career of the Milanese poisoner Aqua Toffana, who although she lived long after what may be called the best period of her art, is said to have disposed of more than six hundred persons during her half-century of practice, before she was publicly strangled at the age of seventy. When cases of poisoning were traced to her, she took refuge in a convent—as her only dangerous rival, the Marquise de Brinvilliers, also did in like straits—and from that point of vantage, the convent authorities refusing to give her up, she went on selling her Acquetta di Napoli for twenty years more. And on every bottle of this deadly poison-tasteless, odourless, without colour—there was painted the image of a saint.

French poisoning on a grand scale is usually supposed to have come, like most of the other arts, from Italy—or such, at any rate, is the opinion of French scholars who trace it confidently to the advent of Catharine de' Medici and her crowd of Italian retainers. Her family had been remarkable even in Italy for its frequent resort to poison and for equally frequent deaths from poisoning—one reason for the equality being, perhaps, the fact that the family had a way of practising upon its own members. The famous "laboratory" in the palace of Cosmo I, which none but he ever entered, has often been supposed to have been devoted to the manufacture of poisons. Cosmo's son, for whom Andrea Bacci wrote his book on the unicorn, died in agony of unascertained cause, followed in fifteen hours by his wife, and it was observed at the time that his brother, Cardinal Ferdinand de Medici, made what seemed undignified haste to divest himself of his robes so as to succeed him. The handsome alicorn mounted in gold which, as we have seen, was given by Pope Clement VII to the bridegroom's family when Catharine de' Medici married the Dauphin, was therefore a most appropriate wedding gift, all these things considered, for it might certainly have been taken as a graceful intimation that Catharine was not expected to practice her family's talents upon her husband's kin—or that, in case she did so, they might be prepared. However this may have been, rumour was still kept busy with her name; she was often charged with the poisoning of the Queen of Navarre in 1572 and even with the death of her own son, the Duke of Anjou, who died very suddenly in 1585, just after his valet had "forgotten" to test his wine with an alicorn.

All the arts blossomed somewhat later in France than in Italy, and it was not until after the middle of the seventeenth century that the Marquise de Brinvilliers, by slaying with poison, and chiefly for money, her father, her husband, her sister, and her two brothers, threatened Italy's "bad eminence". With better luck, or if she had not stolen out of her convent to meet the "lover" who was really an officer of the law, she might have gone as far as Aqua Toffana. The steady increase of criminal poisoning led Louis XIV to establish a committee, the so-called Chambre Ardente, which sat for three years investigating what had become almost a major social problem. But France has never rivalled the secret society of women, mostly young, discovered at Rome in 1659, the sole purpose of which was to kill by poison the husbands of all the members. These women are said to have met regularly at the house of one Hieronyma Spara, who found the drugs and gave directions for the dosing. An archaic touch in the story of this quaint sisterhood, which takes it quite out of the atmosphere of our more chivalrous modern times, is that twelve of the lot were hanged and most of the others were publicly whipped through the streets of Rome.

England was still more backward than France at the time of the Renaissance. The art of poisoning was not one of those brought back by the "Italianate Englishman", although it was among those that Roger Ascham feared, and if it had been it would have found scant encouragement at home. An Act of Parliament passed in 1531 made poisoning treason, and provided that those proved guilty of it should be boiled to death. The first person to suffer this penalty was a certain cook named Richard Roose, convicted of trying—unsuccessfully—to poison the Bishop of Rochester, and two other persons at least were executed in this way at Smithfield before the Act was repealed in 1547. Even in England, however, rumours of poisoning in high places were always flying about. There were several such tales of attempts upon the life of Elizabeth; James I was suspected of having poisoned Prince Henry, and Charles I of having poisoned his father; it was thought by many that Cromwell had done away with the Princess Elizabeth, and Cromwell himself was supposed to have died of poison. Several of the fourteen physicians who waited

DRAGONS AND UNICORNS—FACT? OR FICTION?

upon Charles II gave the opinion that he had been poisoned, and many tales were current as to the culprit.

One has no difficulty in understanding, therefore, how the demand for the alicorn, as for several other articles used to detect the presence of poison, was built up and maintained, and the prices paid for alicorns no longer seem incredible when we think of them with the history of poisoning in mind. All a man hath will he give for his life, and it is a safe inference from what we know that more than one Italian city already groaning under taxation had to melt its silver spoons in order that its lord might pay some northern merchant the sum he asked for an alicorn. The na·ve device of employing pregustators or "tasters" which had been sufficient for the ancient Romans had to be abandoned in a time when, according to general belief, a clever poisoner could compound a drug that would kill in an hour, a week, or a month, as pleasure and convenience might dictate. Belief in the poisoner's powers reached fantastic heights. So sensible and well-trained a man as Ambroise Pare, trusted physician to the Court of France—and, it must be said, to Catharine de Medici herself—thought that it was possible to kill a man by placing poison under the saddle on which he habitually rode. Pope Clement VII, who owned several alicorns and gave away as many more, was thought to have been killed by the odours of a poisoned torch. Poison might be hidden in flowers, in gloves, in rings and bracelets, in cosmetics. How could it be escaped? Almost all the old writers on poisons and their antidotes—an important department of the "Advice to Princes" type of literature—begin by saying that the best security a prince can have is found in living a righteous life and in making no enemies; but this counsel was felt to be unworldly and the practice of it too onerous. There was no real security unless one could find a means of detecting poison the instant it was brought near one, and upon this task, therefore, huge erudition and great sums of money were for a long time expended.

Besides the alicorn, about a dozen different substances and objects were used during the Renaissance in the halls of Italian princes and elsewhere for the detection of poison. These were, in something like the order of importance: the bezoar-stone, the cerastes's horn, snake's-tongue, griffin's claw, terra sigillata, vessels of crystal and of Venetian glass, a'tites or eagle-stone, snake-stone or ophite, the stone called "stellio", the toad-stone, the vulture's or raven's claw hung over a burning candle, rhinoceros horns, walrus tusks, parrots, and various limestone formations having the appearance of horns. Although a consideration of these may seem a digression, it will help to clarify the central problem of the alicorn.

The beaoar-stone was a calculus, composed of calcium phosphate and hair, found in the intestines of certain Oriental sheep, goats, monkeys, and hedgehogs. Similar concretions might have been found, of course, in European animals, but either this fact was not known or else objects found near at hand were not valued. Hunters and plainsmen of the western United States still believe in the magical properties of the "mad-stone", an object of the same kind found in deer and put to similar uses, and there seems to have been an active belief in such objects in Peru before the Spanish conquest. Long known in the Orient and still used there, these stones were brought to Europe in large quantities

DRAGONS AND UNICORNS—FACT? OR FICTION?

by Portuguese traders from India and were often sold for ten times their weight in gold. They were usually enclosed in delicately wrought baskets of gold filigree hung on chains so that they might be dipped into wine. There are frequent references to the bezoar owned by Queen Elizabeth and to many others belonging to European monarchs. During the great plagues in Lisbon bezoar-stones were hired out to sufferers for ten shillings per day.

The cerastes is a small poisonous serpent of the Sahara and Mesopotamia which has two very short protuberances, vaguely like horns, above its eyes. The belief of the ancients was that it buried itself in the sand, leaving only these "horns" above it, and that with them it killed instantly any creature that stepped upon it. The passage quoted above from Petrarch illustrates the use of these horns in the late Middle Ages and the Renaissance, when they were set in elaborate goldsmith's work and placed on the dining-table where all might see them, in the belief that when poison was brought near them they would break into perspiration. The similarity between this belief and that regarding the alicorn is obvious, and a contemporary writer has even ventured to assert that the cerastes gave the original suggestion for the whole unicorn legend—thus solving at a stroke to his own satisfaction a problem which, as he accurately says, "has long perplexed humanity".

Albertus Magnus himself had spoken without complete incredulity of the "virtue" of the cerastes, Peter of Abano gave it his full support, and all later writers on poisons and antidotes echo in chorus, the belief spreading from book to book without the slightest reference to actual experience. The prevalence of the superstition is illustrated by the belief that the gates of Prester John's palace were composed of sardonyx mixed with cerastes' horns, so that no poison could be brought through them undetected.

Even more commonly used than the horns of the cerastes, probably because they were more easily obtained, were snake-tongues. These tongues were suspended, to the number of thirty or more, on elaborate and often costly dining-table ornaments, usually in the form of golden trees, and such languiers or "tongue-stands" are sometimes seen to-day in museums. It was thought that these also perspired in the presence of poison, and because of the belief that they should be kept as dry as possible they were usually placed near the salt—and therefore near the master of the house. In many instances, indeed, the salt-cellar itself was covered with snake-tongues. Powdered snake-tongue was sold in all the apothecaries' shops of Europe during the sixteenth century as an antidote and a protection against poison.

One of the axioms of magical belief everywhere in the world is that an object bearing a close resemblance to another object has the "virtue" or "property" of that other. A curious illustration of this is seen in the use of the stone called "Glossopetra" or "tongue-stone", really the petrified tooth of a shark. "This stone", writes Bo'thius de Boodt, "is so like a tongue in shape that the vulgar not only call it snake's tongue but actually think it is that. . . Many people make much of it for its supposed power against poisons and for keeping off the evil eye. They say that when poison is brought near to it a sweat or dew

DRAGONS AND UNICORNS—FACT? OR FICTION?

breaks out upon it, thus revealing the intended crime."

This recalls the very ancient and still existing belief of the East Indians in a stone with similar properties, sometimes vaguely called in Europe the "Smaragdus", to be found in a serpent's head. Phiostratus relates in his life of Apollonius that the snake-charmer lures the snake out of its hole by incantations, lulls it to sleep, cuts off its head with a hatchet, and then extracts the jewel. This stone or jewel is said to contain "a thin crescent-like fibre which oscillates unceasingly in the centre." In other words, the fibre resembles a snake's tongue, and the resemblance has suggested, in the first place, that it is powerful against poison, and, in the second place, that it is to be found in the head of a snake.

From these stones of the Indian snake the transition is easy to the toad-stones of Europe, commonly worn in finger-rings as amulets and prophylactics. No doubt because of the representations made by those who had them for sale, most of the poison-detecting agents were thought to be very difficult to obtain unless one knew the magic formula, and just as there was only one way of capturing unicorns so there was only one quite correct way of securing toadstones. There were a number of books produced in the late Middle Ages, many of them attributed to Aristotle, which divulged these magic formulae, and in one of these books those who wish to secure a toad-stone are instructed to "put a great or overgrown toad (first bruised in divers places) into an earthen pot, and put this same in an ant's hillock, and cover the same with earth, which toad at length the ants will eat. So that the bones of the toad and stone will be left in the pot." And the test of the toad-stone, to determine whether it was genuine, was equally simple. "You shall know whether the toad-stone called Crapaudine be the right and perfect stone or not. Hold the stone before a toad so that he may see it, and if it be a right and true stone the toad will leap toward it and make as though he would snatch it from you, he envieth so much that a man should have the stone." Most of the toad-stones in actual use seem to have been greenish-brown objects about the size of a large pea, and some were certainly the fossilized teeth of the sting-ray. Finger-rings containing them are still not uncommon.

Similarly used but more difficult to obtain was the "griffin's claw"—in reality the horn of an ibex or a buffalo. There seem to be few exceptions to the rule that when we can trace back the history of a griffin's claw to the time when it came into human possession we come to a saint or some dignitary of the Church, and it is safe to assume a belief that these claws could be secured only by some holy man who cured a griffin of a grievous disease and claimed a claw as his fee. Such a story, which has more than one parallel in folklore, is told of Pope Cornelius in relation to the claw now kept at Cornelimunster on the Inde. In the old Cottonian Library there was a claw inscribed "Griphi unguis divo Cuthberto Dunelmensi sacer", and the supposition is that Saint Cuthbert acquired it in the regular way. Until the French Revolution the monastery of St. Denis had a claw which seems to have had a similar history. All three of those mentioned, and most of those to be seen in various parts of Germany, have been made into drinking-horns. They were thought to act like the beakers mentioned by Ctesias and Aelian when poisoned liquor was drunk from them.

The old belief concerning cups of crystal and of Venetian glass, that they would crack

186

DRAGONS AND UNICORNS—FACT? OR FICTION?

when poison was poured into them, is too familiar to require more than mention. It is a well-known fact, also, that the carbuncle or ruby—the names were commonly interchangeable in the Middle Ages—was thought to have an unerring faculty of detecting poison. More interesting than these was the a'tites or eagle-stone—so-called because, according to Pliny, it was to be found only in the eagle's nest, and was therefore exceedingly rare. The eagle placed it there, as she also sometimes did the amethyst, to watch over her young while she was absent, and it was able to do this because of the great antipathy felt toward it by all serpents. We are told that if a plate containing poison was placed over this stone no man would be able to eat the food upon the plate.

Another belief which carries us far back into primitive magic is that concerning the vulture's foot, an object that seems to have been in common use on the dining-tables of the Middle Ages, perhaps because of its comparative cheapness. The foot was hung in such a way that the claws surrounded the flame of a candle, and it was supposed that whenever poison was brought upon the table it would clutch and extinguish the flame.

Perhaps the most important of all these amulets and prophylactics, considering its great age and universal dispersion, is the terra sigillata, "stamped earth", or earth of Lemnos. This was originally a red clay dug from a certain hill in the isle of Lemnos on the 6th of August in every year, with appropriate ceremonies performed by priests in honour of Diana. Dioscorides informs us that after the clay was dug it was mixed with goat's blood and stamped with a seal bearing the image of the goddess. When properly prepared and sent forth with this hall-mark, the little cakes of clay, a quarter of an inch in thickness and ranging from the diameter of a sixpence to that of a half-crown, were regarded by the ancients, and by the people of the Middle Ages and of the Renaissance as well, as perfect antidotes for all kinds of poison. The clay was also made into cups, which were thought to render harmless the most deadly drugs. This earth was one of the seventy-three ingredients of the theriaca, altogether the most famous and the most astonishing concoction of ancient and mediaeval pharmacy. As the Christian centuries wore on the image of the heathen goddess was displaced by other emblems—among them I have seen the figure of the unicorn—and other clays, even some from England, were found to be quite as effective as those of Lemnos; the pagan ritual and the goat's blood were felt by all good Christians, one need hardly say, to have less than no value; yet, with all these changes, the general faith in the substance held on with surprising tenacity. Writers of the sixteenth century who have only contempt for toad-stones and vultures' claws retain a deep respect for terra sigillata. They had never known it to do the slightest good, but it was mentioned by Dioscorides and it came out of that ancient Greek world which was still regarded, and quite rightly, as the source of almost all sound medical theory.

The two substances remaining to be mentioned, the walrus tusk and the horn of the rhinoceros, point back in the direction of the alicorn. Among the many different objects passed off by charlatans as verum cornu monocerotis, probably the most common was the tusk of the walrus, usually called the "morse" or the "rohart" in old books. I have already mentioned an amusing passage in Hector Bo'thius about the hunting of the wal-

DRAGONS AND UNICORNS—FACT? OR FICTION?

rus among the northern isles. This great fish, he says, swims about for a long time without taking any sleep, but at last, overcome with drowsiness, he turns to the shore, finds a convenient bush or tree, hooks his down-curving teeth over a bough, and falls into a deep slumber. Then the hunters approach and bind him with ropes, and after cutting off his teeth, set him free to grow another pair. The tusks are then straightened artificially and sold as alicorns. Again, we are told by Dr. Giles Fletcher, writing in 1598, that the fish-tooth which is called in Russia the Riba-Zuba is used there, and among the Persians and Bougharians as well, to make the knife and sword-hafts used by noblemen. "Some use the powder of it against poison, as the Unicornes horn. The fish that weareth it is called a morse, and is caught about Pechora." André Thevet asserts that he has actually seen the conversion of walrus tusks into alicorns performed by charlatans of the Red Sea district, and the shrewdest of sixteenth-century writers on the unicorn suspects that the "horns" bought in his day are really marine in their origin.

The walrus tusk was not regarded as a substitute for the alicorn but as the thing itself, and the rhinoceros horn owed much of the vogue it had in Europe to the same estimation. Andrea Marini asserts, indeed, that the rhinoceros horn had no reputation whatever in his time except that which it owed to the unicorn—a situation not without ironic humour for one who realizes how much the legend of the unicorn, and especially the belief in the magic virtues of the horn, owes to the rhinoceros. It seems certain, however, that Marini exaggerates, and that the rhinoceros cup was rather frequently used in Europe by those who had heard of its Oriental reputation. Portuguese merchants would not neglect so attractive a commodity. There is still preserved in the Copenhagen Museum a rhinoceros beaker which Rudolph II of Germany (1575-1612) had prepared for his own use; another was owned by the Medici family, and another still, I believe, by the Visconti of Milan. Many more there probably were, but one cannot distinguish them in the records because they were one and all described as alicorns.

The description of the furniture used at the wedding dinner given by Edward IV for his sister and the Duke of Burgundy illustrates one method of using the alicorn. Like the horn of the cerastes, the snake's tongue, the a'tites, and other objects, it was simply set upon the table, or near it, so that any change in its appearance might be instantly seen. We may imagine that the gaiety of mediaeval feasts was somewhat sobered by the necessity of keeping the eyes fixed upon such objects, and that the grisly suggestions of the vulture's claw might somewhat impede the flow of soul, but the Middle Ages seem to have liked strong contrasts. More commonly, and for a much longer time, the alicorn was used to touch the food and drink before the meal began, being carried about the table by an officer of the household detailed for that important trust. When so employed it was called in mediaeval French "une espreuve a lincorne", and was generally attached to a cord or chain by which it might be hung against the wall when not in use. References to these espreuves are numerous in old inventories, and the descriptions of them often indicate the use to which they were put. Thus we read in an inventory, taken in 1416, of the Dukes of Burgundy: "Une tousche, en quoy a esté mis une piece de lichorne, pour touschier la viande de Monseigneur. Even the inventory of the Emperor Charles V refers to "une touche a licorne, garnie d'or, pour faire essay"—certainly an interesting

DRAGONS AND UNICORNS—FACT? OR FICTION?

article to find in the possession of a man who seems to have eaten himself to death.

One can readily imagine that there was a stateliness in this old ceremony of testing the great man's food and drink that would cause it to be kept up long after the belief in its magical efficacy had been abandoned by intelligent people, and one is not surprised, therefore, to learn that it was maintained in the Royal household of France until 1789, when the Revolution made a clean sweep of all such antiquated customs. To what extent those who saw this ceremony performed at the end of the eighteenth century believed in its supernatural value, and to what extent it was for them merely a graceful ritual, interesting because it was old, we cannot say. Most of them, probably, could not have said themselves. The question, however, is an attractive one because it reveals a situation common to all periods of dying beliefs—and this is to say all periods whatsoever, "for each age is a dream that is dying". Even here, almost at the end of its history, the unicorn continues to illumine the ways of human thought. The ceremony of touching the king's food and drink, in its various effects upon different minds, was closely analogous, we may be sure, to the celebration of the Mass or of any other Christian sacrament. By some, that is, it would be accepted at "face value" and without question; the more sophisticated would feel that although they themselves could not believe in it, yet it would have a wholesome effect upon the simple-minded and would tend to keep them in order; others would think that it ought to be abolished because it had no foundation in fact; a few, the most sophisticated of all, would wish to see it preserved simply because it was old and dignified and had aesthetic charm. As we look out across the Christian world of to-day, are not these the chief varieties of religious opinion that we discover?

Two hundred years before the ceremony was abandoned—with the heroic assistance of Madame Guillotine—Chapelain, physician to Charles IX of France, had said "that he would willingly take away that custome of dipping a piece of Unicorn's home in the King's cup, but that he knew that opinion to be so deeply ingrafted in the minds of men that he feared it would scarce be impugned by reason." Many physicians, he continued, who had themselves no belief in the alicorn felt obliged to prescribe it because, if they did not do so and their patients died, they never had any peace from the surviving relatives. And besides, said he, any man who undertakes to discredit opinions that have been long accepted puts himself in the position of an owl that shows itself in daylight in some prominent place and is persecuted by every other kind of bird. Chapelain and his numerous kind therefore held their tongues, and those who think that the beliefs of the people should never be disturbed will no doubt be charmed with the results—two hundred years were added to the alicorn's lease of life.

Unicorn lore provides an exact parallel also for the feeling of a certain group, well represented in every age, that orthodox belief has a salutary and stabilizing effect upon the public at large, tending to make it patient of conditions that agnostics and free-thinkers might not so quietly tolerate. There is reason to suspect that even in the sixteenth century the more enlightened tyrants of Italy maintained the use of the alicorn, not because they themselves had any faith in its direct action, but rather because they wished others to have such faith, thinking that it would tend to discourage poisoners. This asser-

189

DRAGONS AND UNICORNS—FACT? OR FICTION?

tion is definitely made by Andrea Marini, who wrote freely in Venice, expressing his own mind; it is strongly implied even by Andrea Bacci, who wrote under the patronage of the Medici and therefore without any freedom whatever. Bacci's pen was hired, and his book on the unicorn is a vivid example of what can happen to a man of sense and learning who is pulled one way by his respect for truth and another way by what he takes to be his interests.

According to Aelian, as the erudite were sure to know, the unicorn's horn was properly used only in the form of a drinking-vessel. Here arose a difficulty, for the alicorns of Europe were seldom more than two inches and a half in diameter at the base, so that it was impossible to shape satisfactory beakers from them. The difficulty was evaded by making cups in which a few slices of the horn were inset, or slabs of it were fitted together to form a tankard. Among the objects once belonging to Queen Elizabeth that were given by James I to his queen was "one little cup of unicorn's horn, with a cover of gold, set with two pointed diamonds and three pearls pendent, being in weight 7 ounces". The King of England gave to the Duke of Brittany in 1414: "une grande coupe d'or . . . et y a au fons une licorne et autres choses contre venin". Such citations might be continued indefinitely, but all that one can find show that these cups, like the espreuves and the other objects into which the alicorn was fashioned, belonged solely to the great and wealthy. The unicorn maintained its aristocratic associations almost to the end—and this not merely because of the great price of its horn, but also because only the great fear poison. Seneca had phrased the situation long before in one pregnant line: Venenum in auro bibitur.

Slices of the horn were fitted into the handles of table-knives and salt-cellars, they were shaped into "test-spoons" and sunk in the silver of table dishes, but in all these forms the alicorn was known only to the wealthy. Poorer men used it in powdered form and as a therapeutic. Pharmaceutical ideas were so loose and so uncontrolled by scientific tests that there was no difficulty whatever in this transfer from one department of medicine to the other. Such a transfer, indeed, was inevitable, for the set of beliefs underlying the faith in the alicorn's supernatural properties were just such as would lead to the acceptance of it as a valuable antidote and drug. If it was "indicated" as an antidote against poison, then it seemed to follow that it would be equally good against the so-called "poisonous diseases". Of these the most important was the Plague or Pest.

There is no more pitiful record in the world than that in the scores of books composed during the Middle Ages on methods of avoiding and curing the Plague. It is a record both disgusting and ludicrous, but one's prevailing mood in reading it is that of compassion. Unicorn's horn is certainly the most pleasing of the materia medica mentioned in it, and it is as effective as most. I take up the Monumenta Sinoptica de Peste Preservanda et Curanda, written long after the Middle Ages had closed by John Collis, and published in 1631. This book names thousands of drugs sold over the counters of England and Europe less than three centuries ago as the best means known to science of saving the lives of one's family and friends from the pestilence that never quite died out. Many of these drugs are too foul to name and others too ridiculous to believe in. Hoofs of asses and elks, horns of wild goats and of stags, viper's flesh and Mathiolus's celebrated oil of scorpions, dust of scorpions, powdered swallow's heart—one hardly knows whether to laugh or to weep. For the thought will emerge as one reads that although these people held views about materia medica which we have abandoned—quite recently—yet they loved their children somewhat as we do ours. It was by such means as these that they tried to keep them.

"Noble and powerful against all poisonous and pestilential diseases is the unicorn's horn", says a physician of the time when the Plague took its toll of thousands every year. "Kings and princes and men of wealth all own it, and they should preserve it for the use of future generations. Furthermore, as I know from personal experience, it is highly effective against poisons and all malignant evils." Powdered alicorn was recommended as a specific against the Plague by many of the best physicians of Europe during the sixteenth and seventeenth centuries. In the English version of Johann Schrs(der's important Pbarmacop'ria Medico-Chymica we are told of the "Vertues" of the horn that "it is Sudorifick, Alexipharmacal, and Cordial, hence it is commended good against Poysons, infectious diseases, etc. It is also accounted profitable in the Epelepsie of Infants. The Dose from 4 grains to half a scruple, sometimes a whole scruple and more." According to Andrea Bacci the proper dose is ten grains scraped from the inside of the hornor a piece might equally well be worn as an amulet. Bacci also says that the Cardinal of Trent, a most "public-minded" man, often gave away filings from his alicorn "in cases of suspected poisoning, mushrooms, fever, and pest, for the most part with excellent success". Laurens Catelan warns his readers that the alicorn, whether in the piece or powdered, must never be put into hot water, for this destroys all its virtue, and Conrad Gesner is equally emphatic in saying that only fresh powder can be used successfully. When the daughter of Henry II of France fell ill with smallpox in 1557, Anne de Montmorency sent to her nurse a piece of alicorn with directions that it should be "dissolved" in cold water and drunk. The water commonly called eau do licorne and sold under that name throughout Europe was not made in this expensive way, but merely by standing one end of the horn in a vessel of water, as at St. Denis. Sometimes a hole was bored through the length of the horn and water poured through it, but in either case the water was held to be highly beneficial and found a ready sale. In this way it was made possible to "drink the horn". Intelligent people, however, seem to have preferred to take their alicorn in powdered form. How intelligent these people were may be inferred from a certain illuminating fact of medical history: the English Royal Society of Physicians was required to issue, at intervals, lists of the drugs to be carried by every registered pharmacist in London, and all of the twelve or fifteen lists issued thus officially between 1651 and 1741 named the unicorn's horn. The general editor of the last issue including this drug was no less a person than Sir Hans Sloane. In the edition of 1746 it was tacitly dropped. At about the same time that the Royal Society of Physicians decided to abandon the horn, Hogarth expressed his layman's attitude toward it by placing it in a prominent position in the shop of the quack doctor presented in the series Manage a la Mode.

It must be admitted that the English Society was "not the first to lay the old aside", for Italian and French physicians had been protesting against the alicorn for almost two cen-

DRAGONS AND UNICORNS—FACT? OR FICTION?

turies before this. Andrea Marini had ridiculed the whole belief as early as 1566; Christofle Landré had done all that a courageous and clear thinker could do to kill it even eight years before that; Ambroise Pare, one of the most influential physicians of all time, attacked it repeatedly; Laurent Joubert, another physician to the Court of France, had classed it contemptuously with powdered pearls and potable gold; even Pierre Pomet, a foremost authority, had spoken of it in 1694 as entirely out of date. Decidedly, England did not err on the side of precipitation.

How much responsibility for this lingering of the drug should be attributed to the apothecaries we can only guess. One of the more interesting phases of medical history is that of the relationships between apothecaries and physicians. Often the two parties have been at league, "for ech of hem made other for to winne", but quite as often they have been at strife, and both league and strife might be illustrated, probably, if we knew enough, from the history of the alicorn. One cannot help thinking it significant that forty years after Pare's Discours and almost sixty years after Marini's Falsa Opinione dell' Alicorno, the French apothecary Catelan, who had certainly read both of these opponents of the whole superstition, brought out his Histoire de la Licorne, arguing with apparent conviction not only for the real existence of the animal but for the medical value of its horn. Considering that he was an intelligent man and a leader in his profession, it seems fair to recall that he had alicorn powder to sell and also that he owned a whole alicorn of which he was very proud—though not to such a degree that he would have refused to part with it for a suitable sum of money. All the early opponents of the alicorn were physicians, and no apothecary spoke against it until the time of Pierre Pomet, who had something "just as good" to offer in its stead.

Whatever the apothecaries of Europe may have done to foster the belief we have been tracing, they certainly did little or nothing to establish it, for we have seen that the belief goes back at least to the fourth century before Christ, and it is probably much older still. This can be said, however, only of India, and the question arises, therefore, when and by what means the superstition came into the Western world. Ctesias had made no such assertions about the horn of his onager as those quoted above from European physicians concerning the alicorn. Aeian had spoken only of the beakers made from the horn of his "cartazon". The ancient physicians upon whose works, for the most part grossly misunderstood, mediaeval medicine was chiefly based, had said nothing of this marvellous drug. There is no mention of it in Physiologus, in the patristic writers, in Isidore, or in the Bestiaries. Hildegarde of Bingen, although she seems not to have heard that the alicorn had any peculiar medical value, was apparently the first European writer who thought of the unicorn as possessing magical properties. To her, as I have pointed out, its entire body was medicinal, as that of the rhinoceros was thought to be in India.

From what source is Hildegarde most likely to have derived an idea of this kind? I should say from the Arabian writers whose influence was beginning to be felt, through the medium of Latin translation, in just her time. The unicorn legend had an early and an elaborate development among the Arabs, who dominated European medicine, both for good and for ill, from the beginning of the thirteenth century to the revival of learning,

192

DRAGONS AND UNICORNS—FACT? OR FICTION?

sending out successive waves of influence from the Court of Frederick II, from Salerno, and from many centres in Spain. Adding little to Western surgery, anatomy, or nosology, their chief contribution lay in the field of materia medica, and even this was made possible chiefly by their contacts, direct and indirect, with the Orient. Indian physicians are known to have lived at the Court of Bagdad in the time of Haroun al-Raschid, and there is evidence that they added Oriental ideas to those that Arabic medicine owed chiefly to the Greek tradition. Arabic influence is already discernible in Albertus Magnus and it is controlling in Peter of Abano. Can it be a mere coincidence that these two are among the earliest European writers who show full knowledge of the belief in the alicorn? The probability is that this belief, in its popular form, entered Europe with the Mohammedan invasion of Spain, spreading from Bagdad—whither it had been taken by Indian physicians or brought back by Arabian travellers—to Cordova, Seville, Granada, and finally to Salerno, from whence medical theory radiated through all of Europe.

If this seems no more than a conjecture, it is strengthened, at least, in the definite ascription of the whole belief, by a man who should have known the facts, to Arabian physicians. Andrea Marini makes the charge, with anger and contempt, that the use of the alicorn in medicine was due to the setta de gli Arabi. We should, of course, remember that by 1566 the "arabistes" were in low repute throughout Europe, so that anyone who wished to condemn a medical theory would naturally attribute it to them; but Marini's charge, if that is the right word, is too plausible to be set aside for such reasons, and it is supported by the not infrequent references to Arabian authorities made by European writers on the alicorn.

There is evidence of another kind which, although not conclusive by itself, lends further support to the theory of an Arabian origin for this belief. In the Italian dialects of the fourteenth century and later the unicorn was variously called licorno, liocorno, leocorno, and leoncorno. In French the name has always been licorne or lincorne. I cannot accept the derivation given by Littré's Dictionnaire in which licorne is traced to the whole Latin word unicoma. A tenable etymology is suggested by Alfred Hoare, according to which the ordinary Romance article was prefixed to the Latin coma "and the resulting word was altered, perhaps under the attraction of Leone, lion". Accepting this derivation, we may draw from it two significant deductions. It seems clear, in the first place, that when the basic word licorno—which could mean nothing but "the horn"—was made, the animal to which the horn belonged was unknown. After the development of the unicorn legend the word was applied, not very appropriately, to the animal, and it has done this double service, both in French and Italian, ever since. We shall find it worth remembering that, if the present argument is sound, then "the horn" was known in Italy and was important enough to name in the most vivid and striking way, before any animal was known or imagined to which it could be fitted. The second deduction is that this horn must have seemed in some way impressive to its namers, else they would not have spoken of it with the simple definite article so as to suggest that it was the horn par excellence.

But these are not the only conjectures that may be based upon etymology. Much more commonly used than any of the Italian names for the unicorn cited above, and outlasting them all, is the word alicorno, backed by the Portuguese alicornio. Hoare explains this form without hesitation by saying that it is due to a prefixing of the Arabic article. He refers, of course, to the definite article al, seen in many English words of Arabic origin such as "algebra" and "alcohol". Alicorno, however, is not of pure Arabic origin; it is a hybrid word. The Arabic article has apparently been prefixed to the Romance word licorno already formed, thus giving the word two definite articles fused together. From these facts I think we may infer rather plausibly that the Arabs found when they came to Europe some sort of horn sufficiently remarkable to have attracted attention, and, secondly, that they took enough interest in this horn and made it sufficiently their own so that their capping of its name with an additional definite article from their own language was generally accepted. It seems to me that these etymological considerations, taken together with the evidence to the same effect presented above, make a "strong case" for my theory that the European belief in the alicorn's magical properties was of Arabian origin.

That belief was given considerable impetus, centuries later, by the reports made by Portuguese traders returning from India. The Portuguese were the chief carriers of bezoar-stones—according to contemporary belief because the people of their nation were more afraid of poison than others, but really because they found a huge profit in the trade. They also brought back most of the rhinoceros horns to be found in Europe during the sixteenth and seventeenth centuries, so that they would find it to their interest to spread and deepen the superstitions already existing about horns. Furthermore, they had been, without realizing the fact, in the very land where that superstition had its largest early development and where it was still accepted most widely. There is abundance of contemporary testimony regarding the influence of these traders: "The men of our Portuguese nation", writes Amatus Lusitanus, "who have penetrated the interior of India, are unable to tell us anything about the unicorn itself, but they say that its horn is greatly prized by the Indian kings; and also those who have practised medicine for some time in that country and have then returned home say that in India there is no stronger or more dependable antidote against poison than the horn of the unicorn."

Merely to understand how this idea may have come into Europe gives one a little satisfaction, but one would rather know how so strange a notion ever entered the human mind, and why, once it had found entrance, it was not instantly thrust forth again. Questions of this kind, involving the mental habits of men who lived thousands of years ago, one does well to handle with the least possible suggestion of dogmatic finality. One can only gather all the facts that seem pertinent, enter into those facts imaginatively, strive to think as much as possible in the way of primitive peoples, and then make his conjecture-cautiously, tentatively, as who should say "How will this do?" But whatever the difficulty and danger, the question lies too squarely across our way and is too near the centre and source of unicorn lore to be evaded now.

"Beginning doubtfully and far away", I should like to point out that there has existed from early times and in many parts of the world a vague notion that horns in general, almost any kind of horns, are somehow prophylactic. For ages the most highly valued

DRAGONS AND UNICORNS—FACT? OR FICTION?

drinking vessels, used by kings as well as cow-herds, were made of horn, and it is possible that the belief in the medicinal value of such vessels arose in part from what was said of the wholesomeness of their contents. I have myself encountered in western America the idea that nothing drunk from a cow's horn can ever harm the drinker. Lying even behind this belief there was, and is, the almost world-wide use of horns as charms and amulets, into which I need not go because the subject has been recently treated with ample though somewhat too audacious scholarship. Throughout Italy at the present time, and especially in the south, the "comb"—an amulet representing a single horn and made of coral, silver, nickel, bone, and other materials—is used in many ways as a charm against the evil eye. One sees it even as a watchguard and at the end of a chain hung round the neck and on the coat-lapel. Roman and Neapolitan cab-drivers place it on the headgear of their horses, so suspended that it is constantly in motion and pointing forwards; carters and carriers hang a large single horn under their wagons; in Italian shop-windows one often sees fifty or more of these amulets, certainly more popular than those of any other form, exhibited for sale. Old women of the peasant class frequently wear many of them at once, concealed beneath their clothing. From this ancient superstition some suggestion and support, one cannot say how much, was derived by the notion before us. For the sake of clarity one may allow himself to say that all horns came to be regarded as medicinal because they were vaguely associated with beneficent supernatural powers, although in reality there was no relationship of cause and effect but merely an overlapping. Such overlapping and confusion is unmistakable when one looks, for example, at the pharmacopceia of a Zulu medicine man, which consists usually of nothing but fifteen or twenty short antelope horns tied together by thongs. With this outfit the savage physician attacks all devils and diseases alike, making no distinction between the one group and the other. These horns are charms and medicines at the same time, and they are medicines because—for one can scarcely avoid the word—they are also charms or devil-fighters.

The belief that all horns have medicinal value and that this value is of a supernatural sort lasted on, demonstrably, into modern times. André Thevet, a man of fine intelligence and wide knowledge, could say at the end of the sixteenth century that "quand tout est diet, il ne se trouve guere beste . . . dont la corne n'ait quelque merveilleux effect pour la sauté des bommes." As an example he names the pyrassouppi found in the region of the River Plate, large as a mule and with very long horns which the savages use to cure wounds caused by poisonous beasts and fishes. He says also, as do many other early authorities, that if one burns ordinary stag's horn and scatters the ashes on the ground he will rid the place where they are scattered of all snakes.

Thevet's mention of stag's horn brings us nearer to the centre of our problem, for many writers about the alicorn asserted, during the period when faith in it was breaking down, that the horn of the stag was really quite as effective. Powdered stag's horn was commonly prescribed to the poor as a prophylactic during the whole period of the alicorn's popularity among the wealthier classes, and it is still used in China in the same way. Although all horns whatever were regarded as having medicinal properties, those of the stag were the most important substitute for the alicorn. Now there is no great diffi-

195

DRAGONS AND UNICORNS—FACT? OR FICTION?

culty in tracing the process by which the stag's horn acquired this reputation, and the knowledge gained in tracing it will provide a clue to the solution of our main problem.

In reading the old zoologists one finds a great deal made of "natural enemies", and what is said of them rests upon one of the fundamental conceptions in the mediaeval and ancient theories of nature. Lucretius, to take the most familiar example, tries to explain the material universe as a system of sympathies and antipathies. There was no attempt to get behind the assumed loves and hates of primordial atoms and of all that they composed; no one thought to inquire whether such loves and hates actually existed; they were axiomatic. One assumed that every object in the world had its natural friends and foes, and a main task of science and of magic, during the long period when the two were scarcely distinguishable, was to find out what these were, for one had control over an object and could use it for human ends when its sympathies and antipathies were known. This belief is familiar, yet it is so important for the present discussion that I venture to emphasize it by a quotation.

"By reason of the hidden and secret properties of things", says John Baptista Porta, "there is in all kinds of creatures a certain compassion, as I may call it, which the Greeks call sympathy and antipathy, but we term it, more familiarly, their consent and disagreement. For some things are joyned together as it were in a mutual league, and some other things are at variance and discord among themselves; or they have something in them which is a terror and destruction to each other, whereof there can be rendered no probable reason: neither will any wise man seek after any other cause thereof but only this, that it is the pleasure of Nature to see it should be so, that she would have nothing to be without his like, and that amongst all the secrets of Nature there is nothing but hath some hidden and special property; and moreover, that by this their consent and disagreement, we might gather many helps for the uses and necessities of men, for when once we find one thing at variance with another, presently we may conjecture, and in trial so it will prove, that one of them may be used as a fit remedy against the harms of the other."

This is somewhat to our purpose, but what follows is more so. Porta reminds his readers that the lion is afraid of the cock, that the elephant and the mouse are natural enemies—a belief which is still remembered—and then says: "So likewise those living creatures that are enemies to poisonous things and swallow them up without danger may show us that such poisons [that is the poisonous members of the poison-eating animals] will cure the bitings and blows of those creatures. The Hart and the Serpent are at continual enmity: the Serpent, as soon as he seeth the Hart, gets him into his hole, but the Hart draws him out again with the breath of his nostrils, and devours him. Hence it is that the fat and the blood of Harts, and the stones that grow in their eyes, are ministered as fit remedies against the stinging and biting of Serpents. Likewise the breath of Elephants draws Serpents out of their dens, and they fight with dragons, and therefore the members of Elephants, burned, drive away Serpents. So also the crowing of a Cock affrights the Basilisk, and he fights with Serpents to defend his hens, hence the broth of a Cock is a good remedy for the poison of Serpents. The Stellion, which is a beast like a Lyzard, is an enemy to the Scorpion, and therefore the Oyle of him, being purified, is good to anoint

DRAGONS AND UNICORNS—FACT? OR FICTION?

the place which is stricken by the Scorpion. A Swine eats up a Salamander without danger, and is good against the poison thereof."

This idea of "sympathy" and "antipathy" is encountered everywhere in mediaeval medicine, as it is also, of course, in the history of magic. The Consents and Disagreements, as Porta calls them, are often surprising. In addition to those that he mentions, the goat and the partridge were so sympathetic that they could be prescribed as medicine interchangeably; the ram and the elephant were so antipathetic that elephants always ran away from rams, bellowing with terror; the panther and the hyena were so uncongenial that the mere skin of a dead hyena could put the panther to precipitate flight, and if the skins of the panther and the hyena were hung upside by side the former would soon lose all its hair.

But we must not be drawn aside into these arcana. The pertinent fact before us is that "the stag by nature hates all poysonous things, and therefore either the feet or skin or the homes of a stag, nayled uppon a doore, no Serpent will enter in." Various parts of the stag are accordingly medicinal, and are especially good against the poison of snakes-either for the reason that the stag is a "natural enemy" of snakes or because he eats them and so becomes poisonous himself. To the modern mind these two "reasons" seem quite distinct, as they probably were in origin, but I am not aware that any writer who believed the superstition ever disentangled them; it was not only possible but easy for really acute thinkers to accept both reasons at once, stressing either as occasion served. When the medical action of the stag's horn is explained on the principle of natural antipathy, we have to think of the horn as extremely pure; but when, on the other hand, the principle of sympathy is invoked we are forced to regard it as extremely poisonous in nature. The physicians of four centuries ago could not agree upon the rather fundamental question whether the stag's horn and similar substances were essentially poisonous or essentially pure, but the members of both schools of opinion continued to administer those substances in their medical practice with perfect confidence and probably with good results. When a modern reader first encounters this absurd situation he is moved to what Hobbes calls "a sudden glory" and is tempted to exult a little over the childish fumbling past—but then he recalls the still unresolved conflict between allopathy and homœopathy, which is in essentials the same conflict as that waged in the Middle Ages, and he decides not to laugh.

Medical action by sympathy, as many of the old writers on materia medica explain, requires that the alexipharmical or therapeutic agent shall be of a stronger and more concentrated "virtue" than the thing or condition to be affected, so that it will be active and the other passive. This explains the choice of such supposedly powerful and highly concentrated poison-cures as viper's flesh, the ingredient added to the theriata by one of Nero's physicians. It explains, also, most of the prophylactics and poison-detectors of the Middle Ages and Renaissance that I have named above. The cerastes was thought to carry its poison in its horns; these horns were therefore regarded as exceedingly poisonous, and it was believed that they would have power over any poison less potent and concentrated than that which they contained. Snakes were thought to "bite" with their

197

DRAGONS AND UNICORNS—FACT? OR FICTION?

tongues—a belief held by most people to-day—and therefore snake's tongue, whole or powdered, could detect and cure poison. The vulture's entire body was considered poisonous, and its foot particularly so; all toads were thought venomous, and the stones in their heads, like the snake-stones of India, were held to be concentrated venom. The poisonous nature of the eagle-stone was not so easy to detect or explain, but the eagle does not leave this stone in her nest to guard her young against snakes for nothing; her instinct may be trusted.

In all this mountain of error there was, of course, a grain of sound and precious truth, and no one can fail to do honour to the long struggle of thought which finally isolated the principle similia similibus curantur. This principle, to be sure, was well understood by the ancients and was taught by Galen, who said explicitly that certain poisons attract poison as the magnet does iron. Aristotle pointed out that poisonous reptiles seem immune to poison and can eat one another without suffering harm. Saint Ambrose says explicitly "venenim veneno excludatur". One of the most satisfactory statements of the principle to be found in early writers is that of Antonio Ludovico, who says that nothing except poison can expel poison and that the antidote is not hostile to the poisonous substance, as some suppose, but is "bound to it by invisible chains of everlasting and indissoluble amity."

The principle, then, was sound, and it had long been familiar, but the applications of it are often highly diverting. Thus there was a general belief, lasting until at least 1700, that the elk is a chronic sufferer with vertigo and that he has been able to discover only one thing that will give him any relief. The inconvenience of this will be imagined when one is told that whenever he is pursued by hunters and dogs he has to sit down and place his left hind foot in his left ear to cure himself of dizziness before he can run away. But this infirmity of elks was simply another proof of Emerson's dictum that "Nature is ancillary to man" and also of the proverb: "God works in a mysterious way his wonders to perform." The left hind hoof of the elk was prescribed for centuries as an unfailing specific for vertigo, epilepsy, falling sickness, mal de mer, and dipsomania, with careful directions for distinguishing the left hind hoof from the right. Amulets of this material are still worn in Italy as protection against the falling sickness and the evil eye.

Coming now to our central question, why the alicorn was supposed to sweat in the presence of poison, we may answer, in accordance with what we have learned from the study of stag's horn and other substances, that it does so either because of sympathy or because of antipathy with that poison. Explanation according to the latter principle was of course the more natural one during the centuries when the unicorn was always thought of as a symbol of Christ, as associated with the Virgin, and as a type of purity, but Arabian influence, based upon Galen, seems to have swung opinion over to the other interpretation—that, namely, according to the principle of sympathy, which required that the alicorn be thought of as highly poisonous.

A clear statement of this view is made by Laurens Catelan, although it is not original with him. Those parts of any animal, he begins by saying, are strongest and fullest of the

DRAGONS AND UNICORNS—FACT? OR FICTION?

animal's "virtue" upon which its life depends. In horned animals these parts are the horns. Now it is well known—or so Catelan assumes—that horned animals have a keen appetite for poisonous substances both animal and vegetable, and of course the essence of these substances is drawn into their essential members, their horns. All horns, therefore, are necessarily poisonous in a high degree, for all the poisons that their bearers have eaten is concentrated in them. There is no difficulty in seeing, then, why it is that when all the poison that would ordinarily be distributed through two horns is forced into one it is brought to a very strong focus indeed. The alicorn is clearly one of the most poisonous substances in the world, and with all these facts in mind, Catelan submits, no sensible man can fail to believe the marvels related of it. The alicorn sweats when standing near poison, he thinks, because of a desire to mingle with its like, and when taken as a drug it overcomes and carries off such feebler poisons as arsenic and corrosive sublimate by virtue of its own more powerfully poisonous nature. Why it is that so deadly a substance as this does not kill the patient instantly, how it happens that it can be brought into contact with one's food and drink or worn at one's neck as an amulet with impunity, Catelan and his fellows neglect to inform us.

This theory is too ingenious and has too much of the mark of the clever apothecary upon it for one to accept it as a product of primitive minds, and yet it may contain some primitive elements. Catelan's confident assertion that the unicorn eats snakes and drinks poisoned water implies an intimate knowledge of the animal's habits such as few other writers have claimed, but the assertion is helpful in suggesting that the whole mystery may rest upon a matter of diet. Even those who think of the unicorn as essentially pure sometimes attribute his virtues to the food he eats. Thus Hildegarde of Bingen says that once in every year the animal goes to that land in which the juices of Paradise abound and there seeks out the best herbs, digging them up with his hoof; from these he derives his medicinal properties. It will be remembered that Hildegarde thought the whole body of the unicorn medicinal, and also that the same belief is held in India regarding the rhinoceros. Now we learn from Linschoeten's Voyages that the horns of the rhinoceros are valued in India according to the flora of the district from which they come. "All Rhinocerotes", says the traveller, "are not alike good, for there are some whose homes are sold for one, two, or three hundred Pardawes the piece, and there are others of the same colour and greatness that are sold but for three or four Pardawes, which the Indians know and can discerne. The cause is that some Rhinocerotes which are found in certain places in the countrie of Bengala have this virtue by reason of the hearbes which that place only yeeldeth and bringeth foorth, which in other places is not so." A belief so constant as this, common to both schools of interpretation, may well derive from a source far back in time.

The explanation of the alicorn's "virtue" in terms of "sympathy" and "antipathy" was cogent enough for ordinary minds, but it could not stand the scrutiny of a really thoughtful man such as Andrea Marini. He pointed out that poisons are of many kinds, some hot and some cold, some wet and others dry, and that therefore it was absurd to say that one substance could stand in a relation either of sympathy or of antipathy with all of them at the same time. This contention was unanswerable, and it had a deep influence upon later

DRAGONS AND UNICORNS—FACT? OR FICTION?

writers. Andrea Bacci, whose book on the unicorn appeared in the same year as Marini's, was forced by it to abandon the sympathy-antipathy explanation altogether and to fall back upon a pseudo-Aristotelean forma and essentia which really explained nothing. He also accepted a vague Arabian assertion that alicorn somehow "comforts the heart", but the question as to why it sweats in the presence of poison he confuses and avoids as much as possible, finally leaving it unanswered.

Such light as I have thus far been able to throw upon the mystery of the alicorn's magical properties may be helpful in an attempt to solve the further mystery of what I have called the unicorn's water-conning. We are fortunate in having a description of this performance by one who claims to have been an eye-witness. This is John of Hesse, a priest of Utrecht, who visited the Holy Land in 1389 and had the most extraordinary good luck in the things he saw there. "Near the field of Helyon", he says, "there is a river called Marah, the water of which is very bitter, into which Moses struck his staff and made the water sweet so that the Children of Israel might drink. And even in our times, it is said, venomous animals poison that water after the setting of the sun, so that the good animals cannot drink of it; but in the morning, after the sunrise, comes the unicorn and dips his horn into the stream, driving the poison from it so that the good animals can drink there during the day. This I have seen myself."

One may point out in passing the strange coincidence that John of Hesse should have seen this rare spectacle at just the spot made famous by the miracle of Moses to which it provides so striking a parallel. For the bitter waters of Marah in the Bible story we have here the water poisoned at night by unclean animals; Moses and his staff are matched by the unicorn and its horn; the Children of Israel are represented by the clean animals waiting beside the stream. The two stories correspond in every essential detail, so that John's statement amounts almost to a declaration that he saw the ancient miracle re-enacted symbolically upon the spot.—But this is one of those mysteries into which the lay mind may not hope to pierce.

Leaping now almost five hundred years we find a traveller of the nineteenth century giving almost the same account of the water-conning trait as that given by John of Hesse. "One evening," says he, "as I was sitting among the rocks with a party of natives, the conversation turned upon flags. A man sitting there said to a stranger, 'Why do the English put the wyheed el win, that is the unicorn, on their flag?' and then related the whole story of it as one well known through the length and breadth of the land. 'The unicorn is found in a vast country south of Abyssinia. There the animals, undisturbed by man, live after their own laws. The water does not flow in rivers, but lives in the bosom of the soil. When the others wish to drink, the unicorn inserts his horn into the earth: with this he scoops a pool, satisfies his own thirst, and leaves what he does not require to the rest. So these English have the privilege of first discovering all things and then the rest of the world may come after.'"

In this late version the trait appears somewhat altered and debased: the unicorn does not purify but merely uncovers the water—one should observe, however, that he does this with his horn rather than with his hoof as another animal would—and his service to other beasts is not so much altruistic as accidental. Yet, for all these changes, the story is recognizably the same as that told by John of Hesse and many others.

Regarding the origin of the water-conning trait I shall make one suggestion here and another, somewhat farther reaching, in a later chapter. Popular beliefs about the stag have already served us well and may do so again. This animal, it will be remembered, is devoted to a diet of snakes, and in general he seems to thrive upon it, but sometimes, as Pliny informs us, a snake gets on the stag's back and bites him cruelly, whereupon he rushes to some river or fountain and plunges into the water to rid himself of his foe. Here we have at least a horned animal, a snake, and water brought together. A few sentences from the subtle and fascinating book by Antonio Ludovico from which I have already quoted, will carry us somewhat farther. Stags are accustomed to increase their strength, says he, upon a diet of serpents, but when they are quite saturated with this food, and before they begin to feel the noxious effects of the poison, they go down to the great rivers and there submerge their bodies, leaving only their mouths above the water. They do not drink a drop, however they may suffer with thirst, but remain standing there until the poison is sweated in the form of tears through their eyes, and then they leave. These tears, hardened into balls, fall by the wayside and are gathered by the people of the country, who value them as antidotes for poison. The barbarians call them bezoars.

It may seem that this story, however interesting in itself, leaves us still a long way from the unicorn dipping its horn into the water, but a little reflection will show, I think, that the analogy is rather close. We have already learned that the poison in the unicorn's body is not dispersed, as it appears to be in the stag mentioned by Ludovico, but is concentrated in the horn—the single horn. It seems natural, then, whenever the unicorn goes to the water to seek relief from an excess of poison, if that is indeed his motive, that he should dip the horn alone. Furthermore, it would follow naturally from the poisonous quality of the horn that whatever venom there might be in the water would be dispersed. This, at any rate, is the explanation of the water-conning trait that Laurens Catelan seems to have had in mind, for he says that the unicorn's well-known fierceness is caused by the great pain he suffers constantly on account of the poison in his horn, and that he knows no other way of obtaining relief except that of returning to the poisoned stream by which his pain is partly caused. (There has never been any lack of allegorical possibilities in the unicorn legend; the difficulty is in avoiding them.)

This is not a completely satisfying explanation of the water-conning trait because it gives no clue to the reason why the water is poisonous and it does not include the other animals which, in nearly all versions of the story, wait beside the water for the unicorn's coming. With these details unaccounted for we cannot feel that we have reached the origin of the story, but the passages quoted do carry us as far back toward that origin as any one in the Middle Ages or the Renaissance ever went, and this must suffice at present. We shall encounter the water-conning trait again, and shall be able, if not to "explain" it, at any rate to set it high among the myths and legends that are so ancient as for ever to defy explanation.

DRAGONS AND UNICORNS—FACT? OR FICTION?

CHAPTER VI

THE BATTLE OF BOOKS

FOR somewhat more than a century unicorn lore was a toy of scholarship with which the "leviathans of learning" loved to play. They played awkwardly, as leviathans are likely to do, the sport consisting in a half-jocose and half-ostentatious lavishing of erudition upon a topic which, with all its charm, had even in their eyes little practical importance. They played according to the rules of the scholarly game as they understood them, rallying "authorities" from all past ages, pitting book against book, regurgitating and chewing over again their own enormous reading, seldom subjecting what they read to the simplest tests of sense experience. It was a good time for the literary scholar, this period between the middle of the sixteenth century and the beginning of the eighteenth— a time when a man of great vitality and determination might still hope to read nearly everything that mattered and to write his foot-note in the world's huge Book of Letters. And the men were worthy of their opportunities, for there were giants in those days. Perhaps it is a little hazardous to assert that they played with the unicorn, for certainly they preserve at all times a profound sobriety of manner and style. The herd of whales lashing the surface of the sea in the distance may be engaged on serious business, however much they may seem to be gambolling, but when such mighty men as Thomas Bartholinus and Samuel Bochart unbend their strength upon our topic one can hardly

202

avoid the suspicion that they are merely amusing themselves by riding a favourite hobby-horse. (And if they were, the author of the present book should be the last person in the world to condemn them.)

They attacked what we should regard as a scientific problem largely by literary methods, yet they had something of the modern scientist's faith that no investigation, however remote from any apparent utility, can be valueless if faithfully performed. To some of these writers, however, the unicorn topic was not interesting primarily as "pure scholarship": one of them, at least, sold his learning and dialectic skill to an Italian tyrant who felt that belief in the alicorn on the part of his subjects would be good for his own health; another had an alicorn of his own, worth a large fortune if properly marketed, for sale; several others set themselves to combat a superstition which they thought too expensive and even dangerous; another group felt that if belief in the unicorn should be abandoned all belief in the Word of God would eventually go with it, and therefore they defended the animal with all that fury of religious conviction which their worthy successors now display in defending the first chapter of Genesis. But when all these controversialists are accounted for there remain a select few who approached the topic disinterestedly, concerned only to know the facts. Even these few, however, do not attempt to go behind the facts; not one of them asks himself how and why the human mind ever came to accept so curious a set of beliefs as those concerning the unicorn; not even in the rich and shadowy mind of Sir Thomas Browne did unicorn lore reveal significance reaching beyond itself. The facts had yet to be determined, and scholarship had not yet consciously turned to the tracing of human thought. For these reasons even the best writers on the unicorn missed entirely that aspect of their topic which is to us of primary concern—the only aspect, indeed, which justifies a survey of that topic in the twentieth century.

Between 1550 and 1700 there were published about twenty-five extended discussions of the unicorn, ranging from long chapters or separate tracts to whole books. Nearly all of this writing is derivative, each successive author feeling it necessary to cite, with or without credit given, every major assertion of his predecessors. One who is intensely interested in unicorn lore, or even one who is interested in the literary and scholarly ideals of the later Renaissance, may take a definite pleasure in an exhaustive study of this literature—in discovering the relationship between Bacci and Marini for example, the dependence of Ambroise Pare upon both of these, and in running down the many sources of Aidrovandus and of Thomas Bartholinus—but he can scarcely hope to convey this pleasure to a reader, and he has no right to inflict his minute discoveries upon others. My review of the modern classics of unicorn lore must be as brief as possible.

Sebastian Munster, whose Universal Cosmography appeared in 1550, knew nothing about the unicorn except what he got from the account by Lewis Vartoman, but his illustrator was able to draw from Vartoman's specifications a sightly and credible picture of the animal. Hieronymus Cardan knew a great deal about the unicorn, as about most other things, and his description of the animal, which appeared in the same year as MŸnster's, was frequently quoted by later writers and had an authority almost equal to that of the ancients. In other places, as we have seen, Cardan described the alicorn most exactly and speculated with unusual acumen about the sources of its magic powers. The Zoology of Conrad Gesner, published in 1551, exerted an influence quite out of proportion to its merits. Gesner's account of the unicorn was a mere compendium of what had been previously written on the subject and gave little evidence of original thinking. He suggested, whether for the first time I do not know, that the unicorn may have been destroyed in Noah's flood, and he quoted a letter from one of his many correspondents and collaborators in which a species of unicorn theretofore unknown to science, a native of the Carpathians, was reported and vaguely described. Gesner's book remained the standard work on its topic for almost ninety years, until it was superseded by Aldrovandus, and during that period few readers, even among the learned, would think of doubting what it said about the unicorn.

Pierre Belon, who discussed the unicorn problem at length in 1553, was a man of different stamp—not a compiler of other men's opinions but an observer, an independent thinker, a daring traveller, a zoologist in advance of his times. He was undaunted by authorities and majorities when convinced that they were wrong, using books intelligently, and seldom allowing them to abuse him. The great alicorns of St. Denis and St. Mark's and of royal treasuries puzzled him and won his admiration, but he would not believe in the powers attributed to them, and he was convinced that most of the smaller horns on the market and in the hands of individuals were of marine origin. For shrewdness, clear thinking, and independence of judgment, Belon's account is the equal of anything in unicorn literature with the exception of the book by Andrea Marini.

Of this admirable writer I know nothing except what may be deduced from his book itself, but this is really a good deal. He had a mind that would find itself at home in a few places in the twentieth century, but he must have been very lonely in the sixteenth, even in Venice. His thought is strong, clear, incisive; there is something thrilling in the manly vigour with which he cuts and crashes his way through thickets of superstition; his prose marches forward, every sentence and word an advance, with something like the irresistible tread of John Dryden. There is not one paragraph break from end to end of his book, and there does not need to be, so perfect is the linking of his thought. One sees that he is angry at heart, although his head is clear. He has the mind of a modern scientist and he loves clarity and precision, but he has no tools to work with, he is more hampered by surrounding bigotry and ignorance and lassitude than the scientist of our time, he has not even the support of his own profession. One may surmise that he chooses the unicorn legend for his attack not because of any special animosity toward it, but merely because it seems to him representative of the innumerable follies about him and of a general human tendency to prefer lies to the truth.

Marini begins by deploring that untrustworthiness of the senses which renders the discovery of natural truth so extremely difficult. The mind is acquainted for the most part, he says, not with the essences of things but only with their external "accidents"; and thence arises the variety of sects in all professions, for ambition or presumption leads men to pronounce as certain the conjectures of a moment or to lead others astray by deliberate deceit. Harmful everywhere, this has worked most harm in medicine, in which

DRAGONS AND UNICORNS—FACT? OR FICTION?

that opinion is most popular which most allures and deceives the public. Although the whole profession is guilty here, the Arabian physicians have been boldest in their promises, hoping to prop their failing fortunes by adopting and elaborating popular superstitions. The Arabs have introduced strange drugs, and among them the bezoar-stone and the alicorn, giving it out that these are antidotes for every poison and cures for every incurable disease, notwithstanding that no one knows where these things come from, what they really are, or by whom they were first tried. Things have come to such a pass that no royal treasury is thought complete without its alicorn, and princes are everywhere determined to have one at any price. Clever merchants have not been slow to take the opportunity for deception, seeing that there is no way of making sure what is the true horn. Marini has decided to expose these deceptions partly because he has been asked for his opinion about the unicorn and partly because he dislikes to see men spending great sums for things of no value, and putting trust in drugs that can do them no good.

He proposes, first, to show that we have no certain knowledge of the unicorn, and second, that, even if we had, the animal's horn could not have the powers attributed to it. The first part of his argument is concerned with the wide discrepancies in the unicorn tradition, which convince him that those who have written about the animal have never seen a specimen. The doubt thus cast upon the tradition is increased when one observes the differences in the reputed alicorns of Europe and England. These horns, he believes, have come from different animals, some of them marine, and he suspects that all the alicorns of England have come from the sea, for there is not even a record of a one-horned beast in that country. With a touch of that wonder at the wealth and variety of Nature which was common in his time, he reminds us that the sea is very prolific of animal life and that many of its forms are still unknown. He thinks it likely that the ocean has cast up many objects with the shape and substance of horns.

If the animal is unknown, how can we find and verify the horn? It will be replied that the learned have found certain infallible tests, but Marini asserts that most of these tests are childish and that all are worthless. He admits that powdered alicorn will delay the death of a poisoned pigeon, but says that any other horn will do the same thing by retarding assimilation.

Even if the animal and the horn were both well known, it would be easy to prove that the assertions made concerning the alicorn's properties are come una favola di Romanzi. To say that it is good against all poisons is obviously ridiculous, and an affront to intelligence, for poisons differ so widely in their elements that one substance can be in sympathy or antipathy with only one or two kinds. Poisons operate upon different organs and in various ways, so that no one antidote can counteract them all. The assertion that the alicorn sweats in the presence of poison may be proved a lie by simple experiment, supposing that one can get an alicorn to experiment upon; but we do not need experiment, for reason alone tells us that sweat is an effect of "vegetative vertue", which no horn can have. Marini allows that marble, glass mirrors, and other such objects, collect moisture under certain circumstances, but this is not sweat; it does not come from the intrinsic nature of those objects but from the surrounding humidity.

DRAGONS AND UNICORNS—FACT? OR FICTION?

Coming to the use of powdered alicorn as a medicine prescribed for poisoning, pestilential fever, bites of mad dogs, stings of scorpions, falling sickness, and the like, he admits that it may have some value, though no more than stag's horn. Like all horn, it is "cold and dry" by nature, so that it corrects the putrefactions that are by nature wet and hot. His professional indignation is aroused, however, by the far greater claims of the "Arabistes" that the alicorn can cure all other diseases and even raise the dead to life.

Approaching his close, Marini has of course to face the argument from authority and common consent. It will be objected, he says, that so enduring a fame as that of the alicorn cannot be without foundation, and that it could not last so long unless it contained truth. He points out that the superstitions concerning the Harpies, the Sirens, and the Golden Ass of Apuleius also lasted for a long time. A very slight occasion may give rise, he says, to a lasting belief when no person of intelligence and prestige reveals its emptiness. He cannot be sure how the belief in the alicorn arose, but he conjectures most shrewdly that it must be traced back to the custom of the kings in ancient times who drank their wine from vessels of horn. Some person with a speculative turn of mind may have spread abroad the notion that they did this to escape the danger of poisoning; and it may well be, he says, that these kings connived at the spreading of this report, thinking that it would have a discouraging effect upon poisoners. And this is true, he remarks, "even today, when those Princes who live in constant fear keep on their table pieces of alicorn or the tongues of serpents or other such things, pretending—or perhaps really believing without any evidence—that they will sweat when poison is brought near". Marini ends his book with the hope that he has crushed this superstition and that men of sense will in future leave the alicorn in the hands of charlatans and make use of some more trustworthy means of protection.

Marini was answered at once by a man of greater reputation; he was called a confirmed sceptic and a sworn foe of all believers in horns; the whole tendency of thought in his time and what may be called the "vested interests" were against him. Nevertheless, his book left an indelible mark upon the literature of the unicorn, he found followers almost immediately, and the ruck of writers whose mental habit was a pious echolalia were put to strange shifts because this one man had broken the rules of the game by doing some independent thinking. The Diseorso seems to have been translated into Latin by Aldrovandus, who certainly extended its influence by his careful outline of Marini's argument in a book of his own.

Of Marini's chief antagonist, Andrea Bacci, a good deal is known. He was a professional student of botany and a physician to the Pope, very erudite but not successful in medical practice, so that he seems to have lived in poverty until the Cardinal Azzolino Colonna took him into his household. His numerous treatises show a penchant for recondite topics on the border between magic and science. He had far more learning than Marini and a more poetical mind; the total impression that he makes upon one who reads several of his works together is that of an Italian and somewhat less humorous Sir Thomas Browne; his thought, however, was not active and trenchant, but absorbent, and he loved mystery more than he did the truth.

Bacci's book on the unicorn appeared at Venice in 1566—in the same year and place, that is, as Marini's, and this fact is one of the most curious things about it. Neither of the two writers mentions the other by name or directly alludes to the other's book, yet it is obvious almost at a glance that the two treatises are intimately related. Both begin with an exordium on the inability of reason to discover the essences of natural objects. Bacci presents, and answers, all of the doubts concerning the unicorn named by Marini, and in the same order. Ostensibly, at least, the two writers reach diametrically opposed results: Marini is a sceptic and Bacci would have his readers think that he is a firm believer. I can find no external evidence concerning the relationship between these two books, but internal evidence—most of it too minute to present here—has convinced me that Bacci wrote with the definite purpose of answering and confuting Marini. It seems to me almost certain that he was commissioned to do this by one of his patrons, probably Don Francesco Medici, who feared the weakening of popular belief in the unicorn. For all his grace and skill and learning, Bacci gives everywhere the impression that his pen is hired, his thought dictated, and that he is one of those literary slaves whose miseries were described by Lucian and Aeneas Silvius Piccolomini. He wrote deliberately, I believe, to "keep the Past upon its throne". Did he write dishonestly? Perhaps he could not have answered that question even to his own conscience. He may have felt that a little prevarication, or rather let us say a little stifling of his better thought, would be for the general good. He may have been one of those who honestly believe that multi-millionaires ought not to be poisoned.

If this was indeed his view and if he wrote his book to discourage those who thought otherwise, then it is interesting to observe that he probably failed. The Discorso is dedicated Al Serenissimo Don Francesco Medici, Gran Principe di Toscana; it may have been written in his house and at his instance; it was certainly written with special reference to an alicorn in his possession. Deeply humiliated Bacci must have been, therefore, when this most serene Don Francesco died according to the belief of the time by poison administered by his brother, the Cardinal Ferdinand, who succeeded him. Fifteen hours later died his wife, the famous Bianca Capello, with whom he had carried on amours for years during the lifetime of his first wife, Jean of Austria. The famous alicorn of the Medici and the brilliant Discorso written to corroborate its influence—Bacci says in his Introductory Address that Francesco was almost the author—had failed most dismally.

Bacci's book is clear and orderly in arrangement. "In the first part", says he, "I consider the prime question whether there is such a creature as the unicorn, in regard to which I adduce from one source and another many curious reasonings and finally prove that the animal undoubtedly exists. In the second part we shall decide what sort of animal the unicorn is, and here will be heard the testimony of the ancients and that of all the moderns who have written on the subject so that we may determine what is to be accepted as true. Coming at last, in the third part, to the How and the Why, we shall decide whether the alicorn has any power against poison and how it may be proved that it possesses such power."

DRAGONS AND UNICORNS—FACT? OR FICTION?

Each of the reasons for doubting the existence of the unicorn developed by Marini is considered in a separate chapter with much dialectic skill and adequate learning. Commending those who have expressed doubt not in mere obstinacy but in sincere desire for truth, Bacci points out that the unicorn legend is different from most superstitions in that it has lasted longer and has been shared by the most enlightened minds of all nations. Superstition, he says, lives on the popular tongue alone, but this belief has been maintained by the greatest writers, sacred and profane; furthermore, this belief, instead of growing more monstrous, as superstitions do, has become clearer and simpler and more credible with each succeeding age. The fact that the unicorn is almost unknown does not argue its non-existence but only its rarity. Until recent years the aromatic spices of the East were unknown in Europe; rhubarb and aloes and amber were unfamiliar to the ancients, yet these things existed. We need not wonder that the unicorn is still strange to us when we consider that he cannot be taken alive, that his habit is solitary, that he dwells in remotest mountain fastnesses, and that there are probably very few specimens alive at any one time. The tradition of the unicorn has come down to us precisely as other traditions of actual things have come: first we hear its name from unknown sources and it is confusedly described, but little by little the accounts increase in precision and frequency until we find them everywhere. Notices of the unicorn continue to be confused merely because the beast is very wild and is not found in Europe.

At this point Bacci indulges himself—and at least one of his readers—in an eloquent passage on due gran segreti della natura. The first of these is that she contents herself with producing only a few individuals of those species which are especially distinguished by their beauty, and this she does in order that God Almighty may have the greater glory in His works. We acknowledge His glory when we contemplate the frame of this vast machine the earth, when we consider the ranks of the heavens and the concourse of the stars, the composition of the elements, and how He keeps the earth balanced in the air and sets a limit to the sea. In every created thing there is some marvel, more or less.

In some things God and Nature have shown their power by the manner of their production—as in gems, which are found in the hidden chambers of the hills and yet are composed of the same substance as the stars. Other things are wonderful for the length of time required to make them, such as gold and precious marbles and many kinds of stones. With respect to animals, those necessary to the maintenance of human life are produced in abundance; others, not necessary or even harmful, are produced sparingly, and to these Nature gives the instinct to flee from the sight of men, as we see in lions, dragons, tigers, and basilisks. And then, too, even the rudest mind must be amazed at the divine beauty of some creations, for not even Solomon in all his glory was arrayed like the lilies of the field and the fowls of the air. The emerald itself is vanquished by the marvellous green of certain beetles; no jewel and no work of man's hands can compare with the natural gems, green and gold and red, to be found in certain humble worms and grubs. Other animals are wonderful for their size, such as the elephant and the whale, huge as the hugest ship; others, again, astonish by their smallness, among which Virgil thought the most wonderful was the zenzala, an animal barely visible but which looks like a hippogriff, at once horse and rider and trumpet, both Perseus and Pegasus. Fi-

DRAGONS AND UNICORNS—FACT? OR FICTION?

nally, God and Nature have shown their power by making some things, such as the phoenix and the balsam, exceedingly rare, and thus, apparently, it has pleased the wonder-working Architect and mighty God that the unicorn should be among the rarest works of Nature.

Arguing circularly, Bacci derives from this another "secret". As Nature produces few individuals of the most wonderful kinds and the highest value—witness the phoenix and precious stones—it follows that the unicorn, being so rare, must have great value, and that its horn must have some miraculous virtue (prerogativa). As a manifest proof of this, the animal has a strong instinct for solitude, living in deserts so remote that it seems almost a miracle whenever its horn is found. This horn must be washed down from the desert by great rivers in flood, long after the animal's death; naturally, therefore, it is expensive.

The translation of this passage, which has decided beauty in the original, is justified by the brilliant illustration it gives of a habit of thought common in the Renaissance which made belief in the unicorn easy. Men of Bacci's stamp did not draw back from this or that belief about Nature because it was wonderful; they were too well informed, too cultivated and intellectual, one may as well say too scientifically minded, for that. Wonderful things were precisely what they expected of Nature, just as marvels have been expected, and therefore found, by those minds of our own time that have conceived the answering universes of the atom and of outer space. Those who would condemn Bacci and his fellow-believers on the ground that their assertions about the unicorn were too wonderful for belief are less scientific than they suppose.

Like most of his fellows and like the vast majority of educated people of the present day, Bacci is unscientific rather in his method than in his general mental attitude. He lavishes learning and acute thought upon the problem of the alicorn's alleged properties but says hardly a word about definite experiment, which would have settled his question in one tenth of the time he gives to it. Here we have a most vivid example of the tyranny of mental habit. A scholar, a physician, a trained observer, a man of fine culture and powerful mind, is sitting in a library with an alicorn before him, and he wants to find out whether it responds in any way to the presence of poison. What does he do? He goes to the shelves and pulls down Ctesias, Aristotle, Aeian, Pliny, Solinus, Dioscorides, Avicenna, Albertus Magnus, and twenty or thirty other "authorities", and then sets to work. In the terms of what he finds in these books he thinks with an acuteness of which only a few of the men we now call scientists would be capable; but to think in any other terms, to bring a bit of poison out of Don Francesco's "laboratory" and to set it beside the alicorn to see what would happen—that is quite beyond him. Or perhaps we may say, that would not be "pure scholarship". Perhaps, also, Bacci did not greatly desire to have the truth about the alicorn demonstrated beyond a doubt. He had seen experiments performed upon this alicorn by Don Francesco himself, who, as an amateur chemist, doubtless knew how to get satisfactory results. Bacci was not being paid to test the alicorn but to write a book about it.

DRAGONS AND UNICORNS—FACT? OR FICTION?

I shall not summarize Bacci's rather profound but wholly Aristotelean chapter on the Fondamenti di Tutte le virtu delle cose upon which he bases his conclusion that the operation of the alicorn is due not to its "elementary qualities" nor to its "external accidents" but to its "intrinsic and formal nature or essence" which the mind cannot grasp or understand. This Aristotelian doctrine of "form" or "essential nature"—to which we owe, ultimately, the basic and most obviously false conception of democracy—had lain heavy upon the world of thought for many centuries, as it does upon society to-day. As the intrinsic form of a thing is unknowable, one may say of it almost anything that suits his purpose. Bacci derived from the intrinsic form of the alicorn its alleged powers of detecting poison, just as the philosophers of eighteenth-century France derived from the intrinsic form or essential nature of humanity the equally ludicrous proposition that all men are created free and equal. The very rarity of the alicorn, says he, is proof presumptive that it has extraordinary intrinsic virtue. This virtue may be judged from its substance: like gems, it has much forma in proportion to its materia, and its matter, as in the case of gems, is so pure and splendid and starry that none can deny it a heavenly origin. Its virtue may be seen in the excellence of its external accidents, such as its polished density, its odour and taste and colour. The alicorn is the densest of all horns; it is white, pure, uniform, and single for each animal; it works by its own nature and not by assistance of art; it causes heat yet is not hot; it causes cold, yet it is not cold itself. All this means that it must operate by its intrinsic or hidden virtue.

Marini had rendered it impossible for any intelligent man who read his book to explain the operation of the alicorn in terms of "sympathy" and "antipathy", making clear that no single substance could stand in either of these relations to all poisons whatsoever. Bacci therefore abandons the old explanation but not the belief that the alicorn is good against all poisons. He explains its virtue by invoking an assertion which he says he finds in Avicenna's Treatise on the Heart that alicorn "comforts the heart" and is a powerful cordial. One sees how this might account for the alleged action of the alicorn as a drug, but it does not seem to explain how it could detect and reveal the presence of poison on a rich man's table.

Bacci ends his book with this strange and significant passage: "Whether the alicorn sweats or does not sweat, whether it makes water boil or does not make it boil, the belief that it does so will do no injury to truth and will be for the good of the state. No man of sound mind should seek to disprove these things by rigour of reasoning, but should allow and discreetly admit them—for the sake, at least, of the Princes whom they will please by such favourable opinion. Thus the common good obliges us to write and to persuade the ignorant that what is said of the Alicorn is true, because such a belief discourages wicked men from evil doing by making them think that the virtue of this horn will easily discover their iniquity and bring about their utter ruin."

Thus Andrea Bacci takes his place among the well-intentioned weaklings who throttle their thought for what they make themselves think the social advantage. Did he, after all, believe in the unicorn and its properties, as he often asserts in the body of his book? After one has read his last paragraph it does not seem to matter what he believed. His

DRAGONS AND UNICORNS—FACT? OR FICTION?

patron died, according to contemporary belief, just the death from which Bacci had tried to save him—an apt commentary upon the final value of such endeavours. His book had five editions in twenty-one years, but its influence was far less than that exerted by Marini's Discorso, which has never had more than two. It may seem strange that one who is thankful for every legitimate influence that prolonged the life of the unicorn should be sorry for Bacci's advocacy and regard it as a defection from a higher cause, but almost all the writing ever done about the unicorn has been honest, and that of Andrea Bacci apparently was not. One cannot forget that he was a man of first-rate powers, and that, if it had not been "just for a handful of silver", he might have done better work.

He might have done work equal to that of Ambroise Pare who, with less ability but far more courage and character, left a lasting mark upon scientific thought and won for himself the title "Father of French Surgery". Pare knew the temptations to which his Italian contemporary succumbed, for he was first physician to the Court of France during the period of Catharine de' Medici's regime and apparently a friend to Catharine herself. At a dozen different points we find him standing out against hoary abuses, intrenched superstitions, and ancient ignorances, never failing to act upon and to speak the best he knew through fear that his innovation might be unsafe or untimely. The kings he served used alicorns and bezoar-stones. He did his best to prove to them that such things were useless. In his book on poisons he tells a story which is as well known as anything about him and which illustrates vividly his scientific temper. The king Charles IX, his master, had been given a bezoar in which he had full confidence, but Pare assured him that its reputation was undeserved, suggesting that it be tried on a criminal sentenced to death. The king found that one of his cooks was to be hanged the next day for stealing two silver plates, and this cook gladly agreed to drink poison when he was told by the king that the bezoar would be given him immediately after. The cook died in torment after seven hours, and Pare found by autopsy that the cause of death had been gastroenteritis induced by corrosive sublimate.

The most important of Pare's several passages on the unicorn was written when he was seventy years of age at the request of one of his patients. In 1580 he had successfully treated the Chevalier Christofle des Ursins for an imposthume caused by a fall from a horse, and during his convalescence this patient took great interest in the methods used in his cure, asking particularly why he had not been given mummy to drink. Pare answered this question on both medical and aesthetic grounds, pointing out among other things that it was shameful and infra dignitatem for good Christians to eat and drink the dead bodies of pagans. He was then asked why he had made no use of alicorn, and his reply, which brought in by the way certain remarks about poisons and the pest, was so satisfactory that Christofle begged him to write it all out for the good of humanity. The resulting Discours rests heavily for both matter and method upon Marini, who is nowhere mentioned. It is moderate, sensible, untechnical in vocabulary, obviously addressed to the general public. Although inferior to the books of Bacci and Marini in almost every important respect, it seems to have had almost as much influence as they.

Pare begins as Marini had done by showing that the existence of the unicorn is doubt-

DRAGONS AND UNICORNS—FACT? OR FICTION?

ful, at least on grounds of ordinary evidence. He admits that an acquaintance of his, a physician of Paris named Louys Paradis, has recently given a minute description of a unicorn which he thought he saw at Alexandria, but even this, and all other human testimony put together, does not shake his scepticism. "If it were not for the witness of Holy Scripture, to which we are obliged to adjust all our beliefs", says he, "I should not think that such a creature as the unicorn had ever existed." He then quotes several of the Biblical references and concludes, almost with a sigh: "Il faut donc croire qu'il est des Licornes."

But the Bible says nothing about the medicinal values of the alicorn, so that Pare is left free to deal with that topic in the way of a scientific man. He sets to work to destroy the superstition by appeal to experience, to authority, and to reason. By "experience" he means experiment. He has drawn circles on a table with water in which the alicorn has been soaked for hours, and he finds that scorpions and toads and spiders have no idea of lying down to die inside of such circles but cross and recross the line of alicorn-water at will. Not content with this, he has put a toad to soak for three days in alicorn-water, and at the end of that time he found the toad—regarded in his day, of course, as a highly venomous creature—"aussi gaillard que lors que je l'y mis". He makes short work of the bubble test for "true horn", asserting that the same bubbles are sent up by the horns of cows, goats, sheep, and other beasts, by the tusks of elephants, by the covers of pots, by tiles, and even by wood. He has tried giving alicorn to pigeons poisoned with arsenic, and the pigeons have always died. The assertion that alicorn sweats in the presence of poison is met, as by Marini, with the observation that glass and marble and other substances with smooth surfaces act in the same way—that is, that they condense the surrounding vapours.

Pare attempts to turn the argument from "authority" against his antagonists by showing that Aristotle, Galen, and Hippocrates never mention the medicinal properties of the alicorn, the strength of this contention being that anything ignored by these three supreme authorities in the field of medicine was not worth mentioning. He cites the testimony of eminent physicians of his own day against the alicorn, and says that physicians of repute continue to use it only because their patients demand it. "C'est que le monde veult estre trompe."

Coming to the argument by "reason", Pare accepts Marini's criticism of the alicorn's action by "sympathy" and "antipathy". He goes beyond this and attacks the Arabic theory advanced by Bacci that the alicorn is "cordial" and works by strengthening the heart. Only good blood and good air, says Pare, can do this. Now the alicorn is neither of these, nor is it convertible into either; it is earth, and therefore, according to the old theory of the elements, at the opposite extreme from air; it is dry, while air is moist; it cannot be turned into blood because it contains no flesh or sap. Therefore it cannot affect the heart. Pare believes that the best "alexitery" is to flee from all poisoners as from the plague—"et les chasser du Royaume de France, et les envoyer avec les Turcs et les autres infideles, ou aux deserts inaccessibles avec les Licornes". He did not consider, perhaps, that this drastic policy would have involved the banishment of his royal mistress.

212

DRAGONS AND UNICORNS—FACT? OR FICTION?

At the end of his Discours Pare expresses a hope that those who do not agree with him will bring forward their reasons, for the public good. The wish was gratified. An anonymous champion of the unicorn appeared, reiterated the old superstitions, tried to overwhelm Pare by the weight of authority and tradition and numbers, and—in the way of his kind—treated his antagonist with personal abuse. Pare's reply is a masterpiece of French urbanity. "I say nothing", he writes, "of his apparent animosity, which I suppose must be due rather to his zeal for the truth than to any opinion that he can hold of me"; and at the end of his response he begs his adversary, if he has anything further to advance, "qu'il quitte les animositez, et qu'il traicte plus doucement le bon vieillard."

The adversary had taken his stand upon the mediaeval trust in tradition; the fact that unicorns had been believed in for a long time and were still accepted by the vast majority of men was enough for him. All the wise men of the world, he asserted, have believed in the virtues of the alicorn, and, aside from the fact that we are obliged to accept authority, it is better to err with the wise than to think rightly in opposition to them. To the first of these remarks Pare answers that by no means all the wise men of the world have believed in the alleged properties of the alicorn. To the second highly interesting and representative assertion he makes the equally interesting reply: "I say, on the contrary, that I should prefer to be right entirely alone than to be wrong not merely in company with the wise but even with all the rest of the world." (Quant a la seconde partie, je dy tout au contraire, que j'aimerois mieux faire bien tout seul que de faillir non seulement avec les sages mais mesmes avec tout le reste du monde.) Clearly, a change is coming over the Western world—a change not yet completed.

The adversary's second point, not easily distinguishable from the first, was that the mere length of time during which the alicorn had been used showed that it must be valuable. Although we do not know this adversary's name, we see and know him quite well enough. His true name is Legion, and he has millions of fellows in every age who think that the antiquity of an error converts it into a truth.

Ambroise Pare did not belong to this school; he was accustomed to being in a minority of one and to advancing those "minority reports" which eventually rule the world. "I reply", he says, "that mere duration of time is not sufficient to prove the value of the alicorn. Its vogue is founded upon opinion, but the truth depends upon fact. Therefore it is nothing to the purpose to cite against me the popes and emperors and kings and other potentates who have kept the ailcorn in their treasuries, for such men are not competent judges of the properties of natural things."

A pope not a competent judge of everything in the universe? One is reminded of the contemporary suspicion, certainly well founded, that Pare was a Protestant, and of the probability that he escaped the Massacre of Saint Bartholomew because he was too good a physician for the Court of France to lose. As a Protestant, however, he does accept the authority of the Bible, and when his adversary quotes against him the references to the unicorn in the Old Testament he almost forgets his urbanity. "Any man who tries to bring this argument against me", he says, "merely shows that he wants to quarrel, for there is

213

DRAGONS AND UNICORNS—FACT? OR FICTION?

no one who accepts the teachings of the Bible more faithfully than I do." Thus the champion of personal liberty was imprisoned by authority after all. He accepted the Septuagint's word as the "word of God".

Creditable as Pare's discussions of the unicorn were in method and spirit, they contained little original matter. He depended chiefly upon Marini, but also upon his contemporary and countryman, the famous traveller, André Thevet. This writer's Cosmographie Universelle, an admirable work, very influential and still highly interesting, contained a chapter of first-rate importance about the unicorn. Thevet bases his account upon things he has seen and heard on an island in the Red Sea which was a port of call for many ships trading between East and West, and which swarmed with petty traders of all nations. Here he once met a Turkish ambassador to Abyssinia who showed him a horn, probably that of an oryx, which was thought to grow single upon the animal's brow, but which was decidedly unlike the alicorns of Europe. In the same place and on the mainland near at hand he has seen the tusks of elephants and of walruses artificially straightened by charlatans and tricksters and sold as true alicorns. These and similar observations have made him doubt almost everything that is asserted about the unicorn. The story of the virgin-capture reminds him of the chattering of aged gossips about the winter fire "avec leurs discours du Melusine". He is not to be intimidated by the authority of Pliny, Minster, Solinus, Strabo, and all other such men put together, for, wise and learned as these men were, this tale of the unicorn is not the first not the hundredth of their errors and lies. He says with justifiable pride that if these "authorities" had enjoyed the same knowledge of the world that he himself possesses and had seen the countries that he has traversed they would scarcely have forgotten their duty to such an extent as to hand on to posterity their idle and untested imaginings. It is unlikely, he thinks, that foreigners can know more about the fauna of a country than that country's inhabitants know. He has ranged over the whole territory that the unicorn is said to inhabit and has heard no rumour of its existence. One-horned animals may exist, he thinks, like that one described by his Turkish ambassador, but scarcely any such as the unicorn fabled in Europe. The alicorns of European cathedrals and treasuries are probably, he thinks, the products of such deceitful arts as he saw practised near the Red Sea. He does not doubt that they have medicinal value, but this they share with all other horns whatsoever. The confidence, not to say the swagger, of Thevet is evident in his concluding words: "Voyla donc ce que j'avois de long temps envie d'advertir le Lecteur, pour oster l'opinion mal fondee de plusieurs hommes doctes, tant Grecs que Latins, mesmes des Rois, Princes et Monarques, pour le faict de la Licorne."

From this "vulgar sort of Infidel people", as Edward Topsell called the writers we have just considered, we may now return to the faithful, for it is a curious fact that all the chief sixteenth-century authorities on our topic were sceptical to say the least, and that nearly all those of the seventeenth century were believers. The Reverend Edward Topsell is positively devout, and like a few others of his kind he bolsters his own belief by the conviction that those who do not agree with him must be bad people. All that he requires to prove the existence of the unicorn and the truth of everything ever said of it is the authority of the ninety-second Psalm and of "all the Divines that ever wrote". With these

DRAGONS AND UNICORNS—FACT? OR FICTION?

witnesses on his side he feels dispensed from further argument and expatiates in the meadows of unicorn lore at length, thoroughly enjoying himself. There is little in Topsell's account of the unicorn, however, that is not to be found in Conrad Gesner, and he is interesting chiefly for the quaint vigour of his language.

Laurens Catelan's book on the unicorn was of much greater importance. He was an apothecary of note in Montpellier, a city which in his time (1568-1647) was teaching medicine and pharmacy to all of Europe. Besides succeeding as an apothecary, he collected a rather famous small museum of curiosities which contained an alicorn as its greatest treasure, and it is probable, as I have said, that he wrote his Histoire de la Licorne not so much as a service to science as with the hope of attracting a purchaser. Catelan is seen at his best in his carefully written Disours et demonstration des ingrédients de la thériaque, a valuable book upon a topic of which he was a master. A man of considerable ability and reading, he was both credulous and vain. The chief value of his book on the unicorn is due to the fact that it is the only one of importance written by a practising apothecary.

Catelan divides his book into four parts. In the first he discusses the various names of the unicorn. In the second he treats its appearance, habitat, general characteristics and "virtues" in medicine, giving directions for its chase and capture. The third part is devoted to a fair statement of eighteen objections made by those who think the beast fabulous or the report of its virtues false, and in the fourth division he answers all these objections triumphantly, concluding "que l'animal Iycorne est, et que grandes et merveilleuses sont les venus de sa come, pourveu qu'elle soit de la vraye et legitime." It is certain that Catelan had read both Marini and Pare, for he quotes them both as objectors, but they seem to have disturbed his own beliefs not at all.

A year or two after publishing his book on the unicorn Catelan had the pleasure of showing his little museum to a distinguished physician and scholar from Denmark, one Caspar Bartholinus, who was much interested in the apothecary's specimens of one-horned birds and insects. Horns, and particularly single horns, may be said to have "run in the family" of Bartholinus somewhat as music did in the family of Bach and money in that of Rothschild. Nothing one-horned was alien to Caspar. or to Thomas his son or to Caspar his grandson. They were fascinated all three by the monocerine idea as it had been exemplified by Nature in various species. If Laurens Catelan gave the elder Caspar the first hint for this strange hobby, then that is the best contribution he made to the lore of the unicorn. It seems probable that he did give that hint and that it was partly due to Caspar's visit to the apothecary's museum in Montpellier that unicorn scholarship passed from the south of Europe to the north.

In 1628 Caspar Bartholinus published his little book about the unicorn and related topics. It is a remarkably clear, sensible, and well-arranged little book, as "scientific" as almost any one living at the time could have made it. In forty-eight compact pages it covers every important aspect of unicorn lore, including several never before discussed. The first chapter is concerned with the question whether unicorns exist, and here Caspar sensibly deplores the tendency of some men to deny the existence of things for no bet-

DRAGONS AND UNICORNS—FACT? OR FICTION?

ter reason than that they have not seen them; they would do better, he thinks, to trust authority until a thorough ransacking of the planet has shown conclusively what it does and does not contain. For his part, he has no such difficulties, and he recognizes the existence of unicorned insects, birds, snakes, and even men. Among the larger animals he finds eight different unicorns: the oryx, Garcias ab Horto's African amphibian, the sea-unicorn of the north, the Indian bull, the Indian ass, the Indian horse, the rhinoceros, and the monoceros or unicorn proper. The usual argument from the Biblical references is then made and the correctness of the Septuagint translation upheld.

The next four chapters are devoted to discussion of the sea-unicorn, the horn of the rhinoceros, the alicorns of Europe, and the general characteristics of the true unicorn. The sixth chapter denies without qualification all the magical properties attributed to the horn, chiefly because they do not stand the test of experiment. In a covert reference to Bacci, Caspar says that we ought not to allow our opinion in such matters to be swayed by the authority of princes, which is always less important than the truth—"quae veritati semper est posthabenda". It is evident that the alicorn has moved into a different political atmosphere. Caspar discusses in his concluding chapters the various substances that were sold as "true horn" in his time and ends with a valuable passage on the nature and use of "fossil alicorn".

But the most interesting of the productions of Caspar Bartholinus was his son Thomas Bartholinus the Elder, Professor of Anatomy at Copenhagen and a man of encyclopaedic learning. The De Unicornu Observationes Novae by this son is the most extensive and impressive work ever devoted to the unicorn, and it might have been the best if the author had devoted to it his best powers instead of regarding it as a toy of scholarship. One who knows nothing of Thomas's other books, which are numerous and sound, is likely to think when he glances through the chapter headings of this one that the author was horn-mad. Some of the topics of his thirty-seven chapters are: horned men, the horns of Moses, the causes of horns, horned insects, horned birds and beetles and reptiles and fish, unicorned bulls and asses, the horn of the Holy Cross, the use of horns for beakers, horns as ornaments, horns in medicine, fossil horns. In the second edition of the book this effect of multiplicity is accentuated by a brilliantly executed frontispiece in which a dozen different sorts of unicorns are pictured or represented. The Index Auctorum shows that Bartholinus quotes, in his three hundred and eighty pages from at least six hundred different writers, many of whom are cited many times, and from ten or twelve different languages. This book, the author tells us in his vivacious preface, was written in his youth partly as an act of filial piety—to extend and amplify the work of his father—and partly to while away a tedious interval of time. As I have said, there were giants in those days, and Thomas Bartholinus was one of them. This is the book on the unicorn, more than any other, in which one is convinced that the author is engaged in some sort of erudite play for which we have lost the art and the feeling. The tone of the preface is unmistakably gay and occasionally jocose, and on nearly every later page there is some observation so droll or so almost incredibly erudite as to rouse the suspicion, at least, although we cannot be quite sure, that the unwieldy elephant is wreathing his lithe proboscis to make us sport. The whole work has the look of a giant's jest, and one cannot believe that any

DRAGONS AND UNICORNS—FACT? OR FICTION?

sane man could have written it unless he thoroughly enjoyed the task, saw it in relation to serious concerns, and carried it through somewhat in the spirit of play.

I shall not attempt to make even a brief outline of this extraordinary book, which is really a sort of compact encyclopaedia of unicorn lore. It is enough to say that Thomas expanded in all directions the topics discussed by his father, adding illustration and corroboration from his immense hoard of learning, but extending the thought very little if at all. In regard to thought, in fact, the book is disappointing. Thomas presents the opinions of Caspar without change—holding, that is, that the unicorn exists but refusing to believe in the magical horn, trying to mediate between what he considers the credulity of Bacci and the unwarranted scepticism of Marini. His own son, Caspar, in preparing the considerably amplified second edition, left the matter of the first edition almost unaltered but added passages of his own.

The work of the Bartholini was professional scholarship. In France during the seventeenth century scholarship was almost never professional, and no more vivid contrast can be imagined than that between the exhaustive treatment of unicorn lore by Thomas Bartholinus and the contemporary discussion of the same topic recorded in a work, long since forgotten but worthy of remembrance, called the Recueil General. This consists of two hundred and eighty-seven conferences or public debates on the widest variety of topics, politics and religion alone excluded. One purpose steadily held is to avoid the acrimony, the pedantry and over-emphasis, the excessive citation of authority and dependence upon it, that still and for long after marked and marred academic discussion. Every speaker strives to show himself at once a scholar and a gentleman—one of the most difficult mediations between extremes—and the result, in its moderation and deference and urbane mingling of scholarship with humour, makes an admirable example of what the learned world owes to the French mind. As compared with the records of the English Royal Society, these papers are literature, and indeed I am not sure that the "Bureau" of debaters was not a fictitious device or "frame" of a single author. The two hundred and fortieth conference is De la Licorne.

We have heard the opinions about the unicorn held by the "hirsute scholars in 'us'"; here we learn what was thought on that subject by the educated public, by men who spent their lives in salons rather than in libraries. The two speakers in this debate have read the more important documents of the case. The first, who holds a brief against the unicorn, depends largely upon Pare's Discours, though he may have read Marini also, and he concludes: "ce conte de la Licorne est une fiction". The second speaker, more representative of the popular views, has certainly read Andrea Bacci. He argues shrewdly that the variety of opinions about the unicorn is no proof that the animal does not exist, for we find the same conflicting views about many indubitable beasts and even about God. He chooses the dog as an example and says tellingly that one who knew only the lap-dog could hardly be persuaded that it belongs to the same species as the mastiff. The argument that the Romans never saw the unicorn at their spectacles does not impress him, partly because it is the "argument from silence", and partly because the animal is, almost "by definition", uncapturable. He believes, with Thevet, that all horns are

DRAGONS AND UNICORNS—FACT? OR FICTION?

medicinal, and that the virtue ordinarily distributed through two horns is greatly increased when "united and locked in a single canal, as in the case of the unicorn". In conclusion, he says that occult properties ought not to be denied hastily. We should remember that our knowledge is limited and our reason infirm. Authority, reason, and experiment combine in demonstrating the magical powers of the alicorn.

Ulysses Aldrovandus was the Conrad Gesner of the seventeenth century. His account of the unicorn fills thirty-one folio pages and reviews all the more obvious literature of his time, but he does not commit himself. "Some are doubtful", he says, "whether the unicorn exists; some deny its existence and others affirm it. For my own part, I shall merely report their opinions faithfully, leaving to each of my readers his own freedom of judgment."

We come next to Sir Thomas Browne—always a delightful thing to do, but in this instance somewhat disappointing. His treatment of the unicorn is badly confused; it is based upon Goropius Becanus, but he reads Goropius carelessly. We feel that the topic was almost made for Browne, and we miss, as frequently in the "Vulgar Errors", the full charm and power of his mystery-loving mind. It is disheartening to see this man who thought, quite rightly, that there are not miracles enough, going about to question and discredit one of the best of the few there were left. He has read his Bartholinus, however, to such purpose that he is by no means to be classed among the "vulgar sort of Infidel people". "Wee are so farre from denying there is any Unicorne at all", says he, "that wee affirme there are many kinds thereof. In the number of Quadrupedes wee will concede no lesse then five." But this hopeful beginning is not maintained, for Browne continues: "Although we concede there be many Unicornes, yet are we still to seeke; for whereunto to affixe this home in question, or to determine from which thereof we receive this magnified medicine, we have no assurance . . . for although we single but one and Antonomastically thereto assigne the name of the Unicorne, yet can we not be secure what creature is meant thereby, what constant shape it holdeth, or in what number to be received." Further difficulties are that "this animall is not uniformely described", that the "horne we commonly extoll is not the same with that of the Ancients", that "what hornes soever they be which passe amongst us, they are not surely the hornes of one kind of animall", and that "many which beare that name and currantly passe among us are no hornes at all". Even though we were "satisfied we had the Unicornes horne, yet were it no injury unto Reason to question the efficacy thereof . . . . That some Antidotall quality it may have wee have no reason to deny; for since Elkes hoofs and hornes are magnified for Epilepsies, since not onely the bone in the heart but the horne of a Deere is Alexiphammacall . . . we cannot without prejudice except against the efficacy of this. But when we affirme it is not onely Antidotall to proper venomes . . . but that it resisteth also Sublimate, Arsenick, and poysons which kill by second qualities, that is by corrosion of parts, I doubt we exceed the properties of its Nature, and the promises of experiment will not secure the adventure . . . . With what security, therefore, a man may rely on this remedy, the mistresse of fooles hath already instructed some, and to wisedome (which is never too wise to learne) it is not too late to consider".

218

DRAGONS AND UNICORNS—FACT? OR FICTION?

One sees, in short, that Sir Thomas Browne the poetic scholar, pondering irresponsibly over the contents of Roman urns which no one had thought of converting into merchandise as "mummy", and Sir Thomas Browne the highly responsible physician of Norwich, estimating the practical worth of a "magnified medicine", were two distinct persons. He had to consider his patients as well as his readers.

In the year after that of the "Vulgar Errors" there appeared a book which one wishes that Browne had written. The History of Stones and Gems by Bo'thius de Boodt is one of the more learned productions of a learned age, and all that its author lacked of a complete equipment for his task was imagination. Bo'thius adopts the general position of the Bartholini, holding that the unicorn exists—or, at any rate, that its existence should not be denied until the exploration of the planet has been completed—but that the allegations made about its horn are unfounded.

This position, due to the effort of Caspar Bartholinus to mediate between Marini and Bacci, had become orthodox by the time of Bo'thius. John Johnston advocated it in his important Natural Histoy, and the academic debaters of the second half of the century tended to accept it as axiomatic.

As a usual thing we are safe in assuming, when a given topic is treated in an academic dissertation, that it has lost all the living interest it may once have had, for the learned gentlemen who control the choice of such topics soon develop a sense of smell resembling that of the vulture and the hyena. Intelligent lovers of the unicorn are not delighted, therefore, to find the animal attracting the attention of the universities. In 1660 a Latin dissertation on the unicorn was pronounced at Wittenberg by Johann Frederick Hubrigk, George Caspar Kirchmayer acting as Praeses. Like most successful dissertation writers, Hubrigk avoids, apparently without effort, any suggestion of independent thinking, but his work shows patience, piety, and respect for authorities, so that one feels confident that he secured his degree. His most vigorous utterance refers to a remark of Olaus Magnus in which the unicorn is called a "monster", and to which he responds: "I should have preferred to have Olaus abstain from the use of this word, which seems to cast a slur upon Nature." For the rest, although he does not believe that the horn of the unicorn is a panacea or a universal antidote, he is firmly convinced that the animal exists because the Bible tells him so.

A slightly more important production is the dissertation De Monoceroi'e spoken at Leipzig in 1667 by Johann Homilius. This little work strikes a curiously contemporary note, and indeed, except for the tolerable Latin in which it is composed, it might almost have been written by some university student in Tennessee or Oklahoma who had somehow managed to hear of the doubts cast upon the Bible by modern science and had rushed to the defence of Genesis. Homilius has heard of the infidels who doubt the unicorn, and he wishes them to know that "if this animal were really fabulous it would not be mentioned in so many places of the Holy Scripture". In his belief, the translation of the Septuagint is itself inspired, and he asserts, wrongly, that all the Rabbins and Church Fathers accepted it. Like a true Fundamentalist, he will not allow that the unicorn or any

219

DRAGONS AND UNICORNS—FACT? OR FICTION?

other animal or thing mentioned in the Bible was intended as a symbol. He divides the enemies of the unicorn, and therefore of the Bible, into two groups: those who say explicitly that there has never been such an animal and those who deny it implicitly by leaving it out of their descriptions of the earth's fauna. In the first group he places Saint Ambrose, Apollonius of Tyana, Andrea Marini, and Ambroise Paré—a strange collocation. Those of the second group he does not name. A third division is composed of the writers who admit that the unicorn existed once, but say that he perished in the flood, and upon these last Homilius is very severe. Like Hubrigk, he objects to having the unicorn called a monster, although it is Solinus rather than Olaus Magnus whom he takes to task for the epithet. He treats the question of the alicorn's properties with great caution, neither denying nor affirming them, but quoting authority on either side.

A third dissertation that may be noticed here is that of Christian Vater, pronounced at Wittenberg in 1679. Vater disarms criticism by saying that he is not old enough to add anything of his own to a subject which has perplexed some of the best minds of the time. Like Homilius and Hubrigk, he considers the Bible a more than sufficient proof of the unicorn's existence, though he deigns to quote some secular authority. The only original part of his remarks is that in which he argues that the alicorn is not dead matter, as most of his predecessors had thought, but a living part of the animal.

As one had feared, the appearance of the unicorn in academic circles was an indication that his best days had gone by. Possibly because the second edition of Thomas Bartholinus's De Unicornu, published in 1678, seemed to preclude the possibility of saying anything new on the subject, but more probably because the world had ceased to care about the unicorn, there is no further writing of importance on the topic for a hundred and fifty years. The eighteenth century ignored the unicorn almost entirely feeling, no doubt, that he was a "Gothick" beast, and yet he lingered on at least in the nursery. English children learned their zoology in the eighteenth century from a curious little work by a bookbinder named Thomas Boreman, A Description of Three Hundred Animals, viz. Beasts, Birds, Fishes, Serpents, and Insects, With a Particular Account of the Whale-Fishery, a book which appeared in 1730, and had at least seven editions in the next forty years. The author has some difficulty in making up his three hundred, even with the assistance of the Lamia, the Manticora, the Allocamelus, and several varieties of Dragons. In the first edition the unicorn is the eighth beast, and of him we read: "The Unicorn, a Beast which though doubted of by many writers yet is by others thus described: He has but one Horn, and that an exceeding rich one, growing out of his Forehead. His Head resembles an Hart's, his Feet an Elephant's, his Tail a Boar's, and the rest of his Body an Horse's. His voice is like the lowing of an Ox. His Horn is as hard as Iron, and as rough as any File, twisted and curled, like a flaming sword; very straight, sharp, and everywhere black, excepting the Point. Great Virtues are attributed to it, in expelling of Poison, and curing of several Diseases. He is not a Beast of prey."

One generalization to be made upon this series of monographs is that the last items in it, the academic dissertations, are greatly inferior in acumen and independence to the first. Even allowing for the fact that the academic dissertation is one of the most degraded

220

and degrading forms of written discourse, they are feebler than one would expect. A main reason for this is that they were not written, like Marini's book, freely and with the whole mind. The Ages of Faith in which one believed what one was told had gone by; the brief period of the Renaissance in which a few minds for a few years followed the light of knowledge and reason was gone too. These young scholars were all Protestants, so that they felt obliged to maintain the authority of the Bible; but they belonged also to the seventeenth century, they lived well on the hither side of the great watershed of time raised by the beginnings of modern science, they were aware of certain recently discovered facts that did not seem to square with God's word concerning unicorns. Facts, moreover, were no longer so malleable as they had seemed to the makers of Physiologus; they had taken on a validity of their own quite independent of human desires. The times, in short, were more difficult for a thinking man than those that had gone before. Isidore could accept the unicorn without hesitation because no inconvenient knowledge of facts impeded him; Marini could reject the unicorn almost as freely because he was a physician living in Venice at the end of the Renaissance, and so, for all practical purposes, a pagan; but what could be said on this cardinal topic by young men of the seventeenth century before an audience of Lutherans—by young men seeking academic advancement in a community very literate and very "fundamentalist"? Only such tame and jejune things as Hubrigk and Romulus and Vater did say. The situation was new to them. It is painfully familiar to us.

Nothing if not well read, these young men knew how the unicorn got into their Bibles, and they felt obliged to accept not only the plenary inspiration of the original Biblical text but that of the successive translations as well. If Martin Luther, for example, wrote the word Einhorn in translating Deuteronomy xxxiii. 17, that was equivalent to divine assurance that the unicorn exists, and any doubt on that point might open the way to infidelity as the crevice in a Dutch dike may let in all the sea. If the people who believed this had been considerably cruder and more bigoted than they were, and if they had had the power, they might have enacted "unicorn laws" controlling public education like the so-called "monkey laws" of certain American states, for the controversy was in fact a tiny model of the great quarrel over Darwinian theory. However trifling the issue may seem in comparison, a real conflict was involved between Biblical authority and experience or observation, and this is precisely the conflict that has been going on since the appearance of The Origin of Species and The Descent of Man.

An example of the stress and strain that could be caused by this conflict in earnest minds is found in the writings of Ambroise Pare about the unicorn. When his adversary attempts to overwhelm him with authority and tradition and mere numbers, Pare returns the thrilling reply that he would rather think rightly quite alone than think wrongly with all the rest of the world. One unbroken road runs between that remark and Emerson's Self-Reliance two hundred and fifty years in the future, but it was and is a narrow road, full of obstacles, and few there be that find it. Pare's words sound like a final declaration of intellectual independence, but as such they were premature. As a student of nature and as a thinking man Pare had accumulated several reasons for disbelieving in the unicorn. In one place he wrote explicitly: "The so great variety of dissenting opinions easily

DRAGONS AND UNICORNS—FACT? OR FICTION?

induceth me to believe that this word Unicorne is not the proper name of any beast in the world, and that it is a thing onely feigned by painters and writers." Somewhat later, however, in the Discours, he is obliged to consider the Biblical references to the animal, and these wrench from him the reluctant admission: "Il faut donc croire qu'il est des Licornes." There is a conflict here, and it is being waged inside of one mind. Pare's intellectual condition is that of millions of men who have been drawn one way by know ledge and reason and the whole current of their times and drawn another way by authority, tradition, vested interests, and fear of public opinion. Like them, Pare strove to believe two contradictory things at the same time and not to let the left lobe of his brain know what the right lobe was thinking. We may say that since nothing but unicorns were involved this did not much matter, but Pare and his time were right in feeling that when one begins to doubt the Biblical unicorn there is no convenient place to stop doubting. One might almost say that the cause of Fundamentalism was lost when the unicorn, vouched for by Scripture, was abandoned—for if we cannot trust the translations of the Bible as equally authentic with the original Hebrew, which few Fundamentalists take the trouble to learn, then the door is thrown open to Lower and Higher Criticism, to allegorical interpretations, to scholarship, to facts, to thinking, and, in short, to "infidelity".

The Septuagint's translation of the Hebrew Re'em by the word xxxxxxxxx kept the faith in the unicorn alive somewhat longer than it would otherwise have endured, and that bit of translation may have had an effect even upon trade and commerce and medical theory; but the most interesting of its effects is seen in its production of a minor conflict between the old faith in Biblical authority and the new faith in reason and experiment. One cannot say that the problem thus presented was ever definitely solved. Such problems seldom are. They are forgotten.

"To any ordinary reader", says an author of our own time, "the appearance in the sacred writings of creatures which are nowadays known to have had no real existence is bewildering, and probably not a little unsettling . . . . It is much to be regretted that several monstrosities have been permitted to enter the pages of Holy Scripture." This writer gives it as his "earnest advice" that one whose religious faith is endangered by the Biblical unicorn and basilisk and cockatrice should study some good Natural History-"and his difficulties will be swept away". Thus, for example, a close study of whales, with particular attention to the size of the whale's gullet and its powers of digestion, may be recommended for those who are having "difficulties" with the story of Jonah; and others who are shocked by Jacob's trick with the ringstraked cattle—not by the morality of the tale, of course, but by the notions of heredity involved—may be confidently referred to the Mendelian Law. In Pare's time our notions about Nature were tested by the Bible; in our own time it is still asserted that the Bible will stand the test of our notions about Nature. The sooner we admit that it will not stand any such test the sooner we shall be free to put it to higher uses. "When half-gods go, the gods arrive."

Confronted by such a dilemma as that caused by the conflict between authority and experience, the mind seeks avenues of escape, and one such was found for those who wished to believe both the Biblical unicorn and "science": the suggestion was thrown

DRAGONS AND UNICORNS—FACT? OR FICTION?

out that although there had once been unicorns they had all been drowned in the Flood. I have been unable to discover who first made this suggestion, but there would be no difficulty in naming many who answered him, for he had the usual fate of the peace-maker and was howled down for his pains. "Is it not wrong", says Hubrigk of Wittenberg, "to think that a single species perished and became extinct when such a great God took in hand the charge of all? Over the whole earth it is a common saying that the unicorn perished and became extinct at the time of the Flood, and that not a single individual of the monocerine species survived. We shall correct this iniquity, and with God's help we shall find a means of putting a stop to this universal blasphemy."

The philosophic answer was made by Julius Caesar Scaliger, a man able to bear down almost any opinion by the sheer weight of his prestige. We have God's word, says he, to prove that the unicorn existed at one time, and God cannot lie. If it existed once, then it exists still, for otherwise a vacuum would have been made in nature, which is absurd, for every one knows that nature abhors a vacuum. Therefore unicorns exist. Later writers extended this argument by quoting the Biblical assertion that Noah took with him into the ark representatives of every existing species, and that God then closed the door so that none could get out. They argued also that God's creation was, to begin with, neces-sarily perfect—meaning by this, apparently, that it contained every possible species of animal—and that He would not allow it to decline into imperfection. This cheerful faith in the conservation of species was undisturbed by the discovery of the fossil bones of ani-mals such as the mammoth that were being made at the time throughout Europe.

A possible excuse for the original blasphemer was that a beast with a horn ten feet in length, such as that reported by Albertus Magnus, seemed too large to accommodate in the ark. This difficulty did not occur to the makers of the window in the Church of St. Etienne du Mont in Paris, where the animal is shown snugly housed, nor to the monks who painted cross-sections of the ark in miniature, showing unicorns comfortably munch-ing in their stalls. Nevertheless the difficulty was felt, and the question regarding the room available in the ark exercised several acute minds. Sir Walter Raleigh spent some of his leisure in the Tower making a mathematical calculation that set his own doubts at rest; he shows that the ark contained forty-five thousand cubic feet of space, that there were only eighty-nine non-aquatic species to be got into it, that the total number of indi-vidual beasts it carried—including many very small ones—was only two hundred and eighty, so that there was room and to spare both for them and for their provender. He would have seen no justification for the statement of the Talmud that the Re'em had to be towed behind by a rope tied to its horn.

The idea that the unicorn may have perished in the Flood was probably suggested by the discoveries of fossil remains which began to puzzle Europe in the sixteenth century. What the ignorant thought of these we do not hear; some of the learned thought them the bones of Ajax or of Orestes, but the most widely accepted opinion was that they were the skeletons of Hannibal's elephants. The teeth of the mammoth were attributed to Saint Christopher; but Governor Dudley of Massachusetts, when a mastodon's tooth was found near Albany in 1705, could not be so precise as this because the giants of America had no names. He could only assert that this tooth would "agree only to a human body, for whom the Flood alone could prepare a funeral; and without doubt he would as long as he could keep his head above the clouds, but must at length be confounded with other creatures". The great size and unfamiliar shapes of these remains laid a severe strain upon the faith of some investigators, but the faithful insisted that whatever else they might be they were certainly not the bones of animals that had perished from the earth. "Exactly so many species as were originally created from the protoplasm will endure to the end of the world", says one of these orthodox writers. This was generally considered axiomatic.

In the middle of the sixteenth century Conrad Gesner suggested that the "bones" recently discovered in Germany were the horns of unicorns washed together there during Noah's Flood. This opinion was often ridiculed, but it gained many adherents and had a lasting effect upon materia medica. The belief in fossil unicorn's horn, coming at just the time when such corroboration was most needed, helped greatly to sustain the animal's claims to existence, and this belief lasted well into the nineteenth century. In one of the thousands of books written during that century to combat religious doubt I find these words: "At Castle Rising, near to Lynn Regis in Norfolk, where the sea is making rapid encroachments on the land, in sinking for water there were found at a depth of six hundred feet horns perfectly straight, supposed to be those of the unicorn. These were two feet long, an inch in circumference, and hollow."

The modern reader finds it difficult to make out just what the substances studied and sold and prescribed by physicians under the general name of "fossil unicorn" really were. In some instances they were certainly fossil bones, as in the rather famous find at Quedlinberg Cave in 1663, but the "Hercynian fossil unicorn" mentioned by Gesner and scores of others was probably carbonate of lime in stalactite and stalagmite formations. Others were petrified wood. The distinction between animal, vegetable, and mineral subterranean forms was not dearly made by most writers, although a few had known the truth before the sixteenth century. All kinds were called "fossil unicorn", it was assumed that all had the medicinal values ascribed to the alicorn—for no better reason than that they resembled it—and accordingly we find the lapis ceratites or horn-stone everywhere advanced to an important place in the pharmacopceia. Bo'thius de Boodt, to be sure, ridicules this confusion of substances, saying that he has had more than twenty pieces of the lapis ceratites given him as true alicorn and that most of them were merely petrified wood. He knows how such objects are formed as well as we do, and yet at the end of his account of them he says that all kinds of fossil unicorn have medicinal value against poison, fever, and pest. Caspar Bartholinus tells us that he has used the horn-stone successfully in his practice as a sudorific, for bites of snakes and venomous animals, for fevers and plague, and to "comfort the heart"—in short, for all the purposes for which true alicorn was used. Ole Wurm, a scholar of high attainments, could say precisely the same thing thirty years later.

The seventeenth century did not possess three men better fitted to pronounce upon this topic than Bo'thius de Boodt, Caspar Bartholinus, and Ole Wurm, and all three asserted that the horn-stone had precisely the same medical properties as alicorn. They asserted this, so far as I can see, for no better reason than that the horn-stone vaguely resembled the alicorn, so that they seem to have thought somewhat in the way of the primitive medicine man collecting his magical simples. But Ole Wurm, at any rate, did not believe in the alleged properties of the alicorn itself, and he had done more than any other man to discredit the whole unicorn legend. In other words, he rejected the substance and accepted the shadow. The deeper one delves into unicorn lore the more clearly one sees that its chief interest lies in the revelations it makes of the human mind.

Citation of the praises of "fossil unicorn" might be extended to great length. Daniel Sennert gave it a qualified commendation. Fallopius and Francis Jo'les considered it a sovereign cure for the plague. John Bausch wrote a whole book about its medical properties, and Paul Sachs asserted that "nothing is better than Hercynian unicorn, taken in drink, as a sudorific and for expelling poison, as I know from personal experience". All of these writers, indeed, base their remarks upon actual experience with the drug, and one soon concludes that they cannot all be lying. By a route extending through thousands of years of superstition men had come upon a substance of real medical value. "Fossil unicorn" is not by any means the only example of this. The substance sometimes vaguely called "ossifrage", hollow tubes of carbonate of lime usually found fractured—it was perhaps identical with lapis ceratites—was considered good for broken bones because it resembled them, and it really was so because it contained lime.

In adding "fossil unicorn" to her pharmacopceia Europe was merely trailing once more behind China. For a great length of time one of the most valued medicines of China has been "dragons' bones", the fossilized remains of mastodon and elephant, hippotherium and rhinoceros. When Dr. Henry Fairfield Osborn was excavating for fossils in China in 1923 he heard himself and his company described as "the American men of the dragon bones". The beliefs underlying this ancient superstition may have been similar to those we have found supporting the use of the alicorn, for there seems to have been an opinion that some parts of the dragon, in spite of its general beneficence, are poisonous.

In the year 1663 there was discovered in a limestone quarry near Quedlinberg in Germany the "skeleton of a unicorn". We are told that it was crouched upon its hindquarters with its head thrown back, and that it had on its brow a horn as thick as a human shinbone and seven feet and a half in length. The workmen broke it up and extracted it piece-meal, but the head and horn together with some of the ribs and the spine were handed over to a responsible person and were later accurately described. Somewhat before the middle of the eighteenth century a similar skeleton was found in the so-called

Einhornloch at Scharzfeld in the Harz Mountains, and this one was seen and described by no less a person than the philosopher Leibniz. Admitting that recent treatises and discoveries have caused him some doubts in the past concerning the real existence of the unicorn, Leibniz says that the Quedlinberg skeleton and this of Scharzfeld have converted him entirely. He publishes a drawing, intended to represent his reconstruction of

DRAGONS AND UNICORNS—FACT? OR FICTION?

the animal, which does not "carry conviction". It is interesting enough, however, to find one of the most brilliant minds of the eighteenth century convinced of the unicorn's existence.

DRAGONS AND UNICORNS—FACT? OR FICTION?

CHAPTER VII

RUMOURS

THE first point that research into a doubtful matter should try to determine, as Andrea Bacci wisely observes, is whether the thing in question really exists; and if we were concerned in this book with the unicorn itself rather than with unicorn lore there could be no excuse for having postponed for so long the question concerning the animal's actuality. That question cannot be entirely ignored because the doubts that have been expressed and the affirmations made in reply are themselves an important part of unicorn lore.

To anyone not instructed in comparative anatomy the unicorn is so credible a beast that it is difficult to understand why anyone should ever have doubted him. Compared with him the giraffe is highly improbable, the armadillo and the ant-eater are unbelievable, and the hippopotamus is a nightmare. The shortest excursion into palaeontology brings back a dozen animals that strain our powers of belief far more than he does. What may be called the normality of the unicorn is just as evident when we set him beside the creatures of fancy. Compared with him the griffin is precisely what Sir Thomas Browne calls it, "a mixed and dubious animal".

Yet it is well known that the unicorn has been doubted, and that not by natural infidels like Pare and Marini and Cuvier alone, but by natural believers living far back in the Ages of Faith. Saint Ambrose, for example, disbelieved in the animal for the strange reason that it was not to be found, or so he thought, in nature—"non inveniatur". One might have made sad havoc in the theological creed of Ambrose or any other early Christian by applying that brutal test, and we can imagine the flood of invective he would have poured forth upon the pagan who dared to write "non inveniatur" against the Apostolic miracles. However, I wish to devote this chapter to affirmations, recording the testimony of those who have kept the good faith and of the many others who, having fallen away into agnosticism or free-thinking or positive infidelity, have been brought back

DRAGONS AND UNICORNS—FACT? OR FICTION?

into the fold. The list of these affirmations will necessarily involve some writers that I have mentioned elsewhere.

One of the earliest of these, aside from the Ctesian and the Physiologus traditions, was that of Cosmas Indicopleustes, a Greek of Alexandria who spent his young manhood travelling as a merchant in Ethiopia, the Red Sea, and the Persian Gulf. In his Christian Topography, written about A.D. 5 50, Cosmas writes: "Although I have not seen the unicorn, I have seen four brazen figures of him in the four-towered palace of the King of Ethiopia, and from these figures I have been able to draw a picture of him as you see. People say that he is a terrible beast and quite invincible, and that all his strength lies in his horn. When he finds himself pursued by many hunters and about to be taken he springs to the top of some precipice and throws himself over it, and in the descent he turns a somersault so that the horn sustains all the shock of the fall and he escapes unhurt."

Cosmas's ingenuous admission that he has not seen the living animal inclines one to believe that he did see the brazen images. These must have been figures in the round rather than bas-reliefs, so that their single horns could not well have been due to the wellknown convention of ancient art which often led to the representation of one horn where two were to be understood; we may be fairly confident, therefore, that there existed in Ethiopia during the sixth century of our era an active belief in a one-horned animal. The drawing of this animal which accompanies the text in the Vatican manuscript of Cosmas is more interesting than the description. It shows a beast of the antelope kind, apparently not large, very spirited in bearing, with a horn almost as tall as itself jutting per- pendicularly from between its brows. The moment one sees this drawing the unicorn of Physiologus comes to mind. One remembers that the feat of absorbing the shock of a fall by an elastic or possibly spring-like horn has been attributed also to the ibex, to the African oryx, and to the Rocky Mountain goat. Finally, it is not to be ignored that Cosmas found these brazen unicorns in the palace of a king.

In the year 1206, we are told, the conqueror Genghis Khan set out with a great host to invade India. His army had marched for many days and had climbed through many mountain passes, but just when he reached the crest of the divide and looked down over the country he intended to subjugate there came running toward him a beast with a single horn which bent the knee three times before him in token of reverence. And then, while all the host stood wondering, the Conqueror paused in his march and pondered. At last he said, as we are told in the vivid narrative of Ssanang Ssetsen: "This middle kingdom of India before us is the place, men say, in which the sublime Buddha and the Bodhisatwas and many powerful princes of old time were born. What may it mean that this speechless wild animal bows before me like a man? Is it that the spirit of my father would send me a warning out of heaven?" With these words he turned his army about and marched back again into his own land. India had been saved by a unicorn.

In several versions of the Alexander Romance we read that Alexander's host, while travelling near the Red Sea, met a number of beasts with single horns, sharp as swords, on their foreheads. They were very strong and fierce and charged the host again and

DRAGONS AND UNICORNS—FACT? OR FICTION?

again, but they were killed by arrows. The description is not clear enough to show that they were the unicorns we know.

The Friar Felix Fabri, who went on pilgrimage to the Holy Land in 1483, says that on the twentieth of September in that year he and his company saw standing on a hill near Mount Sinai a large animal gazing toward them. At first they took it for a camel, but their guide told them that it was a unicorn and pointed out the great single horn on its brow, so that they examined it as closely as they could and were sorry that it was too far away to be seen quite clearly. They lingered there a long while watching the beast, which seemed to enjoy the sight of them as much as they did the sight of it, for it did not leave until they did. This beast, the friar adds, is remarkable in many ways: it is exceedingly wild and destroys everything that comes in its way; it sharpens its horn on stones; the horn has a brilliant hue and is set in gold and silver; the animal can be captured only by using a virgin as a decoy.

The most important of all descriptions of the unicorn given by the few who claim to have seen the animal is that of Lewis Vartoman (Ludovico Barthema), of Bologna, who travelled in 1503 through the countries of the Near East. Vartoman's Itinerario is a book of sustained interest and some historical value, although the modern reader is unlikely to share Scaliger's opinion that its author was a man worthy of trust. At the city of Zeila in Ethiopia he saw certain cattle with single horns about a palm and a half in length rising from their brows and bending backward, but much more important than these were the unicorns in a park adjoining the temple at Mecca. There were two of these animals, "shewed to the people for a miracle, and not without reason for the seldomenesse and strange nature. The one of them, which is much hygher than the other, yet not much unlyke to a coolte of thyrtye moneths of age, in the forehead groweth only one horne, in maner ryght foorth, of the length of three cubites. The other is much younger, of the age of one yeere, and lyke a young coolte: the horne of this is of the length of foure handfuls. This beast is of the coloure of a horse of weesel coloure, and hath the head lyke an hart, but no long necke, a thynne mane hangynge only on the one syde. Theyr legges are thyn and slender, lyke a fawne or hynde. The hoofes of the fore feete are divided in two, much lyke the feet of a Goat. The outwarde part of the hynder feete is very full of heare. This beast doubtlesse seemeth wylde and fierce, yet tempereth that fiercenesse with a certain comelinesse. These Unicornes one gave to the Soltan of Mecha as a most precious and rare gyfte. They were sent hym out of Ethiope by a kyng of that Countrey, who desired by that present to gratifie the Soltan of Mecha."

This passage was almost as influential among modern writers as the remarks of Aeian about the unicorn had been during the Middle Ages. One is to observe that the hoofs of Vartoman's unicorns are divided on the fore feet and, apparently, solid behind—a peculiar characteristic faithfully observed by the artist who drew the unicorn picture for Conrad Gesner's Historia Animalium and by all who imitated him. We should observe also that these unicorns came from Ethiopia and that they were sent as a present from one sovereign to another.

DRAGONS AND UNICORNS—FACT? OR FICTION?

I have placed Vartoman, as others do, among those who claim to have seen the unicorn, but although he does say that he saw the one-horned cattle of Zeila, he makes no such assertion about the two animals at Mecca and it has been inferred that he saw these only from the extreme minuteness of his description. Edward Webbe, an Elizabethan traveller whom no one has ever called trustworthy, does not wish to leave his readers in any doubt on this point. "I have scene," says he, "in a place like a Park adjoyning unto prester Iohn's Court, three score and seven-teene unicornes and eliphants all alive at one time, and they were so tame that I have played with them as one would play with young Lambes."

Vincent Le Blanc, who set out on his travels through the Orient in 1567, was still more fortunate, for he declares: "I have seen a unicorn in the seraglio of the Sultan, others in India, and still others at the Escurial. That there are some persons who doubt whether this animal is to be found anywhere in the world I am well aware, but in addition to my own observation there are several serious writers who bear witness to its existence—Vartoman among others, who says that he saw some at the same place in Mecca." In the seraglio of the King of Pegu he saw a unicorn with a tongue "very long and like a file". (This probably means that he had read Marco Polo on the rhinoceros.) He was told that these beasts were tormented cruelly by huge serpents which were very fond of their blood because it had a delicious odour, and that when one of them was wounded in the chase the hunters always sent as much of its blood as they could collect to the king, enclosed in a little box. No one had ever seen the unicorn dip its horn in the water when drinking. A Brahmin told Le Blanc that he had been present at the capture of a very old unicorn which defended itself so fiercely that it broke off its horn on the branch of a tree and which, when it had been taken and bound, was led to the palace of the king; but this animal had been so severely beaten by the hunters for having wounded the king's nephew that it died in a few days. The queens of India, Le Blanc reports, wear bracelets of unicorn bone, and the King of Casubi showed him a horn much lighter in hue than those he had seen elsewhere in the Orient. His remarks are a strange compound of things seen and heard and read thrown together without any attempt at criticism or sorting.

Another Oriental traveller, Dr. Leonard Rauchwolf, who saw the countries visited by Le Blanc a few years after him was told by a Persian "that the Sophi King of Persia had several Unicorns at Samarcand . . . and also in two islands . . . which lay from Samarcand nine Days journey, some Griffins which were sent him out of Africa from Prester John."

In the same year in which Vincent Le Blanc began his travels there was published a famous book on the drugs and spices of India by Garcias ab Horto. Here we find a description of an amphibian unicorn which the author says he has had from men worthy of belief. They have told him that between the Cape of Good Hope and the promontory commonly called Currentes (Cape Corrientes, opposite the southern end of Madagascar) there are to be seen certain animals that live on the land yet take pleasure also in the sea. Although they are certainly not sea-horses, they have equine heads and manes. This beast has a horn two palms in length, and the horn is movable so that it can be turned to right or left and raised or lowered at will. The animal fights fiercely with the elephant and its horn is considered good against poison. A similar animal, called the campchurch, was reported eight years later by André Thevet. This creature, he said, was to be found near the Strait of Malacca, large as a stag and bearing on its brow a horn three feet and a half in length and mobile like the crest of the Indian cock. The horn was efficacious against poison. The campchurch had two web feet like those of a duck which it used in swimming both in fresh and salt water, but its forefeet were like those of the stag. It lived on fish." This André Thevet, one must remember, was a man "worthy of trust." He believed what was told him by a Turkish ambassador about the unicorns of Ethiopia and he thought also that the reindeer had only one horn. Caspar Bartholinus, who had seen reindeer, ridiculed this assertion, but John Johnston, who tried to please everyone in his Historia Naturalis, reconciled Bartholinus and Thevet by showing a picture of the reindeer with the two horns twisted together into one.

We have seen that Ambroise Pare disbelieved in the unicorn as firmly as his faith in the Bible would allow, but his fairness in controversy was such that he quoted against himself the testimony of an acquaintance of his, a physician named Louys Paradis, who said that he had actually seen the animal. This unicorn had been sent to Alexandria, where Paradis encountered it, as a gift to the Great Mogul from Prester John. It was about as large as a boar-hound, though not so slender in body, had a glossy coat like that of the beaver in colour, a slender neck, small ears, and one horn between the ears, very smooth, dark, and only one foot long. The head was short and thin, the muzzle round like a calf's, the eyes were very large and fierce in aspect, the legs lean, the hooves divided like a deer's. The animal was of one colour all over excepting one forefoot, which was yellow. It ate lentils and pease but lived chiefly on sugarcane. Paradis was told by the men who brought it from Prester John that there were many others of the same kind in their country, but that they were so wild that they were hard to capture and that the people feared them more than any other beasts. This account is more impressive in its minuteness and precision even than that of Vartoman, and one is surprised that Pare, who seems to have thought his informant trustworthy, could maintain his disbelief in the face of it.

In reading these accounts one cannot fail to be impressed by the number of unicorns coming from Prester John, who seems to have kept the neighbouring potentates regularly supplied with them. Vartoman's two unicorns came from the Court of Prester John, the numerous specimens seen by Edward Webbe were in a Park adjoining that monarch's palace, the unicorns reported by Leonard Rauchwolf as belonging to the Sophy came from there and so did the single animal seen at Alexandria by Louys Paradis. Let us turn directly to the source of supply and see what records can be found of unicorns in Ethiopia itself.

Most of these records were written by Portuguese and Spanish missionaries to Abyssinia, and they cover a period of about one hundred years. John Bermudez, who went on an embassy to Prester John in 1535, is the earliest member of the group. He says that in the province of Abyssinia, known in his time as Damute, there is found in the mountain districts a very fierce and wild unicorn shaped like a horse and as large as an ass. Marmol Caravaial (often called Marmolius), who wrote forty years later, is much

DRAGONS AND UNICORNS—FACT? OR FICTION?

more specific: "Among the Mountains of the Moon in High Ethiopia", he says, "there is found a beast called the unicorn which is as large as a colt of two years and of the same general shape as one. Its colour is ashen and it has a mane and a large beard like that of a he-goat; on its brow it has a smooth white horn of the colour of ivory two cubits long and adorned with handsome grooves that run from base to point. This horn is used against poison, and people say that the other animals wait until this one comes and dips its horn in the water before they will drink. It is such a clever beast and so swift that there is no way of killing it, but it sheds its horns like the stag and the hunters find these in the wilderness."

Fray Luis de Urreta, whose book on Ethiopia has already proved useful, also tells us that unicorns are found among the Mountains of the Moon. "The reason why so few men have ever seen them", he says, "is that these mountains are almost inaccessible. They are quite different from the pictures of them to be seen in Europe, for they are only slightly smaller than elephants and their feet are like those of the elephant. Their general characteristics remind one of swine, for they love to wallow in the mire. On the brow there is one horn, heavy and large but tapering to a point and black in hue. The animal's tongue is rough with spines that tear whatever it licks like a teasel—an excellent emblem of flatterers! . . . It is true that Saint Thomas and Saint Gregory and other holy men consider this unicorn identical with the Rhinoceros, but we must remember that they were chiefly concerned with moral matters and the welfare of the soul and that it was not their business to distinguish the species of animals."

The most interesting of these travellers in Ethiopia was the Jesuit missionary Jeronimo Lobo (1593-1678). After sailing round the Cape in 1622 and spending some time in the Portuguese colonies of India he went to Abyssinia, the Negus Segued having recently been converted by the Jesuit Pedro Paez. There he spent several years in the district of Damute, where both he and John Bermudea place the unicorn, but in 1632 the Negus fell into heresy and banished all the Jesuit fathers. Lobo was captured by the Turks and sent to Goa to secure ransom money, after which he tried to get the Portuguese viceroy to declare war on Segued with the object of bringing him back to orthodoxy by force of arms. Failing at Goa, Lobo sailed for home, was wrecked and captured by pirates on the way, and laid the grievances of the Christian faith—mingled, perhaps, with others of a more private sort—before the Courts of Lisbon, Madrid, and Rome without avail. Disgusted by this irreligious pacifism, he returned to India and rose to high office in his Order. His last days were spent in Portugal.

Lobo left two accounts of Abyssinia, one of which was translated into French from the unpublished manuscript and out of the French into English by Samuel Johnson in his Grub Street years. This familiar book contains the following passage: "In the Province of Agaus has been seen the Unicorn, that Beast so much talk'd of and so little known; the prodigious Swiftness with which this Creature runs from one Wood into another has given me no Opportunity of examining it particularly, yet I have had so near a sight of it as to be able to give some Description of it. The Shape is the same as that of a beautiful Horse, exact and nicely proportion'd, of a Bay Colour, with a black Tail, which in some Prov-

DRAGONS AND UNICORNS—FACT? OR FICTION?

inces is long, in others very short; some have long Manes hanging to the Ground. They are so Timerous that they never Feed but surrounded with other Beasts that defend them."

It is pleasant to have this passage in Johnson's phraseology, and one would like to know what the man who kept an open mind about the Cock Lane Ghost thought concerning the unicorn. His Dictionary, I think, forbids us to include him among the believers, but in his Preface to the Lobo translation he says that whatever the Jesuit relates, "whether true or not, is at least probable; and he who tells nothing exceeding the bounds of probability has a right to demand that they should believe him who cannot contradict him. He appears to have described things as he saw them, to have copied Nature from the Life, and to have consulted his Senses, not his Imagination."

One is glad to recall Johnson's measured assertion while considering Father Lobo's second passage on this topic, which appears in A Short Relation of the River Nile, edited, or perhaps one may say written, in 1669 by Sir Peter Wyche. The contents of this book are: "A Short Relation of the River Nile; The True Cause of the River Nile Overflowing; Of the Famous Unicorn:—where He is Bred and how Shaped; The Reason why the Abyssine Emperor is Called Prester John of the Indies; A Short Tract of the Red Sea; A Discourse of Palm-Trees." All of this is obviously delectable matter, but the best chapter is that concerning "The Unicorn, the most celebrated among Beasts, as among Birds are the Phoenix, the Pelican, and the Bird of Paradise". This animal is "of the more credit because mentioned in holy Scriptures, compared to many things, even to God made man. None of the Authors who speak of the Unicorn discourse of his birth or Country, satisfied with the deserved eulogiums by which he is celebrated. That secret was reserved for those who travelled and surveyed many countries . . . . The country of the Unicorn (an African creature, only known there) is the Province of Agaos in the kingdom of Damotes; that it may wander into places more remote is not improbable . . . . A Father, my companion, who spent some time in this province, upon notice that this so famous animal was there, used all diligence to procure one. The natives brought him a very young colt, so tender as in a few days it died. A Portuguese Captain, a person of years and credit, told me that returning once from the army with twenty other Portuguese soldiers in company they one morning rested in a little valley encompassed with thick woods, designing to breakfast while their horses grazed on the good grass. Scarce were they sat down when from the thickest part of the wood lightly sprang a perfect horse of the same colour, hair, and shape before described. His career was so brisk and wanton that he took no notice of those new inmates till engaged among them; then, as frightened at what he had seen, suddenly started back again, yet left the spectators sufficient time to see and observe at their pleasure. The particular survey of these parts seized them with delight and admiration. One of his singularities was a beautiful strait horn on his forehead. He appeared to run about with his eyes full of fear. Our horses seemed to allow him for one of the same brood, curvetted and made towards him. The soldiers, observing him in less than musket shot, not able to shoot, their muskets being unfixt, endeavoured to encompass him, out of an assurance that that was the famous unicorn; but he prevented them, for, perceiving them, with the same violent career he recovered the wood, leaving the Portuguese satisfied in the truth of such an animal. My knowledge of this captain makes the

DRAGONS AND UNICORNS—FACT? OR FICTION?

truth with me undoubted. In another place of the same province (the most remote, craggy, and mountainous part, called Manina) the same beast hath been often seen grazing amongst others of different kinds . . . . To this place of banishment a tyrannical Emperor name Adamas Segued sent without any cause divers Portuguese, who from the top of these mountains saw the unicornes grazing in the plains below, the distance not greater than allowed them so distinct an observation as they knew him, like a beautiful Gennet, with a fair horn in his forehead."

More scholarly than any of these writings is the New History of Ethiopia by Job Ludolphus, which appeared in English in 1682. Here one finds a description of a beast "both Strong and Fierce, call'd Arweharis . . . which signifies one Horn. This beast resembles a goat, but very swift of foot. Whether it be the Monoceros of the Ancients I leave to the scrutinie of others . . . . However, the Portugals tell us that the report was not altogether vain, for one of them was seen by John Gabriel in the province of the Agawi in the kingdom of Damota . . . . The description of the Portugueses seems most agreeable to Truth."

Robert Frampton, later Bishop of Gloucester, spent several years of his early life during the middle of the seventeenth century in the Orient, and while there he once met "a great officer of that country they call Ethiopia". This officer told him that "the most remarkable beast they had there was the Unicorn, which, though very wild and rarely taken, he had often seen, and described just as we paint him. And the man being utterly unacquainted with the European fancy made it, if not probable, at least possible that such a beast there might be, though in that little frequented country, not well known by us, it might escape the notice of those few that had been there."

In October 1652 there arrived in Copenhagen an "African legate" by the name of Franciscus Marchio de Magellanes. He was much impressed by the alicorn in the royal museum, especially because it was so different from the horn of the unicorn that was familiar to him in his own land. This horn, he said, came from the Tire Bina, a very fleet and wild beast about the size and shape of a small horse, which lived in the African desert. Shaggy about the head and legs and feet, the animal had a short mane and a tail like that of a horse, but not very full. Its hide, smooth and with very short hairs, was ashen in hue above, with a black line running along its back, and white from the lower jaw to the abdomen. There was a small bundle of hairs on the brow from the midst of which there sprang a single horn to which the hairs adhered. This horn, barely three spans in length, had not the spiral striae seen in European alicorns, but small protuberances running in a straight line from the base to the point. It was of a golden hue and hollow at the root. On the point of this horn there was another bundle of hairs, as large as a man's fist and reddish. The Africans made much of this horn, using it both internally and externally against poison. The legate told his friends in Copenhagen that the Tire Bina always dipped the horn in the water before he drank of it, and that as soon as he did this the water was greatly agitated. The inhabitants were accustomed to dip the horn in their drinking-water in the belief that this made it more healthful. They also used the animal's flesh and the burned hairs of its tail as drugs.

234

DRAGONS AND UNICORNS—FACT? OR FICTION?

These reports of the Ethiopian and African unicorn, buried as most of them were in books that were seldom read, made little impression in northern Europe. In 1625 Purchas felt obliged to say: "As for the Unicorne, none hath beene seene these hundred yeares last past, by testimony of any probable Author (for Webb, which said he saw them in Prester John's Court, is a mere fabler.)" James Primerose, thirteen years later, thought that although the animal was certainly not fictitious it must be excessively rare. Aidrovandus said in 1639 that in spite of the fact that almost the whole surface of the globe had been explored hardly any man dared to affirm that he had seen the unicorn. John Ogilby, the bookseller-poet, by no means so ridiculous a person as Dryden and Pope managed to make him appear, shows in his Africa that his faith is slight. After the middle of the seventeenth century, however, there was a decided tendency, somewhat difficult to explain, toward belief. This is clearly seen in Antony Deussing's monograph on the unicorn and in all the other academic dissertations; but in these the "will to believe" is obviously actuated by fear of the effect that doubt of the unicorn would have upon faith in the Bible.

The eighteenth century, as I have said, was not a good time for unicorns. The general attitude of the period is well expressed in Benjamin Martin's once famous Philosophical Grammar: "The Scripture makes mention of the Dragon and the Unicorn, and most Naturalists have affirmed that there have been such creatures and have given Descriptions of them; but the Sight of these Creatures, or credible Relations of them having been so very rare, has occasioned many to believe there never were any such Animals in Nature; at least it has made the History of them very doubtful."

John Bell of Antermony heard a "credible relation" in Tartary from a native hunter which is worth recording. This hunter said that "in the year 1713, being out a-hunting, he discovered the track of a stag, which he pursued. At overtaking the animal he was somewhat startled on observing it had only one horn, stuck in the middle of its forehead.

Being near the village, he drove it home and showed it, to the great admiration of the spectators. He afterwards killed it and eat the flesh, and sold the horn to a comb-maker. I inquired carefully about the shape and size of this unicorn and was told it exactly resembled a stag. The horn was of a brownish colour, about one archeen or 28 inches long, and twisted from the root till within a finger's length of the top, where it was divided like a fork into two points very sharp."

Faith in the unicorn was at a low ebb in Europe when Anders Sparrmann published in 1783 his account of travels in South Africa. Without asserting that he had seen the animal, Sparrmann gave the impression that the unicorn was not uncommon near the Cape of Good Hope, basing his own belief upon the constant reports of natives and the observation of single horns that were shown to him. Half a dozen other travellers in South Africa during the next half-century reached the same conclusion. Thus Baron von Wurmb writes from the Cape in 1791 that he expects soon to see a unicorn, "which has just been discovered in the interior of Africa. A Boer saw a beast shaped like a horse and with one horn on its brow, ash-gray and with divided hoofs—his observation went no farther. A Hottentot has confirmed this report, and the people in these parts quite generally believe in the existence of the unicorn . . . . The future will decide. Various respectable natives have given their servants orders to bring in one of these beasts alive if possible, or else to shoot one, so that we shall soon see the question settled." Cornelius de Jong, writing two years later from the same region, traces the quest for a South African unicorn to an elderly Dutchman of education and intelligence by the name of Cloete, who was offering three thousand forms to anyone who would bring him a live specimen. The offer was made hopefully, for Cloete and de Jong agreed that the evidence for the presence of the unicorn in the neighbourhood was convincing. Hottentots who could not possibly have heard the European legends about the animal described it exactly and even said that they had drawings of it in their caves and houses.

One of these drawings was seen and copied, a few years later, by the English traveller, Sir John Barrow, who was completely converted by it to a belief in the unicorn. His copy shows the head and neck of a creature with the general appearance of an antelope and with a single horn like that of the gemsbok rising, apparently, from the right side of the brow. This drawing was one of several thousands discovered by Sir John Barrow, all of them as realistic, he says, as the skill of the artists would permit. He makes it clear that in this instance there could be no possible confusion with the rhinoceros, which is also depicted in the South African caves, and he argues earnestly that the long tradition of the unicorn, taken together with what he has heard from the natives of Africa and with this drawing, should be sufficient to compel belief.

A man still better equipped than Barrow to judge this matter, Sir Francis Galton, was almost equally impressed by the evidence. "The Bushmen", says he, "without any leading question or previous talk upon the subject, mentioned the unicorn. I cross-questioned them thoroughly, but they persisted in describing a one-horned animal, something like a gemsbok in shape and size, whose one horn was in the middle of its forehead and pointed forwards . . . . It will be strange indeed if, after all, the creature has a real existence. There are recent travellers in the north of tropical Africa who have heard of it there, and believe in it, and there is surely plenty of room to find something new in the vast belt of terra incognita that lies in this continent."

Among the rather numerous believers in an African unicorn the names of David Livingstone and Dr. Andrew Smith should not be forgotten. The Athenum for December 22, 1860, reviewing The Romance of Natural History, by the father of Edmund Gosse, says that "the unicorn cannot be pronounced a fable, although our national representation of it may prove to be fanciful", expressing belief in a South African species "which appears to occupy an intermediate rank between the massive rhinoceros and the lighter form of the horse". Dr. William Balfour Baikie, the scientist and African traveller, writes in the same journal for August 16, 1862: "The constant belief of the natives of all the countries which I have hitherto visited have partly shaken my scepticism, and at present I simply hold that the non-existence of the unicorn is not proven. A skull of this animal is said to be preserved in the country of Bonu, through which I hope to pass in a few weeks, when I shall make every possible inquiry. Two among my informants have repeatedly

DRAGONS AND UNICORNS—FACT? OR FICTION?

declared that they have seen the bones of this animal, and each made a particular mention of the long, straight, or nearly straight, horn."

These persistent rumours of unicorns in South Africa seem to have revived the belief, which had died down since the seventeenth century, that the animal was to be found in the northern parts of the continent. Dr. Eduard Ruppell was told by the natives of Kordofan, without any question or suggestion from him, that there was in their country a beast about as large as a horse and of the same shape, with reddish smooth hide, divided hoofs, and one long slender straight horn on its brow. Baron von Muller, travelling in the same district in 1848, was told by a native who had provided him with specimens of many other animals, about a beast called a'nasa which he described as resembling a donkey in shape and size but with a boar's tail and a single movable horn. During his travels in Abyssinia

A. von Katte heard repeatedly from soldiers drawn from all parts of the country "that the unicorn really exists in the wild valleys of the mountains. It is true that their reports are not entirely consistent, but neither are they contradictory. Those who assert that they have seen the animal give the same description of it that Pliny left us. They say, that is, that it has the hoofs of a horse and the same shape as a horse, that it is grey in colour and has a strong horn in the middle of its brow. Its size is that of a well-grown ass. They say also that it is very shy and therefore hard to approach. These people find great likeness between it and the unicorn shown on the English arms, but when I showed them a picture of the rhinoceros they said at once: 'That is not it; that is another animal.' . . . I am therefore strongly inclined to believe that the unicorn is really to be found in the high, inaccessible mountains of this country." The vast size and the mystery of the Dark Continent affected the imaginations of thoughtful and trained observers in the nineteenth century somewhat as America had affected the mind of Europe three hundred years before. "In a land like inner Africa", wrote Joseph Russegger, "in which Nature puts forth the strangest forms of life, we may expect that the larger and unknown quadrupeds which we have thought long since extinct will be discovered. Is it not possible that even the unicorn may be found there? Arabs, Nubians, and Negroes told me often and much about this animal, which resembled, according to their descriptions, either an antelope or a wild ass. Their reports were too contradictory and contained too much nonsense for me to reproduce them, but everywhere one hears the refrain that the animal still exists . . . . To regard the unicorn as wholly fabulous and a product of fancy is an absurd and arbitrary position, and we do well to remember that if the elephant and giraffe and camel should once die out they too, on account of their strange forms, would be thought fabulous."

The most interesting account of an African unicorn is that communicated to the Journal Asiatique by F. Fresnel in a letter written in April 1843 and published in March of the following year. Fresnel was a consular agent of France at Djeddah, and his remarks are based, not upon personal observation, but upon the testimony of several Arabs in whose honesty and intelligence he firmly believed. These men had often killed the animal in Dar-Bargou, north-west of Darfour, a district still almost unknown and at the time when the letter was written quite unexplored.

DRAGONS AND UNICORNS—FACT? OR FICTION?

Fresnel's description is very minute. He says that the unicorn is a pachyderm, but insists that it is not the rhinoceros. In appearance somewhat like a wild bull, it has the legs and feet of an elephant, a round and almost hairless body, a short tail, and a single horn one cubit long and movable at the animal's will. This horn springs from between the eyes and not from the end of the nose like that of the rhinoceros. For two-thirds of its length it is of an ashen grey-colour, like the rest of the animal, but the upper third is a vivid scarlet. (One thinks of the splash of scarlet on the end of the horn described by Ctesias, and of the words of Solinus, "de splendore mirifico.") When the unicorn is not disturbed he swings this horn to right and left as he walks, but he can fix it like a bayonet ready for action at a moment's notice. Of vast strength and extremely fierce, he always charges at the first sight of a man, and he charges with intent to kill. He is never taken alive. Fresnel gives a minute account of the method of hunting the beast which one can hardly read without recalling the lion-capture story. One man on foot goes up to the unicorn's lair while his fellows, on horseback and armed with lances, wait at a distance near a tree. As soon as the animal sees the man he plunges toward him, and the man turns and makes for the tree. The mounted hunters lance the beast from behind while he is running, and while he turns to face one after the other, until he drops from exhaustion.

Fresnel has perfect confidence in his sources of information. "There is nothing more animated and honest", says he, "than the descriptions given by a Bedouin, just as there is nothing more false and obviously absurd than those given by the inhabitants of eastern cities or by travellers who are only merchants." His informants had nothing to sell, they said nothing about the horn's medicinal value, they had hunted this beast and killed it, they knew the rhinoceros well and said that this unicorn was quite different. Fresnel was therefore thoroughly convinced that the abou-karn of eastern French Soudan was the same creature as the Hebrew Re'em and the monoceros of Ctesias and the unicorn of Pliny. One is reminded of Samuel Johnson's words with regard to Father Lobo: "He who tells nothing exceeding the bounds of probability has a right to demand that they should believe him who cannot contradict him."

In following the trail of the African unicorn I have neglected chronology and ignored important developments in other parts of the world. The nineteenth century studied the unicorn chiefly "in the field", yet there were a few scholars of the old school who still preferred the methods of the library. E. A. W. Zimmermann, after reviewing all the evidence available in 1780 to a patient German polymath, concluded that the unicorn legend must be founded upon zoological fact. The French geographer Malte-Brun was deeply impressed by the rumours of unicorns emanating in his time from almost the whole continent of Africa, and he decided that although the existence of the animal had not been proved it was certainly not impossible. He said, furthermore—and I think he was the first to express this modern view—that whether unicorns were to be found in Nature or not, the legend concerning them was interesting and worthy of study for its own sake. H. F. Link, a scholar of extraordinary caution and thoughtfulness, reached the conclusion, after many pages of argument, that the unicorn must be accepted as an actual though perhaps an extinct and certainly a very rare animal.

DRAGONS AND UNICORNS—FACT? OR FICTION?

Among these productions of the library one of the most interesting is the *Notice en refutation de la non-existence de la licorne*, by J. F. Laterrade, a professional scientist of literary talent. This monograph is well written and ingenious though not convincing. The author does not assert that unicorns exist but contents himself with arguing that they are not only possible but even probable. In the first place, he says, the description of the animal is in no way fabulous and it contains nothing contrary to Nature; secondly, many authors of repute have written about it in full belief; thirdly, no proof has been found that it does not exist. One does not feel that French acumen is well represented in this argument, for each of Laterrade's three points lies open to attack. Any comparative anatomist would deny his first assertion, which no contemporary and countryman of Cuvier should have allowed himself to make. The historian could name a hundred exploded fallacies that have been supported by authors of repute. As for the third point, absence of disproof is no great assistance toward belief. One might write the word "witches" in place of Laterrade's "unicorns" and get the same results.

In the year after that in which Laterrade's monograph appeared Cuvier himself attempted to give the unicorn the coup de grace. He was probably the first of all the writers on our topic who had scientific knowledge adequate to the problems involved, and, in addition, a clear mind of the highest order. Cuvier is strongly inclined to think the unicorn a fairy tale, although he does not positively affirm this. He believes that it was compounded out of the oryx and the rhinoceros. Speaking as a scientist, he says that any horn growing single would be perfectly symmetrical, and that no such horn has ever been found. A cloven-hoofed ruminant with a single horn, moreover, would be impossible, in his opinion, because its frontal bone would be divided and no horn could grow above the division.

And yet the unicorn legend continued to show surprising vitality, quite as many reports and rumours concerning the animal coming from the Orient as from Africa. Captain Samuel Turner, writing in the first year of the nineteenth century, records an interesting conversation with the Rajah of Bootan. "He had a very curious creature, he told me, then in his possession; a sort of horse, with a horn growing from the middle of his forehead. He had once another of the same species, but it died. I could not discover from whence it came, or obtain any other explanation than *burra dure!* a great way off! I expressed a very earnest desire to see a creature so curious and uncommon, and told him that we had representations of an animal called an unicorn, to which his description answered; but it was generally considered as fabulous. He again assured me of the truth of what he told me, and promised I should see it. It was some distance from Tassisudon, and his people paid it religious respect; but I never had a sight of it." This is an impressive story, but the force of it is somewhat weakened by the paragraph just preceding, in which the Rajah tells his English visitor about a race of men with short, straight tails, so inconvenient that they were obliged to dig small holes for them before they could sit down.

The Quarterly Magazine for December, 1820, quotes a letter from a Major Latter, stationed in the hill country east of Nepal, asserting that the unicorn had been discovered at last in Tibet. The Major writes: "In a Thibetan manuscript which I procured the other day

DRAGONS AND UNICORNS—FACT? OR FICTION?

from the hills, the unicorn is classed under the head of those animals whose hoofs are divided; it is called the one-horned tso'po. Upon inquiring what kind of animal it was, to our astonishment the person who brought me the manuscript described exactly the unicorn of the ancients, saying that it was a native of the interior of Thibet, fierce, and extremely wild, seldom ever caught alive, but frequently shot, and that the flesh was used for food. The person who gave me this account has repeatedly seen these animals and eaten flesh of them. They go together in herds, like our wild buffaloes, and are very frequently met with on the borders of the great desert about a month's journey from Lassa, in that part of the country inhabited by the wandering Tartars." The Asiatic journal, after quoting this letter in December of the following year, remarks: "Our readers are aware that steps have been taken to obtain a complete specimen of the animal supposed to be the unicorn, which is said to exist in considerable numbers in Thibet." Seven years later the same periodical reported that Major Latter was still hunting for the unicorn but had nearly given up hope.

The most famous of earlier travellers in Tibet seems never to have had any doubts. "The unicorn", says Huc, "which has long been regarded as a fabulous creature, really exists in Thibet. You find it frequently represented in the sculptures and paintings of the Buddhist temples. Even in China you often see it in the landscapes that ornament the inns of the northern provinces. The inhabitants of Adtaa spoke of it without attaching to it any greater importance than to the other species of antelopes which abound in their mountains. We have not been fortunate enough, however, to see the unicorn during our travels in Upper Asia."

All this testimony regarding the unicorns of Tibet is illumined by a passage in Colonel Prejevalsky's Mongolia, which throws a beam of light, also, along the whole course of the unicorn legend as we have traced it from the Indica of Ctesias. This passage is concerned with a small, fleet, and very quarrelsome Tibetan antelope known to the Mongols as the orongo and to science as Antholops Hodgsoni. It has slightly recurving black horns, twenty-three inches long, with rings on the anterior surfaces. Prejevalsky says that "the orongo is held sacred by Mongols and Tangutans, and lamas will not touch the meat. The blood is said to possess medicinal virtues, and the horns are used in charlatanism: Mongols tell fortunes and predict future events by the rings on these, and they also serve to mark out the burial places, or more commonly the circles within which the bodies of deceased lamas are exposed: these horns are carried away in large numbers by pilgrims returning from Thibet and are sold at high prices. Mongols tell you that a whip-handle made from one will prevent a rider's steed from tiring. Another prevalent superstition is that the orongo has only one horn growing vertically from the centre of the head. In Kan-su and Koko-nor we were told that unicorns were rare, one or two in a thousand; but the Mongols in Tsaidam, who are perfectly well acquainted with the orongo, deny entirely the existence there of a one-horned antelope, though admitting that it might be found in South-western Thibet. Had we gone farther we should probably have heard that it was only to be found in India, and so on till we arrived at the one-horned rhinoceros."

DRAGONS AND UNICORNS—FACT? OR FICTION?

In the middle of the nineteenth century it was still possible for intelligent people to believe in the unicorn's existence; indeed, if the written records are a trustworthy indication, there seems to have been almost as much belief in the animal at that time as there had been two hundred years earlier, and decidedly more than in the eighteenth century. An amusing evidence of the public interest in the problem is found in a provincial English newspaper: "An Italian gentleman, named Barthema [Lewis Vartoman] said to be entitled to implicit credit, who has just returned from Africa, states that he saw two unicorns at Mecca which had been sent as a present from the King of Ethiopia to the Sultan." This report was of course exactly true, and the only fault that could be found with it was that the news it contained was somewhat over three hundred years old. One of the foremost French archaeologists of the century went out of his way to declare his faith. "In spite of my unfitness to judge in such matters", wrote Charles Cahier, "and in spite of the formal denial by the learned Cuvier of all unicorns past or future, I admit that I do not despair of this animal which is so cried down at present after so many panegyrics. The horn may be movable or not, it may be persistent or caducous, for all this is not important; but I dare to hope that it will be single. The unicorn will have a place in our museums beside the ornithorhyncus, which was quite as improbable as the other before it was brought before us; or he may be placed near the pterodactyls, which would have seemed absurd until the moment when they were found." A scholarly English writer of even more recent date conjectures that the unicorn may be "a hybrid produced occasionally and at more or less rare intervals, a cross between some equine and cervine species." Or the word "unicorn" may be "a generic name for several distinct species of (probably) now extinct animals—creatures which were the contemporaries of prehistoric man and which, before they finally expired, attracted the attention of his descendants, during early historic time, by the rare appearance of a few surviving individuals."

DRAGONS AND UNICORNS—FACT? OR FICTION?

CHAPTER VIII

CONJECTURES

HAVING considered some of the more important arguments and observations that have been advanced to prove the existence or non-existence of the unicorn, we may now assume the role of the sceptic who regards the whole legend as probably a product of the fancy, asking ourselves how the belief first arose. This question plunges us at once into the remote past; it forces us to think as much as possible in the way of men whose mental habit was very different from our own; it is a question, therefore, to which no conclusive answer, carrying final conviction to all, can be expected. I shall arrange my conjectures in the order of plausibility, passing from those one feels tempted to accept immediately to others that may seem at first highly dubious.

Several authoritative scholars have held that the unicorn legend derives entirely from Oriental beliefs about the rhinoceros. This was the opinion of Cuvier, for example, a man whose expert knowledge and good sense command respect, and it is an opinion in keeping with the tendency of our time to prefer the light of common day to "the light that never was". An impressive "case" can be made out for this view.

We have repeatedly seen the rhinoceros crossing the unicorn's path or plunging through the undergrowth in a direction remarkably parallel. Ctesias, Aelian, Pliny, and Isidore mingle large ingredients of rhinoceros with their unicorns. Learned Christian Fathers such as Tertuillan, Jerome, Ambrose, and Gregory reject the unicorn entirely in favour of his doppelganger, and later scholars had to exert constant effort to prevent the animal from slipping down—or back?—into the huge Indian hog. And this is not surprising when one considers that almost exactly the same beliefs were held in India about the one animal as those entertained in Europe about the other, and that from the beginning

242

DRAGONS AND UNICORNS—FACT? OR FICTION?

of the sixteenth century Portuguese commerce made possible a constant infiltration of Oriental superstitions into the Western world. We cannot ignore the fact that Western interest in the alicorn increased at just the time when this infiltration began, and that rhinoceros horns were actually used in Europe, although to no great extent, precisely as alicorns were. A curious illustration of the uncertainty regarding the "true horn" is seen in the fact that the treasury of St. Mark's in Venice contains, beside the two famous alicorns brought from Constantinople and another one of later acquisition, the unmistakable horn of a rhinoceros, hanging with them. In this way the Cathedral assured itself against error, however the learned might eventually decide.

The parallelism between the two traditions may be shown in the words of a famous traveller of the sixteenth century. Linschoeten says of the rhinoceros that "some think it is the right Unicorne, because that as yet there hath no other bin found, but only by hearesay and by the pictures of them. The Portingalles and those of Bengala affirme that by the River Ganges in the Kingdome of Bengala are many of these Rhinoceros, which when they will drinke the other beasts stand and waite upon them till the Rhinoceros hath drinke, and thrust their horne into the water, for he cannot drinke but his horne must be under the water because it standeth so close unto his nose and muzzle: and then after him all the other beastes doe drinke. Their hornes in India are much esteemed and used against all venime, poyson, and many other diseases . . . which is very good and most true, as I myselfe by experience have found."

After reading this passage one is disposed to agree with the assertion of de Laborde that the rhinoceros is the sole source of all the marvellous qualities attributed to the unicorn. One is not surprised to find that Conrad Gesner used Durer's famous drawing of the rhinoceros as the illustration accompanying his account of the monoceros, or that John of San Geminiano could say "Christus assimilatur rhinocerote." Arabian writers constantly described the one animal under the name of the other, and in Europe there seems never to have been a time when some one did not suspect that the two were identical.

It is true that those who thought thus had always vigorous opponents. Andrea Bacci disposed of the notion to his own satisfaction by pointing out that the Romans knew the rhinoceros perfectly and yet believed in the unicorn as a totally different animal. He found the horns of the two animals in the treasury of Don Francesco and characterized that of the rhinoceros, a beast that he seems to have regarded with contempt, as black and thick and vulgar. Julius Caesar Scaliger fell foul of Cardan in this fashion: "By what evil fate does it happen that in spite of the frequent beatings you receive from the rods of grammarians you must now fall under the censure of naturalists? There is no help for you, Cardan, when you describe the monoceros under the heading of rhinoceros, for these two animals are entirely different." This serious charge, like many another that Scaliger brought against his foe, was unjustified, for Cardan had said with all possible clearness that the two animals were quite distinct and that nothing but the vague similarity in their names had caused confusion. But the most amusing of all those who strove to defend the unicorn from this contamination was Luis de Urreta. I have already quoted the

243

DRAGONS AND UNICORNS—FACT? OR FICTION?

passage in which he describes what he calls the unicorn in terms that apply exclusively to the rhinoceros and then refers with an indulgent smile to the belief of "certain holy men", who could not be expected to know better, that the two animals were really the same.

These passages show that the rhinoceros was as mysterious in Europe as the unicorn itself. Familiar to the Romans of the Empire, it was remembered in the Middle Ages chiefly because of a few references in Martial and other ancient writers. For a thousand years Europe forgot what the rhinoceros looks like. There is, to be sure, a curious little figure in the pavement of St. Mark's at Venice—near the Door of the Madonna—which seems, when one first comes upon it, to contradict this statement. This figure, the original of which seems to have been placed here in the thirteenth century, shows the unmistakable head of the rhinoceros with the horn properly placed, although the body is that of a bear, the feet are furnished with claws, and the ears are very large and shaped like those of a bat. The more learned cicerones of St. Mark's always refer to this pavement mosaic as the rhinoceros under the palmtree, explaining that it symbolizes the wrath of God, but they do not tell us why the rhinoceros should stand so near the Madonna's door or how a mosaicist of the thirteenth century happened to know even thus much about the appearance of an Indian beast. Hazardous as it may seem, my conjecture is that the mosaicist did not intend to represent a rhinoceros at all but a unicorn. For an accurate description of the unicorn it is not unreasonable to suppose that he went to his contemporary and fellow-townsman, Ser Marco Polo, recently returned from India where he had seen the rhinoceros in the wild state and had come away with the belief that he had seen the unicorn—although he had to admit (Book III, Chapter) that it "is not in the least like that which our stories tell of as being caught in the lap of a virgin; in fact, 'tis altogether different from what we fancied".

The first rhinoceros seen in western Europe in modern times was brought round Cape Horn in 1498 and taken to Lisbon. The second, much better known and indeed a celebrated animal, arrived in the same city seventeen years later, where it became a great favourite at "the palace of the king" and on one occasion was pitted against an elephant, which it put to ignominious flight. A sketch of it sent to Albrecht DŸrer was converted into the well-known engraving, delightfully inaccurate, which did duty for more than a hundred years in books of zoology. In 1517 this rhinoceros—whose name should have been Ulysses—set forth once more for Rome, intended as a gift to the Pope; but his ship was wrecked off Marseilles and in spite of his gallant effort to swim ashore only the dead body was recovered. The skin was stuffed and sent "to the palace of the King" of France. It was a hundred and fifty years after this that England first acquired a live rhinoceros of her own.

Some of the traits ascribed to the unicorn were almost certainly derived from facts observed by hunters of the rhinoceros. The hide of this beast is impervious to primitive weapons, so that the belief might well get abroad that it could be taken or killed only by stratagem. The people of India and China have long thought, indeed, that their beakers of rhinoceros horn were made of the horns of animals killed by elephants. Until the in-

DRAGONS AND UNICORNS—FACT? OR FICTION?

vention of the modern rifle the Indian rhinoceros had been killed or captured chiefly by great drives, such as that led by Tamerlane, in which many men and horses took part. Although not very swift of foot, the rhinoceros runs more rapidly than its bulk would lead one to expect, and it begins slowly, as early writers said of the unicorn, increasing its speed little by little. With reference to the Western belief that the virgin decoy attracts her victim by her odour it is worthy of remark that the eyesight of the rhinoceros is weak and his sense of smell very keen. The repeated statements that the unicorn belongs in some sense to the king reminds one that even in modern times Eastern potentates have been known to keep the rhinoceros in their parks and to take him with them on royal progresses as a symbol of power and sovereignty. Just as the unicorn came to represent chastity and solitude in Europe and became especially dear, therefore, to Christian monks, so the rhinoceros symbolized chastity and solitude in India and was regarded as a model of the ascetic life. Alkazuwin says concerning the animal's solitude that when it has chosen a grazing ground it will not tolerate the presence of any other beast within one hundred parasangs on any side, and those who know the literature of solitude will understand how readily this trait would be accepted by the Forest Hermits as a mark of holiness and wisdom. Finally, there is to be considered the tradition of the unicorn's great strength which persisted even when the animal was likened by Physiologus to a kid. Does it not seem probable that there is some memory here of the elephant-fighter? Joshua Sylvester, after speaking in high commendation of the elephant, proceeds as follows:-

But his huge strength nor subtle witt can not

Defend him from the sly Rhinocerot,

Who never, with blinde furie led, doth venter

Upon his Foe, but, yer the Lists he enter,

Against a rock he whetteth round about

The dangerous Pike upon his armed snout;

Then buckling close, doth not at random hack

On the hard Cuirasse of his Enemies back

But under's belie (cunning) findes a skinne

Whear (and but thear) his sharpened blade will in.

Even more is claimed for the rhinoceros on the score of medicinal value than for the unicorn, for not his horn alone but his entire body is held to abound with magical virtues. These virtues, it would seem, were regarded as merely brought to a higher potency in

245

DRAGONS AND UNICORNS—FACT? OR FICTION?

the horn, according to a belief that his strength chiefly lay in the member with which he fought and defended himself. The hunting, transport, preparation, and sale of these horns has been one of the more romantic details of Oriental business activity for a very long time, comparable only, so far as the East is concerned, with the commerce in dragon's bones. There are even records showing that Occidental merchants shared in this business. Lying in the Strait of Malacca in 1592, James Lancaster sent commodities to the King of Junsaloam "to barter for Ambergriese and for the hornes of the Abath, whereof the king only hath the traffique in his hands. Now this Abath is a beast which hath one horn onely in her forehead, and is thought to be the female Unicorne, and is highly esteemed of all the Moores in these parts as a most soveraigne remedie against poyson."

Caspar Bartholinus tells us that when he was in Italy about the year 1620 the rhinoceros horn was on sale in several of the larger cities and that it was recommended as a specific against poison and fevers, small-pox, epilepsy, vertigo, worms, impotence, and stomachache. Forty years later Father Lobo could say that this horn, as compared with true alicorn, was "not so sovereign, though used against poison". Pierre Pomet, writing in 1699, asserts that the rhinoceros horn is still used in the belief that it is as effective as alicorn.

This is what one would expect, but it is a little surprising to find precisely the same set of beliefs at the Cape of Good Hope in the eighteenth century, applied there to the white rhinoceros. Whether to attribute this to a prehistoric transmission across the length of Africa or to the influence of the Dutch and Portuguese one is not quite sure. Charles Thunberg writes that in the region of the Cape the horns of the rhinoceros were kept "not only as rarities but also as useful in diseases and for the purpose of detecting poison. The fine shavings of the horns, taken internally, were supposed to cure convulsions and spasms in children, and it was firmly believed that goblets made of these horns in a turner's lathe would discover a poisonous draught by making the liquor ferment."

With these facts and considerations in mind one is strongly inclined to agree with de Laborde that the rhinoceros is the sole source not only of the superstition regarding the alicorn but of the whole unicorn legend. Before committing oneself to the rhinoceros theory, however, there are a few questions that one would like to have answered. How did the unicorn acquire from this animal, so mild and phlegmatic when not molested, his reputation for extreme pugnacity? Does it seem likely that the rhinoceros suggested the unicorn's reputation for extreme fleetness? With the rhinoceros alone in mind, what sense can we make of Topsell's assertion, founded upon good ancient authority, that the unicorn "fighteth with the mouth and with the heels, with the mouth biting like a lion and with the heels kicking like a horse"? Again, what is the connection between the rhinoceros and the unicorn of Physiologus, of which we are told that it is like a kid? Finally, how is it possible to identify an animal of such delicacy and refinement as the unicorn's with the gross, grunting, slime-wallowing rhinoceros? One hesitates to think of him as related to that beast even in the way that the water-lily is related to the mud.

Looking for a way of escape from the almost inescapable evidence accumulated above, one recalls that the rhinoceros was not the only one-horned animal known to or imagined by the ancients. Both Pliny and Aristotle believed that the oryx was a unicorn.

This animal, as we learn from Oppian's poem on the art of hunting, was regarded in the ancient world as extremely formidable both to man and beast. Although it does not look much like a goat to the modern eye, the ancients, with their loose zoological terminology sometimes called it that, and certainly it is far more goat-like than the rhinoceros. The oryx, or rather a bronze figure of one, was probably the original of the drawing of a "monoceros" preserved in an early manuscript of Cosmas Indicopleustes. The nimble and delicate unicorns of mediaeval manuscripts are all of the same general kind—that is, they are all vaguely like antelopes. The painted figure of a unicorn found by Sir John Barrow in a South African cave was clearly that of some sort of antelope. The descriptions of unicorns left us by Vartoman, Thevet, Lobo, Francis Magellanes, Caravaial, Ruppell, and several others, suggest the oryx strongly, and in one of these descriptions-that of Magellanes—the same assertions are made regarding the medicinal value of the horn as those with which we are familiar. The horn of the rhinoceros was not the only one with which this superstition was connected, so that de Laborde may be wrong after all in asserting that it was the source of the whole belief concerning the alicorn. Aelian tells us that it was a custom of ancient hunters to reserve the oryxes they captured as presents for their kings.2' It will be recalled that we have already been obliged to call in a large antelope of some sort to explain the unicorn of Ctesias. In short, almost if not quite as much may be said for the oryx as for the rhinoceros by one trying to find the source of the unicorn legend.

Almost as much has, in fact, been said. Samuel Bochart devoted twenty folio pages of amazing erudition to an attempt to prove that both the Re'em and the unicorn derive from the oryx, basing his argument upon a firm belief—for which he had the authority of Aristotle and Pliny—that all oryxes are one-horned. (Such are the charming results of studying zoology in libraries.) Professor Martin Lichtenstein of Berlin, a far less learned man but better acquainted with antelopes, supported the oryx theory by citation of Egyptian monuments. He reproduced a mural decoration found in the pyramid at Memphis showing five antelopes, one of them certainly intended as a unicorn, led by human figures, the whole scene representing a ritualistic offering. In another plate shown by Lichtenstein we see a god with a saw in one hand holding a one-horned antelope by the other, and the suggestion is that one of the horns has just been cut off. The antelope here shown is apparently the small and graceful dorcas, sacred to Isis, and it is significant, therefore, that in this second plate the god and the antelope stand before that goddess, enthroned. We may perhaps draw the inference that Isis preferred to have her antelopes appear before her with one horn.

Although Lichtenstein does not mention the fact, one cannot help remembering in this connection that the early Christians of Alexandria transferred to the Virgin Mary some of the attributes of Isis, the Egyptian Mother of God, and that even the conventional Christian paintings of Mother and Child are sometimes said to have had this pagan origin. A question grazes the mind whether we have found here the channel by which a

DRAGONS AND UNICORNS—FACT? OR FICTION?

heathen superstition was diverted to the uses of Christian symbolism. (This question arises with unusual emphasis when one stands before the beautiful painting of the Madonna and Child by Stefan Lochner in the Wallraf-Richartz Museum at Cologne. On the Madonna's bosom there is a large jewelled brooch which shows in the middle a seated maiden with a unicorn resting in her lap.) Here, at any rate, we have a unicorn vaguely simile haedo which belongs to the country of Physiologus and is in some way related to a goddess who, in spite of her own practice of incest, was regarded as a patroness of chastity. Bochart's argument would have been stronger if he had admitted a possibility that other antelopes beside the large and fierce oryx may have had some influence upon the unicorn legend. The dorcas is a smaller and more kid-like animal, altogether a more appropriate companion for virgins seated in the woods.

As we shall see, both Pallas and Cuvier admit that the oryx may now and then, as a lusus nafurae, have only one horn, and far more frequent than such "sports" must be the animals that have had one horn broken off in conflict with their fellows. The most important consideration is, however, that when seen in profile the oryx really seems to have only one horn—a fact to which there is abundant testimony and which anyone can test for himself by visiting a large menagerie.

The pertinence of this fact is made clear in a communication that appeared recently in a daily newspaper. Referring to the report that the present Duke of Gloucester had shot an oryx in Tanganyika Territory, the correspondent writes: "The African, even when he is a professional hunter, is not anything of a naturalist. One day a man passed me carrying in the manner of a sceptre or wand of office a long, straight horn. I asked my African companion about the horn and was assured that it was a very rare trophy indeed; it came off a great antelope that was only to be found, and then but rarely, in the desert country far to the North. When I asked whether the owner would not be better off with the two horns instead of with only half a pair, my companion said that the remarkable beast which provided the horn carried only one . . . . Some time later I moved to a part of the country where oryx were to be found. The animal is a very shy beast, not easy to approach. From a distance, and especially when broadside on, he certainly appears to have only one horn. Moreover, the first I saw head-on had, in fact, only one horn. But when I managed to drop that oryx and looked him over I found that, though the beast had only one horn, he had had two; there was a stump of the second, just where one would expect it. Male antelopes at times bicker with one another, and they do it with their horns; one can hear the rattle of them as their wearers battle together. In a bout of the sort the long slender horn is apt to snap off, and that, no doubt, was how the single-horned oryx came to be. Perhaps it was by some such means that the fabulous unicorn found its way into heraldry."

Discoveries of this sort are made many times before they become common property. Sir William Cornwallis Harris made much the same remarks about the oryx seventy years ago, but with important variations. His passage, though wretchedly written and full of errors in statement of fact, deserves partial quotation. "Romance", says he, "aiding the skilful hand of nature with her richest embroidery, has succeeded in investing the group

DRAGONS AND UNICORNS—FACT? OR FICTION?

to which the Oryx belongs with a degree of interest that few other quadrupeds can claim. The figure of the renowned Unicorn can be seen traced in all the ancient carvings, coins, and Latin heraldic insignia; and from our earliest childhood the form of that fabled animal has been made to occupy so prominent a place in our juvenile imaginations that, arriving at years of discretion, we are still almost tempted to regard it as a creature having actual existence. Of all the whimsies of antiquity the Unicorn, unquestionably the most celebrated, is the chimera which has in modern ages engrossed the largest portion of attention from the curious . . . . The alterations required to reduce the African oryx to the standard of the heraldic unicorn are slight and simple, nor can it be doubted that they have been gradually introduced by successive copyists, the idea of the single horn being derived from profile representations of that animal in hasrelief on the sculptured monuments of ancient Egypt and Nubia. Excepting in the position and forward inclination of the horn, the cartazon of the ancient Persians, figured on the monuments of Persepolis and described by Aelian, tallies in every respect so exactly with the Algazel or North African Oryx—as the latter would appear en profile, with the straight and almost parallel horns precisely covering each other—that little question can exist as to that animal having furnished the origin of the design. Accident may indeed have contributed to strengthen the opinion, once conceived, of the existence of the monocerine species, for it is well known that among the savage tribes of Africa the art of twirling, carving, and otherwise adorning the horns of their domestic animals was carried to a singular extent-the most fanciful forms being imparted and the two even sometimes twisted together. It is, however, unnecessary to look beyond the ignorance of the limner and the credulity of the describer, satisfactorily to trace the progress of the whole delusion. . . Both the oryx and the wild ass inhabit the same regions and possess in common the essential attributes of figure, colour, and carriage; nor is it at all unlikely that the mutilation of individuals of the first-named species, by the fracture of a horn, may afterwards have tended to strengthen the belief derived from these imperfect representations . . . . Such would appear to have been the origin and progress of the fable of the Unicorn, from its foundation in ancient Persia to its diffusion over the whole of western Europe; and such, at the present day, is the figure of the fictitious animal forming the sinister supporter of the Royal Achievement of England." The author's painting of the oryx which accompanies this text is more convincing than the text itself.

Already it begins to appear that the difficulty in finding the source of the unicorn legend does not lie in poverty of materials or lack of plausible theories. Quite as convincing an argument can be made for the oryx as for the rhinoceros—indeed a somewhat better one by the test of Physiologus—and either argument looks cogent and final when separately considered. From this fact there seem to be three possible inferences: that the two bodies of belief grew up independently; that the beliefs relating to one of the two animals have been transferred to the other; that both legends are derived from a body of belief lying farther back in time. The first of these possibilities seems to me so nearly impossible that I shall waste no space upon it. The second, although certainly arguable, presents numerous difficulties which I think could not be overcome. One can hardly think, for example, that the medicinal attributes of the rhinoceros could be transferred to the antelope without the transfer of some of its more obvious physical characteristics, of which the unicorn of Physiologus and of Europe is entirely devoid. Neither does it seem probable that the great prestige of the unicorn and of the "treasure of his brow" could have been derived from either of these animals. We are left, then, with the third possibility, that the rhinoceros and oryx legends are indeed related, though not in the sense that one is the parent of the other; they have a common ancestor. Some greater unicorn looms behind them both. We must continue the quest.

It was said of Cuvier that he could reconstruct the skeleton of a prehistoric animal from a single knuckle-bone, and there is just a possibility that the popular imagination has built up the unicornnot the various items of his legend and of what may be called his character alone, for these are obviously products of fancy, but his physical aspect-on the basis of a "horn" which never grew on his brow. A remarkable horn, or an object everywhere so-called, did certainly attract much attention in the Middle Ages, and there can be little doubt what sort of object this was. Representations of it in mediaeval manuscripts show that it had precisely those "anfractuous spires and cochleary turnings" which I see in the ivory stick on the desk before me and which are to be found in no other natural object. This ivory stick is perfectly straight, suggesting that it grew single and alone, as indeed it did. As I have already said, the Italian word licorno, "the horn", was almost certainly made at a time when the object was regarded as independent and no origin for it had been imagined. The rather awkward extension of this word to name the beast from whose brow the horn was supposed to spring suggests that the animal was deduced from the horn. If this could happen in Italy during the Middle Ages it may have happened elsewhere and much earlier. We do not know for how long such objects as my alicorn have been familiar in Mediterranean countries, but the commercial history of the race that chiefly purveyed them stretches back for a very long time. Furthermore, it is not necessary to this conjecture that the kind of horn before me and no other should have always served to suggest the unicorn; there are several horns, particularly those of certain antelopes, so straight and apparently independent as to suggest, when seen singly, that they grew alone. It is a matter not of conjecture but of fact that the single straight horns of antelopes have been used in Tibet during many centuries for magical and ritualistic purposes, and that these sacred horns have been dispersed by pilgrims over a wide territory, acquiring more and more, as they went farther from their source, the reputation of talismans and of being the horns of unicorns. Here we see a unicorn legend in the making.

The highly significant passage that I have quoted from Colonel Prejevalsky shows all the essential phases of the unicorn legend assembled in Tibet, and it shows also how they might be put together. We start, to be sure, with an actual animal, sacred and taboo. Its blood is thought to be medicinal; its long straight horn is used by priests in necromatic and religious rites; it has some sort of symbolism. In this same region there has been, since the time of Genghis Khan and probably for very much longer, a belief in onehorned antelopes. The priests who use the horns in divination may know that they grew in pairs, although they use them singly, but the pilgrims who buy these horns and carry them into the surrounding districts are probably not aware of this. At a distance from the distributing centre everyone is convinced that they are the horns of unicorns. The representations of salesmen praising their wares tend to increase belief in the magic powers of the horns, and this belief grows as it spreads West and East. Tibet lies between Persia, from which we get our first notices of the Western unicorn, and China, which has a highly developed unicorn legend not of native origin. Tibet was included in the "India" of Ctesias.—Why should we look farther for the sources of the unicorn?

There is a possibility, however, and one that must not be ignored, that unicorned animals actually exist in rare instances as lusus naturae. This possibility was urged by Peter Simon Pallas, one of the most competent zoologists of the eighteenth century, who believed that the legend of the unicorn sprang from chance encounters with such one-horned sports. The theory is not unattractive, accounting as it does for the universal belief that the unicorn is exceedingly rare and also for the facts that it has been reported from many different parts of the world and has been described as resembling a wide variety of animals. A nineteenth century scholar points out that there are antelopes whose horns are joined for the first few inches from the base, and he asks what is to prevent nature from prolonging this juncture, now and then and as a freak, throughout the entire length. These speculations are brought into the region of fact by an authentic record of a onehorned animal. In his Natural History of Oxfordshire Robert Plot describes several sheep with six or eight horns kept in his time by Lord Norreys at Ridcot; "and there was one other sheep", says he, "that excelled them all in being a Unicorn, having a single horn growing in the middle of its forehead, twenty-one inches long, with annulary protuberances round it and a little twisted in the middle. There was, to be sure, another little horn growing on the same head, but so inconsiderable that it was hid under the wool."

This Oxfordshire unicorn seems to have been a freak, but others have been produced artificially by the deliberate man-handling of horns, of which there has been a good deal, early and late, in various parts of the world. "Among us", says a modern writer, "the horn does not seem capable of much modification, but a Kaffir can never be content to leave the horns as they are. He will cause one horn to project forward and the other backward. Now and then an ox is seen in which a most singular effect has been produced. As the horns of the young ox sprout they are trained over the forehead until the points meet. They are then manipulated so as to make them coalesce, and so shoot upwards from the middle of the forehead, like the horn of the fabled unicorn."

This passage is corroborated by another in a more recent book which seems to bring the unicorn almost to one's door: "Few domestic sheep are more remarkable, or have given rise to more controversy, than the Indian one-horned or unicorn-sheep, of which the first living specimens ever seen in this country formed part of a large collection of Nepalese animals presented to King George V when Prince of Wales, that were exhibited at the London Zoological Gardens in the year 1906. Although receiving the name of unicorn-sheep, these animals really possessed a pair of horns, for if we examine one of their skulls and remove the horn-sheath from its bony support it will be noticed that the latter is composed of two quite separate structures . . . . There appears to be a certain amount of mystery regarding the origin of these creatures, and some doubt as to whether their peculiar horn-formation is not the outcome of artificial manipulation." A letter from

DRAGONS AND UNICORNS—FACT? OR FICTION?

the British Resident at the Court of Nepal is then quoted in which these words occur: "There is no special breed of one-horned sheep in Nepal, nor are the specimens which have been brought here for sale natural freaks. By certain maltreatment ordinary two-horned sheep are converted into a one-horned variety. The process adopted is branding with a red-hot iron the male lambs when about two or three months old on their horns when they are beginning to sprout. The wounds are treated with a mixture of oil and soot and when they heal, instead of growing at their usual places and spreading, come out as one from the middle of the skull . . . . I am told that the object of producing these curiosities is to obtain fancy prices for them from the wealthy people in Nepal." The original writer then continues: "Notwithstanding the above explanation, the majority of naturalists are inclined to doubt whether a true understanding has even yet been arrived at concerning these sheep, for it has been pointed out that the mere fact of searing the budding horns would not result in those appendages sprouting out at the summit of the skull instead of towards the side, and moreover, if there is any secret attending their production it has been remarkably well kept from the ever-prying eyes of zoologists. It is true that the horns of a young animal might be induced to grow together by binding them up, but in that case we should expect the bony supports to be bent aside at their bases as a result of the unnatural strain put upon them, whereas on the contrary, those of the unicorn sheep arise in quite a straight manner from the skull."

Whatever the process may be there is no doubt that the thing is done, and for the present purpose the motive is more important than the method. The British Resident at Nepal says that the artificial unicorns of that country are produced "to obtain fancy prices", but we should like to know why a sheep with one horn is thought to be worth more than a sheep with the normal equipment, and also why such a sheep was thought a suitable gift for the Prince of Wales. Some light is thrown upon this question by the fact that the tribe of Dinkas, who live just south of the White Nile, not only manipulate the horns of their cattle as the Kaffirs do but use this practice as a means of marking the leaders of their herds. One can readily believe that the practice is one of great antiquity and that it was used as the Dinkas use it in many parts of the world during the pastoral ages. In the minds of primitive men living a pastoral life the leader of a flock or herd is a valuable possession and he is also a natural emblem of sovereignty and supreme power. We have already seen that the unicorn has been used as such an emblem in lands far apart and during a great stretch of time, the remarkable vision in the Book of Daniel providing the most striking instance. It seems possible, therefore, that what I may call the unicorn idea, the notion that one-horned animals exist in Nature, arose from the custom of uniting the horns of various domestic animals by a process which is still in use but still mysterious to the civilized world. Here may be the explanation of the one-horned cows and bulls that Aelian says were to be found in Ethiopia and of the unicorned cattle reported by Pliny as living in the land of the Moors. The cows with single horns bending backward and a span long seen by Vartoman at Zeila in Ethiopia may have been of this sort. The one-horned ram's head sent to Pericles by his farm-hands may have been that of the leader of their flock, and so a perfect symbol of that leadership in Athens which, according to Plutarch's interpretation, they wished to prophesy for their master. Finally, the mysterious one-horned ox mentioned three times over in the Talmud as Adam's sacrifice to Jehovah may

DRAGONS AND UNICORNS—FACT? OR FICTION?

have been the most precious thing that Adam possessed, the leader of his herd of cattle. -Once more the question rises whether there is any need of seeking further.

One goes on seeking for the source or sources of the unicorn legend partly because other explanations of it, perhaps not so immediately plausible as those just considered but quite as able to stand scrutiny, continue to suggest themselves. Another reason for continuing the search is that none of the suggestions thus far made is completely convincing. They suggest no sufficient reason why the single horn—whether found alone or on the head of a beast, whether growing naturally or as the product of artifice—should have attracted so much attention and should have won such prestige as the horn of the unicorn has long had. Even if we accept one or all-for this too is possible—of the suggestions put forth above we feel that they are not primary or fundamental because they do not explain the strange fascination exercised by unicornity (if I may venture the neologism) upon the mind. They require explanation in their turn by something lying behind and towering above them all.

Among the ruins of the Palace of Forty Pillars at Persepolis, on the left-hand side of the western staircase constructed by Artaxerxes III, there is a bas-relief showing the figure of a lion with teeth and claws fastened upon a one-horned animal of uncertain species resembling at once a bull, a large antelope, and a goat. Three other treatments of the same subject are found in the corresponding positions, the figure of the unicorned animal varying slightly from one to another. During the last century and a half these bas-reliefs have been studied, minutely by many competent scholars and the suggestion has been made repeatedly that they may have some bearing upon the problem of the unicorn.

No purpose would be served by a full survey of this extensive literature. I may say, however, that there has been much discussion concerning the species represented by the unicorn, some contending that it was intended for a goat, others that it is an antelope, and still others that it is certainly a wild ass. For my own part, dependent as I am upon the numerous photographs and drawings, I am chiefly impressed by the confidence in his own opinion displayed by each of the contenders, for it seems obvious to me that the animal was intended by the sculptor—who could be realistic enough when he chose, judging from his lion—to represent a composite beast in which ass and goat and antelope and bull were included. One of the most interesting of the conclusions upon which there is fairly general agreement is that Ctesias was influenced by these figures in writing his description of the unicorn. There seems to be no reason why we should not accept this opinion, provided that we see how little it signifies. Ctesias probably saw the bas-reliefs and others like them at Susa, and one cannot say that his one-horned onager is utterly unlike the rather nondescript animal of the Persepolis sculptures; but he certainly did not derive from these figures his precise ideas about the colours of the horn and of the astragalus, about the use of the horn by Indian princes, or about the unicorn's habitat and characteristics. From the bas-reliefs of Persepolis he could have got little more than a belief that there existed somewhere—and why not in "India", the home of wonders?—a beast vaguely resembling the wild ass that he had seen in Persia but, unlike the local variety, furnished with a single horn. For the appearance and properties of this horn he would have had to inquire elsewhere.

Ctesias may well have accepted these figures as those of unicorns, but did the sculptor intend that they should be so understood? This is a question which one would suppose that any thoughtful person sitting down before the present problem would try to answer first of all, but on the contrary the question is not even stated or grazed for over a hundred years by any of the writers engaged in the main discussion. Niehbuhr, Rhode, Ker Porter, Heeren, Lassen, and Robert Brown all tacitly assume that all representations of animals in ancient sculpture that look like unicorns were intended as such. This strange ignorance or ignoring of an obvious art convention vitiates some of their results and weakens confidence in their powers of observation.

The statement is often made that the artists of Egypt, the Euphrates, and Persepolis knew nothing of perspective and that they always showed two legs for four, one ear and one horn for two, through sheer inability to represent the third dimension. This statement is untrue. There was an artistic convention—which grew up, probably, before the technic of representing perspective was mastered—allowing the artist to show one horn or ear instead of two when representing animals in profile, but this convention was by no means universally followed, and the fact that ancient artists were not consistent in observing it lends some excuse to the enthusiasts named above who found unicorns everywhere in ancient art, on coins and seals and gems as well as in sculptures, somewhat as Sir Thomas Browne found quincunxes.

The fact that the sculptors of the ancient world sometimes showed two horns in representing animals in profile must not be taken as proof that when they showed only one they had in mind an actual unicorn. Far more important for our purpose than the sculptor's intention, however, is the effect of his work upon the public mind, the interpretation put upon it by ignorant laymen. We have just seen that several acute modern scholars, most of them students of ancient art, were convinced that the one-horned figures of Persepolis were intended to represent unicorns. If this was true of them, what are we to expect of ignorant men, for whom graphic and plastic art is always a record of actuality? Millions of ignorant men saw the unicorn bas-reliefs at Persepolis and Susa, and millions more saw others almost exactly like them at Nineveh and Babylon, for these figures, like almost everything else in Persian sculpture, were derived from the remote Euphratean past. If these millions had not believed in unicorns before they saw the figures, we may be quite sure that they did believe after they had seen them. Whatever the original artists meant to do, this is a part of what they accomplished: either they corroborated an already existing belief in the unicorn or else they gave the first hint leading to that belief.

Those who doubt whether this is possible will do well to read Jean Wauquelin's Merveilles d'Inde, in which it is perfectly evident that the six-handed men, the horned women, and the griffins with lions' paws, all regarded by the fifteenth-century author as actual creatures, derive ultimately from the symbolic monstrosities of Indian religious art. It has even been suggested, quite credibly, that the griffin itself was the imaginative

DRAGONS AND UNICORNS—FACT? OR FICTION?

creation of Indian tapestry workers and that the Greeks, seeing these tapestries at the court of Persia and elsewhere, thought the figures on them represented real animals and described the animals in words as best they could. The fact that esoteric symbols are constantly subject to exoteric interpretation, that symbolic images are almost everywhere regarded by most people as idols and these idols as physically present deities, is familiar to every student of the history of religion, and purely artistic representations of animals—if indeed there were any such in the times of which we are speaking—were subject to similar misinterpretation. We have seen that Arabian travellers, finding certain figures carved on rhinoceros horn, thought that they grew naturally in the horn, and that when Sir John Barrow, a highly educated traveller of the nineteenth century, found in South Africa a cave painting of an antelope showing only one horn he could only infer that one-horned antelopes must exist in Nature. The numberless millions of Persepolis and the Euphrates valley, who lived all their lives with powerful representations of one-horned animals constantly before them, may have been no more intelligent and cautious and critical.

Not only on the great public monuments were such apparently one-horned animals to be seen; figures of them were spread broadcast through the known world by the constant use of them on sealcylinders in Persia, Assyria, Babylon, Chaldea, and Elam. The spread of these cylinders was not confined even to the wide territory in which for many centuries they were in daily use, for the figures upon them, impressed on tablets of clay, were employed to identify and protect personal property, so that they must have had a dispersion similar to that of modern trade-marks. Almost indestructible by weather, sealcylinders made over four thousand years ago lasted on into a time when the symbolism they at first conveyed was quite forgotten. Everywhere they went—and they went everywhere—they suggested the existence of one-horned animals, and they suggested also that these animals were in some way highly important. If there had been no belief in the unicorn before the use of these emblems on seal-cylinders or independent of it, they alone would have been sufficient to suggest and develop such a belief.

But the unicorn, like das Ewig Weibliche, lures us on and on. Although it seems likely that faith in the animal was corroborated by seal-cylinders and profile figures in bas-relief, I should be sorry to think that his first emergence wore such "hues of hap and hazard", that he was born of a mere blunder. If the facts point to that conclusion we must of course accept them, but I am not sure that they do. I venture to suggest that the ignorant millions of Persepolis and Nineveh and Babylon might have been justified and right in accepting these figures as representations of unicorns, and that the artists who made them intended that they should be so accepted.

I am well aware that this suggestion is counter to expert opinion. Early writers upon the one-horned figures at Persepolis and elsewhere assumed unanimously, as I have said, that they were always intended to represent unicorns, and later writers have assumed with the same unanimity that they never were. The second assumption seems to me hardly less hasty than the first. No one doubts that there was a widespread and long-enduring artistic convention by which one horn was commonly depicted to represent

DRAGONS AND UNICORNS—FACT? OR FICTION?

two, but this convention was often ignored, and furthermore its existence does not prove that none of the animals represented as unicorns were ever intended as such. Conclusive evidence of a pre-Ctesian belief in the unicorn would be given by a full-face figure dating from before the time of Ctesias and showing only one horn, but I am not aware that such a figure exists. We can do fairly well without it.

Strong probability that the unicorn legend is older than Ctesias and older than the Palace of Forty Pillars is indicated by many of the facts already discussed, but there is no need of resting the present argument upon anything in the slightest degree uncertain. It can be shown that animals clearly described as unicorns held a high position in the religion of Persia.

The basic idea of Zoroastrian religion is an intensely conceived dualism worked out in the moral sphere as a perpetual conflict between forces of good and of evil captained respectively by the primal gods Ormuzd and Ahriman. The forces comprise and the struggle involves not human beings alone but the whole animal creation, part of which is regarded as belonging to the god of virtue and light, part to his rival. All the creatures or "servants" of Ormuzd consider it their highest duty to cherish others of their own kind and to destroy the creatures of Ahriman. The division of the animal kingdom into pure and impure creatures is made, of course, according to the utility or hostility of different species to mankind. Thus the horse and the ass stand high among the servants of Ormuzd, but highest, king and progenitor of all, is the bull. The chief of the impure animals is either the martichore or the lion. In many primitive beliefs, probably in most, the snake is of good omen, primarily because a need is felt of placating it, but Zoroastrianism shows what seems to most modern minds the natural attitude in regarding it as evil, at war with all pure animals, who kill it when they can.

In the sacred writings of Persia there are several references to an animal of Ormuzd's creation that is of utmost importance to the present problem. The context of one of these, a passage almost modern in feeling, brings together for adoration the beneficent forces and elements of nature, and then come the words: "We worship the Good Mind and the spirits of the Saints and that sacred beast the Unicorn which stands in Vouru-Kasha, and we sacrifice to that sea of Vouru-Kasha where he stands." In another context, not unlike the sanitation chapters in Leviticus but on a much higher level, there is mention of water polluted by the creatures of Ahriman—that is to say, presumably, stagnant water, always mysteriously dangerous in a country such as Persia. But Ormuzd has provided against this danger, for "the three-legged ass sits amid the sea Varkash, and as to water of every kind that rains on dead matter. . . when it arrives at the three-legged ass he makes every kind clean and purified with watchfulness." The most important text reads thus: "Regarding the three-legged ass they say that it stands amid the wide-formed ocean, and its feet are three, eyes six, mouths nine, ears two, and horn one. Body white, food spiritual, and it is righteous . . . . The horn is as it were of pure gold, and hollow. . . . With that horn it will vanquish and dissipate all the vile corruption due to the efforts of noxious creatures. When that ass shall hold its neck in the ocean its ears will terrify, and all the water of the wide-formed ocean will shake with agitation . . . . If, 0 three-legged ass! you were

256

DRAGONS AND UNICORNS—FACT? OR FICTION?

not created for the water, all the water in the sea would have perished from the contamination which the poison of the Evil Spirit brought into its water through the death of the creatures of Ahuramazd."

These passages throw at least a glimmer of welcome light upon more than one aspect of the unicorn problem. Here we have an ass, although a supernatural and symbolic and celestial one, with a single horn, and that horn when dipped in water is thaumaturgic in its power against poison. Ctesias, physician to the Court of Persia, may have had something other than travellers' tales and bas-reliefs to work upon in his account of the one horned ass, and in any case he was not the inventor of the unicorn. That animal has now definitely escaped from human records into timeless myth.

It will be recalled that after a laborious effort to explain the unicorn's water-conning trait in the terms of mediaeval theories of medicine I was obliged to abandon that problem—promising, however, to return to it later. The tentative explanation advanced at the end of the fifth chapter gave no clue, as I said, to the reason why the water is poisonous, and it did not include the other animals which, in nearly all versions of the story, wait beside the water for the unicorn's coming. The Bundahis suggests unmistakably that the water is poisonous because the impure creatures of Ahriman have in some way made it so, and it makes clear also that the animals waiting beside the water are the pure creatures of Ormuzd expecting the advent of their champion and preserver.

Lest there should linger any doubt that the three-legged ass of the Bundahis and the unicorn of Europe are of the same stock, let us place beside the third quotation just above, the account given by John of Hesse of the water-conning which he says he saw beside the bitter waters of Marah: "Even to-day the venomous animals poison the water after the going down of the sun, so that the good animals cannot drink of it; but in the morning after sunrise comes the unicorn, and he, dipping his horn in the stream, expels the poison so that during the daytime the other animals may drink." This is the unicorn of Europe in his most characteristic action, but this is precisely the action also of the three-legged ass. John of Hesse even speaks of animalia bona and animalia venenosa exactly as though he were a Zoroastrian worshipper of Ormuzd instead of a Christian priest, and it would be hard to find a stranger tangle of cultures and beliefs than his Christian use of an ancient Persian symbol to illustrate and enforce a Hebrew tale. How glibly we talk about "melting-pots" as though they had been invented in our own day!

With every wish to avoid the appearance of dogmatism, I cannot even pretend to doubt that the horned ass of the Bundahis and the unicorn of the West belong to the same tradition. But here we seem to have come, at last, to something final. I cannot trace the three-legged ass—that is the unicorn, with a less euphonious name—to his origin, for he fades into the clouds of mythology and the distance blots him out. One may say that he bears some resemblance to the horned horse of Indra and to the snake-killing horse of Pedu, but these surrogates, if such they are, merely take him farther away. So little is known and heard of him in Persian literature that he is probably an importation from another culture, and it seems likely that his legend is older than the Avesta. James

257

DRAGONS AND UNICORNS—FACT? OR FICTION?

Darmesteter regards him as one of the many personifications of the storm-cloud, and so considered by the people of a thirsty land a beneficent creature and a serpent-killer. Angelo de Gubernatis identifies him with the gandharvds of Hindu myth who guard the sacred soma in the midst of the waters. However this may be, the sea of Varkash in the midst of which he stands represents either the ocean as contrasted with the Persian Gulf, or else, more probably, the "waters of the firmament." He is called three-legged for purely symbolical reasons, either because he is supposed to stand on air, earth, and sea, or because his reign is to endure for three Zoroastrian ages. As the guardian of the pure animals and chief antagonist of Ahriman he is usurping the position of the Primitive Bull which, according to the Avesta, is at the head of Ormuzd's creation. This usurpation carries one's thought back to the long controversy over the question whether the one-horned animal of the Persepolis bas-reliefs was intended to represent a bull, a goat, or an ass. Possibly the sculptor intended that it should represent all three of these and stand for the entire animal kingdom of Ormuzd. The pollution in the waters which the three-legged ass is said to destroy or disperse by dipping its horn need not be taken literally, for the myth is symbolic in every detail. It may represent the darkness of night dispersed by the first beams of dawn or by moonlight; it may stand for drought overcome by the golden horn of the lightning; ultimately, however, it is an emblem of evil overcome by good.

Like the unicorn of Europe, the three-legged ass is a symbol of purity and a champion of those oppressed by the devil. In him the Christian makers of Physiologus had ready to their hand a perfect emblem of a Saviour sent into the world for the healing of the nations, and the fact that they chose instead of this the trivial and inept tale of the virgin-capture merely shows again how puerile they were.—But perhaps they were not given the choice, for the Persian tale may have been one of the very few myths and legends that were never heard in Alexandria.

It is natural to suppose that the three-legged ass must have been a glorification of some actual animal, perhaps the onager of the Persian plains; and if that were so he would not stand at the end of our quest but would be merely another point of departure; his attributes, however magnified, would be those of some terrestrial creature which we should feel obliged to find. Fortunately for the present investigation, the mythopceic fancy did not work in this way. Difficult as the conception may be to us, the worshippers of the three-legged ass, instead of atributing to him the characteristics of actual asses, derived what they took to be those characteristics from what they knew of him, their divine prototype. The wild ass merely performs on earth the role created for him by the three-legged ass of Varkash, and if he kills serpents that is only because his celestial prototype destroys the poison that Ahriman has spread in the sea, annihilating evil-doers with his golden horn. One might say, perhaps, that the three-legged ass is the Platonic idea to which all actual asses strive to conform. They are the shadow of which he is the substance. For this reason the myth of the three-legged ass may be regarded as one source of the unicorn legend.

But this is not the only unicorn referred to in the sacred literature of Persia. We are told that the race of goats is divided into five orders of which sheep-goats form the sec-

258

ond, and that these are subdivided into five kinds, the second of which is the Koresck, which has "one great horn and dwells upon separate hills and takes its pleasure there." We know also that the Koresck is of the fold of Ormuzd because it is said in the same passage that he educated one of the Zend kings. This helps to explain the fact that several of the one-horned animals represented at Persepolis have cloven hoofs and look far more like goats than like either the bull or the ass. From the time of Aristotle to that of the British College of Heralds scholars have been perplexed by the unicorn's combination of caprine with equine characteristics. The unicorn of Albrecht DŸrer, for example, is a horse in most respects, but it has cloven hoofs and a goat's beard, and so has the unicorn of the British Royal Arms. This confusion, preserved by a surprising tenacity of tradition, may have been due originally to the effort of Zoroastrian artists to represent not any single species of animal but a combination of several species which they regarded as the leaders of the pure creation.

In thinking of the one-horned figures at Persepolis we are not to ignore the fact that they are grouped about the royal palace, just as were the four brazen unicorns seen by Cosmas Indicopleustes about the four-towered palace of the King of Ethiopia. The King of Persia was regarded as the general overseer of the realm of Ormnad, and it was natural that his chief lieutenant, the king of pure beasts, should be associated with him. The relationship between unicorns and royalty is brought out again by the fact just mentioned that one of the Zend kings was reared by a Koresck. It may be implied by the symbolism of the Persepolis bas-reliefs, for we find that the same animal—closely resembling a lion but possibly intended to represent the martichore as well—which is seen springing upon the unicorn in some scenes is shown in others fighting with the King, who drives a sword through his body. Heeren and Porter would have us believe that this familiar group was originally intended merely to exhibit the King's prowess as a hunter; to me it seems symbolic of the final victory of Ormuzd, just as the other scene represents, I think, his temporary defeat. The sculptors would scarcely have dared to show the King overcome even by the powers of darkness, and this may be the reason why they used his animal representative for the first scene; but it was natural that he should appear in person when victorious. In any case, the King here takes the place of his chief subaltern. Even at Persepolis kings and unicorns stand side by side, reminding one of the phrase recurring so frequently in the Bestiaries: "They lead him to the palace of the king."

The four brazen unicorns seen by Cosmas about the palace in Ethiopia may have been stationed there primarily as symbols of sovereignty, but it is probable that they had another more important function—that of guardians. For this belief I can advance no coherent evidence, yet I am more confident of it than of many assertions that I have "documented" heavily. I might show that the seal-cylinders on which apparently one-horned animals were so frequently represented were used not as trade-marks and substitutes for signatures only but as amulets, and I might speak of the human heads of stone equipped with formidable single horns that are set up at the corners of Chinese houses to keep away demons. In Italy to this day single horns set in heavy blocks of wood are placed against open doors, and I have seen in Italy three little bronze unicorns made and used for the same purpose. A dozen such parallels and examples would not amount to proof,

DRAGONS AND UNICORNS—FACT? OR FICTION?

but they may produce conviction. Recent excavations have shown that almost every private house in Nineveh and Babylon was protected against invasion from the unseen world not only by charms and ritual but by symbolic figures of various kinds buried in the floor or placed above the lintels. Now the king's house needed special attention because he bore the brunt of every attack from the forces of evil, and whatever harm came to him was a national calamity. Here I think we find a hint for the explanation of the colossal stone bulls that guarded the palaces of Assyria-bulls with human heads and faces of majestic power. The unicorn belongs with these. As the one-horned bull protects the herd of which he is the leader and as the three-legged one-horned ass protects the pure creation, so the unicorn protects the king and thereby the people. He is a devil-fighter.

Thus far we have paid no attention to the total scene, represented four times over in great prominence at Persepolis, in which a beast resembling a powerful lion attacks an apparently one-horned animal probably intended, as we have seen, to stand for the ass and goat and bull. Consciously begging several questions at once, I shall call these animals the lion and the unicorn. The delineation of their conflict was remarkably popular over a great extent of territory and of time. One sees it continually and with only slight variations on cylinder-seals of Babylon and Assyria, on coins of Mycene, and on objets d'art of uncertain origin that were spread through Europe and Asia during the Middle Ages by Scythian traders. The inference is that it had more than a decorative value and was widely recognized as a symbol. But a symbol of what?

Here and there in the unicorn literature of Europe one finds references to a clever ruse employed by the lion in capturing unicorns. Little is made of this story because it has not the sanction either of Physiologus or of the Greek and Latin authorities, and as it has no Christian significance it seems to have been crowded out by the story of the virgin-capture, yet it may be much older than the Holy Hunt allegory and may have served for ages as a religious symbol in the East.

Several European writers assert that this story was first told in "a letter written in Hebrew by the King of Abyssinia to the Pope of Rome". This seems at first a rather obscure reference, and one has not much hope of discovering the letter referred to in the voluminous correspondence of the Holy See; but a little reflection breeds a little encouragement and one turns again to the celebrated "Letter of Prester John", which may be read, if not in Hebrew, in every important language of Europe. Half-way through the French version upon which I happen to pitch occur the words: "Item sachez quen nostre terre sont les licornes qui ont sur le front une corne tout seulement; & en y a en touts maniers, cest assavoir de vers de noirs & aussi de blancs. Et occissent le lion aucune foys mais les lions les occisent moult subtilement, car quant la licorne est lasse elle se met du coste dung arbre & le lion va entour & la licorne le cuide frapp de sa corne, & elle frape larbre de si grant vertu quelle ne le peut oster; adonc le lion la tue."

The Latin original of this passage seems to have been the source of all later European versions, such as that of Edward Topsell, who says of the unicorn: "He is an enemy to Lions, wherefore as soon as ever a Lion seeth a Unicorn, he runneth to a tree for succour,

DRAGONS AND UNICORNS—FACT? OR FICTION?

that so when the Unicorn maketh force at him, he may not only avoid his horn but also destroy him; for the Unicorn in the swiftness of his course runneth against a tree, wherein his sharp horn sticketh fast. Then when the Lion seeth the Unicorn fastened by the horn, without all danger he falleth upon him and killeth him."

Although this story never took deep root in Europe it had sufficient vitality to spring up there, with variations, in the literature of the people, as we see in the following tale:

"'Before you win my daughter and the half of my kingdom,' said the King, 'you must accomplish yet another heroic deed. You must capture a unicorn that is at large in the wood and doing great harm there.'

"The tailor took a halter and an axe and started for the wood, telling the party that was with him to wait outside. The unicorn came in sight immediately, and made for the tailor as if to gore him without ceremony.

"'Steady, steady,' cried the tailor. 'Not so quick!'

"He stood still and waited till the animal was quite close, and then sprang nimbly behind a tree. The unicorn made a frantic rush at the tree and gored it so firmly with his horn that he could not get it out again, and so was caught.

"'Now I've got you, my fine bird,' said the tailor, coming from behind the tree. He put the halter round the beast's neck, cut its horn out of the tree, and when all this was done led the animal home to the king."

If this has always been an idle and meaningless tale then it is a very strange one. It is so odd, so unlikely to occur to the free excursive fancy, that one suspects a symbolic significance. But what significance? Can this question be connected with that other, which we have left in suspense, concerning the symbolism of the lion and unicorn bas-reiefs at Persepolis and their innumerable congeners? They too present a version of the lion-capture story although they show, perhaps because of the limitations of plastic art, only the denouement. We may be able to answer the two questions together more easily than we could either one of them separately.

As I have pointed out, the one-horned figures at Persepolis were imitations, both in subject and treatment, of others at Nineveh and Babylon. These in their turn were by no means original, for recent diggings at Ur of the Chaldees have shown that precisely the same conventional treatment of horned animals and the same interest in them that we have seen at Persepolis existed as far behind Persepolis in time as it lies behind us. On the lid of a toilet-box found at Ur there is worked in gold and lapis-lazuli exactly the same subject as that presented in the gigantic bas-relief under the staircase at Persepolis—a lion gripping with teeth and claws the hind quarters of a one-horned beast. A shell plaque of amazing delicacy in this collection shows two one-horned goats standing back to back on either side of a tree, and another shows a creature with the body of a goat and the

261

DRAGONS AND UNICORNS—FACT? OR FICTION?

head of a man, in profile and one-horned, with a foreleg thrown over the shoulder of a similar monster seen full-face and with two horns.

Looking at these objects from the city of Abraham, one realizes that, beautiful as they are, they were produced in a time long antecedent to any nonsense about art for art's sake and were certainly not intended as mere ornaments. Each of them had a meaning and was a compact symbol or metaphor in a language now lost to us. That meaning was evidently an important one, for the pattern or theme of the lion and unicorn conflict can be shown to have endured in art for at least twenty-five hundred years, and that of the two unicorned goats on either side of the tree for somewhat longer. Is it possible to make a plausible guess at the meaning these objects had for their makers? The scholars who are best equipped to answer this question are precisely those most reluctant to hazard even a conjecture. Gazing at these ancient unicorns, however, one cannot help recalling that they come from a region which we have always considered, perhaps because of our ignorance, the very cradle of astrology. Is it possible that the lion and the unicorn (I continue, consciously, to beg the question), so strangely brought together in that dim past, were solar and lunar emblems? Well aware as I am of the bad reputation earned for all such theories by the wild excesses of the "solar myth" euhemerizers of the nineteenth century, I am willing to give this possibility its chance.

That there is some kind of connection between the moon and the unicorn is not a theory but a fact. To be convinced of this one need scarcely look farther than the miserere seat in the Parish Church of Stratford-on-Avon which shows the figure of a unicorn with a crescent moon over its head. On ancient cylinder-seals the crescent moon frequently appears in conjunction with figures of animals which, whatever the original intention, are represented with single horns. Selecting characteristics of the unicorn at random we see that the animal may be likened to the moon, as the astrologers see it, in several ways: The unicorn is commonly, though not always, thought of as white in body; it is an emblem of chastity; it is very swift; according to the best authorities it cannot be taken alive. The animal is most readily associated with the new or crescent moon, which might indeed seem to dwellers by the sea to be leading the stars down to the water and to dip its own horn therein before they descend. The crescent moon has been used for ages to represent both celestial motherhood and virginity, whether of Ishtar, Isis, Artemis, or the Madonna. In all his pictures of the Assumption at Madrid Murillo painted the crescent moon over Mary's head. Old alchemical charts commonly designate the figure of Luna by placing in her right hand a single horn. The ki-lin, or unicorn of China, is commonly represented in bronze, bearing a crescent moon among clouds on his back.

These matters may seem little to the purpose, and I mention them merely for their cumulative force; but when we turn to consider the unicorn's medicinal properties and to ask what parallel these may have in old beliefs about the moon we discover something more significant. According to astrological belief and also that of magic and early medicine, the moon's phases exercise controlling influence upon all "humours", including not only the waters of the earth but the juices of plants and the blood of animals and of man. The close relationship between the moon and the tides, well known if not well

DRAGONS AND UNICORNS—FACT? OR FICTION?

understood from very ancient times, may have suggested this idea which later attained a surprising extension and complexity. Alkazuwin asserts that the vigour of all animals grows with the waxing moon, that the milk of kine and the horns of beasts and even the whites of eggs increase with it, that during the first half of every lunar month more snakes come from their holes than in the second half and that their venom is more deadly. He recounts also the belief, still current in rural England, that trees planted in the waning moon seldom come to any good. Physicians of the Middle Ages foretold the results of illnesses and regulated their treatments with constant attention to the moon's phases.

But this mere swaying and increasing of tides and humours by the new moon, although it has intimate connections with medical theory, does not bring us closer to the unicorn's magic power of dispelling poison. For the parallel to that we must look to another astrological belief. It was thought by early astrologers, and therefore by most educated Europeans of four centuries ago, that the moon, either by virtue of its proximity to earth or by the swiftness of its course, purifies the air of the noxious vapours supposed to rise from the earth during the night. The belief in these poisonous fumes, which correspond to the venom of Ahriman in the Bundahis myth and to that left floating in water by serpents in the unicorn legend, is still strong enough to keep tightly closed at night the windows of three houses in every five throughout rural England, Europe, and America, but the faith in the moon's purifying power does not seem to have survived. That faith was destroyed, apparently, and the moon came to be regarded as positively unwholesome in her influence, by the same turn of thought that made many theorizers regard the unicorn's horn, once the very emblem of purity, as essentially poisonous. At first the moon's effect in dispersing noxious vapours was explained partly by the speed and proximity of her course which enabled her to fan the air and keep it in motion, and partly also by reference to her essential purity. "As Albumasar sayth, the mone clensyth the ayre, for by his contynuall mevynge he makyth the ayre clere & thynne. And soo yf mevynge of the spere of the mone were not the ayre sholde be corrupte wyth thyckenesse & enfeccion that sholde come of out-drawynge by nyghte of vapours & moystures, that grete corrupcion shold come thereof." 69 The more common and less learned view of the ancient world was, however, that the moon acted upon poisons by simple "antipathy", she herself remaining pure. By the time of Ptolemy the Geographer this opinion seems to have changed, in accordance with changes going on in medical theory, and the moon's effect upon noxious vapours was attributed to her "sympathy" with them; it was apparently ascribed to the high potency of poison in her own essence which enabled her to draw all lesser poisons into herself. Using the jargon of later times, her action was no longer explained by the principle of "allopathy", but was regarded as "homoeopathic". For a long period, however, the two explanations overlapped and were used alternately as occasion served, just as they were in discussions of the alicorn's medicinal action and just as a modern physician may turn from one theory of medicine to the other with no feeling of inconsistency. We may surmise that the shift was not due so much to passage of time as to differences of latitude and climate, for the moon has always seemed beneficent and pure in the southern lands from which astrology came, but in northern countries it has usually been thought unwholesome, sinister, dangerous, while remaining unquestionably therapeutic.

DRAGONS AND UNICORNS—FACT? OR FICTION?

The pertinence of all this to the problem now in hand, whether the moon and the unicorn can be in any way identified with each other, is made clear by Ptolemy and two of his commentators. We are told in Ptolemy's Tetrabiblon that the chief influence of the moon is exercised upon "humours", and that it is able to wield this influence because it is nearer to the earth than other heavenly bodies and so can draw vapours from the earth into itself. In another place the same author remarks that the moon is saturated with the exhalations of the earth. The Arabian astrologer known to Europe as Albumasar doubted these assertions, holding that the earth's vapours cannot rise higher than sixteen stadia—less than two miles—and that the moon is considerably farther away than that. Albumasar was triumphantly answered by Cardan, who says in his amplified translation of Ptolemy that we can actually see the moon drawing vapours and that she does this not by contact and immediate absorption, like a sponge, but by innate and essential power acting at a distance like the power of a magnet upon iron. In other words, her action is due to her forma, and is exactly analogous to that attributed by Andrea Bacci to the alicorn.

One comes upon these passages and fits them into their place with something like the thrill a mason may feel when he sees his keystone slip smoothly down between the two halves of an arch on which he has been labouring with secret doubts of final success. (The petty triumphs of literary research are so minute and they are so commonly made in large libraries, where one is not allowed to shout "Eureka!" above a whisper, that this bit of confession may be pardoned.) For is not the belief in the moon's power to absorb poisons rising from earth during the darkness closely similar to the belief in the unicorn's water-conning? Does it not recall the vivid picture of the three-legged ass dipping his golden horn into the waters of the firmament and dispelling their corruption? One's fancy, warmed by exercise, rushes on into the Middle Ages and the Renaissance, almost ready to believe that in these ancient superstitions about the moon there may be found a source for the beliefs concerning the unicorn.

When fancy rushes forward at such speed, however, it is always well that some other faculty of the mind should hold back. Solar and lunar hypotheses, as we ought to know by this time, are dangerously seductive sirens, and many a tall ship has gone on the rocks just here, so that the voyager who will not stop his ears should lash himself to the mast. And yet I have agreed to give this hypothesis its chance. No harm can be done by a merely tentative and experimental assumption that the unicorn of the lion-capture story once stood for the moon. Let us make this assumption and see whither it will lead.

If the unicorn is to represent the moon, then the lion, a common solar emblem, should of course represent the sun, and we have only the tree left to be explained. Trees are involved in several problems concerning the unicorn. Many descriptions of the virgin-capture specify that the maiden must be seated either in a wood or under a tree, and nearly all the mediaeval illuminations place her there. Professor Otto Wiener has advanced an ingenious theory that in the original form of the story the animal was captured by the tree itself, and in the story now before us the tree does take the place of the virgin as the lion takes that of the huntsman and his dogs. Unicorned animals are often found on Assyrian cylinder-seals grouped with a single conventionalized tree in symbolical ar-

DRAGONS AND UNICORNS—FACT? OR FICTION?

rangement. This tree of the cylinder-seals is usually called the Tree of Fortune, but it seems to be ultimately indistinguishable from the Cosmogonic Tree, the Tree of the World, springing from the nether darkness and holding the earth and heavenly bodies in its branches, familiar in the myths of many peoples but best known to us by the Scandinavian name Yggdrasil. If the lion and unicorn are to represent sun and moon they will need no less a tree than this as the scene of their encounter.

We are now prepared for a bald statement of the solar-lunar theory concerning the lion-capture, and I make it in the words of that theory's most enthusiastic exponent: "The Lion-sun flies from the rising Unicorn-moon and hides behind the Tree or Grove of the Underworld; the Moon pursues, and, sinking in her turn, is sun-slain." In other words, just as the lion of our story slips behind the tree to avoid the unicorn's onrush, so the sun goes behind the Tree of the World, or perhaps into that western grove called the Garden of the Hesperides; and as the unicorn is caught by the horn so the moon is held fast during the interlunar period—at which time, as many myths assert, the sun eats it up.

To this audacious theory the cautious critic objects at once that the moon is two-horned and that a far more fitting emblem for her is the common one of the bull or cow; and yet the young crescent moon standing upright in the sky does suggest a single horn, and if we are to do justice to the lunar theory it is of the crescent moon that we must think, in spite of the awkward fact that only the old moon is slain by the sun. It is possible, furthermore, that the unicorn may symbolize a normally two-horned creature such as a bull or cow whose horns are being constantly brought together and twisted into one as the herdsmen of Africa still twist the horns of their herdleaders. To a pastoral people it may have seemed that the moon was thus marked out as the leader of the herds of the sky that follow her down to the sea, but do not drink until she has dipped her horn.

Robert Brown, the chief contender for this lunar theory, makes much of the fact that the "unicorns" of Assyrian sculpture and gems and seals are for the most part "regardant" -that is, that they are shown with heads turned and looking backward. This is indeed a remarkable characteristic of these puzzling figures. Careful examination of hundreds of examples shown by Felix Lajard shows that almost but not quite all of the animals shown in profile and with two horns are looking forward, whereas almost all of those shown with only one horn are regardant. In explanation of this Brown says: "The unicorn-goat [that is, the moon] during the first half of its career bounds forward from the sun, at which and the earth it looks back, and hence it is regardant; during the second half of its career it bounds back toward the sun, looking back to the point whence it has begun to return."

Brown also finds significance in the fact that many of these creatures are shown touching or nearly touching the symbolic tree with their horns, and that their heads are invariably turned toward this tree. From this topic he turns, naturally, to the mysterious "Horn of Ulph", which is probably the most remarkable relic in unicorn lore.

This large drinking horn was given to the Church of Saint Peter, now York Minster, in the ninth century by a certain Prince of Deira named Ulph as a token of his donation to

DRAGONS AND UNICORNS—FACT? OR FICTION?

that church of all his lands; the See of York still holds by virtue of this horn several valuable estates called Terrae Ulphi. The designs carved upon it, wherever and whenever they were made, are ancient and Euphratean in ultimate origin, highly symbolistic, apparently Byzantine in style. We may account for this fact, if we like, by recalling the influence of the Orient and the Near-East upon Scandinavian art which was made possible by the great overland routes, or we may explain it by reference to the activity of Scythian traders. At any rate, the designs include the favourite theme of the lion leaping upon a horned beast—in this case apparently a fawn. What is far more important, they include the symbolic Tree of the World and an unmistakable unicorn ; for there can scarcely be any doubt that the artist who carved this design was thinking of one horn and not of two. The end of this horn is embedded in, or at least is touching, the tree, so that the figure represents exactly the symbol of the setting moon already discussed. The body and legs and head are those of a cow or bull, but there are two additional details that prove beyond a doubt, in Brown's opinion, that the figure is a moon-emblem: the creature's tail is converted into a serpent by being equipped with a snake's head at the end, and beneath its belly there emerges from the earth the head of a dog. Now it is a fact remarkable in this connection that the goddess Hecate Triformis appears in the Argonautica in the three forms of horse, dog, and snake, which are usually interpreted as representing respectively the full, the waning, and the crescent moon. If the unicorn of the Horn of Ulph—which Robert Brown manages to call a ''horned horse''—does stand for the moon, its one horn must symbolize the two horns of the crescent coalesced.

This Horn of Ulph, one must admit, is an awkward obstacle for those who are determined not to believe anything that goes by the name of solar and lunar interpretation. And indeed such incredulity is often made to look like mere prejudice, for there are of course many myths based upon primitive attempts to explain the apparent motions of sun and moon. Robert Brown's effort to show that the unicorn legend is one of these is at least impressive in spite of its awkwardness and extravagance. If Brown had brought to bear such corroborative evidence as I have cited from Ptolemy and Cardan concerning early beliefs about the moon and if he had related his theory to the total sweep of the unicorn legend, I do not say that he would have established his thesis, but at any rate he would have left less room than he did for another book in English about the unicorn.

I find that I have suggested eight possible sources for the unicorn legend: the rhinoceros, the oryx, the separate horn, the freak of nature, horn-twisting, a misinterpreted art convention, the three-legged ass, and lunar myth. For each of these I have argued faithfully as though, for the time being, I believed in it alone. The fact is that I believe in them all, and I see no more necessity that the unicorn legend should have sprung from a single source than that the Nile should rise in a single spring or that an oak with fifty arms should have a single root. It is true that one stream out of all the many that are braided together at last in the Nile comes from farthest back in the mountains, so that all the others are reduced to the rank of affluents and tributaries, but men quarrelled and explored for ages before they could decide which stream that is. Similarly, there may have been a primitive unicorn, a unicorn almost divine, of which the rhinoceros and oryx were only the unworthy avatars, so nobly conceived that every object and creature that called it to

DRAGONS AND UNICORNS—FACT? OR FICTION?

mind—separate horns, single-horned sports, cattle with twisted horns, bas-reliefs that suggested one-horned animals—aroused a kind of awe, so holy that it gave rise to a Persian myth. The influence of these subsidiary sources may have been to revive the earlier belief when it was languishing and to provide fresh nuclei round which ideas that had at first no connection with them might cluster. The rhinoceros and the oryx, for example, may have been at first mere earthly representatives of the supreme unicorn, as the onager of Persia was a representative of the three-legged ass, acquiring later in popular belief some of the characteristics of their great progenitor, which was then forgotten. But through all these languishings and revivals the unicorn has maintained an amazing consistency. From beginning to end of his long history he has been wild, fleet, chaste, solitary, and beneficent.

And now, having pursued the unicorn through the ages and seen him take refuge at last in the sky, we may end our search for the source of his legend. We end it not because we have plucked out the heart of his mystery but because there is no farther to go, seeing that we cannot enter the dark, brooding heart and mind of early man. The unicorn escapes us at last, as we should wish, for "he is not to be taken alive". Like every other thing or idea that we pursue to the limits of our powers and knowledge he goes forth into mystery.

DRAGONS AND UNICORNS—FACT? OR FICTION?

CHAPTER IX

CERTAINTIES

THE zoologists of four hundred years ago believed that every terrestrial form of animal life had a marine counterpart. When men began to think, in the seventeenth century, that the land-surface of the globe had been fully explored and yet no unicorn was any where discovered, it was natural, therefore, that they should seek the animal beneath the ocean waves. They were justified by at least a partial success: the alicorn, whose origin had been concealed so long by the mists and dangers of the northern seas and by that old fear of the Atlantic sedulously propagated two thousand years before by Phoenician merchants, was traced at length to its source. The method of this discovery and the effects of it upon commerce and medicine and scholarship, the coincidence of it with the dawn of modernity, the light it threw backward over the way we have come these things, which make up perhaps the most interesting department of unicorn lore, are what we have left to consider.

Near the end of an exceedingly dull history of Iceland I find a vivid passage relating how Arnhald, the first Bishop of that country, was wrecked off the west coast of it in the year 1126, barely escaping with his life. There is a marsh on the mainland, the narrator tells us, near the spot where the shipwreck occurred, and this marsh was in his time still called the Pool of Corpses because of the many bodies of drowned sailors washed ashore there after the disaster. "And there also were found, afterward, the teeth of whales (dentes balenarum,) very precious, which had gone down with the ship and then had been thrown on shore by the motion of the waves. These teeth had runic letters written on them in an indelible red gum so that each sailor might know his own at the end of the voyage, for they had apparently been tossed into the hold helter-skelter as though intended merely for ballast."

To one reader, at least, that passage is not merely vivid but thrilling, for these "whales' teeth" were indeed very precious. Shakespeare's Clarence saw no greater wealth in his gorgeous dream of the under-sea than this that went down with the Bishop of Iceland

DRAGONS AND UNICORNS—FACT? OR FICTION?

eight hundred years ago and was found again in the Pool of Corpses. The fact that each man had his name written on the teeth he owned shows that they were already valuable, but this was in 1126; their market value was to increase for five centuries until they were worth ten times their weight in gold. The "whales' teeth" found in the Pool of Corpses were the "true unicorns' horns" of kings' treasuries.

How many cargoes such as this were brought safely to port in later years no one can say, for they belonged to a business in which it did not pay to advertise. There were not enough of them, at any rate, to glut the market, nor did they come in frequently enough to attract the slightest attention in Europe. Four hundred and fifty years after Arnhald's shipwreck there were scarcely more than twenty famous alicorns in Europe, and although these were very famous indeed no one had the faintest notion of their origin. If the situation had been planned and prepared by a master of salesmanship it could not have been arranged more admirably.

Four hundred and fifty years pass by, and in 1576 Sir Humphrey Gilbert presents to Queen Elizabeth his famous argument to prove that there must be a north-west passage to Cathay. He has to meet the arguments in favour of a north-east passage made by Anthonie Jenkinson, one of which is that a unicorn's horn has been picked up on the coast of Tartary. Whence could it have come, Jenkinson asks, unless from Cathay itself? Sir Humphrey replies: "First, it is doubtful whether those barbarous Tartarians do know an Unicornes horne, yea, or no: and if it were one, yet it is not credible that the Sea could have driven it so farre, being of such nature that it will not swimme . . . . There is a beast called Asinus Indicus (whose horne most like it was) which hath but one horne like an Unicorne in his forehead, whereof there is great plenty in all the north parts thereunto adjoyning, as in Lappia, Norvegia, Finmarke, etc. And as Albertus saieth, there is a fish which hath but one horne in his forehead like to an Unicorne, and therefore it seemeth very doubtful both from whence it came and whether it were Unicorne's horne, yea, or no."

In the following year Martin Frobisher set forth on his second voyage to discover a north-west passage, and during this voyage his men discovered, in the words of Master Dionise Settle: "A dead fish floating, which had in his nose a horn straight and torquet, of length two yards lacking two inches, being broken in the top, where we might perceive it hollow—into the which our sailors putting spiders, they presently died. I saw not the trial thereof, but it was reported to me of a truth, by the virtue whereof we supposed it to be the sea-unicorne."

Eleven years later one of these "fish" was washed ashore on the coast of Norfolk so that England had only herself to blame if she continued to pay Danish fishermen the huge sums at which alicorns were then held. Englishmen did continue to pay such prices, however, and the credit for discovering, or at any rate for publishing, the true nature of the alicorn went to another nation.

The dead "fish" found by Frobisher's company belonged to the same species of whales

DRAGONS AND UNICORNS—FACT? OR FICTION?

from which the "teeth" collected by Bishop Arnha]d's sailors had come, and that species was of course the narwhal—monodon monoceroc. The adult males of these marine mammals, from ten to eighteen feet in length, have single teeth or tusks of pure ivory extending for half their length from the left side of the upper jaw, pointing forward and a little downward. The fact that they are seldom seen south of Greenland explains the success of Scandinavian fishermen in keeping their lucrative secret for at least five centuries. Even after these animals had been closely examined and described by scholars of Copenhagen and Amsterdam curious misapprehensions concerning them held on well into the eighteenth century. In particular, it took over a hundred years to quell the belief that the narwhal's tusk was a "horn" and that it sprang from the middle of the forehead.

A well-written and sensible book published in 1665, for example, makes this assertion: "Comme la Licorne de terre a une corne aufront, cette Licorne de mer en avoit aussi une parfaitement belle au devant de la teste." Thus far all is clear, but the reader is somewhat confused when he finds in the same chapter a good description of the actual narwhal. It happened that just when the author of this book, César de Rochefort, was writing the revision of his chapter on the Licorne de Mer for a second edition there arrived at Rotterdam a Flemish ship from Davis Strait which had on board many narwhals' tusks-"une quantité bien considerable de ces dens ou cornes de ces Poissons qu'on appelle Licornes de Mer". From these sailors he may have gained his correct notions of the narwhal, but he hands on to his readers without prejudice both the narwhal and the Licorne de Mer, giving pictures of both. According to the economical customs of the times, these pictures did service in several other books, propagating error wherever they went. They were used by de la Martini?re, for example, in his popular Voyage des pays Septentrionaux, where confusion is worse confounded by the addition of a vigorous woodcut depicting the capture of a Licorne de Mer. The author informs us that he saw this capture—pretty certainly that of a cetacean because the harpoon was used—with his own eyes, and that he studied the head carefully, yet he allowed his engraver to place the "horn" in the middle of the brow. Furthermore, he says of the creature caught just after this one that it had no horn but that this was atoned for by the fact that its teeth were "beaucoup plus grosses". Now the fact is that the narwhal has only two teeth; in the young and in females both are rudimentary and in adult males one is enormously developed into the tusk. Unless de la Martini?re's second licorne was a walrus I can make no sense of his passage, and even in that case it remains mysterious how an intelligent man can "study" the head of a narwhal and still believe that its "horn" springs from the brow.

The unicorn was "an unconscionable time adying". No sooner was the narwhal discovered by Europeans—putting the legendary beast, as one might have thought, in deadly danger of being explained away—than they made a horn of its tooth and placed that horn where the horn of a unicorn ought to be. For was not the narwhal the Licorne de Mer, the unicorn of the sea? The rest followed, in spite of ocular evidence. A man who was by no means a fool could "study" the head of a narwhal, seeing clearly with his eyes if not with his mind that the creature's tusk issued from the upper jaw, and yet when he came to give directions to his engraver he was tricked by a mere word, the word "Licorne", into making that tusk a horn. There is no more vivid example of our inveterate

DRAGONS AND UNICORNS—FACT? OR FICTION?

tendency to see only what we expect to see, to think in terms of labels and phrases, to ignore the unfamiliar, to let the present be ruled by the past. One may judge what progress knowledge of the narwhal had made in England by the year 1721 from this definition: "Unicorn Whale-A fish eighteen feet long, having a head like a horse and scales as big as a crown piece, six large fins like the end of a galley oar, and a horn issuing out of the forehead nine feet long, so sharpe as to pierce the hardest bodies."

About one hundred years later still "a sea-unicorn's horn, seven foot and a half long" was to be seen at a coffee-house in Chelsea. Thomas Roscoe was at this time working at his translation of Cellini's Memoirs in far-off Liverpool, and when he came across a note in which Cellini's Italian editor, Carpani, says that the unicorn is a wholly fabulous animal he wrote: "From all we hear of the fine specimen of a unicorn's head—an unique, we suppose, now in London—the Italian commentator will soon be obliged to change his tone."

These are the words, be it observed, of a highly educated Englishman of the nineteenth century.

Dutch and Danish scholars had told the world everything of importance about narwhal tusks and their relation to the traffic in alicorns two hundred years before the time of Roscoe. They had, to be sure, a definite advantage of position, for ships from the northern seas with narwhal tusks in their cargoes were frequently calling at Copenhagen and Amsterdam, but their chief advantage was that they read everything without believing all that they read, that they were insatiably curious, and that they were rather more disposed than any other body of scholars in Europe to try all things and to hold fast only what seemed to be true.

Several early writers attribute to Pierre Belon, the sixteenth-century traveller and zoologist, the first identification of the alicorn with the narwhal's tusk. Feeling that such a discovery would be an important addition to the claims this bold and brilliant man already has upon memory, I have searched his writing for confirmation, but all that I find is his assertion that the alicorn is often merely the "dent de Robart". This is not quite the same thing as the narwhal discovery, for the rohart is the walrus or morse, concerning whose tusks Hector Bo'thius had made the same assertion some time before. Olaus Magnus, Archbishop of Upsala, came closer to the truth in saying that "the monoceros is a sea-monster that has in its brow a very large horn wherewith it can pierce and wreck vessels and destroy many men". Perhaps we have here the literary origin of the Licorne de Mer celebrated by de Rochefort and de la Martini?re, but Olaus Magnus is not entitled to the rank of discoverer for Albertus Magnus was in advance of him by several centuries. Closer to the fact than either of these remarks is the brief statement of Amatus Lusitanus—who makes an excellent showing everywhere by the unicorn test—that some fraudulent merchants "sell whale bones in place of unicorns' horns". Andrea Marini, writing in 1566, suggests that the sea, "which often breeds animals very like those of the land, and much more numerous", is the source of most of the alicorns of Europe, and he suspects that all of those in England are of marine origin because "there is not even a

271

record of a one-horned beast in that country". It seems probable to him that the sea has cast up many objects with the shape and substance of horns, and he even knows that there is "a sea-unicorn which has, as it were, a single horn," though just what this horn is he cannot say. Three years later the excellent Goropius of Antwerp goes a step beyond Marini. After a close description of a great narwhal's tusk which was before him as he wrote, one of three exposed for sale, he speculates about its origin: "I sometimes suspect", says he with the caution of a scholar, "that this is the horn of some fish, because many remarkable horns are found among fishes and also because this horn at Antwerp was brought from Iceland. And yet it occurs to me, on the other hand, that this island is not far from the Pole, and that animals may be much more numerous there because of the absence of men, wherefore it is not absurd to suppose that the horn comes from a beast after all."

The men thus far named had only glimmerings of the truth. We may learn from them by what slow processes the way is prepared for a slight advance in knowledge, how subject the knowledge once gained always is to relapses, and with what difficulty it was disentangled from old errors.

William Boffin, the English voyager, came a little closer in a letter written in 1615 concerning the north-west passage: "As for the Sea Unicorne", says he, "it being a great fish having a long horne or bone growing forth of his forehead or nostril (such as Sir Martin Frobisher in his second voyage found one) in divers places we saw of them, which if the home be of any goode value, no doubt but many of them may be killed." Not much credit is due to Boffin for these remarks, however, for he has not made up his mind whether the "horn" grows from the brow or the nostril and he does not know whether it is "of any goode value".

The earliest clear statement of all the essential facts that I have found is that of the great geographer Gerard Mercator. In one of his discussions of Iceland he says: "Among the fish is included the Narwhal. Anyone who eats its flesh dies immediately. It has a tooth in its head which projects to a length of seven cubits, and some sell this tooth as unicorn's horn. It is considered good against poison. The beast is forty ells in length." Caspar Bartholinus, who wrote seven years later, in 1628, did not know so much as this, for he still calls the tusk a horn, and if Mercator's statement had been somewhat ampler full credit for the discovery would be due to him. As it is, the man to whom that credit should be given acknowledges that Mercator had made a prior announcement of his own conclusions.

This man is Ole Wurm, Regius Professor of Denmark and a zoologist and antiquarian of high attainment. Perhaps the most important event recorded in unicorn lore was his public delivery at Copenhagen in 1638 of his Latin dissertation on the narwhal's tusk. The dissertation was called forth by a dispute among the merchants of Copenhagen about the true nature and origin of the substance they were selling as unicorn's horn—a quaint and antique situation indeed, when it is considered that the learned Professor was appealed to, so far as one can see, not for purposes of advertisement but actually to decide

DRAGONS AND UNICORNS—FACT? OR FICTION?

the question. If any of the alicorn merchants of the city expected Professor Wurm to put patriotism before truth and to "remember who paid his salary", they must have been grievously disappointed, for his remarks were decidedly "bad for business". He began with a careful description of the alicorns to be seen in his time all over Europe, everywhere regarded and highly treasured as horns of unicorns. So far are they from being such, he then says, that they are not horns at all. They have neither the substance, nor the shape of horns and they are not set in the animal's cranium as horns are. He asserts that they have all the characteristics of teeth and that teeth they must be called. In his third section Ole Wurm declares that the alicorns of Europe are the teeth of narwhals, citing as evidence the cranium of a narwhal, which he has recently examined. This cranium he describes, and also the tusk projecting from the left side of the upper jaw, with painstaking exactness. He concludes by saying that in the future those who do not care to deny the authority of witnesses and even of their own senses will be obliged to admit that the alicorn is really the tooth of the narwhal.

One might suppose that after such a public statement of the facts, iterated as it was by the author himself and by many others, the vogue of the alicorn would have ceased and the whole unicorn legend would have begun to die away. On the contrary, the dissertation seems to have had little more effect at first than such productions usually have. Public faith in the unicorn was unshaken. The trust of physicians and princes in the alicorn remained. It is true that the price of narwhals' tusks fell off sharply at about this time, but that was chiefly due to a glutting of the market. I have shown that the tusk was to be used in the royal household of France for one hundred and fifty years after Ole Wurm's dissertation was delivered and printed; it was to be kept on the official pharmacopoeia of London for more than a century to come; good physicians continued for a long time to speak highly of its medicinal virtues. Ignorance and mental indolence, better known as conservatism, may have been chiefly responsible for this, but they were assisted by these two facts: the disclosure of the marine origin of most alicorns did not by any means disprove the existence of the terrestrial unicorn; on the contrary, if there was a unicorn of the sea it seemed to follow necessarily that there was one of the land as well. Further, the proof that the alicorns of Europe were whales' teeth did not cause people to abandon the belief in their medicinal virtues, for it seemed natural to suppose that the sea-unicorn would have all the properties attributed to his counterpart of the land.

We may infer that Ole Wurm's dissertation had little effect even in his own land from a remark made by de la Martini?re about the disposition of the two "horns" taken by his company to which I have already referred: "One of the Principals of the Company was ordered by the rest in all their names to present to his Majesty [Frederic III of Denmark] the two sea-horses horns that we brought home with us, which his Majesty received as a most estimable present, supposing they had been Unicornes Horns, of the virtues of which so many authors had written. He ordered them presently to be laid up among the best of his rarities, promised the Company to do them what benefit he could, and presented the bearer with a Chain of Gold with his Picture hanging to it, and forgave him his Customes besides." One can only surmise, reluctantly, that Frederic III did not read all the works of his Regius Professor.

DRAGONS AND UNICORNS—FACT? OR FICTION?

The two "horns" presented on this occasion to the King of Denmark are heard of again in the Travels of Dr. Edward Browne, son of Sir Thomas. "Two such as these", he writes, "the one ten foot long, were presented not many years since to the King of Denmark, being taken near to Nova Zembla." But this Edward Browne is a scoffer, and his testimony is valuable chiefly as showing how plentiful alicorns became towards the end of the seventeenth century. He asserts that he has "seen some full fifteen feet long, some wreathed very thicke, some not so much, and others plain: some largest and thickest at the end near the Head; others are largest at some distance from the Head; some very sharp at the end or point, and others blunt. My honoured Father Sir Thomas Browne had a very fair piece of one which was formerly among the Duke of Curland's rarities, but after that he was taken prisoner by Douglas it came into the hands of my Uncle Colonel Hatcher, of whom my Father had it. He also had a piece of this sort of Unicornes Horn burnt black, out of the Emperor of Russia's Repositorie . . . . I have seen a walking Staffe, a Sceptre, a Scabbard for a Sword, Boxes, and other Curiosities made out of this Horn, but was never so fortunate as from experience to confirm its medical Efficacy against Poisons, although I have known it given several times and in great quantity. Mr. Charleton hath a good Unicorn's Horn. Sir Joseph Williamson gave one of them to the Royal Society. The Duke of Florence hath a fair one. The Duke of Saxony a strange one, and besides many others I saw eight of them together upon one table in the Emperor's treasure, and I have one at present that for the neat wreathing and the elegant shape gives place to none. But of these Unicorns' Horns no man sure hath so great a Collection as the King of Denmark; and his Father had so many that he was able to spare a great number of them to build a magnificent Throne out of Unicorns' Horns."

This alicorn throne of Denmark was in its time one of the chief wonders of Europe, and if Edward Browne mentioned it to show how cheap the material had become he did not choose a good example. It was begun by Frederic III and was long used as the Coronation Chair, the legs and arms and all the supporting pieces being made of alicorn. (If the construction of such thrones was at all common in the remoter past then it is clear why all captured unicorns were led at once "to the palace of the king".) Christian V was crowned in this chair in 1671 and the officiating bishop remarked: "History tells us of the great King Solomon that he built a throne of ivory and adorned it with pure gold, but your Majesty is seated on a throne which, though like King Solomon's in the splendour of its materials and shape, is unparalleled in any kingdom." Whatever might be said of the learned professions, Church and State had not abandoned the unicorn.

The dissertation of Ole Wurm did not shake the faith of Europe, as I have said, in any serious degree. Belief in the medicinal value of narwhal tusk remained as strong as ever- and Ole Wurm, like Caspar Bartholinus, seems to have shared this belief himself. And after all this was a sensible attitude, for the substance remained the same that it had always been, although a few persons now called it by a new name and thought of it as coming from another part of the world. César de Rochefort, in the passage in which he speaks of the cargo of tusks just arrived at Amsterdam from the northern seas, remarks that they are certain to bring a great price because all the most celebrated physicians and apothecaries, having tested them in various ways, assert "qu'elles chassent le venin,

DRAGONS AND UNICORNS—FACT? OR FICTION?

et qu'elles ont toutes les memes proprietez qu'on attribue communement a la Corne de la Licorne de terre". And this in 1665 was still approximately true.

Eleven years after that date appeared the curious monograph by Paul Ludwig Sachs, M.D., the main purposes of which are to show that the unicorn really exists, that its true name is "narwhal", and that the narwhal's "horn"—for Sachs rejects all theories about "teeth"—has at least the alexipharmic if not the magic properties formerly attributed to the alicorn. So much he has himself proved by repeated scientific experiments, and he quotes in corroboration of his belief a dozen of the most prominent physicians of the time who used the "horn" in daily practice. Taking his point of view, one smiles with sympathy at his pious outburst by way of peroration: "Therefore we cannot sufficiently adore and wonder at the marvellous goodness of God, who has brought forth for us things useful and beneficial to our health not only from the bowels of the earth and from the mountain-tops but even from the abysses of the sea. In the sea the unicorn is found. Those precious objects which have long been kept like pearls in the treasuries of princes and which our forefathers vainly sought among the wild forests and mountains of Africa and America are now brought to us from the ocean waves. This miraculous and never-enoughto-be-praised horn forces us to cry out with the royal prophet: 'Praise the Lord from the deep, ye whales and all abysses; yea, all creatures, praise the Lord. Hallelujah!"

The remarks of Pierre Pomet on this topic are considerably more restrained. He has no more belief in the terrestrial unicorn than Paul Sachs had, and rather less confidence in the tusk, yet he hands on de Rochefort's Licorne de Mer, together with the inevitable picture, in addition to the narwhal, leaving the reader to suppose that there were two marine creatures with this medicinal horn. Nicolas Lemery, another French pharmacist of wide influence, says much the same things in 1733, although he tacitly ignores the Licorne de Mer. He asserts that the narwhal tusk strengthens the heart, induces perspiration, cures epilepsy, and is "propre pour resister au venin". These are exactly the same claims that had been made two hundred years before for the unicorn's horn, although nearly a century had passed since the appearance of Ole Wurm's dissertation. Lemery says that the reason for the alicorn's great rarity in former days was that the narwhal was then unknown, "mais depuis qu'on a peché beaucoup de ces poissons, cette corne n'est plus guéres rare; on en trouve chez plusieurs Marchands coupées par troncons".

The remark of Lemery that by the year 1733 the alicorn was much more common than in former times leads one to ask what had been the narwhal tusk's commercial history. The materials for an answer to this interesting question are few, partly because that history belongs to a time when no trade records were kept and partly because those concerned had no desire that their transactions should be generally known. What little can be said on this topic, therefore, must be based primarily upon inferences.

One of the inferences to be drawn from the few facts at our disposal is as unquestionable as it is significant. I have already spoken more than once of the fact that in mediaeval pictures of the unicorn found in illuminated manuscripts that go back to the twelfth century, the animal's horn almost invariably shows the characteristic striae, the "anfractuous spires and cochleary turnings", which are found on no object in nature except the narwhal's tusk. Now when we consider that the narwhal is almost never seen south of Greenland that the seas in which it swims were utterly unknown to Europeans in the twelfth century—or, for that matter, in the fifteenth—and that its tusk will not float, we can reach only one conclusion: narwhal tusks have been articles of merchandise for at least eight hundred years. The same conclusion is indicated by the remarkable passage quoted above in which Arngrimr Jonsson records the loss, in 1126, of a cargo of tusks collected among the gulfs of Iceland. A study of the Mediterranean trade carried on during the Middle Ages in Scandinavian bottoms will show that there would be no difficulty, when once such tusks reached Norway or Denmark, for them to find their way into the treasure chests of Europe.

How much farther than that they went, and how much earlier than 1126 they set out on their travels, is harder to say. The overland routes by which the trade of Scandinavia was carried into Russia and southward toward the Black Sea must have absorbed many of them, and the tradition that the two alicorns of St. Mark's in Venice were taken at the division of spoils from Constantinople in 1204 is therefore, in itself, not incredible. In Arabia they had apparently ousted the rhinoceros horn as early as the fourteenth century, for Alkazuwin says that the unicorn has "one horn on his head, sharp at the point and thicker at the bottom, with raised striae outside and a hollow within". We may be fairly sure, however, that the tusks did not reach China in considerable numbers until the legend of the Ki-lin was complete, for there is no evidence of acquaintance with them in the descriptions and representations of that animal. Whether they gave rise to the Italian word licorno one cannot certainly say. One does not see how they could have had any dispersion whatever in Europe or Asia before the seas about Iceland became known at least to a few adventurers, and it is this fact, among others, that makes Aelian's word xxxxx so tempting to the historic imagination. If we translate that word cautiously and conservatively by "rings", as I have done, then it is fairly certain that Aelian had in mind the horn of an antelope; but if we translate it by "spirals"—a sense in which it was used by Aristotle, with reference to snail-shells, and also by Aelian himself—then we must think of narwhal tusks as brought back from Ultimate Thule in the third century of the Christian era.

One thing is perfectly evident regarding this traffic: it never amounted to a regular trade. So much is made clear by the great prices commanded by the tusks in the sixteenth century, after they had been known for at least four hundred years. Even if we allow fifty per cent. for the goldsmith's work upon the Horn of Windsor or upon that for which Pope Julius III paid ninety thousand scudi, it is clear that the tusks had enormous rarity value. In the middle of the sixteenth century there were probably not more than fifty whole tusks in all of Europe and Great Britain, although the smaller pieces were more numerous, and these, seeing that they were precious and almost indestructible, represented certainly a large part of the total importation from the beginning. Taken together with the huge prices and the fact that the supply was almost unlimited this paucity is somewhat perplexing. We can scarcely believe that the middlemen who conducted

DRAGONS AND UNICORNS—FACT? OR FICTION?

the sales had the economic foresight and knowledge which would have made them refrain from glutting the market. Perhaps we need only remember that the voyage to Iceland and Greenland was a different thing in the centuries of which we are speaking from what it is now, that means of advertisement were almost entirely lacking, and that the number of persons who would be practically interested, so to speak, in alicorns was always narrowly restricted. Furthermore, the maintenance of high prices for the tusks is partly explained by the fact that just when they began to be more plentiful in Europe a fresh impetus to the belief in their medicinal value was contributed by Portuguese travellers returning from India. The rhinoceros was introduced to Europe at about the same time, and it was felt that his horn would not meet the specifications because it was too short and not at all like the alicorns represented in pictures. Narwhal tusks on the other hand corresponded exactly, and for the best of reasons, with pictures of unicorns' horns that had behind them almost the authority of revelation.

We may be quite as certain of one other thing about this traffic: during the earlier centuries it did not involve conscious deceit on the part of anyone. The seamen of the North who collected the tusks may not even have known under what name and with what representations concerning their value they were finally sold. Those who conducted the final sales may not have been aware, in the earlier centuries, of the tusks' origin. Even if they had been aware of this, their notions of zoology and of materia medica were certainly no clearer than those of the scholars and physicians whose opinions we have examined, and they would have felt entirely justified in selling for ten times its weight in gold a substance for which such miraculous powers were everywhere asserted and accepted. There was a definite though restricted demand for alicorns, but there was no general agreement as to just what these were. Rhinoceros horns had a considerable following and walrus tusks, artificially straightened, had probably a greater; fossil bones and petrified wood and even stalactites were used in large quantities; after the end of the fourteenth century, however, the tooth of the narwhal defeated all competitors and was accepted by the experts as "true unicorn". A busy merchant could not trouble himself about such niceties. The public wanted unicorns' horns; his business was to give the public what it wanted and to get the best price he could.

Before it established itself above all rivals the narwhal's tusk met with some opposition, as we have seen, from those who knew what the ancients had said about unicorn's horn. The chief objection was to its colour, for both Pliny and Aelian had said that the true horn was black. Bo'thius de Boodt disposed of most of the horns to be seen in his time by saying that they were not of the right colour, and Amatus Lusitanus advised his readers to purchase the black variety—antelope or rhinoceros horn—when it could be had. Pietro della Valle, again, although much interested in the tusk shown him by Captain Woodstock, who had found it in Greenland in 1611, could not agree that it was the true horn, for this, if he remembered his Pliny correctly, had been described as black. Another objection to the narwhal tusk was that it was not large enough, even at the base, to permit its being made into beakers such as those used by Indian potentates; but this difficulty was evaded by fitting together several lamin sliced from the tusk and so constructing a tankard not unlike a German stein, or by inserting a single piece of the tusk in a cup made of other

DRAGONS AND UNICORNS—FACT? OR FICTION?

materials.

During the seventeenth century, however, those who had narwhal tusks for sale were confronted by more serious difficulties and objections. A probing, curious, sceptical spirit was spreading through northern Europe, inciting men to ask questions that had never been asked before and to deny beliefs that had been held for ages—beliefs that were still held, of course, by all but one or two in the million. Those who were infected by this new spirit laid a novel emphasis upon what they called "experience" and we call experiment, rating the evidence it provided almost as highly as that given by "authority" and by "reason". Not quite so logical as the Schoolmen, nor quite so erudite as their own immediate predecessors—although their book-learning was still enormous in comparison with that of those whom we call scientists to-day—they sought for evidence not so much in authority and tradition and the consent of the ages as in what they were more and more disposed to call "facts". Such a spirit was not good for the traffic in narwhal tusks. Very slowly but surely it diffused throughout Europe an intellectual climate in which the unicorn could not feel at home.

Like all transformations in the fundamental habits of our thought, this change was very gradual. Recent news from Tennessee and Oklahoma shows that it is far from complete to-day, and Europeans may reach the same conclusion upon evidence gathered nearer home. The mass of men, quite unaffected by Ole Wurm of whom they had never heard, went on buying powdered alicorn for more than a hundred years after his dissertation was delivered, went on drinking alicorn-water, went on believing what they were told as they always had done and as they always will do. Thomas Bartholinus certainly exaggerates the influence of the Danish discovery when he implies that it stopped the traffic in narwhal tusks. "Our merchants would have filled whole ships with this pretended horn", says he, "and would have sold it all through Europe as true alicorn, if the deceit had not been detected by experts." Thus it is that scholarship constantly tends to over-estimate its own influence. The fact seems to be that if anything like whole cargoes of narwhal tusks had ever been brought to Europe they must have been brought at about the time when Bartholinus was writing, and in Danish ships. No; the scholars of Denmark may have done their best to kill the goose that laid their country's golden eggs, but the goose declined to die. All the little that may have been lost in British and European markets by Ole Wurm's unpatriotic disclosures was made up by new markets in Russia—or rather by old Russian markets first developed by the Scandinavian overland traders. When these were gone, there were still others, as we shall see, in lands much farther off where Latin dissertations were never read.

For all this, the difficulties encountered in selling the tusks at anything like the old prices did certainly increase as the seventeenth century wore on. Pietro della Valle gives us some significant information on this topic in his account of the efforts to dispose advantageously of the tusk found by Captain Woodstock. As he was bound to do by the terms of his agreement, the Captain turned this tusk over to his Company of Merchants, who sent it at once to Constantinople for sale. The best offer made for it there was only two thousand pounds. Hoping to get more than this, the Company sent it to Russia, where about the same amount was offered, and in Turkey the bids were even lower. (The fact that no effort was made to sell the tusk in western Europe is significant.) At last it was cut into small pieces and disposed of bit by bit, realizing a total sum of only twelve hundred pounds.

Even clearer evidence that the market was rapidly falling is found in de la Peyrere's Relation de Groenland, which first appeared in 1647. "'Tis not long since", says this garrulous writer, "that the Company of New Greenland at Copenhagen sent one of their agents into Muscovy with several great pieces of these kind of horns, and amongst the rest one end of a considerable bigness, to sell it to the Great Duke of Muscovy. The Great Duke being greatly taken with the beauty thereof, he shewed it to his Physician, who, understanding the matter, told the great Duke 'twas nothing but the tooth of a fish, so that this agent returned to Copenhagen without selling his commodity. After his return, giving an account of the success of his journey, he exclaimed against the physician who had spoiled his market by disgracing his commodities. 'Thou art a half-headed fellow', replied one of the directors of the Company, as he told me since. 'Why didst thou not offer two or three hundred ducats to the physician to persuade him that they were the horns of unicorns?'" If we have been right in saying that there was no conscious deceit in the earlier history of the traffic in tusks, that period is now definitely past.

There are several references to this Copenhagen Company of Greenland Merchants to be found in unicorn literature, although not so many as one could wish. It seems to have enjoyed something like a monopoly in the traffic for a time, and during a still longer period Denmark kept the business in her control. We read in Purchas His Pilgrims, for example, that in 1561 "a citizen of Hamburg begged the gift of a unicornes horne found in the ice of Iceland, and sold it after in Antwerp for some thousands of Florins. When this came to the King of Denmarkes eares he ruled that no Germaine should winter in Iceland in any cause." Another record shows that "in the year 1606 a company of merchants in Copenhagen sent two ships into the straits under the patronage of the Chancellor Christian Fries, and they traded with the natives . . . . On this voyage the ship's company brought back the teeth or horns of the unicorn fish, which at that time were unknown, and were valued at twelve hundred pounds a piece in Copenhagen, and were sold in Russia for a great price as the horns of the land-unicorn."

Although there was certainly a "period of depression", we are not to suppose that the unicorn, after his millenniums of glory, was snuffed out by a dissertation, or even that the traffic in his alleged horn was permanently disabled by the discovery that it was really the tooth of a small whale. Superstition is armed in triple bronze against all mere learning, and as for trade and commerce we should know that they will use science for their own ends precisely as far and as long as they find it lucrative. We reckon ill when we ignore the enterprise shown by modern business in finding and exploiting new markets. When it was found that western Europe would absorb no more alicorns at the old prices they were sent to Constantinople, Turkey, and Russia, and when even these markets began to fail others were discovered to take their places. One of the more amusing events in unicorn lore is the emergence of the alicorn, late in the eighteenth century, in the

DRAGONS AND UNICORNS—FACT? OR FICTION?

trade of the Far East.

The story is told by Charles Peter Thunberg, a traveller and botanist whose account of the medicinal use of rhinoceros horn in South Africa I have already quoted. He visited Nagasaki in 1775—at a time, that is, when the Dutch factory on the neighbouring island of Dezima still held a monopoly in the Japanese trade. This monopoly, which began in 1601, had formerly been of immense value, two voyages sufficing to make a Dutch captain wealthy for life; but it had recently fallen away for the sad reason that the Japanese had learned from their European visitors a few elementary tricks of trade. Among the articles imported by Japan in 1775 were camphor, tortoise-shells, spectacles, glass and mirrors, watches, chintz, and "unicorns' horns". The collocation is instructive.

"Unicorn's horn", writes Thunberg, "sold this year on Kambang very dear. It was often smuggled formerly, and sold at an enormous rate. The Japanese have an extravagant opinion of its medical virtues and powers to prolong life, fortify the animal spirits, assist the memory, and cure all complaints. This branch of commerce has not been known to the Dutch till of late, when it was discovered by an accident. One of the chiefs of the commerce here, on his return home, had sent out from Europe, amongst other rarities, to a friend of his who was an interpreter, a large, handsome, twisted Greenland unicorn's horn, by the sale of which this interpreter became extremely rich and a man of consequence. From that time the Dutch have written to Europe for as many as they could get, and made great profit on them in Japan. At first each catje [threequarters of a pound] sold for one hundred kobangs or six hundred rixdollars, after which the price fell by degrees to seventy, fifty, and thirty kobangs. This year, as soon as the captain's wide coat had been laid aside and prohibited [to prevent smuggling] all the unicorn's horn was obliged to be sold on Kambang, the open market of Dezima, where each catje fetched one hundred and thirty-six rixdollars . . . . The thirty-seven catjes four thails which I had brought with me were therefore very well disposed of for five thousand and seventy one thails and one mas [the 'thail', in money, is about the equivalent of one rixdollar], which enabled me to pay the debts I had contracted and, at the same time, to expend one thousand two hundred rixdollars on my favourite study."

Here we may close this inadequate outline of the narwhal tusk's commercial history, not because there is nothing left to say, but because we should find chiefly disillusionment in pursuing the research until we came to the hogsheads crammed with alicorns that may be seen stored to-day in the London docks. And here, too, we may as well end our sketch of the lore of the unicorn, although certainly not for lack of further materials. It is something to have shown how it happened that, perhaps on account of a curious set of beliefs about the moon worked out ages ago by Mesopotamian astrologers, a European scholar of the eighteenth century was able to equip himself for his botanical studies by selling bits of narwhal tusk at twelve rixdollars an ounce to credulous Orientals.

At any rate, I have accounted for the long, straight stick of ivory that lies before me on the table.

280

DRAGONS AND UNICORNS—FACT? OR FICTION?

CHAPTER X

REFLECTIONS

I

RELIGIOUS history presents few stranger possibilities than this, that the beast sculptured on the staircases at Persepolis may have come at last, after as many changes as the Old Man of the Sea went through, to stand depicted in the windows of Christian cathedrals; that the three-legged ass may have been transformed eventually into a symbol of Christ; that a lunar myth of Mesopotamia may have produced after two thousand years an allegorical representation of the central Christian mystery. Whether these changes ever occurred or not, the unicorn has preserved through all his long history a character that would have made them possible.

For the most part we have made the beasts of fancy in our own image—far more cruel and bloodthirsty, that is to say, than the actual "lower animals". The dragons of the West-

DRAGONS AND UNICORNS—FACT? OR FICTION?

ern world do evil for evil's sake; the harpy is more terrible than the vulture, and the were-wolf is far more frightful than the wolf. Almost the only beast that kills for the pure joy of killing is Western civilized man, and he has attributed his own peculiar trait to the creatures of his imagination. There are a few exceptions, however, to this rule that our projection of ourselves is lower than the facts of Nature, and the unicorn—noble, chaste, fierce yet beneficent, altruistic though solitary, strangely beautiful—is the clearest exception of all. The unicorn was not conceived in fear. Our early sense of Nature's majesty and mystery is revealed in him. If he came from Ur of the Chaldees, where the moon was a friend to man always contending against the demoniacal sun and the powers of darkness alike, his constant benevolence is more readily understood; but whatever may have been his first local habitation and whatever was his original name, this "airy nothing" was born and bred in the human mind. There are times when one takes hope and comfort in remembering the fact.

II

"Whoever has followed the development of a single department of knowledge", says Nietzsche, "finds in its history a clue to the understanding of the oldest and commonest processes of all intellectual life. There one finds the premature hypotheses, the idle fictions, the absence of distrust, the lack of patience, and the good stupid will to believe. Our senses learn late, and never fully learn, to be subtle, dependable, and cautious instruments of knowledge."

The legend of the unicorn is so old and it has been since its dim beginnings so close to human hearts and bosoms that it illustrates vividly Auguste Comte's three stages of intellectual "progress": the theological, the metaphysical, and the positivistic. Tracing it through the centuries, we have seen it remodelled again and again by the changing Zeitgeist or adjusting itself anew to the time-climates into which it has strayed. The historian of thought might find this legend, indeed, a serviceable thread upon which to arrange his generalizations, and it would save him from Comte's error, and ours, of supposing that the successive stages of human thought are stages of progress in the sense of amelioration. We do not think better about the unicorn than the men who made the myth of the three-legged ass; we think differently.

Although the conception of the unicorn does us credit, the total history of the animal's legend does not flatter our modern pride. In his beginnings, wherever and whatever they may have been, the unicorn was a symbol of beneficent power inhabiting the poetic imagination. The symbol expanded into myth and this myth was debased into fable. The unicorn next became an exemplum of moral virtues, then an actual animal, then a thaumaturge, then a medicine, then an article of merchandise, then an idle dream, and, last stage of all, an object of antiquarian research. Relics of the earlier stages are discoverable in the later, but what is most apparent is the steady intrusion of fact upon fancy and the invasion of what was once a sanctuary by the positivistic temper. We are accustomed to regard the growth of this temper as unqualified gain, and it has indeed brought us many advantages that no sensible man or woman would forgo, but it has not been

DRAGONS AND UNICORNS—FACT? OR FICTION?

good for unicorns or for the many holy and beautiful things that unicorns may be taken to represent. There are some quite sober moods in which one may sum up all the unquestionable advantages of modernity and calmly decide that he would "rather be a pagan suckled in a creed outworn".

Or, for that matter, a Christian of the ages when that name still connoted a rich and sufficient and poetic faith. It is true that the Middle Ages moralized the unicorn, thus contributing their share to his degradation, for Christianity inherited from the later Stoics a feeling that all nature is a vast copy-book of maxims designed for mankind's edification, a sort of subsidiary revelation of moral truths. Two thousand years have not quite rid us of that error: Wordsworth did not escape it, and even Emerson revealed his clerical upbringing by the na·ve assertion that "Nature is ancillary to man". It was indeed a "pathetic" fallacy, but there are moods in which one would rather believe in even an emasculated and homiletic unicorn than in none at all.

It is not that the men of the Middle Ages who believed in the unicorn were less intelligent than we; their intelligence was trained in a different direction. A modern scientist might make the same havoc among the scientific beliefs of the Schoolmen that the Connecticut Yankee made in King Arthur's Court, but it would by no means follow that he had a better mind than that of Duns Scotus or Thomas Aquinas, any more than it follows that Mark Twain's low-bred Yankee is superior to the champions of chivalry. We care for facts, and are comparatively careless about ultimate meanings; the Middle Ages were regardful of meanings and careless about facts.

The Middle Ages saw the spiritual and physical worlds as two aspects of one thing— a view made easier by their revival of the latonic doctrine of microcosm and macrocosm. We feel confident—although another century of scientific thought may convince us of error—that this view is hostile to the interests of science, but we should not be quite so sure that it is hostile to the interests of men and women. "By depriving objects of their share in the spiritual ife of man," says Mr. Aldous Huxley, "by leaving to them only such characteristics as can be measured, physicists of the seventeenth and eighteenth centuries made possible the advance of modern science. world regarded from the introvert's point of view, a subjectivized world, is unamenable to science. It may be picturesque and agreeable, but it is not a world for physicists and mathematicians."

Probably not, although this does not seem a serious objection to such a world, and one hopes that we have not yet fallen so low as to test the worth of this "world" and that by asking whether it has been made safe for mathematicians and physicists. Quite as reasonably ne might demand assurance that a given world is safe for unicorns. But it is to Mr. Huxley's closing remark on this topic that I should like to call special attention: "The scientific theories of the Middle Ages were fruitless theories." Of course they were that in the sense that further scientific theories could seldom be deduced from them, yet there are other things to be asked about a theory than whether it is prolific of corollaries and consequences after its own image. We may ask, for example, how it is related to the total complex of human hopes and fears; and if, like the theories of the physicist and the

DRAGONS AND UNICORNS—FACT? OR FICTION?

mathematician, it has been carefully disassociated from these, then its fruit, however abundant, will be to us like Dead Sea apples and will furnish forth a Barmecide Feast. The scientific theories of the Middle Ages were not like this. They were framed, unconsciously, with human "values" always foremost in thought. When we have begun to correct our own extreme tendency in the opposite direction we can afford to be severe with them for this, but in the meantime we do well to remember that...

There are two laws discrete,

Not reconciled,-

Law for man, and law for thing;

The last builds town and fleet,

But it runs wild,

And doth the man unking.

III

Is there no choice possible, then, except that between a docile and unquestioning acceptance of authority on the one hand and a world of physicists and mathematicians on the other? Because Ole Wurm has demonstrated that alicorns are really the teeth of whales, must we abandon the unicorn altogether? I do not see the necessity.

The higher and the enduring values of a belief—the faiths that we call religious provide the best examples—do not depend at all upon its congruity with actual fact, but upon its sway over the human heart and mind. They are grounded not upon fact, but upon what even we may perhaps still call "the truth". The question of historicity and actuality with regard to gods and unicorns is a relatively trifling matter which may be left to antiquarians and biologists, for both the god and the unicorn had a business to perform greater than any mere existence in the flesh could explain or provide a basis for. We wrong ourselves when we insist that if they cannot make good their flesh-and-blood actuality on our level we will have none of them.

The unicorn came to stand for Christ, and for that reason if for no other we can scarcely avoid passing in thought from the symbol to the symbolized. Here are two great and beautiful legends, to say no more than that, neither of which could have lived so long in the world if it had not contained a truth far higher than any historic or zoological fact could help us to understand. But legends and truths of this kind are in grave danger in a world increasingly adjusted to the requirements of physicists and mathematicians; there is question whether they can hold out against our tendency to accept no truths except those the senses seem to warrant—which is to say, no truths whatever, but only facts. The legend of the unicorn was assailed three centuries ago on the side of fact, and it gradu-

284

DRAGONS AND UNICORNS—FACT? OR FICTION?

ally withered because there was no longer any sufficient capacity for a faith unsustained by the senses. That attack could never have been made if the unicorn had not first been dragged from the fastnesses of the imagination to take his chances in the mob of animals whose only claim upon our attention is that they happen to exist. Three centuries from now, if we continue to make the question of fact decisive where it should have least weight, the legend of Christ may be as outworn as that of the beast that was once His appropriate symbol. For the decline of the unicorn began with the affirmation that the animal must exist in nature, and just so, as Matthew Arnold saw with painful clearness, religion is declining because it has based its claim upon fact, or supposed fact, which is now crumbling. Our best hope seems to lie in the faith expressed by Arnold himself that in the years coming on poetry will be an ever surer and surer stay.

END

DRAGONS AND UNICORNS—FACT? OR FICTION?